Summary of Contents

HTML Utopia: Designing Without Tables Using CSS

by Dan Shafer

and Rachel Andrew

HTML Utopia: Designing Without Tables Using CSS

by Dan Shafer and Rachel Andrew

Copyright © 2006 SitePoint Pty. Ltd.

Technical Director: Kevin Yank
Expert Reviewer: Richard Rutter
Managing Editor: Simon Mackie
Technical Editor: Craig Anderson
Printing History:
   First Edition: May 2003
   Second Edition: April 2006

Editor: Georgina Laidlaw
Index Editor: Bill Johncocks
Cover Design: Jess Mason
Cover Layout: Alex Walker
Latest Update: July 2006

Published by SitePoint Pty. Ltd.

424 Smith Street Collingwood
VIC Australia 3066.
Web: www.sitepoint.com
Email: business@sitepoint.com

ISBN 0-9752402-7-7
Printed and bound in the United States of America

About the Authors

Dan Shafer is a highly respected web design consultant. He cut his teeth as the first web-master and Director of Technology at Salon.com, then spent almost five years as the Master Builder in CNET's Builder.com division.

Dan gained widespread recognition as a respected commentator on the web design scene when he hosted the annual Builder.com Live! conference in New Orleans. He has designed and built more than 100 web sites and is regarded as an expert in web user experience design and implementation.

The author of more than 50 previous titles on computers and technology, Dan lives in Monterey, California, with his wife of almost 25 years, Carolyn, and their Shiitzu dog, Albert Einstein.

Rachel Andrew is web developer and director of web solutions provider edgeofmyseat.com. When not writing code, she writes *about* writing code and is the coauthor of several books promoting the practical usage of web standards alongside other everyday tools and technologies. Rachel takes a common sense, real world approach to web standards, with her writing and teaching being based on the experiences she has in her own company every day.

Rachel lives in the UK with her partner Drew and daughter Bethany. When not working, they can often be found wandering around the English countryside hunting for geocaches and nice pubs that serve Sunday lunch and a good beer.

About the Expert Reviewer

Richard Rutter lives and works in Brighton, UK, where he is co-founder and Production Director for web consultancy Clearleft.[1] Richard has been designing and developing web sites for nigh on ten years and regularly harps on about web standards, accessibility, and mountain biking on his weblog.[2]

About SitePoint

SitePoint specializes in publishing fun, practical, and easy-to-understand content for web professionals.

Visit http://www.sitepoint.com/ to access our books, newsletters, articles, and community forums.

---

[1] http://www.clearleft.com
[2] http://www.clagnut.com

This book is dedicated to One
Mind, in the knowing that It
is all there is.

—*Dan Shafer*

Table of Contents

Preface

I've been around the Web for a while now—some might say I've been here from the beginning. And one thing that always bothered me about the Web was its inherent inability to disentangle content from presentation. The interconnectedness of it all meant that, to produce a web site, you needed not only to have something to say, and some graphical design skills to make the presentation of that message look good, but you also needed to be a bit of a programmer. Initially, this "programming" was a pretty lightweight task: HTML markup, when all is said and done, isn't really programming. Still, it's more than just writing words and using a word processor to format them, or conceptualizing a display for a page—digitally or otherwise.

It's no surprise, then, that designers who had clear ideas about how they wanted their web pages to look were frustrated by the need to create complex sets of deeply nested tables even to *approximate* their visions. As designers created increasingly complex ideas, and web browsers diverged further and further from even the merest semblance of compatibility, the Web threatened to collapse under its own weight. Serious designers began lobbying for a complete break from HTML to some new approach to the Web. Chaos reigned.

The Holy Grail of the Web, back then, was the notion that authors should write, designers should design (and code HTML), and programmers should ... well ... program. Those boundaries had not been clear in the first few years of the Web.

Then, along came Cascading Style Sheets (CSS), the subject of this book. The governing forces of the Web, through the World Wide Web Consortium, better known as the W3C,[1] addressed the problem with the proposal that we divide presentation instructions and the structural markup of content into two separate kinds of files.

Things haven't been the same since, thank goodness! Now we can (mostly) separate what we say from the way it's presented to the user in a browser. I wager that most of today's web developers are fairly comfortable with CSS, and would be no more likely to think of embedding presentational instructions in their HTML than they would to consider mixing 23 fonts on the same web or print page.

---

[1] http://www.w3.org/

Since CSS emerged, dozens of books have been written about it. So when Site-Point approached me to write a CSS book, my first thought was, "Who needs another CSS book?" But as they began to reveal their vision to me, it made sense. It was indeed time for a book that took a different tack, based on the extensive experience of the web design community.

This book is different from the rest in two fundamental ways.

First, it focuses on the question of how to use CSS to accomplish some of the successes that web designers have spent significant amounts of time and energy to create using nested tables. In other words, this book doesn't try to start from scratch and become a CSS tutorial. Instead, it's a sort of introductory CSS design guide.

Second, it starts at the outside and works its way in. Most, if not all, other CSS books focus first on the little pieces: the attributes, values, and tags that comprise the syntax of CSS. They then explain how to put those pieces together into a web site.

This book begins by looking at how CSS should influence the overall design of a site, and how to put the CSS framework in place before you begin to deal with individual HTML elements and their styling.

Who Should Read this Book?

As I wrote this book, I had in mind web designers with at least a little experience building sites, who are curious about how CSS can help them become more effective designers. It's aimed at the beginner to intermediate designer. I'll assume a strong grasp of HTML, but that's about it.

What's in this Book?

Chapter 1: *Getting the Lay of the Land*
This first chapter serves as a brief introduction to CSS and the main concepts that we'll discuss throughout the rest of the book. If you haven't used CSS at all before, or you want to ensure that you understand the concepts fully before you get started, this chapter is a great place to start.

Chapter 2: *Putting CSS into Perspective*

In this chapter, we begin to use CSS in practical ways, and to discuss why we might want to use CSS rather than old-style methods like font tags for text styling, and tables for layout.

Chapter 3: *Digging Below the Surface*

Picking up the pace, we start to look in some depth at how CSS works. Here, we consider the different ways in which we can add CSS to our documents, we discuss CSS selectors and rules, and we investigate the various shorthand properties that will help us streamline our CSS files. We'll also come to grips with the concept of inheritance. This chapter ensures that you understand the terminology and syntax we'll be using, which will make it easier for you to follow examples in this book and elsewhere.

Chapter 4: *Validation and Backward Compatibility*

In this chapter, we discuss how we can validate our documents and style sheets to ensure that they comply with the published specifications. We also find out a bit about the practicalities of ensuring our sites' backward compatibility with older browsers or devices.

Chapter 5: *Splashing Around a Bit of Color*

This chapter looks closely at the ways in which colors can be applied to text and other objects, as well as to page backgrounds. It will discuss how to describe colors, where to use them, and how to make them work together to achieve specific effects.

Chapter 6: *Working with Fonts*

This chapter examines the question of how fonts can be used properly in CSS-based web design. After an explanation of how CSS deals with fonts at the most abstract level, we'll look at the use of standard and nonstandard fonts in web pages. Finally, we'll discuss some guidelines for the selection of font families and sizes for your page designs.

Chapter 7: *Text Effects and the Cascade*

This chapter builds on Chapter 6, where we looked at text in terms of fonts and their related style properties. Here, we'll explore a range of other ways in which we can style text, and spend time looking at links and lists, in particular.

Chapter 8: *Simple CSS Layout*

We start this chapter by creating a simple two-column layout. Along the way, we discover how to use absolute and relative positioning techniques in CSS layouts; how margins, padding, and borders work together; and how we can put all of these techniques into practice by creating a fully functional two-column layout.

Chapter 9: *Three-column Layouts*

Out first task in this chapter is to add a third column to the layout we created in Chapter 8. We then discuss the issues that arise when we want to add a footer that runs along the bottom of a multiple-column layout like ours. Along the way, we'll find out how to use the `float` property to create multi-column layouts, and how to create full-length columns using CSS. We'll also consider some of the issues that surround these types of layouts.

Chapter 10: *Fixed-width Layouts*

In this last chapter, we'll create a fixed-width layout that's centered in the user's browser window. As we progress, we'll look at techniques for styling data tables effectively, and discuss one method by which you can enable your users to choose a different layout if they find your fixed-width layout difficult to read.

Appendix A: *CSS Miscellany*

This appendix provides a brief description of some of the more obscure parts of CSS that weren't covered in detail earlier in the book, including the "at-rules" and aural style sheets. It also introduces the concept of DHTML as a launching point for further reading.

Appendix B: *CSS Color Reference*

This appendix provides a comprehensive list of all (official and unofficial) color names in CSS, along with their hexadecimal and RGB equivalent values.

Appendix C: *CSS Property Reference*

This sizeable appendix contains a complete reference to all CSS properties at the time of writing. It includes a practical example for each property (when appropriate) and gives an indication of the level of support browsers provide for that property.

Bibliography

The Recommended Resources listed here include books and web sites. The bibliography is by no means exhaustive; it's more of a list of our own favorite references—resources that we, personally, have found helpful over the years—than a reference to every resource on the topic.

The Book's Web Site

Located at http://www.sitepoint.com/books/css2/, the web site supporting this book will give you access to the following facilities:

The Code Archive

As you progress through the text, you'll note a number of references to the code archive. This is a downloadable ZIP archive that contains complete code for all the examples presented in the book. It also includes a copy of the *Footbag Freaks* web site,[2] which we use as an example throughout the book. You can get it from http://www.sitepoint.com/books/css2/code.php on the book's web site.

Updates and Errata

No book is perfect, and we expect that watchful readers will be able to spot at least one or two mistakes before the end of this one. The Errata page, at http://www.sitepoint.com/books/css2/errata.php on the book's web site, will always have the latest information about known typographical and code errors, and necessary updates for new browser releases and versions of the CSS standard.

The SitePoint Forums

If you'd like to communicate with us or anyone else on the SitePoint publishing team about this book, you should join theSitePoint Forums.[3] In fact, you should join that community even if you *don't* want to talk to us, because there are a lot of fun and experienced web designers and developers hanging out there. It's a good way to learn new stuff, get questions answered (unless you really enjoy being on the phone with some company's tech support line for a couple of hours at a time), and just have fun.

The SitePoint Newsletters

In addition to books like this one, SitePoint offers free email newsletters.

---

[2] http://www.footbagfreaks.com/
[3] http://www.sitepointforums.com/

The SitePoint Tech Times covers the latest news, product releases, trends, tips, and techniques for all technical aspects of web development. The long-running *SitePoint Tribune* is a biweekly digest of the business and moneymaking aspects of the Web. Whether you're a freelance developer looking for tips to score that dream contract, or a marketing major striving to keep abreast of changes to the major search engines, this is the newsletter for you. *The SitePoint Design View* is a monthly compilation of the best in web design. From new CSS layout methods to subtle Photoshop techniques, SitePoint's chief designer shares his years of experience in its pages.

Browse the archives or sign up to any of SitePoint's free newsletters at http://www.sitepoint.com/newsletter/

Your Feedback

If you can't find your answer through the forums, or you wish to contact us for any other reason, the best place to write is `books@sitepoint.com`. We have a well-manned email support system set up to track your inquiries, and if our support staff is unable to answer your question, it comes straight to us. Suggestions for improvement—as well as notices of any mistakes you may find—are especially welcome.

Acknowledgements

First and foremost I must acknowledge the author of the original edition of this book, Dan Shafer, for the solid CSS tutorial that makes up the first half of the book. His original work still stood as an excellent introduction to the subject almost three years later, and updates were required simply due to the passing of time and the evolution of browsers since the first edition of this book was produced.

Thanks must also go to the team members at SitePoint—especially to Simon Mackie—for their expertise and support in guiding this book to completion. Also, thanks to expert reviewer Richard Rutter, who helped greatly in ensuring that outdated advice was excised from the original manuscript, and that I didn't add any inaccuracies of my own!

Finally, and as always, thanks to Drew and Bethany for putting up with me and supporting me through yet another book project. I love you both.

—Rachel Andrew

1

Getting the Lay of the Land

We can look at Cascading Style Sheets (CSS) from a number of contextual perspectives. I prefer to view them as a correction to a fundamental mistake that was made at the beginning of Web Time, back in the old days of the early 1990s, when Tim Berners-Lee and the pioneering web builders first envisioned the beginnings of the Web.

What was that mistake?

To meet the requirements of the Web's initially limited purpose (its original intent was to allow a small number of nuclear physicists using disparate systems at various locations to share vital experimental data), it was not necessary to separate a page's content (the information contained in the document) from its presentation (the way that information is displayed). However, Berners-Lee didn't envision the massively popular, wildly commercialized, extensively morphed Web that emerged from his core ideas in the early 1990s—I doubt that anyone could have.

So, the mistake was a lack of foresight, rather than an oversight. But it was a mistake nonetheless.

CSS in Context

Almost as soon as the Web became popularized by the emergence of early graphical web browsers (such as the wildly popular Netscape Navigator), the designers of early web sites became aware of a problem. The method by which the web browser displayed information stored in HTML files was not within the designers' control. No, it was primarily the users who were in charge of how the web pages they visited would appear on their systems.

While there were many, including myself, who thought this was A Good Thing, designers were beside themselves with concern. From their perspective, this constituted a fundamental flaw. "Users don't know anything about good design," they argued. If the designers couldn't control with great accuracy things like colors, fonts, and the precise, pixel-level positioning of every design element on the web page, their creations could easily end up as ugly travesties in users' browsers. Most designers, accustomed to print and other fixed layouts that afforded them complete control over what the user saw, found ways to bend the Web to their will.

Lest I incur the ire of every designer reading this book, let me hasten to add that I don't think this was A Bad Thing. It is certainly the case that designers know more about how content should be displayed for users than do the users themselves. Things like spacing, color combinations, and other design elements affect readability and usability. My point has much less to do with who should have been in charge, than it does with the actions to which designers were more or less forced to resort in order to achieve at least some measure of control.

Soon, expert designers discovered that they could use tables to gain significant control over the presentation of content to users. By laying out tables within tables within tables, they could position quite precisely any design element that could be contained within a table cell. And that encompassed almost everything.

The first desktop publishing-style web page design tool, NetObjects Fusion, enabled designers to lay out pages with a high degree of precision. It generated complex, table-based HTML, which resulted in web pages that were as close as possible to the designer's original vision.

We never looked back.

But tables weren't intended to be used as layout tools, so while they were effective, they were also horribly inefficient. We'll explore some of the shortcomings and disadvantages of using tables for layout tasks a little later in this chapter; for now, just know that everyone, including the designers who used the techniques, understood pretty well how clumsy a solution they really were.

The Basic Purpose of CSS

After a brief series of skirmishes at the beginning of the Web's development, the question of who should control the overall appearance of a page or site ended with the designers as victors. Users, after all, care more about usability, accessibility, and convenience than the nitty-gritty details of design techniques.

Yet designers found themselves hard-pressed to identify very good, standards-compliant ways to provide their customers—and their customers' users—with great designs that were also effective and efficient. Thus, they were forced to rely largely on tables.

However, as time passed and the use of tables to lay out web pages became increasingly complex, even the design community became uneasy. Maintaining a web page that consists of a half-dozen or more deeply intertwined tables is a nightmare. Most designers prefer not to deal with code—even simple HTML markup—at such a level of detail.

Into the breach stepped the World Wide Web Consortium, better known as the W3C,[1] a body founded by Tim Berners-Lee to oversee the technical growth of the Web. They saw that separating the content of a site from its presentation (or appearance) would be the most logical solution. This would enable content experts—writers, artists, photographers, and programmers—to provide the "stuff" that people come to a site to see, read, or experience. It would also free the design experts—artists, graphic designers, and typographers—to determine a site's aesthetics independently of its content.

The result was CSS.

Why Most—but Not All—Tables Are Bad

Why is the table not suited to being a design mechanism? There are numerous reasons, but the ones we're most concerned with in this context are:

❏ They result in load times that are longer than necessary.

---

[1] http://www.w3.org/

- They encourage the use of inefficient "placeholder graphics" that further slow performance.

- Their maintenance can be a nightmare in which even minor changes break the entire layout.

- They can cause the page to become inaccessible to those who are not using a graphical web browser.

Tables Mean Long Load Times

Most people don't know that web browsers are deliberately designed to ensure that each table downloads as a single entity. None of the material that's contained in a table will be displayed until all the contents of that table are downloaded to the client machine and available for display.[2]

When the original, intended purpose of tables is taken into account, this makes sense. Tables were designed to display ... well, tables of data. Each cell contained a value that was being compared to, or related with, the values of other cells in the table. Isolated bits of data appearing quasi-randomly would not do; the table was a single, integrated entity.

When designers began to rely on tables to contain all or most of the content of a web page, they were also saddled with the consequences of this design decision. In addition to the apparent delay that many users experience as a result of tables displaying all at once, the sheer volume of HTML code that's required to create web page layouts with nested tables can also add load time due to the increased page size. Table-based layouts almost certainly account for more user concern over long page-load times than any other single factor.

Avoiding this significant load time would obviously be A Good Thing.

Use of Transparent Images Slows us Down

Even when using tables as layout mechanisms, designers could not quite attain the detailed level of control they wanted over page design. Sometimes, for instance, a designer might need a bit more breathing room around one part of a table cell—something for which tables do not allow. This kind of precision was un-achievable.

---

[2]Cascading Style Sheets Level 2 (CSS 2) includes a property called `table-layout` that alters this behavior, with several important caveats. Refer to Appendix C for details.

Early on, someone came up with the notion of creating a `transparent.gif` image file—a tiny GIF image that had no visible content. By creating table cells that contained these transparent images, we could force extra vertical and horizontal "space" into tables whose cells were designed to remain in close proximity to one another.

The problem is that, given a table with dozens (or even hundreds) of these images, and depending on a variety of other factors, the performance impact of transparent GIFs on a web page can be significant. More importantly, though, this technique often restricts the page to a fixed pixel size, and clutters the page with images that are irrelevant to the meaning of the page content. This severely impacts the ability of users with disabilities to make sense of table-based sites, as we'll see later.

Maintaining Tables is a Nightmare

The third reason why most tables are bad is that maintaining a complex array of deeply nested tables is a nightmare. If you use tools such as Macromedia Dreamweaver or Adobe GoLive to manage your sites and their designs, generally you can ignore the messiness of the nested tables that make the design possible. But even these tools are not foolproof, and when they "mess up" (to use a highly technical term), amending the unsightly pages they create can be quite a challenge.

If you're like most designers, and you wouldn't be caught dead using an HTML-generating tool because you feel you gain more control and understanding if you hand-code everything, then you'll be familiar with the maintenance problem.

The difficulty arises because, by necessity, tables have a fairly complex set of tags—even if they aren't embedded within other tables. And when we have nested tables, well, we've got a clear case of the uglies, all right.

The situation is further complicated by the fact that, unlike programming editors, HTML editors generally do not force or support the clean indentation of code. So, finding the start and end points for a given table, row, or cell turns out to be what software folks call a "non-trivial task." While it's true that a competent HTML coder or designer could make this problem more tractable, it's never really solvable, no matter what we do.

Tables Cause Accessibility Issues

The fourth reason why tables are bad lies in the way non-graphical browsers—such as the screen readers used by many visually impaired users—read an HTML document. When a text-only device reads the content of a site, it starts at the top and works down the page line by line. When it comes to a table, it starts at the first (top-left) cell, then continues along the top row, then moves to the second row, and so on. In the case of a table that's used correctly, for tabular data, this is rarely a problem. However, where nested tables have been used to display chunks of text in the desired layout, that content can become nonsensical when read in this manner.

When it's Okay to Use a Table

There's one notable exception to the cardinal rule that Tables Are A Bad Thing.

If you have tabular data, and the appearance of that data is less important than its appropriate display in connection with other portions of the same data set, then a table is in order. If you have information that would best be displayed in a spreadsheet such as Excel, you have tabular data.

In general (though, undoubtedly, there are exceptions to this rule as well), this means that the use of tables should be confined to the presentation of numeric or textual data, not graphics, multimedia data types, forms, or any other interactive user interface components.

What is CSS, Really?

Now that we've established that an important role of CSS in designers' lives is to free us from the drudgery of using tables for page layout, let's take a look at what CSS really is.

The most important word in the label "Cascading Style Sheets" is the middle one: "style." "Cascading" becomes important only when we get into fairly complex style usage, while the word "sheet" is a tad misleading at times. So, even though we mean Cascading Style Sheets in the broadest and most accurate sense, we'll focus not on the cascading or sheet-like nature of these beasts, but on their role in determining the styles of our web pages and sites.

Styles are defined as **rules**. These rules tell any web browser that understands them (i.e. any browser that supports CSS) how to display specific types of content structures when it encounters these structures in delivering a web page to a user. We call this visual display of a web page the way the browser **renders** the page.

To understand how styles affect the appearance of a web page, we need to understand what happens to a web page in the absence of any style rules.

Figure 1.1 shows how the browser displays a page when its author hasn't specified any style rules. Each browser has a default way of displaying web pages using its own internal style sheet. So, a first-level heading enclosed in <h1> and </h1> tags will be displayed using a relatively large font in black, because that's dictated by the browser's style sheet. The "default" font that's used may vary between browsers, and can be affected by user-defined settings as well.

Figure 1.1. Normal browser page display behavior

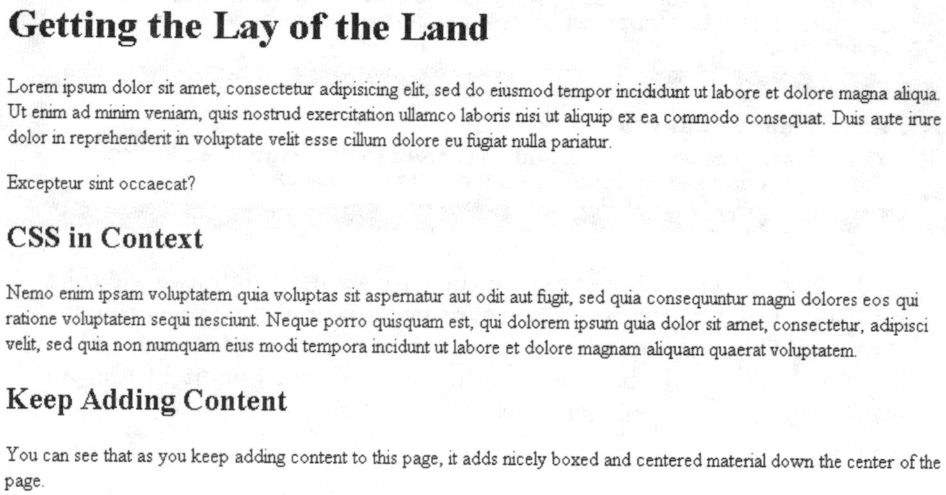

Getting the Lay of the Land

Lorem ipsum dolor sit amet, consectetur adipisicing elit, sed do eiusmod tempor incididunt ut labore et dolore magna aliqua. Ut enim ad minim veniam, quis nostrud exercitation ullamco laboris nisi ut aliquip ex ea commodo consequat. Duis aute irure dolor in reprehenderit in voluptate velit esse cillum dolore eu fugiat nulla pariatur.

Excepteur sint occaecat?

CSS in Context

Nemo enim ipsam voluptatem quia voluptas sit aspernatur aut odit aut fugit, sed quia consequuntur magni dolores eos qui ratione voluptatem sequi nesciunt. Neque porro quisquam est, qui dolorem ipsum quia dolor sit amet, consectetur, adipisci velit, sed quia non numquam eius modi tempora incidunt ut labore et dolore magnam aliquam quaerat voluptatem.

Keep Adding Content

You can see that as you keep adding content to this page, it adds nicely boxed and centered material down the center of the page.

Figure 1.2. The browser displaying a page with a style rule in effect

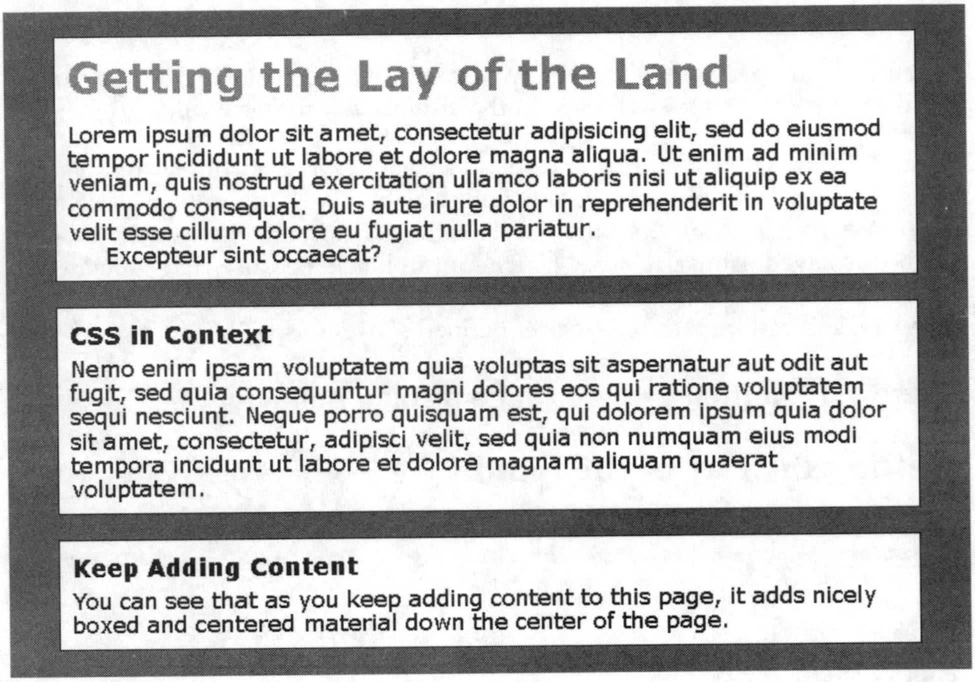

> # Getting the Lay of the Land
>
> Lorem ipsum dolor sit amet, consectetur adipisicing elit, sed do eiusmod tempor incididunt ut labore et dolore magna aliqua. Ut enim ad minim veniam, quis nostrud exercitation ullamco laboris nisi ut aliquip ex ea commodo consequat. Duis aute irure dolor in reprehenderit in voluptate velit esse cillum dolore eu fugiat nulla pariatur.
>
> Excepteur sint occaecat?
>
> **CSS in Context**
>
> Nemo enim ipsam voluptatem quia voluptas sit aspernatur aut odit aut fugit, sed quia consequuntur magni dolores eos qui ratione voluptatem sequi nesciunt. Neque porro quisquam est, qui dolorem ipsum quia dolor sit amet, consectetur, adipisci velit, sed quia non numquam eius modi tempora incidunt ut labore et dolore magnam aliquam quaerat voluptatem.
>
> **Keep Adding Content**
>
> You can see that as you keep adding content to this page, it adds nicely boxed and centered material down the center of the page.

Figure 1.2 depicts what happens when the page's author defines style rules. An author-defined rule overrides the browser's own internal style sheet rule for that element, and the new style takes over. Even if the user has defined his or her own settings for this element, those wishes usually will not be honored (though there are some intriguing exceptions to this generality, which we'll discuss much later in this book).

Parts of a CSS Rule

Every style consists of one or more rules. Figure 1.3 shows a CSS rule with all the parts labeled.

Figure 1.3. The parts of a CSS rule

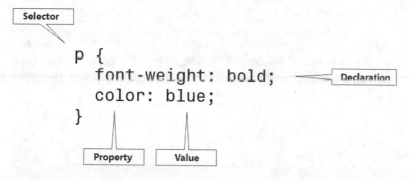

Each rule has two parts:

1. a **selector** that defines the HTML element(s) to which the rule applies

2. a collection of one or more **declarations**, made up of a **property** and a **value**,[3] which describe the appearance of all the elements that match the selector

The property tells the browser which element is being defined. For example, `font-weight` tells the browser that this declaration defines the weight of the font. After the colon that separates the two parts of a declaration, we see a value that will be applied to that property. If a value of `bold` followed the `font-weight` property, it would make the weight of the font in that document bold. Each declaration must be followed by a semicolon, with one exception: the semicolon that follows the last property is optional and may be omitted. In this book, though, we'll always add the optional semicolon. I encourage you to adopt this habit, as it's much easier to train yourself always to add the semicolon than it is to remember when it is and is not required. This approach also makes it easier to add properties to an existing style rule.

Here are a few examples of increasingly complex CSS rules, with the parts identified so that you can fix this syntax clearly in your mind. This is the only real syntax issue you must understand in order to master CSS, so it's important!

---

[3]Many books and articles about CSS get confused when it comes to this terminology, using these terms interchangeably, or calling declarations "attributes." In this book, I used the W3C-endorsed terminology of "declarations," "properties," and "values." I reserve the name "attributes" for attributes of HTML tags.

```
h1 {
  color: red;
}
```

The selector, h1, indicates that this rule applies to all h1 headings in the document. The property that's being modified is color, which refers to the font color. The value we want the color property to take on is red. Chapter 5 and Chapter 6 explore fonts and coloring in CSS in greater detail.

```
p {
  font-size: small;
  color: green;
}
```

The selector, p, indicates the style rule should be applied to all paragraphs in the document. There are two declarations in the rule. The first, which sets the property font-size, sets the size of the font in all paragraphs in the document to small. See Chapter 3 for an explanation of this and other measurement issues in CSS. The second property, color, is set to green. The result of this rule is that all paragraphs in the document will appear in a green, "small" font.

```
p {
  font-family: 'New York', Times, serif;
}
```

Again, this rule deals with paragraphs, as is evidenced by the p selector. This time, the selector affects the font family that is used to display text. The new wrinkles in this example are that it includes a list of values for the font-family property, and one of those values is enclosed in quotation marks.

The font-family property is one of a handful of CSS properties to which you can assign a list of possible values, rather than a single, fixed value. When you use a list, commas must separate its individual members. In this case, the font-family value list tells the browser to use New York as the font if the user's machine has it installed. If not, it directs the browser to use Times. And if neither of these fonts is available on the user's system, the browser is told to default to the font used for serif type. This subject is covered in more depth in Chapter 6.

Whenever a value in a list includes spaces (as is the case with the font named "New York"), you must put that value into quotation marks. Many designers use single quotation marks for a number of reasons, not least of which is that they're slightly easier to type, but you can use either single or double quotation marks.

Types of CSS Rules

We can categorize and think about CSS rules in several possible ways:

❑ First, we can think of the different types of properties that can be defined. For example, different properties affect the color of elements, their positions within the browser window, and so on.

❑ We can also consider the types of elements that can be affected using CSS, and specifically, how certain elements can be targeted.

❑ Finally, there is the issue of where the style rules are defined.

Let's take a brief look at each of these categorizations, so that you have a good overview of the organization of CSS rules before you embark on a detailed study of their use.

Which Properties can CSS Rules Affect?

CSS rules can include properties that affect virtually every aspect of the presentation of information on a web site. A complete reference to these properties is presented in Appendix C.

Which Elements can CSS Affect?

Stated another way, this question asks, "How, specifically, can a CSS rule target a piece of information on a web page for special presentation?" CSS allows the designer to affect all paragraphs, but how can you confine that impact to certain, specific paragraphs? Is this even possible?

The answer is "yes." Through various combinations of selector usage, the designer can become quite specific indeed about the circumstances under which a style rule is enforced. For example, you can assign rules so that they affect:

❑ all elements of a specific type

❑ all elements of a specific type that are assigned to a common group or class

❑ all elements of a specific type that are contained within other elements of a specific type

❑ all elements of a specific type that are both contained within another specific element type and assigned to a common group or class

❑ all elements of a specific type only when they come immediately after an element of some other type

❑ only a specific element of a specific type that is assigned a unique ID

Chapter 3 includes a detailed discussion of all the CSS selectors you can use to achieve these kinds of precision targeting.

Where can CSS Styles be Defined?

Finally, you can define CSS styles in any of three places:

❑ inside the HTML (such style declarations are called **inline declarations**)

❑ between `<style>` and `</style>` tags inside the `head` element (this is called an **embedded style sheet**)

❑ in an external CSS file, also called an **external style sheet**

Inline Declarations

You can style any element by listing style declarations inside that element's `style` attribute. These are referred to as inline declarations because they're defined inline as part of the document's HTML. You can assign a `style` attribute to almost all HTML elements. For example, to make a second-level heading within a document appear in red text and all capital letters, you could code a line like this:

```
<h2 style="color: red; text-transform: uppercase;">An Unusual
    Heading</h2>
```

If you follow the advice in this book, you won't use many inline declarations. As we'll see, separating content from presentation is one of the big advantages of CSS, and embedding styles directly in HTML tags defeats that purpose. Inline declarations are mainly useful for rapid prototyping—quickly applying style properties to a particular element to experiment with an effect before giving the properties a more permanent place in an embedded or external style sheet.

Embedded CSS

Specifying style properties in an embedded style sheet is an approach that's often used by beginning web designers and those just learning the techniques involved in CSS design. It's not my favorite method, but it does have the virtue of being easy to deal with, so you'll see it used from time to time in this book.

To embed a style sheet in a web page, we place a `style` element in the head of the document's HTML and fill it with style rules, as shown here in bold:

```
<!DOCTYPE html PUBLIC "-//W3C//DTD XHTML 1.0 Strict//EN"
    "http://www.w3.org/TR/xhtml1/DTD/xhtml1-strict.dtd">
<html xmlns="http://www.w3.org/1999/xhtml">
  <head>
    <title>CSS Style Sheet Demo</title>
    <meta http-equiv="Content-Type"
        content="text/html; charset=iso-8859-1" />
    <style type="text/css">
      h1, h2 {
        color: green;
      }
      h3 {
        color: blue;
      }
    </style>
  </head>
```

The CSS rules contained in the style block apply to all the designated parts of the current document. In this case, the first rule directs the browser to display all level one and two headings (`h1`, `h2`) in green. The second rule displays all level three headings (`h3`) in blue.

Notice that each rule starts on a new line, and each declaration within the rule appears indented within braces on its own line. Strictly speaking, this layout isn't required, but it's a good rule of thumb that improves the readability of your code, especially if you're used to the look of JavaScript code.

External CSS

Finally, you can define CSS rules in a file that's completely separate from the web page. You can link to this file by including a `link` element in the head of any web page on which you want to implement those styles.

```
<!DOCTYPE html PUBLIC "-//W3C//DTD XHTML 1.0 Strict//EN"
    "http://www.w3.org/TR/xhtml11/DTD/xhtml1-strict.dtd">
<html xmlns="http://www.w3.org/1999/xhtml">
  <head>
    <title>CSS Style Sheet Demo</title>
    <meta http-equiv="Content-Type"
        content="text/html; charset=iso-8859-1" />
    <link rel="stylesheet" type="text/css" href="corpstyle.css" />
  </head>
```

In this example, the file `corpstyle.css` contains a set of styles that have been linked to this page. Here's what the contents of this file might look like:

File: **corpstyle.css**

```
h1, h2 {
  color: green;
}
h3 {
  color: blue;
}
```

This is my preferred way to use CSS, for a number of reasons.

First, this is the least "locked-in" of the three basic methods designers can use to insert styles into a web page. If you define an external style sheet file, you can apply it to as many pages of your site as you want, simply by linking to the style sheet from each page on which you want it used. Using external CSS also makes your site a lot easier to maintain: changing the appearance of an element that appears on every page of your site is a simple matter of modifying the shared `.css` file. If you use embedded or—worse yet—inline styles, you'll have to change every single page on which the element appears.

Second, external style sheets are treated as separate files by the browser. When the browser navigates to a new page that uses the same style sheet as a previous page, that external style sheet will not be downloaded again. Therefore, pages that use external styles are quicker to load.

Last, but not least, external style sheets are simply more professional. By using them, you demonstrate an understanding of the importance of the separation of content from presentation, and you make it much easier to discuss your style sheets, share them with colleagues, analyze their effects, and work with them as if they were a serious part of the site's design, rather than an afterthought.

A Simple Example

Now that you have a basic overview of what CSS is all about, why it exists, and why it's an important technique for web designers to adopt, where's the proof? Let's look at an example of a small but not overly simplistic web page (see Figure 1.4).

Figure 1.4. A sample web page demonstrating embedded styles

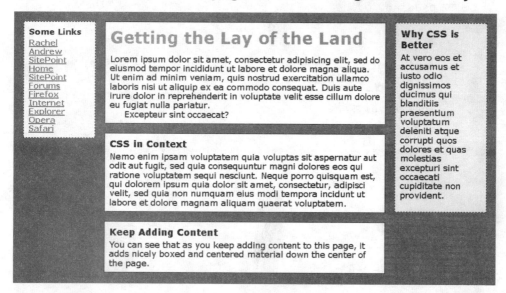

Here's the HTML that will produce that page if we use embedded CSS. Don't let the complexity of the code intimidate you—by the end of Chapter 3 you should be able to infer the meaning of most of it without my help. For now, you can download the code archive from the book's web site and marvel at the results in your browser. The file is called ch1sample.html.

File: **ch1sample.html**

```
<!DOCTYPE html PUBLIC "-//W3C//DTD XHTML 1.0 Strict//EN"
    "http://www.w3.org/TR/xhtml11/DTD/xhtml1-strict.dtd">
<html xmlns="http://www.w3.org/1999/xhtml">
  <head>
    <title>Basic 3-Column Sample Page</title>
    <meta http-equiv="Content-Type"
        content="text/html; charset=iso-8859-1" />
    <style type="text/css">
```

```
body {
  background-color: teal;
  margin: 20px;
  padding: 0;
  font-size: 1.1em;
  font-family: Verdana, Arial, Helvetica, sans-serif;
}
h1 {
  font-family: Verdana, Arial, Helvetica, sans-serif;
  margin: 0 0 15px 0;
  padding: 0;
  color: #888;
}
h2 {
  font-family: Verdana, Arial, Helvetica, sans-serif;
  margin: 0 0 5px 0;
  padding: 0;
  font-size: 1.1em;
}
p {
  font-family: Verdana, Arial, Helvetica, sans-serif;
  line-height: 1.1em;
  margin: 0 0 16px 0;
  padding: 0;
}
.content>p {
  margin: 0;
}
.content>p+p {
  text-indent: 30px;
}
a {
  color: teal;
  font-family: Verdana, Arial, Helvetica, sans-serif;
  font-weight: 600;
}
a:link {
  color: teal;
}
a:visited {
  color: teal;
}
a:hover {
  background-color: #bbb;
}
/* All the content boxes belong to the content class. */
```

```
    .content {
        position: relative;
        width: auto;
        min-width: 120px;
        margin: 0 210px 20px 170px;
        border: 1px solid black;
        background-color: white;
        padding: 10px;
        z-index: 3;
    }
    #navleft {
        position: absolute;
        width: 128px;
        top: 20px;
        left: 20px;
        font-size: 0.9em;
        border: 1px dashed black;
        background-color: white;
        padding: 10px;
        z-index: 2;
    }
    #navleft ul {
        list-style: none;
        margin: 0;
        padding: 0;
    }
    #navright {
        position: absolute;
        width: 168px;
        top: 20px;
        right: 20px;
        border: 1px dashed black;
        background-color: #eee;
        padding: 10px;
        z-index: 1;
    }
    </style>
</head>
<body>
    <div class="content">
        <h1>Getting the Lay of the Land</h1>
        <p>Lorem ipsum dolor sit amet, consectetur adipisicing elit,
            sed do eiusmod tempor incididunt ut labore et dolore
            magna aliqua. Ut enim ad minim veniam, quis nostrud
            exercitation ullamco laboris nisi ut aliquip ex ea
            commodo consequat. Duis aute irure dolor in
```

```
        reprehenderit in voluptate velit esse cillum dolore eu
        fugiat nulla pariatur.</p>
    <p>Excepteur sint occaecat?</p>
</div>
<div class="content">
    <h2>CSS in Context</h2>
        <p>Nemo enim ipsam voluptatem quia voluptas sit aspernatur
          aut odit aut  fugit, sed quia consequuntur magni
          dolores eos qui ratione voluptatem  sequi nesciunt.
          Neque porro quisquam est, qui dolorem ipsum quia dolor
          sit amet, consectetur, adipisci velit, sed quia non
          numquam eius modi tempora incidunt ut labore et dolore
          magnam aliquam quaerat voluptatem.</p>
</div>
<div class="content">
    <h2>Keep Adding Content</h2>
    <p>You can see that as you keep adding content to this page,
        it adds nicely boxed and centered material down the
        center of the page.</p>
</div>
<div id="navleft">
    <h2>Some Links</h2>
    <ul>
      <li><a href="http://www.rachelandrew.co.uk/"
          title="Rachel Andrew's personal site">Rachel
          Andrew</a></li>
      <li><a href="http://www.sitepoint.com/"
          title="SitePoint Home Base">SitePoint Home</a></li>
      <li><a href="http://www.sitepoint.com/forums"
          title="SitePoint Discussion Forums">SitePoint
          Forums</a></li>
      <li><a href="http://www.mozilla.org/firefox"
          title="Firefox at The Mozilla Foundation">Firefox</a>
          </li>
      <li><a href="http://www.microsoft.com/ie"
          title="Internet Explorer at Microsoft's Site">Internet
          Explorer</a>
      <li><a href="http://www.opera.com/"
          title="Opera Home Page">Opera</a></li>
      <li><a href="http://www.apple.com/safari"
          title="Safari on Apple's Web Site">Safari</a></li>
    </ul>
</div>
<div id="navright">
    <h2>Why CSS is Better</h2>
    <p>At vero eos et accusamus et iusto odio dignissimos
```

```
          ducimus qui blanditiis praesentium voluptatum deleniti
          atque corrupti quos dolores  et quas molestias excepturi
          sint occaecati cupiditate non provident.</p>
     </div>
   </body>
</html>
```

Summary

You should now understand the historical and technological contexts in which CSS has emerged, the major problems it is designed to solve, and how it works on a superficial level. You also know why tables aren't suited to being used as a web page layout device, even though they have other perfectly valid uses.

In addition, you can identify both the parts of a CSS rule, and at least three ways in which these rules can be applied to your web pages.

Chapter 2 drills more deeply into the prospective issues surrounding CSS. It clears up some of the misconceptions you may have about this technology, and describes some of the important issues you'll have to take into consideration because of the way web browsers work (or don't) with CSS rules.

2

Putting CSS into Perspective

In Chapter 1, we took a 10,000-foot view of CSS. We began by looking at why using tables for web page layout is generally a bad idea. Then, we examined the types of CSS rules, and which aspects of a web page our style sheets could affect.

This chapter provides an overview of CSS's place in the web development cosmos. First, we'll discuss what CSS can and can't do for you. We'll spend a little time examining the advantages of CSS design, and see how using CSS can help you to create better sites by doing things that old-style tables and spacer GIFs can't do.

After a quick look at how CSS interacts with the ever-shifting world of web browsers, we'll discover how we can create CSS that accommodates those browsers that don't provide full support for CSS standards, either because they predate the standard, or they tried to support the standard but got it wrong.

What can CSS Do?

Recall from Chapter 1 that one of the key advantages of CSS is that it separates the *content* of a web site from its *appearance* or *presentation*. This separation is important because it allows us to create web sites that enable writers to create the *information* the web site is intended to convey, while leaving the *design* of the site—how it looks and how it behaves—to designers and programmers.

It follows, then, that CSS would be useful for defining the *appearance* of a site, but not necessarily for dictating its *behavior*.

However, like many such generalizations, this statement is true only most of the time. Why? Because the dividing line between appearance and behavior is necessarily fuzzy.

For example, as we'll see when we develop our layouts in the second part of this book, CSS can be used effectively to create context-sensitive menus, along with other elements of the interface with which your users will interact. You may be familiar with menu designs whose interactivity relies heavily on JavaScript, or some other scripting language, but we'll learn some techniques that avoid scripting, while allowing us to do some fairly creative things with navigation.

Later on, this book provides detailed instructions and examples of how you can alter the appearance of colors, fonts, text, and graphics using CSS; the rest of this section provides some ideas about the kinds of tasks for which you can use CSS. My intention here is less to teach you how to do these things than it is to whet your appetite and start you thinking about the possibilities …

Color and CSS

You can use style sheet rules to control the color of any HTML element that can be displayed in color. The most common elements for which you'll find yourself setting the color are:

❑ text

❑ headings (which are really a special form of text)

❑ page backgrounds

❑ background colors of text and headings

This may not seem like much, but knowing when and how to apply color to these elements—and, perhaps more importantly, how to combine the use of color in interconnected elements—can really expand your web design capabilities.

Figure 2.1. Black-and-white version of fall holiday page

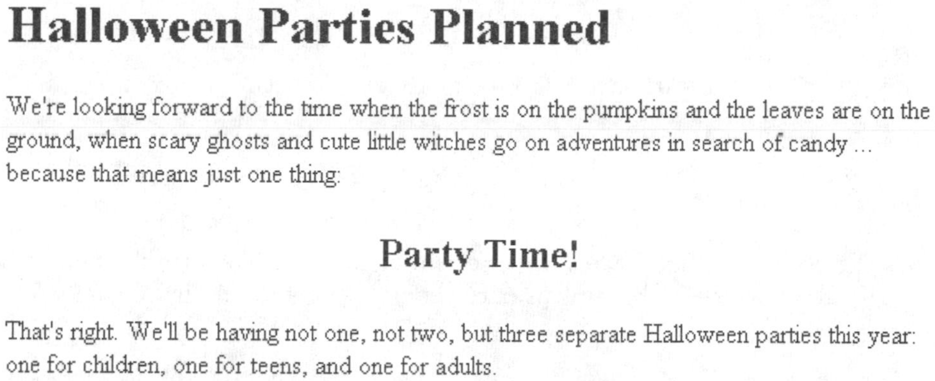

Halloween Parties Planned

We're looking forward to the time when the frost is on the pumpkins and the leaves are on the ground, when scary ghosts and cute little witches go on adventures in search of candy ... because that means just one thing:

Party Time!

That's right. We'll be having not one, not two, but three separate Halloween parties this year: one for children, one for teens, and one for adults.

The simple act of changing the color of all the text on a page, then providing a colored background for that text, can turn a fairly ordinary-looking web page (Figure 2.1) into one that has a completely different feel to it. Figure 2.2 shows what the page in Figure 2.1 looks like if we simply choose colors appropriate to a holiday theme—yellow text on a black background. Figure 2.3 shows the opposite effect: black text on a yellow background. While you could argue that these alternative layouts aren't as readable as the black and white original in Figure 2.1, you'd have to admit that the two variations are more interesting to look at.

Figure 2.2. Yellow-on-black version of fall holiday page

Halloween Parties Planned

We're looking forward to the time when the frost is on the pumpkins and the leaves are on the ground, when scary ghosts and cute little witches go on adventures in search of candy ... because that means just one thing:

Party Time!

That's right. We'll be having not one, not two, but three separate Halloween parties this year: one for children, one for teens, and one for adults.

Here's the style rule that creates the effect in Figure 2.2. As you can see, it's fairly straightforward, yet the result of its use is certainly dramatic.

```
body {
  color: yellow;
  background-color: black;
}
```

As we'll see in Chapter 5, naming the colors you want is just one of several ways to define color in CSS.

Here's the style rule that creates the effect in Figure 2.3. No surprises here: it's the opposite of the code that was used to generate the look in Figure 2.2.

```
body {
  color: black;
  background-color: yellow;
}
```

Figure 2.3. Black-on-yellow version of fall holiday page

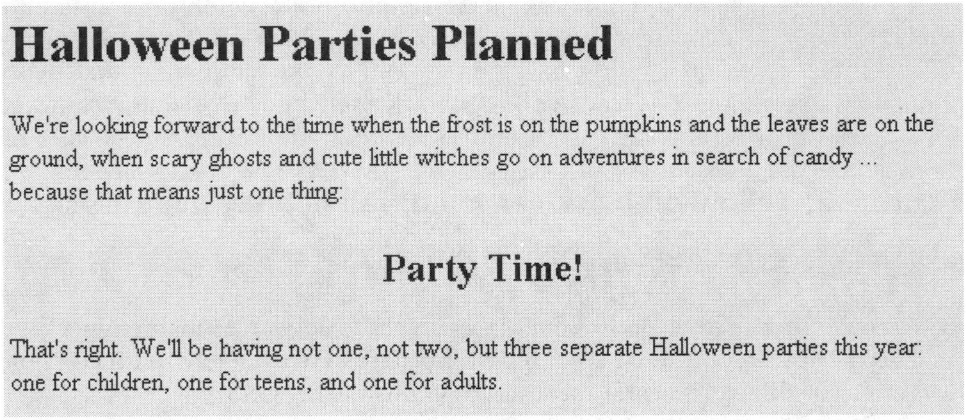

Halloween Parties Planned

We're looking forward to the time when the frost is on the pumpkins and the leaves are on the ground, when scary ghosts and cute little witches go on adventures in search of candy ... because that means just one thing:

Party Time!

That's right. We'll be having not one, not two, but three separate Halloween parties this year: one for children, one for teens, and one for adults.

Maybe you find the use of a starkly contrasting color for the entire background of a page a bit overwhelming. Figure 2.4 shows another variation on the text color theme. Here, we've provided yellow text on a black background only behind the headings on the page. The rest of the page's background color, and all non-heading text, remains unchanged from the original design in Figure 2.1.

Figure 2.4. Yellow-on-black headings on fall holiday page

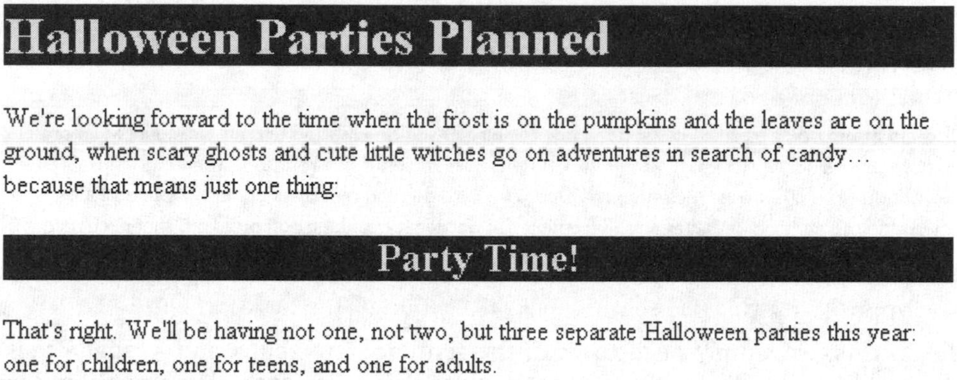

Halloween Parties Planned

We're looking forward to the time when the frost is on the pumpkins and the leaves are on the ground, when scary ghosts and cute little witches go on adventures in search of candy... because that means just one thing:

Party Time!

That's right. We'll be having not one, not two, but three separate Halloween parties this year: one for children, one for teens, and one for adults.

Here's the style rule that generates the heading effect shown in Figure 2.4.

```
h1, h2, h3, h4, h5, h6 {
  color: yellow;
  background-color: black;
}
```

Notice that we didn't have to do anything fancy, like put the headings inside `<div>` and `</div>` tags, or create a rectangular box around them. In the view of the web browser, the heading is a **block level element**, which occupies the full width of the space in which it resides, by default. So, if you give a heading a `background-color` property, that property will apply to the entire horizontal block that contains the heading.

CSS provides a range of other advantages to the color-conscious designer, but we'll leave those details to Chapter 5. Our purpose here is merely to touch upon the variety of things you can expect to accomplish using CSS.

Fonts and CSS

In Chapter 1, we saw a number of examples that used fonts in CSS style rules. From that exposure, you're probably comfortable with defining the fonts in which you want the body text and headings of various levels to be displayed.

You can apply fonts to smaller amounts of text by enclosing that text within `<span>` and `</span>` tags (a subject we'll treat in detail in Chapter 9), then applying style properties to the span. You might use this approach, for example, to highlight a sentence in the middle of a paragraph, as shown in Figure 2.5.

Figure 2.5. Highlighting an important sentence

Lorem ipsum dolor sit amet, consectetur adipisicing elit, sed do eiusmod tempor incididunt ut labore et dolore magna aliqua. Ut enim ad minim veniam, quis nostrud exercitation ullamco laboris nisi ut aliquip ex ea commodo consequat. Duis aute irure dolor in reprehenderit in voluptate velit esse cillum dolore eu fugiat nulla pariatur. Excepteur sint occaecat cupidatat non proident, sunt in culpa qui officia deserunt mollit anim id est laborum.

To do this, we simply need to wrap the sentence in <span> and </span> tags, then add a style rule for the new span. Note that these span elements should be used sparingly, and that there are a number of issues to consider before you apply these techniques—see Chapter 8 and Chapter 9 for all the details. Below is the HTML that was used to create this effect.

```
<p>Lorem ipsum dolor sit amet, consectetur adipisicing elit, sed
   do eiusmod tempor incididunt ut labore et dolore magna aliqua
   <span class="important">Ut enim ad  minim veniam, quis nostrud
   exercitation ullamco laboris nisi ut aliquip  ex ea commodo
   consequat.</span> Duis aute irure dolor in reprehenderit in
   voluptate velit esse cillum dolore eu fugiat nulla pariatur.
   Excepteur  sint occaecat cupidatat non proident, sunt in culpa
   qui officia  deserunt mollit anim id est laborum.</p>
```

You can target a particular span by adding an id or class attribute (we'll look at this in more detail in Chapter 3), then adding the id or class to the selector, as shown here:

```
.important {
  font-weight: bold;
  background-color: yellow;
  color: red;
}
```

One type of HTML text element to which it's sometimes quite useful to apply font rules is the list. We generally create lists in an effort to call specific attention to several items that are related to one another, and using a font style to set the list off even more clearly from the text can be a good technique. Figure 2.6 shows a list that has been set in a font that contrasts with the main text of the page, and is bold. The list stands out from the page, calling attention to itself as being particularly important.

Figure 2.6. Highlighting an important list

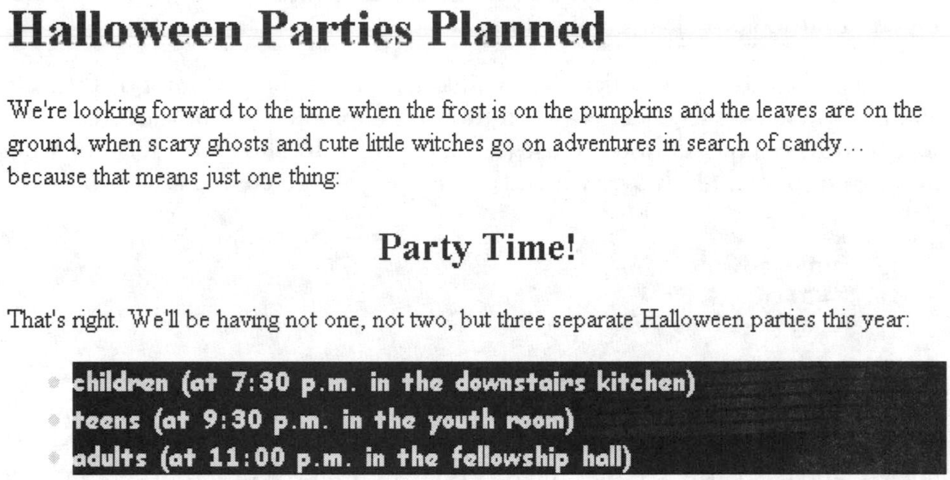

Halloween Parties Planned

We're looking forward to the time when the frost is on the pumpkins and the leaves are on the ground, when scary ghosts and cute little witches go on adventures in search of candy... because that means just one thing:

Party Time!

That's right. We'll be having not one, not two, but three separate Halloween parties this year:

- children (at 7:30 p.m. in the downstairs kitchen)
- teens (at 9:30 p.m. in the youth room)
- adults (at 11:00 p.m. in the fellowship hall)

Once we've identified this list in HTML using an `id` attribute, we can style it by adding a rule to our style sheet.

```
<ul id="partylist">
  <li>children (at 7:30 p.m. in the downstairs kitchen)</li>
  <li>teens (at 9:30 p.m. in the youth room)</li>
  <li>adults (at 11:00 p.m. in the fellowship hall)</li>
</ul>
```

The rule now looks like this:

```
#partylist {
  font-family: 'Comic Sans MS', Arial, Helvetica, sans-serif;
  font-weight: bold;
  color: yellow;
  background-color: black;
}
```

Dynamic Pseudo-classes and CSS

One of the more interesting effects that you can create with CSS involves the use of the "hover" effect on text. By defining a CSS style rule that changes the appearance of text when the user pauses the cursor over that text, you can create an effect that looks a bit like animation.

Unfortunately, this effect works only on link text in Internet Explorer 6, although in other browsers—such as Firefox and Internet Explorer 7[1]—you can create this effect on other elements. You can use the `hover` **pseudo-class** to determine what will happen to a text link over which the user pauses the cursor, as shown here:

```
a:hover {
  background-color: blue;
  color: white;
  font-size: x-large;
}
```

Figure 2.7 shows what happens when the user positions the cursor over a link to which this style rule is applied. While you can't tell that the color of the text has changed, you can easily see that the text is larger than the other links around it.

Figure 2.7. Applying a dynamic pseudo-class to a hovered link

Halloween Parties Planned

We're having parties all over the place for this holiday. Whether you're an <u>adult</u> or a <u>child</u>, we've got you covered!

This effect feels a bit like an animated graphic in a menu where the buttons are programmed to change when the user's mouse hovers over them—it's a technique that we'll learn more about in Chapter 9.

Changing Text Size in `:hover` Styles

You may be tempted to change the size of the text in a link when the user hovers their mouse over it—it does make very obvious to the user which link

---

[1] At the time of writing, Internet Explorer 7 is still in beta testing, so no guarantees can be made of its final functionality.

they currently have selected. However, this is generally considered bad practice, as changing the size of text in the middle of a document will typically move other elements of the document around, potentially confusing the user. It's much better to use background and font colors to make such distinctions.

Images and CSS

Images are placed on a web page using the HTML <img /> tag. With CSS, we can only affect relatively minor aspects of an image's display, but that doesn't mean we can't control anything interesting.

Like any other object in a web page, an image can always be enclosed inside a div element and positioned arbitrarily on the page. We can also affect the border around an image, as well as its alignment, again by embedding the image in a div element, then using a style to alter the appearance of that containing div.

Figure 2.8 shows what would happen to an image placed alongside text on a page, in the absence of any CSS instructions. The image appears at the left edge of the page and it is aligned with one line of text, which shares its baseline with the bottom of the image. Subsequent lines of text appear below the image.

Figure 2.8. An image and text to which CSS styles haven't been applied

Subscribe to One of Our Journals Now... and Save!

Shown here is a selection of some of the many magazines and journals we have available for subscription as part of our annual fund-raising drive. As a matter of fact, we have just about every magazine and journal you could ever hope to find or subscribe to. If you already get enough magazines, we can arrange to renew your current subscription when it expires and still get credit for your purchase. We both win. You don't miss out on any issues of a proven favorite magazine, and Charities International gets the benefit of your contribution.

One thing for which CSS is particularly helpful is forcing text to flow gracefully around inline images. Using the float property (which is covered in detail in Chapter 8), you can "float" an image on a page in such a way that the text placed beside it will wrap around the image nicely. Figure 2.9 shows what happens if we position the image using the `float` property. Note how the text flows smoothly around the side of, and then under, the image. This is almost certainly closer to the design effect we want than the example shown in Figure 2.8.

Figure 2.9. Positioning an image and text with help of `float`

Subscribe to One of Our Journals Now... and Save!

Shown here is a selection of some of the many magazines and journals we have available for subscription as part of our annual fund-raising drive. As a matter of fact, we have just about every magazine and journal you could ever hope to find or subscribe to. If you already get enough magazines, we can arrange to renew your current subscription when it expires and still get credit for your purchase. We both win. You don't miss out on any issues of a proven favorite magazine, and Charities International gets the benefit of your contribution.

To do this to all the images in your site, add the following rule to your style sheet:

```
img {
  float: left;
}
```

Multiple Style Sheets, Users, and CSS

It is possible to define more than one style sheet for a given web page or site; we'll look at how alternate style sheets can be used in the course of creating projects later in the book. Some modern browsers (such as Firefox and Opera) allow the user to select from additional style sheets if they have been created. These "alternate" style sheets can be used to display larger font sizes or higher contrast designs for users who have specific accessibility needs.

With a bit of scripting, you can automate that selection process and create an adaptable site that several different categories of users can experience appropriately. We won't be covering this kind of scripting in this book, but if you're interested, Paul Sowden's article, "Alternative Style: Working With Alternate Style Sheets",[2] on A List Apart is a great place to start.

Advantages of CSS Design

I've already touched on a number of the powerful features of, and reasons for, using CSS for site layout. In this section, I'll formalize those arguments and present them all in one place. Not only do I hope to convince you of the merits of CSS, but I aim to give you the tools to sell *others* on the technology.

In the cutthroat world of freelance web development, you will often be called upon to explain why you will do a better job than other developers bidding on the same project. If CSS layout is one of the tools in your web design arsenal, the sites you build will benefit from the advantages presented here. Many of these advantages go well beyond ease of development, and translate directly to extra value for your clients. Let them know about this—it just might make the difference between winning the contract and losing out to a designer who lives and breathes table-based design.

Increased Stylistic Control

Perhaps the major selling point of CSS is that it lets you control many aspects of the appearance of your site that simply cannot be controlled with pure HTML (for example, creating hover effects on links). For a complete reference to the style properties that can be controlled with CSS, see Appendix C.

In addition to the number of properties that it puts at your fingertips, CSS allows you to apply those properties to the available HTML page elements more uniformly than would be possible using other techniques. For instance, if you wanted to use HTML to put a visible border around part of the page, you'd need to use a table to do it, because pure HTML lets you add borders to tables only. Not only does CSS give you greater control over the look of the border (it can be solid, embossed, dotted, or dashed; thick or thin; any of a multitude of colors; etc.), it lets you add a border to *any* page element—not just tables. The design rationale behind CSS aims to give the designer as many options as possible, so, generally speaking, a property can be applied at any point at which, potentially, it could make sense to do so.

---

[2] http://www.alistapart.com/articles/alternate/

CSS simply has more properties that can be applied to more page elements than HTML has ever offered. If you had to choose between CSS and HTML as a means for specifying the design of your site, and your decision was based solely on which approach would afford you the most visual control, CSS would win outright. Despite this, it is common practice to use HTML for design wherever possible, and to resort to CSS whenever an effect is needed that HTML cannot produce. While the appearance of sites designed with this rationale is just as good as any others, by taking this approach to design, we miss out on all the other advantages of CSS.

Centralized Design Information

As I've already explained, the best way to use CSS in the design of a web site is to write one or more .css files to house all your style code, and then to link those files to the appropriate pages with the HTML <link /> tag. This approach ensures that everything to do with the *look* of your site can be found in one place, and is not jumbled up with the *content* of your site.

The idea is that you should be able to change the content of your site without affecting its look, and vice versa. In traditional web design, where HTML tags and attributes are used to specify the way things look in the browser, the code for these two aspects of your site are mixed together, so anyone who wants to modify one of these must understand both, or risk breaking one while making changes to the other. The look and the content of the site are said to be **coupled**.

This principle of keeping code that serves different purposes in different places is known in the programming world as **decoupling**. If a site's style and content are decoupled, a web designer can modify the look of the site by editing the .css file(s), while a content editor can add content to the site by editing the .html files.

Even more significant than facilitating organization and teamwork, this separation of code reduces code duplication. In HTML-based design, if you want the title of every article on your site to display in a large, red font, you have to put <font> and </font> tags around the text inside the relevant h1 element on every one of your site's article pages. With CSS-based design, you can specify the font properties for every h1 element in one place, which saves on typing. And, should you decide to change the appearance of these headings, you have only to modify the .css file instead of each and every .html file, which saves your sanity! These differences are illustrated in Figure 2.10.

Figure 2.10. Centralizing design code with CSS

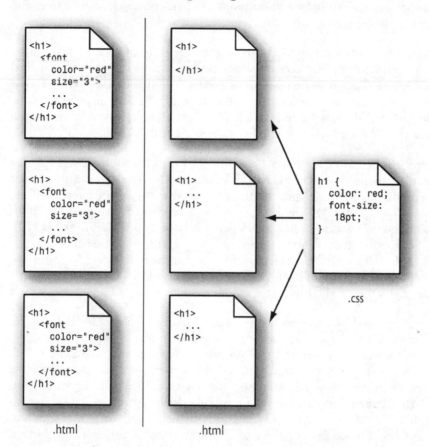

If you look closely at Figure 2.10, you'll see that, in addition to the organizational advantages described above, the browser has less code to download. On heavily designed sites, or sites with hundreds of pages or more, this reduced download time can have a significant impact both on the user experience, as well as your bandwidth costs.

Semantic Content Markup

When you use `.css` files to decouple the content from the appearance of your site, as I've just described, a curious thing begins to happen to your HTML. Because CSS affords you complete control over the appearance of page elements, you begin to choose tags because they describe the structure and meaning of elements of the page, instead of how you want them to look. Stripped of most or all of the presentational information, your HTML code is free to reflect the **semantics** of your site's content.

There are a number of reasons why this is a desirable state of affairs, key among them the fact that decoupling content from design makes it very easy to find things when you're changing the content of your site. The easiest way to spot a CSS-based site is to use the View Source feature in your browser—if you can make sense of the code within ten seconds, chances are that you're not dealing with a site that uses table-based layout and other non-semantic HTML.

Your web site will be easier for potential visitors to find through search engines if it's marked up with semantic HTML, because the fewer presentational tags the search engine has to wade through to analyze your site, the easier it will be for it to index the content. As we'll see, CSS lets you control the position of an element in the browser window almost independently of its position in the HTML document. So, if you have a newsletter subscription form, or some other lengthy chunk of HTML that won't mean a whole lot to a search engine, feel free to move its code to the end of your HTML document and use CSS to ensure that it's displayed near the top of the browser window.

Increasingly supported by modern browsers is a feature of the HTML `link` element[3] that lets you restrict a linked style sheet so that it affects a page only when that page is displayed by a certain type of browser. For instance, you could link three `.css` files to a page: one that defined the appearance of the page on a desktop browser, another that dictated how the page will look when printed, and yet another that controlled the display on mobile devices such as Internet-connected Personal Digital Assistants (PDAs). Only by using semantic markup, and allowing the CSS to take care of the display properties, is this sort of content repurposing possible.

Last, but certainly not least, are the vast accessibility improvements that a site can gain by using semantic markup. We'll discuss these in detail in the next section.

Accessibility

Should you ever have the opportunity to observe a visually impaired individual browsing the Web, I highly recommend you do so. Alternatively, get yourself

---

[3]Specifically, the `media` attribute.

some screen reader software, switch off your monitor, and see for yourself what it's like.

Web sites that use tables, images, and other non-semantic HTML for layout are extremely difficult for visually impaired people to use. Their screen reader software will typically read the page aloud, from top to bottom. It's not unusual for a modern, table-based web site to inflict 30 seconds or more of nonsense upon the user before the actual content begins. An example of some of what a screen reader would output for a table based site is shown below:

> Table with one column and five rows, Table with three columns and one row, Link, Graphic, slash logo underline main dot gif, Table end, Table with two columns and one row, Link, Graphic, slash nav underline about underline us dot gif, Link, Graphic, slash nav underline site underline map dot gif, Table end, Table end, Table with one column and twenty-six rows, Table with one column and seventeen rows ...

Now, if you think that sounds mildly annoying, imagine having to listen to it for each and every page of the sites that you visit!

CSS-based design and semantic markup nearly eliminate this aural garbage, because they ensure that every tag in the document has a structural meaning that's significant to the viewer (or listener). An aural browser ignores the visual formatting properties defined in the CSS, so the user need not listen to them.

On a site that used semantic markup, for example, a visually impaired user would never have to wonder if a word was bold because it was more important, or just because it looked better that way. Elements that were displayed in bold for design reasons would have that property assigned using CSS, and the aural browser would never mention it. Elements that needed additional impact or emphasis would be marked up using the semantically meaningful strong and em elements, which are displayed, by default, as bold and italic text in visual browsers, yet also convey meaning to a screen reader user, as they tell the device to emphasize the phrase.

A complete set of guidelines exists for developers who are interested in making their sites more accessible for users with disabilities. The Web Content Accessibility Guidelines 1.0[4] (WCAG) is recommended reading for all web developers, with Guideline 3[5] focusing on the idea of avoiding presentational markup in favor

---

[4] http://www.w3.org/TR/WCAG10/
[5] http://www.w3.org/TR/WCAG10/#gl-structure-presentation

of semantic markup. As we create projects later in this book, we'll discuss some of these issues more fully.

Standards Compliance

The WCAG isn't the only specification that advocates the use of CSS for the presentational properties of HTML documents. In fact, the latest HTML standards[6] themselves are written with this in mind.

The World Wide Web Consortium[7] (W3C) is the body responsible for publishing recommendations (de facto standards) relating to the Web. Here are some of the W3C Recommendations that relate to using semantic markup and CSS:

HTML 4[8]

The latest (and last) major revision of the HTML Recommendation marks all non-semantic elements and attributes as **deprecated**.[9] The font element, for example, is clearly marked as deprecated in this standard. Under the description of deprecated elements, the Recommendation has this to say:

> In general, authors should use style sheets to achieve stylistic and formatting effects rather than HTML presentational attributes.

XHTML 1.0[10]

XHTML is a reformulation of HTML 4 as an XML document type. It lets you use HTML tags and attributes while enjoying the benefits of XML features (including the ability to mix tag languages, custom tags, etc.).

This Recommendation includes the same tags and deprecations as HTML 4.

Web Content Accessibility Guidelines 1.0[11]

As described in the section called "Accessibility", the WCAG Recommendation strongly recommends using CSS and semantic markup in web design to improve accessibility. I'll let the Recommendation speak for itself:

---

[6] http://www.w3.org/MarkUp/#recommendations

[7] http://www.w3.org/

[8] http://www.w3.org/TR/html4

[9] A deprecated element or attribute is one that has been tagged for removal from the specification, and which therefore should not be used. For a document to comply strictly with the specification, it should not use any deprecated tags or attributes.

[10] http://www.w3.org/TR/xhtml1/

[11] http://www.w3.org/TR/WCAG10/

Misusing markup for a presentation effect (e.g. using a table for layout or a header to change the font size) makes it difficult for users with specialized software to understand the organization of the page or to navigate through it. Furthermore, using presentation markup, rather than structural markup, to convey structure (e.g. constructing what looks like a table of data with an HTML PRE element) makes it difficult to render a page intelligibly to other devices.

Many web developers believe that strict standards compliance is an idealistic goal that is rarely practical. One of the primary goals of this book is to demonstrate that this is not true. Today's browsers provide strong support for CSS and produce more consistent results when they are fed standards-compliant code. While bugs and compatibility issues still exist, they are no more insurmountable than the bugs that face designers who rely on noncompliant code. In fact, once you have valid, standards-compliant code, fixing bugs and compatibility problems can be easier—as you have the starting points of a valid document and style sheet, and just need to find out why the browser display differs—and a lot of help is available on the Web to help you to do that.

Browser Support for CSS

At the time of writing, the browsers employed by the vast majority of web users provide sufficient CSS support to make CSS layouts a viable and sensible choice. The usage of really old browsers—such as Netscape 4—has dwindled to a point where supporting them to the full (i.e. so that these users can access the complete design and functionality of your site) is unnecessary. That said, it's perfectly possible to design sites so that your layout degrades gracefully in older browsers, ensuring that no users are denied access to your content

Designing sites to meet web standards, and constructing them using CSS, should enable you to communicate with more users: they'll be able to access the content whether they're using the latest version of Firefox on a desktop computer, a PDA or phone, an old version of Netscape, or a screen reader. We'll explore some of the ways in which we can optimize site access for various browsers in Chapter 4.

Summary

In this chapter, we explored the primary uses of CSS, and discussed the advantages of designing sites using Cascading Style Sheets. Chapter 3 focuses on the "how" of CSS: we'll see how rules are included in tags as inline style rules, embedded in pages as embedded style sheets, and loaded from external style sheet files. We'll also investigate in more detail the various selectors and structures of CSS rules, and the units and values you'll use in all rules that require specific measurements.

3

Digging Below the Surface

This chapter completes our look at the "mechanics" of CSS: the background you need to have in order to work with the technology. It covers six major topics:

❑ a quick review of the three methods we can use to assign CSS properties to HTML documents

❑ the use of shorthand properties to group the values for a related set of properties within a single statement

❑ the workings of the inheritance mechanism in style sheets

❑ the structure of a style, including variations on the use of selectors to determine with great precision exactly what is affected by a style

❑ the units and values that can appear in styles to express sizes, locations, and other properties, and how they're used

❑ CSS comments, which can be used to place human-readable notes in your CSS code

Applying CSS to HTML Documents

In Chapter 1, we discussed three methods for applying style sheet properties to HTML documents. Let's briefly review them here.

inline styles

We can use the `style` attribute, which is available for the vast majority of HTML elements, to assign CSS properties directly to HTML elements.

```
<h1 style="font-family: Helvetica, Arial, sans-serif;
    color: blue;">Welcome</h1>
```

This method is best reserved for times when you want quickly to try out one or more CSS properties to see how they affect an element. You should never use this method in a practical web site, as it avoids almost every advantage that CSS has to offer.

embedded styles

We can use the `style` element in the `head` portion of any HTML document to declare CSS rules that apply to the elements of that page.

```
<style type="text/css">
h1, h2 {
  color: green;
}
h3 {
  color: blue;
}
</style>
```

This form of CSS offers many advantages over inline styles, but is still not as flexible or powerful as external styles (discussed below). I recommend that you reserve embedded styles for use when you're certain that the styles you're creating will be useful only in the current page. Even then, the benefit of separate code offered by external styles can make them a preferable option, but embedded styles can be convenient for quick-and-dirty, single-page work.

external styles

We can use a `<link />` tag in the head portion of any HTML document to apply the CSS rules stored in an external file to the elements of that page.

```
<link rel="stylesheet" type="text/css" href="mystyles.css" />
```

External styles are the recommended approach to applying CSS to HTML, as this technique offers the full range of performance and productivity advantages that CSS can provide.

Using Shorthand Properties

Most properties take a single item as a value. When you define a property with a collection of related values (e.g. a list of fonts for the `font-family` property), the values are separated from one another by commas, and if any of the values include embedded white space or reserved characters, such as colons, they may need to be enclosed in quotation marks.

In addition, there's a special set of properties called **shorthand properties**, which let you use a single property declaration to assign values to a number of related properties. This sounds more complicated than it is.

The best-known shorthand property is `font`. CSS beginners are usually accustomed to defining font properties one by one:

```
h1 {
   font-weight: bold;
   font-size: 90%;
   line-height: 1.8em;
   font-family: Helvetica, Arial, sans-serif;
}
```

But CSS provides a shorthand property, `font`, that allows this same rule to be defined much more succinctly:

```
h1 {
   font: bold 90%/1.8em Helvetica, Arial, sans-serif;
}
```

You can do the same with properties such as `padding`:

```
h1 {
   padding-top: 10px;
   padding-right: 20px;
   padding-bottom: 10px;
   padding-left: 5px;
}
```

We could replace the above declaration with the following shorthand:

```
h1 {
  padding: 10px 20px 10px 5px;
}
```

The values are specified in a clockwise order, starting at the top of the element: from top, to right, to the bottom, then left.

All shorthand properties are identified in Appendix C.

How Inheritance Works in CSS

Before you can grasp the syntax and behavior of CSS rules, you need a basic understanding of **inheritance**, and how it's used in CSS.

Think of a family tree. Your great-grandfather is at the top of the tree, followed by his children, including his only son (your grandfather). Below your grandfather is your mother and her siblings, and then, beneath her, there's you, your siblings, and your children. Some of your features, such at the color of your hair and eyes, would be inherited from your ancestors—perhaps you have your mother's hair color, but your grandfather's eyes. Other features may not be passed on in this way. Your son may be far taller than anyone else in the family.

Just as everyone in your family fits into your family tree, every element on an HTML page belongs to the document's inheritance tree. The root of that tree is *always* the html element.[1] Normally, the html element has only two direct descendants in the inheritance tree: head and body.

Figure 3.1 shows a simple HTML inheritance tree for a small document.

As you can see, the document has in its head the standard title and link elements, the latter of which probably links to an external style sheet. It also includes a meta element (most likely to set the document's character set).

The body element has five children: an h1, an h2, a p element (labeled p_1 so we can refer to it easily), a div, and an unordered list (ul) element. The div element, in turn, contains two paragraph elements, one of which has an emphasis (em) element, while the other contains an anchor (a) element. The ul element includes three list item (li) elements; one of these includes an emphasis (em) element, while another contains the paragraph element labeled p_4.

---

[1] This is even true of documents written to older versions of the HTML standard, in which the html element was not required.

Figure 3.1. A simple HTML inheritance tree

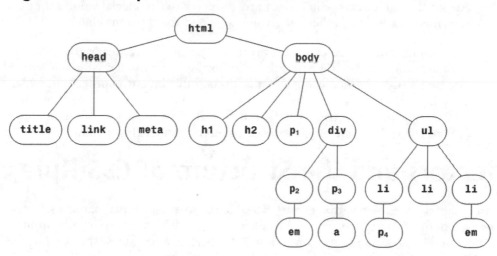

Each element in an HTML document (with the exception of the root html element) has a **parent** element. This is the element that directly precedes it in the tree. In Figure 3.1, p_1's parent is the body element. Likewise, p_1 is said to be a **child** of the body element.

Most elements in an HTML document will be **descendants** of more than one element. For example, in Figure 3.1, the paragraph element p_1 is a descendant of the body and html elements. Similarly, the paragraph element p_2 is a descendant of the div, body, and html elements. This notion of element hierarchy is important for two reasons:

❑ The proper use of some of the CSS selectors you'll work with will depend on your understanding of the document hierarchy. There is, for example, an important difference between a descendant selector and a parent-child selector. These are explained in detail in the section called "Selectors and the Structure of CSS Rules", later in this chapter.

❑ If you don't supply a specific value for an element's property, in many cases, that element will take the value assigned to its parent. Consider the example document shown in Figure 3.1. If the body element had a declaration for the font-family property and p_1 did not, p_1 would inherit the body element's font-family. In contrast, setting the width property of an element will not directly affect the width of its child elements. font-family is an **inherited property**; width is not.

The properties that are inherited—and those that are not—are indicated in Appendix C. However, you can set any property to the special value `inherit`, which will cause it to inherit the value assigned to its parent element.

This inheritance issue can become tricky when you're dealing with fairly complex documents. It's particularly important when you're starting with a site that's been defined using the traditional table layout approach, in which style information is embedded in HTML tags. When a style sheet seems not to function properly, you'll often find that the problem lies in one of those embedded styles from which another element is inheriting a value.

Selectors and the Structure of CSS Rules

In Chapter 1 we learned that every CSS style rule consists of two parts: a selector, which defines the type(s) of HTML element(s) to which the style rule applies; and a series of declarations, consisting of properties and values, that define the style.

So far, we've seen only simplistic selectors. Typically, they've contained only one element:

```
h1 {
  font-size: 120%;
  text-transform: capitalize;
}
```

We've encountered one or two instances where a single rule is designed to apply to more than one kind of HTML element:

```
h1, h2, h3 {
  font-size: 120%;
  text-transform: capitalize;
}
```

In this section, we'll take a look at all the different kinds of selectors that are available to you in CSS.

Universal Selector

The **universal selector** matches every element in the document. It has very little practical value by itself, but the universal selector can come in handy in specific situations involving, for example, attribute selectors, which I'll explain later in this section.

In this example, all elements in the page are given a text color of red:

```
* {
  color: red;
}
```

Element Type Selector

The **element type selector** is the most common selector. It specifies one HTML element type with no qualifiers. In the absence of other style rules that might apply to the element type provided in the selector, this rule applies to all such elements on the page.

In this example, we specify the text and background color of all hyperlinks in the current document. They will appear as white text on a green background.

```
a {
  color: white;
  background-color: green;
}
```

Class Selector

To apply a style rule to a potentially arbitrary group of elements in a web page, you'll need to define a class in the style sheet, then identify the HTML elements that belong to that class using the `class` attribute.

To define a class in a style sheet, you must precede the class name with a period. No space is permitted between the period and the name of the class.

The following style sheet entry defines a class named `special`.

```
.special {
  font-family: Verdana, Helvetica, Arial, sans-serif;
}
```

Then, we add `class="special"` to the elements that we want to adopt this style.

```
<h1 class="special">A Special Heading</h1>
<p class="special">This is a special paragraph.</p>
```

You can write your class so that it applies only to a particular type of element. In the following example, we create the same `special` class, but this time it applies only to paragraph elements.

```
p.special {
  font-family: Verdana, Helvetica, Arial, sans-serif;
}
```

If you define an element-specific class such as the `p.special` example above, then associate that class (in this case, `special`) with an element of any other type, the style rule simply does not apply to that element.

An HTML element can belong to multiple classes: simply list those classes (separated by spaces) in the `class` attribute:

```
<p class="special exciting">Paragraph! Of! Stuff!</p>
```

ID Selector

An **ID selector** lets you target a single HTML element within a page. Like a class selector, an ID selector must be defined in the style sheet and included explicitly in the HTML tag. Use the # symbol to identify an ID selector in the style sheet,[2] and the `id` attribute to give an element an ID. IDs must be unique within a document; no two HTML elements in a single document should have the same ID.

This style sheet rule defines a rule for an element with the ID `unique`:

```
#unique {
  font-size: 70%;
}
```

The code below uses the HTML `id` attribute to indicate the element that will be affected by the rule above:

```
<h4 id="unique">This will be a very tiny headline</h4>
```

For example, if you had five `<div class="sidebar">` items on your page, but you wanted to style differently the one responsible for displaying your site's search box, you could do so like this:

---

[2]Optionally, you can confine the ID's use to an element of a specific type by preceding the # with the HTML element's tag name (e.g. `div#searchbox`). But, since you can have only one element with the specific ID within a document, it seems silly to confine it to a specific element type.

```
div.sidebar {
  border: 1px solid black;
  background-color: yellow;
}
#searchbox {
  background-color: orange;
}
```

The search box would then appear in your HTML as shown here:

```
<div id="searchbox" class="sidebar">
  <!-- HTML for search form -->
</div>
```

Now, since the `div` has `id="searchbox"` and `class="sidebar"` attributes, all the sidebar declarations will be applied to the search box, but it will take its `background-color` from the `#searchbox` rule. The guidelines for cascading overlapping rules (discussed in Chapter 9), in combination with the ID selector, let you avoid having to redefine all the sidebar properties in a special `searchbox` class.

However, you could just as easily define a class and apply it to the exceptional element (the search box, in this example). This approach is more flexible, although perhaps not as efficient in terms of code space. For example, imagine you've identified a class or other rule that applies to all level-three headings except one, and you've used an ID selector for the exception. What do you do when a redesign or content change requires one more such exception? The ID selector solution breaks down immediately in that situation.

Pseudo-element Selector

This and all the remaining selectors in this section require a browser that supports the CSS 2 specification, such as Firefox, Safari, Opera, or Internet Explorer 7. Some features, such as the `:hover` pseudo-class, are supported by some older browsers, but their implementations are not complete.

Pseudo-element selectors and pseudo-class selectors are unique among the CSS selectors in that they have no equivalent HTML tag or attribute. That's why they use the prefix "pseudo" (meaning "false").

So far, the CSS specification has defined only three pseudo-elements: `first-letter`, `first-line`, and `first-child`. While the first two of these phrases mean something to us humans, it's ultimately up to each browser to interpret them when rendering HTML pages that use these pseudo-elements. For example, does `first-line` mean "first sentence," or does it mean the first physical line that's displayed—a value that changes as the user resizes the browser? The `first-child` pseudo-element, on the other hand, is not browser-dependent. It refers to the first descendant of the element to which it is applied, in accordance with the HTML document hierarchy described in the section called "How Inheritance Works in CSS".

To define a pseudo-element selector for a style rule, precede the pseudo-element name with a colon. Here's an example:

```
p:first-letter {
  font-face: serif;
  font-size: 500%;
  float: left;
  color: gray;
}
```

This creates a drop-caps effect for the first letter in every paragraph on the page, as shown in Figure 3.2. The first letter in each paragraph will be five times larger than the usual type used in paragraphs. The `float` style property, which we discuss in Chapter 8, ensures the remaining text in the paragraph wraps around the enlarged drop-cap correctly.

Figure 3.2. Creating a drop-caps effect using the `first-letter` pseudo-element

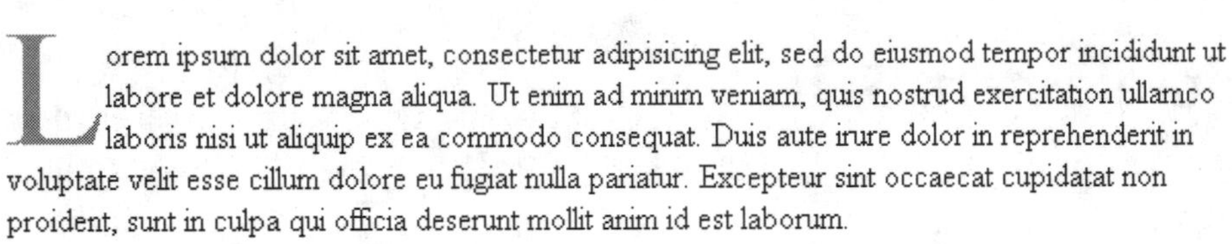

Lorem ipsum dolor sit amet, consectetur adipisicing elit, sed do eiusmod tempor incididunt ut labore et dolore magna aliqua. Ut enim ad minim veniam, quis nostrud exercitation ullamco laboris nisi ut aliquip ex ea commodo consequat. Duis aute irure dolor in reprehenderit in voluptate velit esse cillum dolore eu fugiat nulla pariatur. Excepteur sint occaecat cupidatat non proident, sunt in culpa qui officia deserunt mollit anim id est laborum.

Pseudo-class Selector

A **pseudo-class selector** is exactly like the pseudo-element selector, with one exception. A pseudo-class selector applies to a whole element, but only under certain conditions.

The current release of CSS 2 defines the following pseudo-classes:

❑ hover

❑ active

❑ focus

❑ link

❑ visited

❑ lang

A style sheet, then, can define style rules for these pseudo-classes as shown in the example below. You may remember that we've already seen a rule that uses the hover pseudo-class.

```
a:hover {
  color: green;
}
```

All anchor tags will change color when the user mouses over them. As you can see, this means the pseudo-class selector comes into play only when the user interacts with the affected element.

The lang pseudo-class[3] refers to the setting of the lang attribute in an HTML element. For example, you could use the lang attribute shown below to define a paragraph in a document as being written in German:

```
<p lang="de">Deutsche Grammophon</p>
```

If you wanted, for example, to change the font family associated with all elements in the document that were written in German, you could write a style rule like this:

```
:lang(de) {
  font-family: spezialitat;
}
```

lang vs language

Be careful not to confuse this lang attribute with the deprecated language attribute that used to be used to set the scripting language used in pages.

---

[3]Be aware that browser support for the lang pseudo-class is still very scarce. It's covered here mainly for the sake of completeness.

Descendant Selector

As we've discussed, all HTML elements (except the html element) are descendants of at least one other HTML element. To apply a CSS style rule to an element only when it's a descendant of some other kind of element, we can use a **descendant selector**.

A descendant selector, such as the one shown in the following style rule, restricts the applicability of the rule to elements that are descendants of other elements. The scope of the descendant selector is determined by reading the rule from right to left. Spaces separate the element types.

```
li em {
  color: green;
}
```

The style rule identifies that a color of green will be applied to any text contained in an em, or emphasis, element *only* when the emphasized text is a descendant of a list item.

In the fragment below, the first em element will be displayed in green characters; the second will not, as it doesn't appear within a list item.

```
<ul>
  <li>Item one</li>
  <li>Item <em>two</em></li>
</ul>
<p>An <em>italicized</em> word.</p>
```

It's important to note that the descendant relationship need not be an immediate parent-child connection. Take this markup, for example:

```
<div class="sidebar">
  <p>If you have any questions, <a href="contact.html">please call
    our office during business hours</a>.</p>
</div>
```

The following style rule would apply to the anchor element even though it focuses explicitly on a elements that are descendants of div elements. This is because, in this case, the a element is the child of a paragraph that's contained in a div element.

```
div a {
  font-style: italic;
}
```

Parent-child Selector

A **parent-child selector** causes a style rule to apply to element patterns that match a specific sequence of parent and child elements. It is a special case of the descendant selector that we discussed above. The key difference between the two is that the pair of elements in a parent-child selector must be related directly to one another in a strict inheritance sequence.

A parent-child relationship is specified in a selector with the "greater than" sign (>).

Below is an example of a parent-child relationship.

```
body > p {
  font-weight: bold;
}
```

In the example below, this rule will only affect para2, as para1 and para3 are not direct descendants of the body element.

```
<body>
  <div class="sidebar">
    <p id="para1">This is the sidebar.</p>
  </div>
  <p id="para2">Welcome to the web site! Here's a list:</p>
  <ul>
    <li>
      <p id="para3">This is the first paragraph in the list. It's
        also the last.</p>
    </li>
  </ul>
</body>
```

As of this writing, Internet Explorer for Windows (up to and including version 6) distinguishes itself by being the only major browser that does not support parent-child selectors. Because of this, careful use of descendant selectors is far more common, and the parent-child selector is often abused to specifically create styles that do not apply to Internet Explorer for Windows.

Adjacent Selector

Adjacency is not related to inheritance. Adjacency refers to the sequence in which elements appear in an HTML document. As it happens, adjacent elements are always siblings, but it's their placement in the document, rather than their inheritance relationship, that is the focus of this selector. This point is demonstrated in the HTML fragment below:

```
<h1>This is important stuff!</h1>
<h2>First important item</h2>
<h2>Second important item</h2>
```

The first h2 heading is *adjacent* to the h1 heading, but the second h2 heading is not adjacent to the h1 heading.

The adjacent selector uses the + sign as its connector, as shown here:

```
h1 + h2 {
  margin-top: 11px;
}
```

This style rule would put 11 extra pixels of space between the bottom of an h1 heading and an h2 heading that followed it immediately. It's important to recognize that an h2 heading that follows a paragraph under an h1 heading would not be affected.

As of this writing, Internet Explorer for Windows (up to and including version 6) remains the only major browser that does not support adjacent selectors, although support is planned for Internet Explorer version 7. Because of this, the adjacent selector has not yet found widespread use in practical web design.

Attribute Selectors

The group of selectors I'm lumping together as **attribute selectors** are among the most interesting of all the CSS selectors, because they almost feel like programming techniques. Each attribute selector declares that the rule with which it is associated is applied only to elements that have a specific attribute defined, or have that attribute defined with a specific value.

There are four levels of attribute matching:

[*attribute*]   matches if the attribute *attribute* is defined at all for the element(s)

[*attribute*="*value*"]	matches only if the attribute has a value of *value*
[*attribute*~="*value*"]	matches only if the attribute is defined with a space-separated list of values, one of which exactly matches *value*
[*attribute*|="*value*"]	matches only if the attribute is defined with a hyphen-separated list of "words," and the first of these words begins with *value*

You might, for example, want to apply style properties to all single-line text input boxes (<input type="text" />) in your document. Perhaps you want to set their text and background colors to white and black, respectively. This style rule would create that effect:

```
input[type="text"] {
  color: white;
  background-color: black;
}
```

The third variation of the attribute selector described above searches the values assigned to an attribute, to see whether it contains the word you've specified (i.e. a value in a space-separated list).

For example, during the development of a web site, various graphic designers may have inserted some img elements with temporary placeholder alt attributes, with the idea of returning to them later to finish them. You could call attention to the existence of such tags with a style rule like this:

```
img[alt~="placeholder"] {
  border: 8px solid red;
}
```

This selector will find all img elements whose alt attributes contain the word "placeholder," and will put an eight-pixel red border around them. That ought to be hard to miss!

The fourth variation really is useful only when you're dealing with the lang attribute. Typically, the lang attribute takes on a value such as en or de. However, it can also be used to define the regional dialect of the language being used: en-us for American English, en-uk for British English, etc. This is when the [*attribute*|="*value*"] selector comes into its own. It enables you to isolate the first portion of the lang attribute, where the language that's being used is defined. The other portions of the hyphen-separated value are ignored.

As you've probably come to expect by now, attribute selectors are not supported by Internet Explorer for Windows versions 6 and earlier. As with other advanced selector types, this has prevented the widespread adoption of attribute selectors, despite their obvious usefulness.

Selector Grouping

To apply a style rule to elements of several different types in an HTML document, we use selector grouping, separating with a comma the element types to which the rule is to be applied.

Here's a simple example of this type of selector:

```
h1, h2, h3 {
  font-family: Helvetica, Arial, sans-serif;
  color: green;
}
```

The elements in the selector list need not be of the same type or even the same level of specificity. For example, the following style rule is perfectly legal. It applies a specific style to level-two headings (h2) and to paragraphs whose class is defined as special:

```
h2, p.special {
  font-size: 22px;
}
```

You may include a space between the comma-separated items, though this is not necessary.

Expression Measurements

Most of the values we define in a CSS rule include measurements. These measurements tell the rule how tall or wide something is to be, so it follows that you'll most commonly use measurements when working with fonts, spacing, and positioning.

There are two types of measurements: absolute and relative. An absolute measurement (e.g. setting a font-size to 18px, or 18 pixels) tells the browser to render the affected content 18 pixels tall.[4] Technically speaking, it tells the browser to

---

[4]Again, if I wanted to be terribly precise, I would say that a pixel is actually a relative measurement, because its meaning is relative to the display medium on which the page is produced. But, in this

use the specified font and scale its character height so that the font's overall height is 18 pixels. Chapter 8 includes an explanation of font height and width.

Relative measurements, on the other hand, instruct the browser to scale a value by some percentage or multiple, relative to the size of the object before the scaling takes place. The example below defines a style rule in which all fonts in paragraphs on the page should be scaled to 150% of the size they would have been without this style:

```
p {
  font-size: 150%;
}
```

If you knew that, in the absence of such an instruction, the text of all paragraphs on the page displays at a size of 12 pixels, you could also accomplish the same thing this way:

```
p {
  font-size: 18px;
}
```

Generally, you should use the relative sizing values whenever you can. This technique works better than absolute sizing when the user has set preferences for font sizes, and in situations in which multiple style sheets could be applied. It's also more accessible, as visually impaired users can more easily increase the font size on the page by configuring their browsers' preferences.

All **length values** (the term used by the CSS specification to describe any size measurement, whether horizontal or vertical) consist of an optional sign (+ or -), followed by a number (which may include a decimal point), followed by a unit of measurement. No spaces are permitted between the number and the unit of measurement.

---

context, "relative" means "relative to some other value in the style rule or in the HTML," and in that sense, pixels are absolute.

Absolute Values

Table 3.1. Absolute values supported in style sheets

Style Abbreviation	Style Meaning	Explanation
in	inch	Imperial unit of measure; 2.54 centimeters
cm	centimeter	
mm	millimeter	
pt	point	1/72 inch
pc	pica	12 points, or one-sixth of an inch
px	pixel	One dot on the screen

Table 3.1 shows the absolute values that are supported in CSS style sheets, and where they're not obvious, the values' meanings.

When a length of zero is used, no unit of measurement is needed. 0px is the same as 0. It doesn't make sense to give a unit of measurement when the length is zero units, because zero is the same distance in any unit of measurement.

Whenever you need to supply an absolute measurement for the size or position of an element in a style sheet rule, you can use any of the above abbreviations interchangeably. Each of the following rules should produce precisely the same result:

```
font-size: 1in;
font-size: 2.54cm;
font-size: 25.4mm;
font-size: 72pt;
font-size: 6pc;
```

Pixels pose an entirely different set of issues. A pixel is one point on a screen that can be on or off, displaying any color that is needed. If you set your monitor's display to a resolution of 800 pixels by 600 pixels, a pixel corresponds to 1/600 of the screen height. On a 15-inch display, the height is about 10.5 inches and the width is a little more than 13 inches.[5] A 12-pixel font display on that monitor would turn out to be about 1/50 of the 10.5-inch height of the display, or just a little more than one-fifth of an inch.

Many designers set their font sizes using pixels in the belief that this prevents site users from increasing the font size using their browser settings, because Internet Explorer does not allow the resizing of text set in pixels. However, most other browsers do allow the user to resize text set in pixels. A common issue arises with sites whose designers haven't realized that fonts set using pixels can be resized in other browsers: often, the text will appear to expand out of fixed-size boxes. From the point of view of accessibility, if users need a larger font size and have increased the text size in their browsers accordingly, we should support this choice regardless of which browser they're using; thus, we should avoid setting text heights using pixels. Creating designs that work well even if users have increased the text size in their browsers is part of the process of designing for the Web. The use of pixels to size text should be avoided.

Relative Values

Because of the problems posed by the use of any absolute value, the most flexible way to approach measurements for style rules is to use relative units of measurement. Principally, these units are em and percentage, although some people prefer to use the more obscure ex measurement. The em measurement is so named because it refers to the width of an uppercase "M" in the given font, but in practice, it's equal to the font-size of the current font. The ex measurement is based on the height of the lowercase "x" character in a font (more commonly known as the x-height of the font) and is far less common than the em.

Both the em and the percentage generate font sizes based on the inherited or default size of the font for the object to which they're applied. In addition, ems and percentages are 1:100 equivalent. A size of 1em is identical to a size of 100%.

This description begs the question, "What's the default or inherited font size for a particular HTML element?" The answer is: it depends.

Prior to the emergence of Opera 5 for Windows, browsers set the default values for all fonts as part of their startup processes. Users had no control. The browsers

---

[5]High school math would lead you to predict a nine- by 12-inch screen, but unfortunately, 15-inch monitors don't normally have a full 15 inches of diagonal screen space. Perhaps computer manufacturers don't study Pythagoras.

defined a default, and web designers overrode the defaults willy-nilly, as they saw fit. The user took what was presented.

Then, along came the idea of user choice—a development that, not surprisingly, was facilitated by the emergence of CSS. Essentially, the developers of the Opera browser created a local style sheet that users could modify and set their own defaults to use. The Opera developers also defined a nice graphical user interface through which users could set preferences for these styles.

This was great for users, but web designers found themselves in a quandary. If, for example, you assumed that browsers were going to default body text to a 12-point font size[6] (which was the de facto standard before the user-controlled preferences era), you could set a style to apply a `1.25em` scaling to the text and get a 15-point font size for the text in question. It was nice and predictable.

But now, a `1.25em` scaling applied to a font tells the browser to increase the size of the font to 1.25 times (or 125% of) its default size. If the user has set up his or her browser to show standard text at a height of 16 points, your `1.25em` transformation brings the size up to 20 points.

When you stop to think about it, though, that's probably just fine. The user who chooses a larger base font size probably needs to see bigger type. If you want type that would otherwise be at 12 points to display at 14 for some good reason, then it's not unreasonable to expect that this new user will benefit in the same way from seeing the font used in this particular situation increase from his or her standard 16 points to 20.[7]

Most of the time, there's not really a reason to muck around with the user's settings for font sizes, so changing them arbitrarily isn't a good idea. Before you apply this kind of transformation to a segment of text in your web design, ask yourself if it's really necessary. My bet is that, nine times out of ten, you'll find it's not.

I would be remiss if I didn't point out that some pitfalls are inherent in the use of relative font sizes. Under some circumstances, relative font values can combine and multiply, producing bizarre results indeed.

---

[6]Just in case you were wondering, pixel sizes and point sizes are not equivalent, and the ratio between the two varies between browsers and operating systems. For example, the 12-point default font size used by most Windows browsers was rendered at 16 pixels on that platform. `12pt` is equivalent to `16px` on Windows browsers.

[7]If that's not the case, you probably want to rethink your reason for boosting the font size in the first place.

For example, let's say that you define style rules so that all text that's bold is displayed at 1.5em and all italic text is displayed at 1.5em, as shown below.

```
.bold {
  font-weight: bold;
  font-size: 1.5em;
}
.italic {
  font-style: italic;
  font-size: 1.5em;
}
```

In your document, these styles are used together in a number of different ways, as shown in this markup:

```
<p>This is normal, <span class="bold">this is bold,</span>
  <span class="ital">this is italic,</span>
  <span class="bold ital">this is bold and italic,</span> and
  finally, <span class="bold">this is bold,
  <span class="ital">then italic</span></span>.</p>
```

When you nest[8] these styles, the resulting text will display at 2.25em (1.5em × 1.5em). This problem arises with child elements, which inherit from their parent container elements the computed values for measured properties, not the relative values. This is relatively easy to avoid, but if you overlook it, the results can be quite startling, as Figure 3.3 illustrates.

Figure 3.3. Relative measurements gone haywire

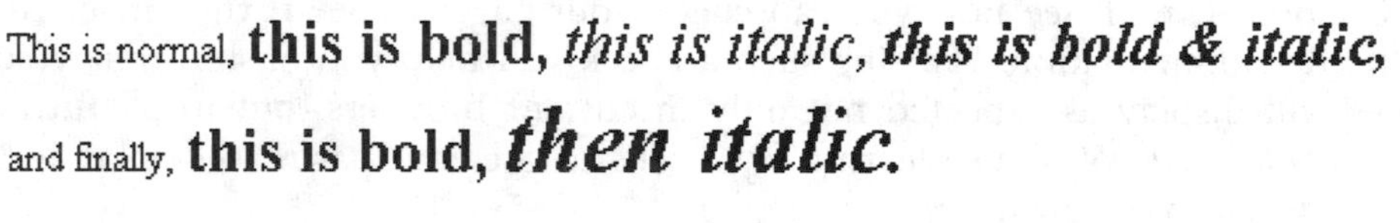

This is normal, **this is bold,** *this is italic,* ***this is bold & italic,*** and finally, **this is bold,** *then italic.*

CSS Comments

You're probably already familiar with the concept of **comments** in HTML:

```
<!-- this is an HTML comment -->
```

---

[8]Nesting is the process of putting one element inside another. For example, we say that a span inside another span is nested.

Comments allow you to include explanations and reminders within your code. These are ignored entirely by the browser, and typically are included solely for the developer's convenience. If you've ever had to make changes to code that hasn't been touched in a few months, I'm sure you can appreciate the value of a few well-placed comments that remind you of how it all works.

CSS has its own syntax for comments. In HTML, a comment begins with `<!--` and ends with `-->`. In CSS, a comment begins with `/*` and ends with `*/`:

```
<style type="text/css">
  /* This rule makes all text red by default. We include
     paragraphs and table cells for older browsers that don't
     inherit properly. */
  body, p, td, th {
    color: red;
  }
</style>
```

If you know much JavaScript, you'll recognize this syntax, which can be used to create multiline comments in that language as well. However, unlike JavaScript, CSS does not support the single-line double-slash (`//`) comment style.

Summary

This chapter ended our overview of CSS technology with a tour of some of the syntactic and structural rules of CSS styles. Along the way, it explained the basic ideas involved in HTML document inheritance.

In Chapter 4, we'll see how you can check your pages to see if they meet the W3C Recommendations. Passing such a check will help you ensure that your pages will display as expected not only in current browsers, but in all future browsers as well. We'll also learn a few tricks to get your pages to display in a usable way in older browsers.

4   Validation and Backward Compatibility

This chapter discusses two related topics. It begins with a description of the use of W3C and other CSS-validation tools and techniques to ensure that your CSS designs create valid pages. As you migrate existing table-centered designs to CSS, validation will be helpful in pointing out areas where you haven't quite lived up to CSS expectations.

The second part of the chapter focuses on some small changes you can make to valid CSS pages so that they will display as correctly as possible in older or incompatible browsers. It discusses the main types of browser problems that you may encounter, how to use the `@import` rule to avoid some potential pitfalls, and how to define a page's `DOCTYPE` to gain more direct control over the rendering of that page.

Validating your CSS

It's vital that you validate all your external style sheets, as well as all your HTML pages that use internal style sheets. It's not just easy to do—it's free. If you submit a page (or multiple pages) to the W3C's CSS validation service, and they pass, you can put a nifty little icon like the one in Figure 4.1 on your page.

Figure 4.1. A Valid CSS badge

To submit a style sheet or HTML page for validation, just go to http://jigsaw.w3.org/css-validator/. The page you'll see looks like Figure 4.2.

Figure 4.2. The main page of the W3C's CSS validator

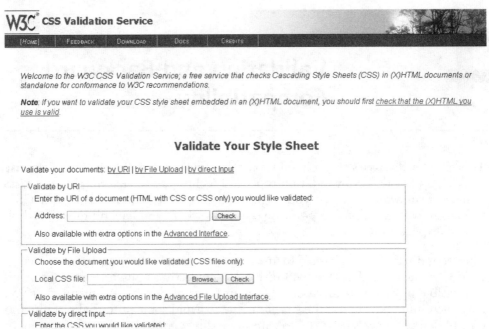

Scroll down this page if necessary, and you'll see that three options are available: you can submit a URL for validation, upload a file from your computer for validation, or enter some CSS to be validated.

The simplest way to validate your CSS is by entering a URL. You can enter the URL of your CSS file, or the URL of any HTML page. In the latter case, the validator will load and check any externally linked style sheets, in addition to looking over the CSS contained within the HTML document itself.

If your CSS is contained in a file on your hard drive, the easiest way to validate it is by uploading the file. The validator won't be able to see any of the linked files on your hard drive, so you'll have to upload all of the files that contain CSS one by one.

The forms on the validator's home page perform validation using the default settings, but we can change these options by using one of the advanced interfaces, which are linked from the bottom of each form. One of these advanced interfaces is shown in Figure 4.3.

Figure 4.3. One of the W3C CSS validator's advanced pages

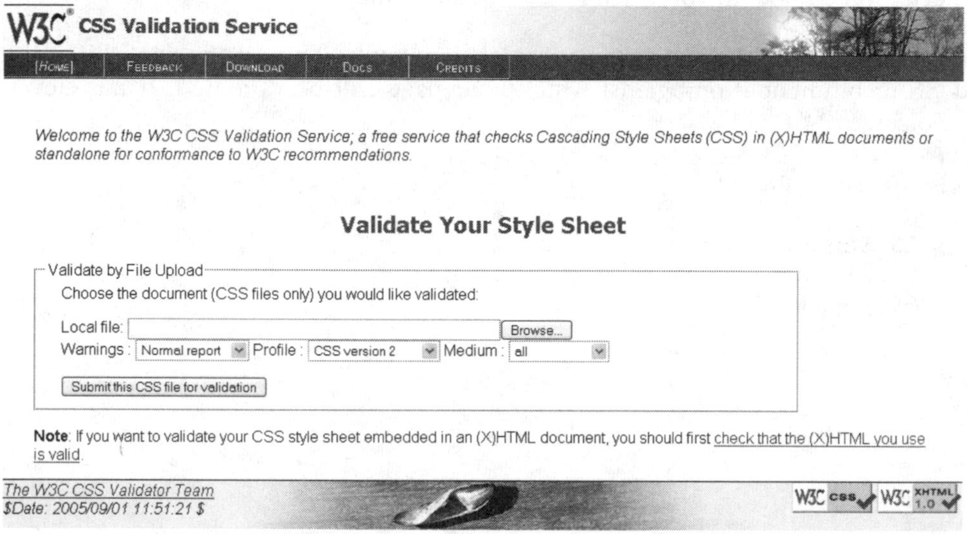

The validation form contains three drop-down menus:

The first, labeled Warnings, determines how significant a mistake must be before the validator includes it in the litany of warnings it produces as part of its report. It has four options:

☐ All

☐ Normal report

☐ Most important

☐ No warnings

Warnings are not the same as errors. If your page contains CSS errors, it won't validate. But it's possible for a page to validate and still contain markup that's either deprecated or used in inadvisable ways. For example, the CSS validator warns you if you set the color of text and background elements within a block to the same color. This doesn't make the CSS wrong, but it can have an undesirable effect when the page is rendered.

By default, this drop-down is set to "Normal report," and unless you have some experience or a specific reason to believe that level of warning won't serve your needs, I recommend you leave it at its default value.

The second drop-down on the page is labeled Profile. This setting determines the CSS recommendation against which your page will be validated. It has eleven choices:

- ❏ No special profile

- ❏ CSS version 1

- ❏ CSS version 2

- ❏ CSS version 2.1

- ❏ CSS version 3

- ❏ SVG

- ❏ SVG Basic

- ❏ SVG Tiny

- ❏ Mobile

- ❏ ATSC TV profile

- ❏ TV profile

The first few options are self-explanatory—they allow you to select the specific version of the CSS standard to which you're validating your markup. The other options, such as SVG, mobile, and TV profile, refer to other uses of CSS, and can be ignored for our purposes.

By default, the validator sets this to CSS version 2. However, I would advise you set it to CSS version 2.1, as it's the latest version of CSS with widespread browser support.

The final drop-down list, labelled Medium, lets you specify the media type for which this style sheet is intended.

When you've set the options you require, click the Check or Submit button to submit your CSS for validation. After a brief pause, the validator will let you know if your page contains valid CSS. If so, it will provide you with a link to the badge shown in Figure 4.1, so you can put the graphic on your page. Alternatively, if the validator encounters errors in your CSS, it will tell you what you need to fix in order to make your page's CSS valid.

It's important to note that if you're validating your CSS from an HTML document, the validator must be working with a correct HTML page. Specifically, what is called the "document parse tree" must be valid, or the CSS validator will not be able to work as it should.

You'll see a note to this effect on the CSS validation page, alongside a link to the main W3C validation page on which you can submit the page for HTML validation prior to using the CSS validator. Note that "valid" HTML requires the inclusion of all of the document prologue elements, including DOCTYPE and a character encoding label. If your page lacks either of these, you'll be told that the validator cannot proceed until these points are fixed.

Adjusting for Backward Compatibility

When we move on to create our CSS layouts, we'll create CSS (and the related XHTML) documents that validate and display correctly in the latest versions of modern browsers. While even these modern browsers still have bugs and rendering inconsistencies, these issues are more of a problem when you're dealing with slightly older browser versions, which may still be in common usage. As our development progresses, we'll explore the various ways in which we can avoid cross-browser issues altogether while building layouts; in this section, we'll discuss some of the techniques you can use to deal with existing cross-browser issues.

When you're working to address existing cross-browser issues, you're likely to run into three separate scenarios:

❑ browsers that do not support CSS at all

❑ browsers with poor or badly implemented CSS support

❑ relatively modern or recent browsers that, while effectively rendering most CSS, provide inconsistent support—or lack support entirely—for certain parts of versions 1 and 2 of the CSS specification

Browsers that Do Not Support CSS

Of the major browsers, the following offer no CSS support whatsoever:

❑ Opera (Version 3.5 and earlier)

❑ Netscape Navigator (Version 3.x and earlier)

❑ Internet Explorer (Version 2.x and earlier)

There are also text-only browsers—such as Lynx—that display only the text of the page, ignoring both CSS and images.

In practice, the usage of browsers that do not support any CSS is minimal. For anyone who uses one of these browsers, a CSS layout coupled with a semantic document may well deliver a far better experience than a design that uses a mish-mash of presentational HTML and CSS: users will, at least, be able to access content that's structured in a meaningful way. Therefore, when it comes to browsers that do not support CSS, we should be concerned that our content is accessible to them.

Browsers with Poor or Badly Implemented CSS Support

While browsers that don't support CSS are not much of an issue, browsers that support CSS, but in a strange or dysfunctional manner, are far more problematic. The browser that caused the greatest number of problems in this area was Netscape Navigator version 4.[1] The problem with browsers that support CSS badly is that, in such browsers, a perfectly well-built, valid page can render so badly that it's not readable by the user.

---

[1]When we talk about Netscape 4, we mean all versions of Netscape Navigator that begin with 4: from 4.0 to 4.8.

Many developers stopped worrying about Netscape 4 as its market share has dwindled. However, it is possible to block this browser's view of style sheets completely, so that the Netscape 4 user sees the same display as users of browsers that don't support CSS at all.[2]

Two Ways to Block Netscape 4 from Style Sheets

There are two ways to prevent Netscape 4 from seeing the style sheets that are applied to a particular page. Either of these approaches will cause the browser simply to ignore all CSS-related information stored in the external style sheet, and to display the page as it would routinely.

Using the `@import` at-rule

The first approach is to use a CSS at-rule called `@import`.[3] An **at-rule** is a special kind of CSS directive (or command, if you prefer) that starts with an "at sign" (@). These are used inside styles in a document or, less frequently, in externally linked style sheets. Because Navigator 4 doesn't understand these commands, it ignores them.

To link an external style sheet called `corpstyle.css` to a page, we add a `link` element to the head of the document, like this:

```
<link rel="stylesheet" type="text/css" href="corpstyle.css" />
```

But, to cause Netscape 4 to ignore this externally linked style sheet, we create an embedded style sheet instead, and use an `@import` rule to reference the external style sheet:

```
<style type="text/css">
  @import url(corpstyle.css);
</style>
```

Notice that the name of the style sheet is supplied as an argument to the `url` operator.

Blocking Internet Explorer Version 4

While Netscape 4's interpretation of the CSS specifications is the furthest from the mark, Internet Explorer 4's implementation isn't too crash-hot,

---

[2]It's also possible to design your pages so that they function in Netscape 4, but we won't be dealing with that option in this book.
[3]The other at-rules are described in Appendix A.

either. You can use the `@import` trick to block a style sheet from Internet Explorer 4, but you need to use a different form of the at-rule, as shown below.

```
<style type="text/css">
  @import "corpstyle.css";
</style>
```

Using the `media` Attribute

The other simple way to stop Netscape 4 from seeing a style sheet is to take advantage of an error in the way the browser interprets the `media` attribute of the `link` element. The `media` attribute is optional, and generally is not included, but if it is, and if it contains a value other than `screen`, Netscape 4 ignores it. Here's an example of how we can use this error to our advantage:

```
<link rel="stylesheet" type="text/css" href="corpstyle.css"
  media="all" />
```

Generally, you should use `all` as the value for the `media` attribute if you want Netscape 4 to ignore the style sheet. However, you may be more comfortable using `screen` along with some other value, such as `screen, print`, which will also have the desired effect on Netscape 4.

Identifying and Dealing with Problems

Just about the only way to identify CSS markup that will break your layout in older browsers is to use a compatibility chart, and to go through your documents in search of offending properties. You can find a comprehensive CSS property reference, including browser compatibility information, in Appendix C. But, since books tend to slip out of date faster than online information, here are some good online references.

A good web browser compatibility chart can be found at Westciv's web site.[4] This company publishes a CSS editor and other web design tools, and maintains this chart as a service to its customers and prospects. I've generally found the data here to be current and accurate.

If you look down the Netscape 4 columns in either of the Westciv charts, or peruse Appendix C, you'll see the aspects of CSS design that tend to be problematic for Netscape 4.

---

[4] http://www.westciv.com/style_master/academy/browser_support/

Among the most pronounced areas of nonconformance are:

☐ the cascade itself

☐ `font-variant`

☐ backgrounds (particularly positioning and attachment)

☐ word and letter spacing

☐ `vertical-align`

☐ most of the box-related CSS properties, in particular, floats and margins (these properties are discussed in Chapter 8)

☐ much border-related control

☐ `list-style` properties

Other less obvious errors abound, as well. For example, Netscape 4 incorrectly causes an element to inherit the font size set in the parent element, rather than the relative value, when relative units are used (see Chapter 7).

In general, I'd advise you to spend as little time as possible worrying about Netscape 4 support, and very little energy trying to get your pages to display well (let alone perfectly) in this flawed browser.

Bugs in Modern Browsers

Even if you feel that you can safely ignore these older browsers, you'll find that dealing with browser-related CSS bugs and inconsistencies is an inevitable part of CSS design. Just as those of us who learned to design web sites using tables had to learn "tricks" to get the nested tables to display in the way we wanted, so too do we need to learn how to deal with a variety of cross-browser issues when working with CSS.

The most prevalent browser currently in use is Internet Explorer 6, which is an older browser than the latest versions of Firefox, Safari, and Opera, and its support for CSS is lacking when compared to these newer browsers. A significant number of people continue to use older versions of Internet Explorer—versions 5.0 and 5.5—which have additional problems where CSS is concerned. Therefore, a site that validates and works well in the latest version of Safari on the Mac, or in

Firefox, may well display several problems when viewed in Internet Explorer. Other browsers are not immune to strange bugs, either.

Sometimes, it's possible to get around a bug or other issue by approaching the layout from a slightly different angle. There are often several ways to achieve the same visual result in CSS, and if you can make a change and get it to work consistently across all of your target browsers without resorting to CSS hacks, that's a far better end result than sticking with your original method and needing to include a raft of hacks to get it to work in a particular browser. If you have a very specific issue, you'll probably find that a quick search on Google will turn up some information about it, and often, a simple way to fix it.

If all attempts fail, and you're left with a specific issue that you need to resolve for one browser, you might consider using a CSS hack or filter to give that particular browser the different rules it needs in order to display your layout effectively. However, hacks should be seen as a last resort, and used as sparingly as possible.

My recommendation is that you should develop your site using a browser that's the closest to the specifications as possible. I tend to develop using Firefox, which has frequent update releases and useful add-ons such as the Web Developer Toolbar. By using a standards-compliant browser, you should end up with a layout that works well and complies with the specification, leaving you free then to turn your attention to other, less compliant browsers. And if, using this approach, you find that you have a display issue, you have the assurance that you're working from a solid starting point: a layout that has valid CSS and works well in a browser that's known to be relatively standards compliant. Internet Explorer bugs are very well documented, so if you stumble upon one of these, you're likely to find the answer by searching around, and trying out a few techniques.

In the course of developing the layouts in this book, we'll use this method of developing in Firefox first, then testing in other browsers. We'll address the issues of CSS hacks and browser discrepancies as we meet them.

Keep the Quirks: DOCTYPE Switching

Web pages that are coded to display in one of the earlier browsers may look ugly—or fail to display at all—in later browsers that do support CSS. Badly formed HTML, which earlier browsers forgave, breaks in newer browsers that must render HTML more meticulously because of the strict rules that come with standards like CSS. The opposite is also true, as we've seen. Pages designed to display well in recent and new browsers may not display well, or may fail to display at all, in older browsers.

Internet Explorer versions 5 (for Macintosh) and 6 (for Windows), Firefox and Safari browsers support a technology called **DOCTYPE Switching**. Simply stated, this technology allows these browsers to adapt their display characteristics based on the document type declaration, or DOCTYPE declaration, at the beginning of a web page.

I should point out that this DOCTYPE declaration has always been recommended for inclusion in web pages. Most web designers have ignored the advice, and web design tool manufacturers have failed to enforce it. As a result, updating all your current web pages with a DOCTYPE declaration may be a bit of a task. If you're using a good editor or design tool, the burden won't be too onerous.

A browser that supports DOCTYPE Switching gives the appearance of supporting two different modes: a standards-compliant mode, called Strict mode, and a "Quirks" mode. As you can probably guess, the former is more strict about its interpretation of tags and CSS instructions than is the latter.

You can add a DOCTYPE declaration as the first statement in every web page you've written. If the page uses style sheet rules, whether embedded, external, or both, it is recommended that you provide a Strict DOCTYPE like this one for the HTML 4.0 standard:

```
<!DOCTYPE HTML PUBLIC "-//W3C/DTD HTML 4.0//EN"
    "http://www.w3.org/TR/html4/strict.dtd">
```

The equivalent DOCTYPE for the newer XHTML 1.0 standard is:

```
<!DOCTYPE html PUBLIC "-//W3C//DTD XHTML 1.0 Strict//EN"
    "http://www.w3.org/TR/xhtml1/DTD/xhtml1-strict.dtd">
```

If one or more pages on your site does *not* support CSS, but requires older-style styling using embedded HTML tags, the following DOCTYPE statement will ensure that most browsers that support DOCTYPE Switching will render the page cleanly and correctly:

```
<!DOCTYPE HTML PUBLIC "-//W3C//DTD HTML 4.0 Transitional//EN"
    "http://www.w3.org/TR/html4/loose.dtd">
```

If you prefer to adhere to the new XHTML 1.0 standard, this is the DOCTYPE you want:

```
<!DOCTYPE html PUBLIC "-//W3C//DTD XHTML 1.0 Transitional//EN"
    "http://www.w3.org/TR/xhtml1/DTD/xhtml1-transitional.dtd">
```

Notice that the second pair of DOCTYPE declarations refer to the "transitional" versions of the two standards. The result is that browsers that support DOCTYPE Switching technology act in Quirks mode, and again, display the documents correctly even if there are standards compliance issues with the page's HTML.

If you find that, when working with a valid document, you see layout differences between modern browsers, one of the first things to check is that the page is running in Strict mode on both browsers. Unfortunately, Internet Explorer requires a little mangling of the DOCTYPE declaration before it will switch into Quirks mode. In addition to specifying the transitional version of HTML 4.0, you must leave out the URL portion of the DOCTYPE to enable Quirks mode:

```
<!DOCTYPE HTML PUBLIC "-//W3C//DTD HTML 4.0 Transitional//EN">
```

Any HTML DOCTYPE that specifies a URL, and any XHTML DOCTYPE whatsoever, will put Internet Explorer into standards-compliant mode, so if you do want it to operate in Quirks mode, you must use this last DOCTYPE. For full details, consult the article CSS Enhancements in Internet Explorer 6[5] on MSDN.

Most browsers (including Internet Explorer) will also go into Quirks mode if the DOCTYPE declaration is missing; however, as both the HTML and XHTML standards specify that this declaration is required, I don't recommend that you omit the DOCTYPE statement.

In this book, I've endeavoured to present 100% XHTML 1.0 compliant markup, except where it was necessary to show code for older browsers. Every sample document in this book begins the same way:

```
<!DOCTYPE html PUBLIC "-//W3C//DTD XHTML 1.0 Strict//EN"
    "http://www.w3.org/TR/xhtml1/DTD/xhtml1-strict.dtd">
<html xmlns="http://www.w3.org/1999/xhtml">
  <head>
    <title>Page Title Here</title>
    <meta http-equiv="Content-Type"
        content="text/html; charset=iso-8859-1" />
```

As you can see, the DOCTYPE declaration on the first line will ensure that modern browsers operate in standards-compliant mode.

---

[5] http://msdn.microsoft.com/library/en-us/dnie60/html/cssenhancements.asp

XML DOCTYPE Switching Bug in Internet Explorer

XML purists may wonder why our XHTML documents don't start with an XML version declaration like this:

```
<?xml version="1.0" encoding="iso-8859-1"?>
```

Indeed, the XML standard prescribes that a document should begin with a `<?xml ... ?>` processing instruction, which is followed by the XHTML `DOCTYPE`.

Unfortunately, when a document begins with `<?xml ... ?>`, or anything else—including white space—before the `DOCTYPE`, Internet Explorer version 6 does not see the `DOCTYPE` and lapses into Quirks mode. For this reason, you must leave out the XML version declaration to get the best CSS support from all browsers in wide use.

Thankfully, the XML standard allows you to omit the processing instruction if you're happy with the default settings—which, in the case of most XHTML documents, we are.

Summary

In this chapter, we saw how to validate CSS and XHTML documents, and discussed the issues surrounding browser support and backwards compatibility. This chapter served as an introduction to the issues that we'll encounter in the second half of the book, as we create our CSS layouts.

5

Splashing Around a Bit of Color

In this chapter, we take a close look at color: we'll explore the application of color to text and other objects, and review page background colors. We'll also discuss how colors are described, where we can apply them, how we can use them together to achieve specific effects, and a range of other techniques.

However, we begin this chapter with a discussion of one of the most basic of color concepts. Good designers must understand the conflicts that can arise between the way we believe a page should look, and the constraints placed on that page's appearance by users.

Who's in Charge?

Under the rules of CSS, user settings trump designer specifications every time. While it's important to keep this in mind, this knowledge doesn't give us any insight into how to design a site with this rule in mind.

How can you build your site to look its best, regardless of users' own settings? You can't!

Figure 5.1. Firefox's color preferences panel

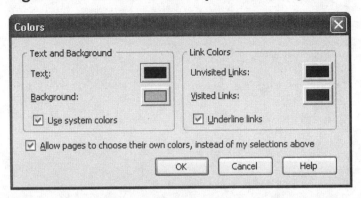

Figure 5.2. Firefox's font preferences panel

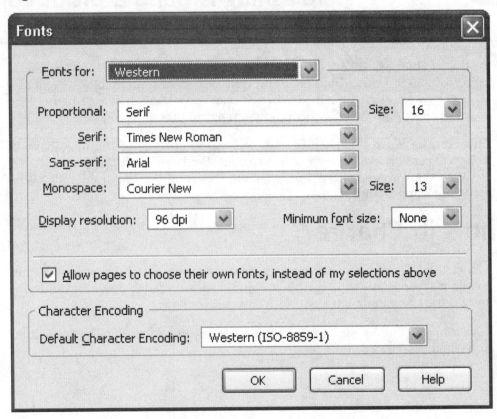

It's very easy for users to set their own browser preferences. All modern browsers have simple preference-setting panels for colors and fonts; those of Firefox are shown in Figure 5.1 and Figure 5.2.

The dialog in Figure 5.1 allows the user to set colors for pages' backgrounds and text, as well as the colors of visited and unvisited links. The dialog shown in Figure 5.2 allows you to set the browser's default font for serif, sans-serif, and monospaced text. Both dialogs offer checkboxes that allow the user to stop web pages' design specifications from overriding their own preferred settings.

Many browsers also allow users to define their own style sheets, and tell the browser to use these style sheets to override any styles it finds on incoming pages.

For example, let's assume that a user has set the following style:

```
h1 {
  background-color: black;
  color: white;
}
```

Now, imagine that the user opens a page with the following style rule:

```
h1 {
  background-color: yellow;
  color: black;
  font-family: Helvetica, Arial, sans-serif;
}
```

In this situation, the page's `font-family` will be used, but the page's `color` and `background-color` will be overridden by the user's settings.

As you read all the information that follows in this part of the book, then, keep in mind the caveat, " … unless the user overrides your settings." I won't bore you by reminding you of this rule repeatedly.

Color in CSS

Elements that can be displayed in colors defined through style rules are:

❑ backgrounds

❑ borders

❑ text

❑ links

❑ outlines

I've listed that last one for the sake of completeness. Outlines are not supported by the majority of browsers available today, so we won't spend time discussing them here. Refer to the `outline` property in Appendix C if you're curious.

How to Specify Colors

We can use several methods to specify a color for any CSS property that accepts color values:

❑ descriptive color names

❑ system color names

❑ RGB decimal values

❑ RGB hexadecimal values (including a three-character shorthand)

❑ RGB percentage values

The most human-readable way to specify colors in HTML is to use key words that are reserved for describing those colors. Officially, only 16 descriptive color names are supported in HTML and CSS,[1] yet virtually all modern browsers support a range of 140 color names first suggested by Netscape in the early days of the Web.

These 140 colors, along with their RGB equivalents, can be found in Appendix B. The 16 official descriptive color names are:

❑ `black`

❑ `white`

❑ `aqua`

---

[1]Although the HTML and CSS specifications define 16 standard color names, the Web Content Accessibility Guidelines 1.0 [http://www.w3.org/TR/WCAG10-CSS-TECHS/#style-colors] published by the W3C recommend that numerical values, not names, are used to define colors.

- ❏ blue

- ❏ fuchsia

- ❏ gray

- ❏ green

- ❏ lime

- ❏ maroon

- ❏ navy

- ❏ olive

- ❏ purple

- ❏ red

- ❏ silver

- ❏ teal

- ❏ yellow

Whether or not you use the 124 other named colors is up to you. Given that they are not officially supported in any W3C documentation, there is the potential risk that some future browser may not support them. Also, the way in which those colors render on some browsers and operating systems cannot easily be determined, other than by detailed testing. Frankly, I don't see much of a risk, and I use these names a great deal. The descriptive color names give me some idea of what I'm likely to see, even before I view my page in a browser.

In addition to those descriptive color names, there's also a set of 28 **system color names**. These names, such as AppWorkspace, correspond to different parts of the graphical user interface (GUI) that's presented by the operating system. The actual color associated with each of these names is, therefore, operating system-specific, and potentially is subject to user preferences. Using these color names, you can create web interfaces that match users' operating system GUIs. A complete list of system color names is presented in Appendix B.

Colors are rendered on computer monitors using combinations of three basic colors—red, green, and blue—in various intensities. We can use these three colors to define a seemingly endless range of other hues in two ways:

❏ Use the `rgb` function to supply a set of three comma-separated values that define the mix of the three basic colors.

❏ Supply a hexadecimal value as a three- or six-character string. Such strings are preceded by the pound sign, also known as the hash symbol (#).

For example, if you wanted to specify the color blue for a particular element in a CSS style rule, you could do it in any of the following ways:

```
color: blue;
color: rgb(0, 0, 255);
color: rgb(0%, 0%, 100%);
color: #0000ff;
color: #00f;
```

Note that you can use the three-character hexadecimal approach only when the six-character version consists of three matching pairs (i.e. #abc is equivalent to #aabbcc).

You've probably figured out that the decimal and hexadecimal values in the above represent the presence of no red, no green, and the maximum amount of blue. Black is represented by the value #000000 (or, in shorthand, #000) and white is represented by the value #ffffff (or, again in shorthand, #fff). If you prefer the `rgb` function, black is `rgb(0,0,0)` and white is `rgb(255,255,255)` or `rgb(100%,100%,100%)`.

Sometimes, simply by looking at a color value—or, perhaps more easily, looking at two color values side by side—we can figure out how to modify that color to achieve a different effect. For example, if we've defined a color as #ff7f50, but when we look at it, we decide it needs to be a bit more blue, we can just increase the value of the last two digits to, say, #ff7f70.

The level of precision that hexadecimal specifications afford over combinations of red, green, and blue is the reason why web designers with artistic backgrounds tend to favor this approach.[2] If you're working in a graphics application, you should be able to check the hexadecimal code of a given color within the design

---

[2]There are over 16.7 million possible combinations of the 256 levels of red, green, and blue in CSS, and therefore, over 16.7 million possible individual colors.

package, and use that code in your CSS. However, if you're putting together a simple web site in Notepad, you might find it easier to use color names.

Selecting and Combining Colors

The selection of color combinations that work well is a key part of a site's graphical design. If you've ever put a chartreuse background next to an image with a dark-blue background, and then ran screaming for the exit when the page displayed, you have some idea of the difficulty of the task.

The selection of colors becomes an important issue primarily in two situations: when you have adjacent objects with colored backgrounds and you want to avoid a clash, and when you have colored text on colored backgrounds and you want to ensure readability.

A number of basic artistic principles are involved in selecting colors that complement one another. Everything starts with the color wheel. The color wheel is discussed at countless places on the Web, but the clearest and most concise explanation I've found was written by the makers of a program called Color Wheel Pro™, in an article called "Color Theory Basics.[3]"

Essentially, we start with a color wheel that includes the range of colors from which we want to choose. Colors that are adjacent to one another on the color wheel are said to be "harmonious" colors that look good together. Choosing two or three adjacent colors on a color wheel, and applying those colors to large areas such as backgrounds and menus, can produce very pleasing aesthetic effects.

For greater vibrancy, we'll want to select colors that are opposite one another on the color wheel; such pairs of colors are said to be "complementary." To find more great color combinations for your designs, move an equilateral triangle around the middle of a color wheel, and use combinations of the colors that lie at the triangle's corners.

Some graphics and web design programs include palettes and other interfaces to allow you to select colors without knowing their RGB or hexadecimal codes. These aids make it much easier to experiment with color combinations, and to determine what works and what doesn't.

Laying colored text over colored backgrounds can be especially problematic. A process of trial and error can be incredibly time consuming, but often, the specific

---

[3] http://www.color-wheel-pro.com/color-theory-basics.html

effect we want isn't achievable without some effort. However, help is available on the Web! One of the best places I know of is Pixy's Color Scheme Generator:[4] click on the different colors in the color wheel to view color schemes based on your selection.

This tool also features a drop-down list of different kinds of color blindness, each of which corresponds to a filter. By selecting one, you can see how your chosen scheme will look to people with that kind of color blindness. After playing with this drop-down list, you'll realize that there are many different types of color blindness that can cause people to have difficulty distinguishing between colors.

As well as avoiding color combinations that cause content to become unreadable, it's important to ensure that your site is not designed so that the only way users can understand certain information is by its color. For example, using different colored icons without accompanying text labels might mean that some users can't distinguish the difference between those icons. Another service that shows how your site looks to colorblind users is Vischeck.[5]

Discovering new color combinations that may defy conventional wisdom, but work well together regardless, is one of the most interesting areas of creative exploration in web design. Don't limit yourself to the accepted combinations that everyone uses.

Setting body Color

Often, you won't define a color for the body element either inline or in a style sheet rule. By default, most browsers will display black text on a white or gray background, and for many layouts, that's fine. However, be aware that users who have set their browser's default background colors to something other than white will see your page in that color. To remind themselves to set page background colors in CSS, many designers set their own browsers' default backgrounds to garish colors!

But, if you need to define a different color combination, you can define a color for all the text that appears on a page using a style sheet entry like this:

```
body {
  color: red;
}
```

---

[4] http://wellstyled.com/tools/colorscheme2/index-en.html
[5] http://www.vischeck.com/

I don't recommend you use this approach exactly as shown above, even when you wish to declare all the fonts on a page (or site) to be a specific color. Why? Because, in CSS, there's a fundamental rule from which you should never deviate: *if you set a foreground color, always set a background color, and vice versa*. You can never know whether or not the user has set a specific background color against which your carefully chosen text color will look like mud. Or—worse yet—users may have defined a background color that's exactly the same as your foreground color. In this case, they'll see what appears to be a blank page.

So, if you decide to declare a foreground color using the `color` property, combine it with a `background-color` declaration, as in this example:

```
body{
  color: white;
  background-color: maroon;
}
```

Note, too, that if you set a `color` property for the `body` element, it will apply to all the elements that are nested inside that element (including headings, paragraphs, and lists, among other things), unless you override it (or your users' preferences trump you).

Transparency, Color, and User Overrides

We can ensure that the background color of any HTML element is identical to that of the page's body. To do this, we declare its `background-color` as `transparent`:

```
#transbox {
  color: white;
  background-color: transparent;
}
```

In fact, the value of `background-color` is `transparent` by default; it is not inherited from the parent element. This ensures that an image background assigned to an element will display continuously through child elements, rather than being displayed again in alignment with each child.

Why would we explicitly declare a background color of `transparent`? Most commonly, we'd use this approach in cases where we've declared a `background-color` property for a particular type of HTML element (such as paragraphs), but we have one or more specific *types* of paragraphs for which we want to display transparent backgrounds.

This issue of "default" background color gets sticky when users change their own settings. For example, if a user defines a local style sheet, the settings in that style sheet—including background colors—may override yours. Fortunately, very few users change their browsers' default settings, so your page settings will usually win out, with browser defaults handling those elements for which you don't specify any styles. For example, the default background color for the body of a page is white or gray. However, if you define the background color of the body to be transparent, then all bets are off. As the W3C puts it in its CSS specification, in such cases, "the rendering is undefined."

Figure 5.3. Using color to create attention-getting cautions and notes

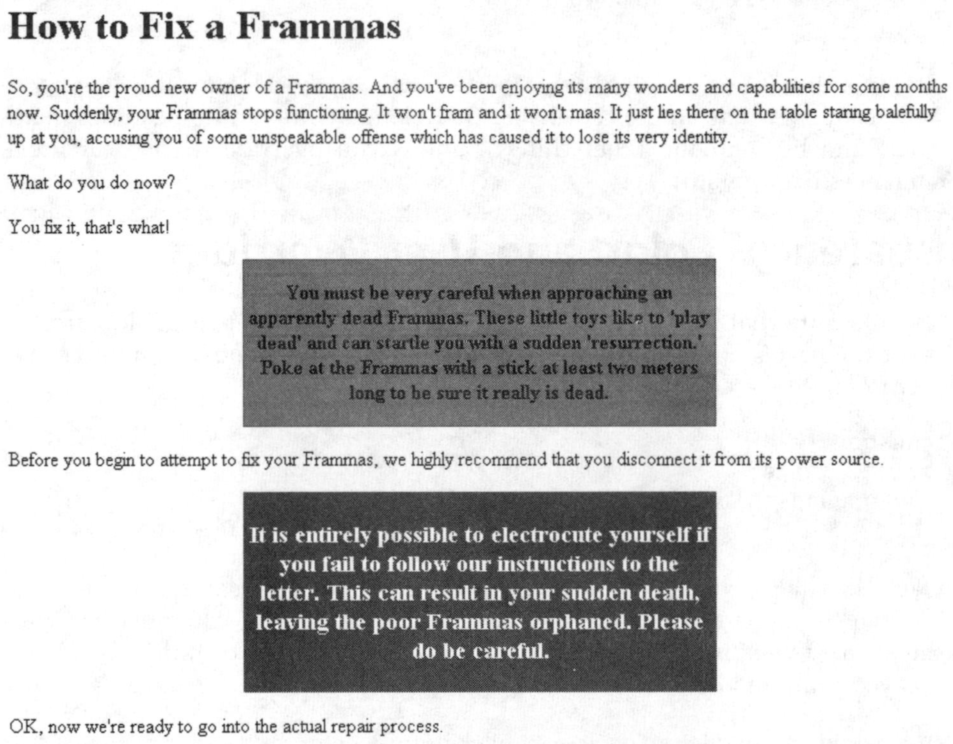

How to Fix a Frammas

So, you're the proud new owner of a Frammas. And you've been enjoying its many wonders and capabilities for some months now. Suddenly, your Frammas stops functioning. It won't fram and it won't mas. It just lies there on the table staring balefully up at you, accusing you of some unspeakable offense which has caused it to lose its very identity.

What do you do now?

You fix it, that's what!

> You must be very careful when approaching an apparently dead Frammas. These little toys like to 'play dead' and can startle you with a sudden 'resurrection.' Poke at the Frammas with a stick at least two meters long to be sure it really is dead.

Before you begin to attempt to fix your Frammas, we highly recommend that you disconnect it from its power source.

> It is entirely possible to electrocute yourself if you fail to follow our instructions to the letter. This can result in your sudden death, leaving the poor Frammas orphaned. Please do be careful.

OK, now we're ready to go into the actual repair process.

Interesting Uses of Color

Coloring text, backgrounds, and borders is all well and good—and not terribly complicated—but other than aesthetic benefits, what does it give us? In this section, I'll outline three specific examples in which specific color combinations are applied to produce useful results.

Warnings and Cautions

In online documentation, often it's useful to call specific attention to pieces of information that are of particular importance to the reader. Printed manuals, generally produced in black-and-white, rely on typographic techniques—boxes, bold or italic type, special fonts, and the like—to accomplish such attention-getting.

On a web page, where color can be used more freely, we can apply these typographic techniques in combination with colored text and backgrounds to create notices that grab readers' attention more effectively than usually is possible in print. Often, table-based layouts are used to create these kinds of effects. Let's see how we can take advantage of CSS rules to accomplish the same result, which is shown in Figure 5.3.

The HTML for the page shown in Figure 5.3 looks like the markup below. I've used bold to indicate where the style sheet for this page is invoked.

File: **frammas.html (excerpt)**

```
<!DOCTYPE html PUBLIC "-//W3C//DTD XHTML 1.0 Strict//EN"
    "http://www.w3.org/TR/xhtml1/DTD/xhtml1-strict.dtd">
<html xmlns="http://www.w3.org/1999/xhtml">
  <head>
    <title>A Cautionary Demo</title>
    <meta http-equiv="Content-Type"
        content="text/html; charset=iso-8859-1" />
    <link rel="stylesheet" href="frammas.css" type="text/css" />
  </head>
  <body>
    <h1>How to Fix a Frammas</h1>
    <p>So, you're the proud new owner of a Frammas. And you've
        been enjoying its many wonders and capabilities for some
        months now. Suddenly, your Frammas stops functioning. It
        won't fram and it won't mas. It just lies there on the
        table staring balefully up at you, accusing you of some
```

```
          unspeakable offense which has caused it to lose its very
             identity.</p>
      <p>What do you do now?</p>
      <p>You fix it, that's what!</p>
      <div class="caution">
         <p>You must be very careful when approaching an apparently
             dead Frammas. These little toys like to 'play dead' and
             can startle you with a sudden 'resurrection.' Poke at
             the Frammas with a stick at least two meters long to be
             sure it really is dead.</p>
      </div>
      <p>Before you begin to attempt to fix your Frammas, we highly
          recommend that you disconnect it from its power
          source.</p>
      <div class="danger">
         <p>It is entirely possible to electrocute yourself if you
             fail to follow our instructions to the letter. This can
             result in your sudden death, leaving the poor Frammas
             orphaned. Please do be careful.</p>
      </div>
      <p>OK, now we're ready to go into the actual repair
          process.</p>
   </body>
</html>
```

As you can see, I've identified two classes: caution and danger. I used classes, rather than identifiers, because it's quite likely that I'll have more than one instance of each of these kinds of notes in a document, and identifiers are limited to one usage per page.

Here are the CSS definitions of the two classes:

File: **frammas.css (excerpt)**

```
.caution {
  text-align: center;
  font-weight: bold;
  background-color: gray;
  color: black;
  margin-left: 25%;
  margin-right: 25%;
  border: 1px solid red;
}

.danger {
  text-align: center;
  font-size: 1.2em;
```

```
  font-weight: bold;
  background-color: red;
  color: white;
  margin-left: 25%;
  margin-right: 25%;
  border: 3px solid red;
}
```

There's nothing new here. Each class defines a background and text color combination that's designed to attract attention. Each is positioned so that it stands out from the page. As you can see from this example, when we use CSS, the HTML code becomes much easier to read and maintain than it would be if we used nested tables to accomplish the same task.

Coloring Alternate Rows and Adding Cell Borders in Data Tables

While we're learning how to avoid the use of tables for page layout purposes, we must remain appreciative of the situations in which tables are a perfectly legitimate tool. Displaying tabular data is a task that should still be entrusted to HTML tables.

However, we can make what might otherwise be fairly ordinary tables into more readable and attractive page elements with the help of a little CSS. Figure 5.4 shows an admittedly stark example of a table presented in HTML. Obviously, few of us would publish a web page with such a sparse table design, but it serves as a good starting point for this discussion.

Figure 5.4. A starkly ordinary table design

Row 1, Cell 1 Row 1, Cell 2 Row 1, Cell 3

Row 2, Cell 1 Row 2, Cell 2 Row 2, Cell 3

Row 3, Cell 1 Row 3, Cell 2 Row 3, Cell 3

Row 4, Cell 1 Row 4, Cell 2 Row 4, Cell 3

Row 5, Cell 1 Row 5, Cell 2 Row 5, Cell 3

Row 6, Cell 1 Row 6, Cell 2 Row 6, Cell 3

Row 7, Cell 1 Row 7, Cell 2 Row 7, Cell 3

Among this table's problems are its complete lack of borders, and the fact that it's hard to keep your place within the table rows as you read its contents. We can address both issues with some simple CSS magic.[6]

Below is the HTML for a modified version of the above page; as you can see, I've defined a couple of trivial CSS rules here. This is a case in which an external style sheet is probably overkill, though it may still constitute good design practice.

File: **table.html** (excerpt)

```
<!DOCTYPE html PUBLIC "-//W3C//DTD XHTML 1.0 Strict//EN"
    "http://www.w3.org/TR/xhtml1/DTD/xhtml1-strict.dtd">
<html xmlns="http://www.w3.org/1999/xhtml">
  <head>
    <title>Coloring Rows in a Table</title>
    <meta http-equiv="Content-Type"
       content="text/html; charset=iso-8859-1" />
    <style type="text/css">
      .odd {
        background-color: lightgrey;
      }
      .even {
        background-color: white;
      }
      table {
        border: 1px solid black;
        border-spacing: 0;
      }
      td {
        padding: 4px 6px;
        border: 1px solid black;
      }
    </style>
  </head>
<body>
  <table>
    <tr class="odd">
      <td>Row 1, Cell 1</td>
      <td>Row 1, Cell 2</td>
      <td>Row 1, Cell 3</td>
    </tr>
    <tr class="even">
```

---

[6]Actually, this example is somewhat contrived. For historical reasons, web browsers will display tables with a one-pixel border by default, so Figure 5.4 actually represents a table that has had its default borders removed, either with CSS or through the now-deprecated (but common) practice of setting the border attribute of the table to 0.

```
            <td>Row 2, Cell 1</td>
            <td>Row 2, Cell 2</td>
            <td>Row 2, Cell 3</td>
         </tr>
         <tr class="odd">
            <td>Row 3, Cell 1</td>
            <td>Row 3, Cell 2</td>
            <td>Row 3, Cell 3</td>
         </tr>
         <tr class="even">
            <td>Row 4, Cell 1</td>
            <td>Row 4, Cell 2</td>
            <td>Row 4, Cell 3</td>
         </tr>
         <tr class="odd">
            <td>Row 5, Cell 1</td>
            <td>Row 5, Cell 2</td>
            <td>Row 5, Cell 3</td>
         </tr>
         <tr class="even">
            <td>Row 6, Cell 1</td>
            <td>Row 6, Cell 2</td>
            <td>Row 6, Cell 3</td>
         </tr>
         <tr class="odd">
            <td>Row 7, Cell 1</td>
            <td>Row 7, Cell 2</td>
            <td>Row 7, Cell 3</td>
         </tr>
      </table>
   </body>
</html>
```

I've simply defined two classes, odd and even, in an embedded style sheet, then labeled alternate rows of the table to correspond to those styles. I've also defined a basic style rule that surrounds the table in a one-pixel black border. Because table cells inherit their default border from the parent table, each cell is also surrounded by a one-pixel border; the net result is a two-pixel line between and around every table cell. The results of our markup are shown in Figure 5.5.

Obviously, this display is much more readable, and while it isn't a final solution, it gives us a much more pleasant starting point from which to begin additional work on the table.

Figure 5.5. Coloring table rows alternately, and adding cell borders, with CSS rules

Row 1, Cell 1	Row 1, Cell 2	Row 1, Cell 3
Row 2, Cell 1	Row 2, Cell 2	Row 2, Cell 3
Row 3, Cell 1	Row 3, Cell 2	Row 3, Cell 3
Row 4, Cell 1	Row 4, Cell 2	Row 4, Cell 3
Row 5, Cell 1	Row 5, Cell 2	Row 5, Cell 3
Row 6, Cell 1	Row 6, Cell 2	Row 6, Cell 3
Row 7, Cell 1	Row 7, Cell 2	Row 7, Cell 3

With some of the less frequently used aspects of table definitions in HTML, such as header (`th` and `thead`) and grouped columns (`colgroup`), you can create some professional-looking and eminently readable tables of data. We'll work on a more complete and complex data table in the final chapter of this book.

Background Images

By now, you should feel fairly comfortable assigning background colors to elements using the `background-color` property, so let's move on to assigning background images, which is done with the `background-image` property and the `url` function, as this markup shows:

```
body {
  background-color: white;
  color: black;
  background-image: url(fish.jpg);
}
```

The `url` function can be used to specify any image file, similar to the way you'd use the `img` element's `src` attribute.

If you define a graphic as the background for a page—as we have in the example above—that graphic will repeat, or tile, itself to fill up the entire browser viewport. As you scroll through the document, the image will also scroll along. This is the normal behavior of backgrounds, as Figure 5.6 illustrates.

Figure 5.6. Normal background image behavior

Something Smells Fishy...

Tip **Always Specify a Background Color with a Background Image**

Whenever you specify a background image which will appear underneath other content, you should specify an appropriate background color. This color will display while the image is loading, and will appear for site users who have disabled images in their browsers.

However, you can use CSS to change both the tiling and scrolling characteristics of images. You can define the graphic so that, rather than tiling, it simply appears once, wherever you position it. More interestingly, you can instruct the background graphic to remain in place while other objects that are placed on top of it, including text, effectively scroll over it.

Figure 5.7. Fixed background image displaying behind unscrolled text

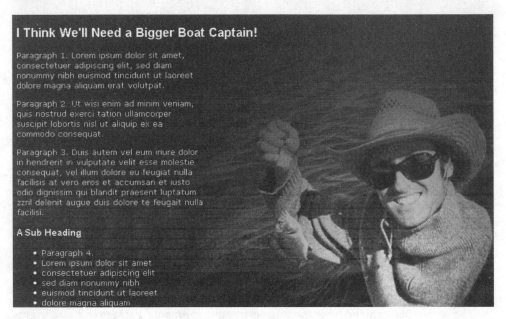

Figure 5.7 and Figure 5.8 show this effect as clearly as it can be shown on a "dead" page. Figure 5.7 shows how the page looks before any scrolling takes place. You can see that the picture of our happy fisherman is positioned in the lower right of the page.

In Figure 5.8, the numbered list has scrolled down several items, but as you can see, the fisherman image that serves as the background for this text remains firmly fixed in place.

Here's the CSS rule that produces the fixed background effect demonstrated in Figure 5.7 and Figure 5.8:

```
body {
  background-color: #30293f;
  color: white;
  background-image: url(fisherman.jpg);
  background-repeat: no-repeat;
  background-attachment: fixed;
  background-position: right bottom;
}
```

Figure 5.8. Scrolled text leaving fixed background image in place

The `background-repeat: no-repeat` declaration stops the background image from tiling. Whenever this declaration is used in conjunction with a `background-image` declaration, only one instance of the image will appear in the background. Other values that `background-repeat` can take on are `repeat`, which is the default value, and `repeat-x` and `repeat-y`, which repeat the image horizontally and vertically respectively.

The `background-attachment` property controls whether or not the background image scrolls with the content. By default, it's set to `scroll`, but it can also be set to `fixed` to achieve the effect we see with our fisherman image.

Finally, the `background-position: right bottom` declaration puts the image in the bottom-right corner of the browser window. This property usually takes two keyword values: the first value controls the horizontal position and can be `left`, `center`, or `right`; the second value controls the vertical position, which can be `top`, `center`, or `bottom`. The default value of the `background position` property is `left top`.

You can use a percentage, instead of these keywords, for either value. In that case, the first value determines the image's horizontal position, where `0%` places the image right up against the left edge of the browser window, and `100%` places it on the right edge. Accordingly, the second value determines the image's vertical position: 0% indicates the top of the window, and 100% indicates the bottom of the browser window. These values aren't limited to 0% or 100%—you can make use of any value in between. For example, the following declaration would put your background image in the lower-right quarter of your background, but it wouldn't be flush against the corner of the browser window.

```
background-position: 80% 80%;
```

As you can see, CSS gives us *a lot* of control over background images! All of these properties can be set using the background shortcut property, which is covered in Appendix C.

Summary

This chapter discussed how to use CSS rules to apply color to web pages. After considering who controls the colors a web page ultimately displays—designer or user—we learned how to specify colors in CSS. We then pondered the questions of color selection and combination, specifically considering the ways in which these decisions impact on colorblind users.

The chapter then focused on some practical applications of color: setting body color, dealing with transparency, and using color to make tables easier to read and elements like warnings and cautions more eye-catching and effective. Finally, we discussed how CSS can be used to add background images to your document and took a tour of the properties that can be used to exert a great deal of control over them.

In Chapter 6, we'll start looking at how we can spruce up our site even more by using different fonts and applying effects to them.

6

Working with Fonts

This chapter examines the question of how to use fonts properly in CSS-based web page design. After an explanation of how CSS deals with fonts, I'll offer some guidelines on choosing font families and sizes for your page designs.

How CSS Deals with Fonts

With the emergence of CSS, the HTML `font` element was deprecated in favor of using style sheets, which provide a greater degree of control in a more manageable format.

CSS provides great flexibility in our work with fonts. While HTML limits you to working with only seven standard font sizes, CSS allows you to specify font sizes in a number of different ways, providing a nearly unlimited range of sizes. In addition, CSS formalizes the ability to define a fallback, or default, font that can be used if none of the fonts you specify in a style rule are available on users' machines. This capability existed with the deprecated `<font>` tag in HTML, but the list of defaults was never officially standardized.

With CSS, we also get the ability to change the **weight** of fonts (e.g. bold or normal), alter their **style**s (e.g. italic or oblique), and even to declare a font to display in small caps.

The CSS properties you'll work with in this chapter include:

- `font-family`

- `font-size`

- `font-style`

- `font-variant`

- `font-weight`

- `font` (shorthand property)

The `font-family` Property

A font family is simply a collection of fonts. The members of a font family vary only by features such as weight and orientation. For example, the font family Times contains fonts named Times Bold and Times Italic, both of which are based on the font Times Roman.

The issue of applying font families to web pages is tangled up with the question of using supported and/or unsupported fonts—a question to which an entire section of this chapter is devoted. Here, I'll cover font families briefly, but we'll explore the subject in much greater detail later in this chapter.

You can use the `font-family` property to assign a list of specific and generic font families to any HTML block or element. Usually, we supply a list of specific fonts—separated from one another by commas—and end the list with a generic font that is to be used if none of the specified fonts are available. Here's how that looks:

```
font-family: Helvetica, Arial, sans-serif;
```

Font families are used in the order in which we list them in the rule. In the above example, the browser will look to see if the user has Helvetica installed. If so, the text affected by this style rule will be shown in Helvetica. If Helvetica isn't present on the user's system, the browser will look for the next font, Arial. If it finds Arial, it uses it. If it doesn't find Arial, the browser uses whatever is defined as the browser's default sans-serif font.

Generic Fonts

It's worth pausing here to discuss how the browser gets its default sans-serif font, and other generic font settings. Every browser with CSS support has preset defaults for the following generic font families:

- ❏ `serif`

- ❏ `sans-serif`

- ❏ `monospace`

- ❏ `cursive`

- ❏ `fantasy`

When the browser encounters one of these generic font families, it will match it with an appropriate font. For example, a browser running on Windows may substitute Times New Roman for `serif`, Arial for `sans-serif`, Courier New for `monospace`, and so on.

In serif fonts, such as Times New Roman, a small decoration or tail is added to the ends of many of the strokes that comprise each letter, helping to define those strokes. Sans-serif fonts, such as Arial, have no such decorations. Typically, the strokes of a sans-serif font are straight and of uniform width. In monospace fonts, each letter of the alphabet is as wide as all the others, much like the effect that old typewriters used to create. A cursive font is intended to mimic the connected-character style of handwriting. A fantasy font is a more decorative or fancy style of font.

Artistic views differ over which fonts look better on a web page. Many people believe that serif fonts are easier to read because the small extenders along the bottoms of the letters give the eye something to follow as users read across a line. Others argue that a sans-serif font is easier to read on a computer monitor. Unfortunately, a discussion of these issues is beyond the scope of this book.

Figure 6.1 shows a sample of each of the three most popular generic font families. As you can see, they're quite different from one another.

Figure 6.1. Samples of serif, sans-serif, and monospace fonts

This is a sentence in a serif font.

This sentence, on the other hand, is in a sans-serif font.

`Finally, this is a sentence in a monospace font.`

The user may be able to change these default fonts through preference settings in the browser. If that's the case, then all bets are off. Under such circumstances, the generic specification of `sans-serif` can't even guarantee that a sans-serif font will be used. If the user has overridden the default value for `sans-serif` to display a monospaced font, for example, they will see monospaced text wherever a `font-family: sans-serif;` declaration takes effect.

Regardless of how the browser arrives at its default setting for a generic font, that font will be used only when other fonts that appear before it in a list are not available.

If the name of a font family that you want to specify contains embedded spaces, you'll need to enclose that family name in quotation marks, as shown here:

```
font-family: "New Century Schoolbook", Baskerville, serif;
```

Note that, while you'll usually want to include fonts of the same type (`serif`, `sans-serif`, `monospaced`, etc.) in your list, it's not mandatory that you do so. You can legally specify, for example, a list of specific font families that includes a sans-serif family, a serif family, and uses `monospace` as the default. I'm not sure why you'd want to do this, but it is possible.

What is fantasy?

It's a good question, but one that doesn't have an easy answer.

The current CSS Recommendations don't describe what any of these generic font families should look like, other than providing a simple example. That's not really a problem for `serif`, `sans-serif`, `monospace`, or to a lesser extent, `cursive`, all of which are self-describing, but `fantasy` is described only as "decorative."[1] What this actually means is anyone's guess, and the makers of the various web browsers have taken some pretty wild guesses. Internet Explorer tends to display `fantasy` text in a font similar to Blackadder ITC (a font that comes as part of Microsoft's Office package, and is very difficult to read at small sizes). Firefox displays the text in Showcard Gothic (another Microsoft Office font), which is dramatically different from Internet Explorer's choice. Safari displays Papyrus; though more common than the others, this font also looks very different than either of them.

For now, it's probably best to steer clear of using the `fantasy` generic font family unless you're sure you want a dramatic, decorative font and you're displaying the text in a large size.

The `font-size` Property

Setting font size is one of the most troublesome aspects of web design, because browsers vary widely in the ways they understand and apply the key concepts that determine how fonts will be sized for display. Before we explore this issue any further, let's take a look at the official definition of the ways in which you can determine the size of a font on a web page.

You can specify the font size you wish to use by selecting from a collection of seven constants:

- ❏ `xx-small`

- ❏ `x-small`

- ❏ `small`

- ❏ `medium`

- ❏ `large`

- ❏ `x-large`

- ❏ `xx-large`

These constants define what are referred to as **absolute** sizes, but as we'll see, in practice, absolute sizes are not "absolute" in the usual sense of that word. Another

---

[1]This description was added to the CSS documentation in version 3, which is still a working draft at the time of writing. This description could be improved in the future to provide more predictable results for web designers.

way to define absolute font sizes is to specify a length value in units, such as pixels or points.

Relative font sizes can be defined in three ways: using the constants `larger` and `smaller`; using the relative measurement of ems; or using a percentage value.

HTML Sizes vs CSS Sizes

In the days before CSS, designers often assigned font sizes using absolute or relative values from one to seven. You could specify a size of +1 (meaning you wanted the font to be one "level" higher than the default font size for that element), -1 (to create a font one "level" smaller than the default font size for that element), or 1 (one of seven absolute values, with no sign).

The fact that there were seven such values in HTML, and there are now seven absolute size constants in CSS, has led some people to conclude that there must be a one-to-one correspondence between those two scales. In fact, there is no connection between the two. Specifying `<font size="7">` in HTML will not necessarily produce the same result as `font-size: xx-large;` in a CSS rule.

Variability across Browsers and Platforms

Unfortunately, the effect of these different absolute font sizes varies greatly from one browser to the next, as shown in Figure 6.2. There, the same web page's contents are shown as rendered by a number of different browsers, browser versions, and platforms.

Given such variability between browsers, platforms, and even versions of the same browser, how in the world can you achieve anything like a predictable design using fonts on your web pages?

The short answer is that there is no way to accomplish this, short of using graphics or Adobe Acrobat PDF files to render and display your pages. It's inevitable that your pages will look somewhat different across these variable platform/browser/version combinations.

So, if you can't achieve complete consistency, what's the best way to approximate it? As a first step, use CSS rules rather than the deprecated `font` element to define the fonts in your designs. The W3C is always working on ways to overcome the limitations in web page rendering, and given the CSS support that's provided in current browsers, we're already moving closer to the ideal of accessible, yet predictable, font sizes.

Figure 6.2. Discrepancies between browsers using absolute size constants to display text

xx-small	xx-small	xx-small	xx-small
x-small	x-small	x-small	x-small
small	small	small	small
medium	medium	medium	medium
large	large	large	large
x-large	x-large	x-large	x-large
xx-large	xx-large	xx-large	xx-large

| **Internet Explorer 6** | **Internet Explorer 5** | **Safari** | **Firefox** |

Beware of Sizing Fonts Using Pixels

Using pixel measurements to set text size does result in a fairly consistent experience across browsers, but unfortunately, using pixels to set font size means that site visitors will be unable to resize the font using the browser settings in Internet Explorer. Obviously, this is an accessibility issue. You might like the look of tiny text—you may even find it perfectly readable—but a user with poor eyesight may need to increase the text size to read it comfortably. Therefore, it's best to use a method of text sizing that enables users of all browsers to resize text.

Relative to what?

When you use relative font sizes, such as ems or percentages, or the relative constants `larger` and `smaller`, you need to understand the base measurement to which they relate. In Chapter 3, we learned that em measurements tell the browser to render text in a size that's a multiple or fraction of that base measurement. Thus, a `font-size` setting of `1.5em` tells the browser to blow up the font size to 1.5 times the base measurement, and a font size of `0.5em` tells the browser to shrink the font size to half the base measurement.

What is the base measurement?

In the case of text that's contained directly in the body of a document, the base measurement is the browser's default font size. If the default setting for text in a browser is, for example, 12 points, then a font-size setting of 1.5em produces 18-point type.

For text inside other elements, the base measurement used by relative font sizing is the `font-size` of the element's parent container, rather than the size of the element's default font, as you may have expected. You might, for example, expect that if you define a particular class or instance of an `h1` tag to have a `font-size` of `1.5em`, you'd end up with a heading that was one and a half times the size of all other `h1` headings. In reality, the font size will be 1.5 times that of the parent element of the `h1` in question. Figure 6.3 demonstrates this concept by showing two headings, for both of which the document body is the parent element. The top heading is a standard `h1`. The second is an `h1` that's been defined as having a `font-size` of `1.5em`. Not quite what you might expect, is it?

Figure 6.3. Relative font size produces unexpected results if you make a wrong assumption

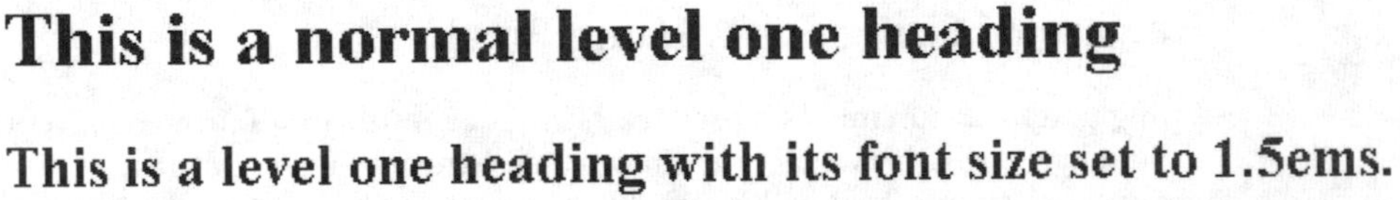

This is a normal level one heading

This is a level one heading with its font size set to 1.5ems.

Figure 6.4 shows how defining a `font-size` of `1.5em` in a `span` of text within an `h1` heading affects that `span`'s size. The word "Important" is 1.5 times as large as the other words in the heading because the heading is the `span`'s parent element.

Figure 6.4. Using a relative font size inside an h1 element to produce a predictable result

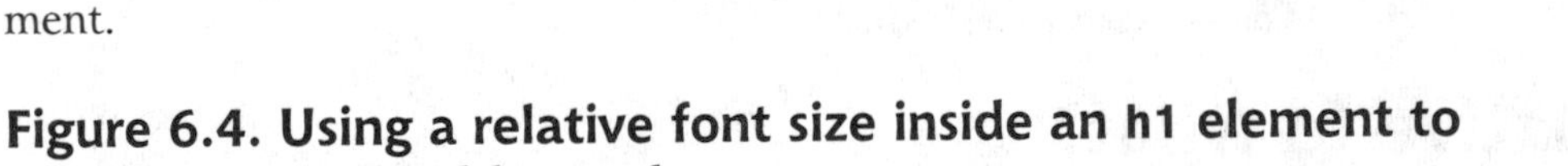

This is an important heading.

Other Font Properties

The `font-style` Property

The `font-style` property determines whether the text inside an element is rendered in an italic, oblique, or roman (or normal) font style. For all practical purposes, italic and oblique are identical.

Italics

If you're interested in typography, it's worth noting that if there's an italic font available in the font family, then it is used. Otherwise, the browser will take the Roman font and slant it itself. Also, if oblique is specified, but only an italic font is available, then the italic font is used, and vice versa.

The `font-variant` Property

In its current incarnation, the `font-variant` property has only one effect: it determines whether text should be displayed in small-caps format. In an ideal world, font families would contain a small-caps font, and the browser would use that font. Unfortunately, this is very, very rarely the case. Rather, current browsers render lowercase letters as capital letters with a smaller size than that used for the main font.

Figure 6.5 demonstrates the `font-variant` property set to a value of `small-caps`. The only other value this property can take is `normal`.

Figure 6.5. Using the `font-variant` property with a setting of `small-caps`

LOREM IPSUM

Note that in Internet Explorer prior to version 6, small-caps type is rendered as all-caps, without any difference in character size.

The `font-weight` Property

In the context of CSS font control, weight refers to the boldness of the characters. The `font-weight` property can take two types of values: relative and absolute. Relative values are `bolder` and `lighter`. Absolute values range from 100 (lightest) to 900 (boldest) in 100-unit increments, and also include the shortcut names normal (equivalent to 400) and bold (700). This set of values is actually more fine-grained than any current browser can support. The Adobe OpenType™ font standard does allow for nine levels of boldness in a font family; however, I have yet to see a practical application of all these levels.

As is the case with other relative measurements in CSS properties, these relative settings are based on the setting of the parent of the element affected. Because neither browsers nor fonts support the full range of nine different settings for the font-weight property, you'll find that two or more adjacent values usually produce identical output on the screen.

The font Shorthand Property

This shorthand property allows you to set multiple font-related properties in one CSS declaration.

As with other CSS shorthand properties we've seen, values are separated from one another by spaces, with commas used in multiple-value situations. Here's an example of a reasonably complex font description in CSS:

```
h3 {
  font: bolder small-caps 22px Arial, "Lucida Console", sans-serif;
}
```

Notice that the font size (22px) and the font family list are included in the definition of the style in sequence at the end of the list of properties. You must always include at least the font-size and the font-family property values, in that order, as the final (or only) values in the font shorthand property.

The above CSS rule produces the output shown in Figure 6.6.

Figure 6.6. A heading produced by a style rule calling for 22-pixel bolder small-caps font

LOREM IPSUM DOLOR SIT AMET

Use of the font shorthand property involves a couple of intriguing subtleties that are worth noting. First, you can add the line-height property to the font declaration by placing a forward slash (/), followed by an additional valid size or number, after the setting for the font size. We'll cover line-height in greater detail in Chapter 7. Here's an example:

```
p {
  font: small-caps 12px/2em Arial, "Lucida Console", sans-serif;
}
```

The bold type in the above code fragment instructs the browser to render paragraph text in a 12-pixel font and to set the line height to double the height of the font. Figure 6.7 shows what a paragraph looks like without the added line-height value. Figure 6.8 shows what it looks like when we add the two ems of line height.

Figure 6.7. Font without the addition of line spacing

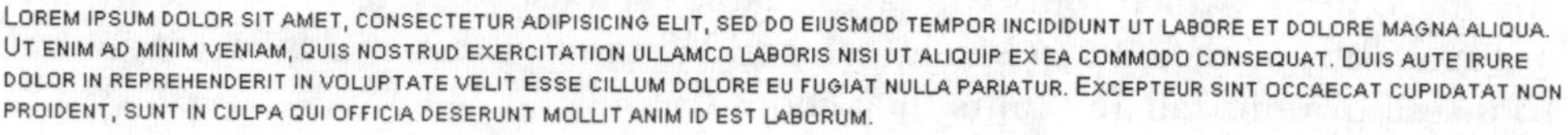

LOREM IPSUM DOLOR SIT AMET, CONSECTETUR ADIPISICING ELIT, SED DO EIUSMOD TEMPOR INCIDIDUNT UT LABORE ET DOLORE MAGNA ALIQUA. UT ENIM AD MINIM VENIAM, QUIS NOSTRUD EXERCITATION ULLAMCO LABORIS NISI UT ALIQUIP EX EA COMMODO CONSEQUAT. DUIS AUTE IRURE DOLOR IN REPREHENDERIT IN VOLUPTATE VELIT ESSE CILLUM DOLORE EU FUGIAT NULLA PARIATUR. EXCEPTEUR SINT OCCAECAT CUPIDATAT NON PROIDENT, SUNT IN CULPA QUI OFFICIA DESERUNT MOLLIT ANIM ID EST LABORUM.

Figure 6.8. The same text with a 2em line-height property value

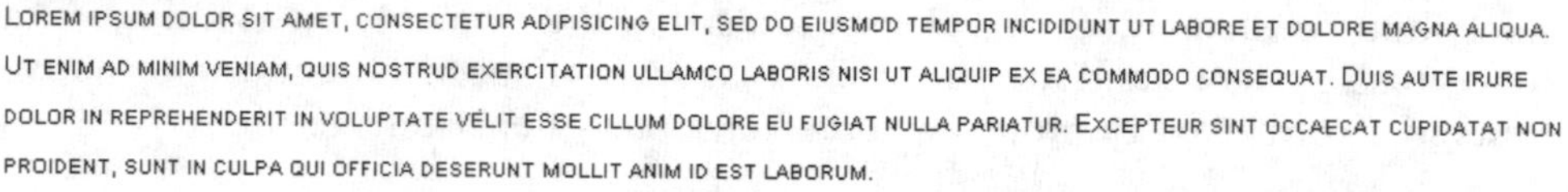

LOREM IPSUM DOLOR SIT AMET, CONSECTETUR ADIPISICING ELIT, SED DO EIUSMOD TEMPOR INCIDIDUNT UT LABORE ET DOLORE MAGNA ALIQUA.

UT ENIM AD MINIM VENIAM, QUIS NOSTRUD EXERCITATION ULLAMCO LABORIS NISI UT ALIQUIP EX EA COMMODO CONSEQUAT. DUIS AUTE IRURE

DOLOR IN REPREHENDERIT IN VOLUPTATE VELIT ESSE CILLUM DOLORE EU FUGIAT NULLA PARIATUR. EXCEPTEUR SINT OCCAECAT CUPIDATAT NON

PROIDENT, SUNT IN CULPA QUI OFFICIA DESERUNT MOLLIT ANIM ID EST LABORUM.

CSS 2 introduces the concept of a font constant that you can use when you're creating user interfaces and want to match user expectations based on their browsers and operating systems. Theoretically, these constants will use the font defined by the browser or operating system as the base from which they create the appearance of the text to which they are applied. These constant values may be assigned to the `font` shorthand property, as they represent a particular combination of values for all of the font properties. The constants are:

❑ `caption`

❑ `icon`

❑ `menu`

❑ `message-box`

❑ `small-caption`

❑ `status-bar`

Before you use this feature, you'll want to check the browser compatibility information in Appendix C, as not all browsers support these constants.

Standard and Nonstandard Font Families

Earlier, when we discussed the `font-family` property, I indicated that a deeper discussion of standard and nonstandard fonts was requisite to a complete understanding of the issue of font families. This section provides that background.

What do we mean by **standard fonts**? There's no CSS standard or specification that determines which fonts will be available on a user's system. Different fonts are available, by default, to Macintosh and Windows users, and all users are free to install or uninstall any fonts they choose.

However, some fonts are widely available on both platforms, along with alternatives that are sufficiently similar across those platforms to allow us to specify them safely and predictably. Table 6.1 lists fonts that are available on Windows and Macintosh systems, and are so similar that we can specify them as alternative fonts in a `font-family` property, and receive fairly consistent results.

Table 6.1. Font commonality between Windows and Macintosh platforms

Generic Font	Windows	Macintosh
`sans-serif`	Arial, Lucida Sans, Trebuchet MS, Tahoma, Verdana	Arial, Geneva, Helvetica, Helvetica Neue, Lucida Grande, Tahoma, Trebuchet MS, Verdana
`sans-serif`	Impact	Headline A
`monospace`	Courier New	Courier New, Courier
`serif`	Times New Roman, Georgia, Palatino Linotype	Times New Roman, Times, Baskerville
`cursive`	Comic Sans MS	Comic Sans MS, Chalkboard, Marker Felt
`sans-serif`	Impact	Headline A
`fantasy`	Papyrus	Papyrus

In addition to the fonts in Table 6.1, Microsoft once offered a free collection of downloadable TrueType fonts from its web sites. Due to licensing issues, Microsoft discontinued the collection's availability, but thanks to a quirk in the original licensing, it was determined that anyone who had legally downloaded these fonts could redistribute them. As a result, they're now available at http://corefonts.sourceforge.net/. Additionally, these fonts are available in a form that works on Unix and Linux machines. They are:

❏ Andale Mono

❏ Arial and Arial Black

❏ Comic Sans MS

❏ Courier New

❏ Georgia

❏ Impact

❏ Times New Roman

❏ Trebuchet MS

❏ Verdana

❏ Webdings

A significant percentage of the systems in use today have these fonts installed, so they can be used, if not with absolute certainty, at least with some confidence.

Specifying Font Lists

As you know, when we define a `font-family` style rule, usually we supply not one font, but a list of fonts separated by commas. Fonts that contain spaces must be enclosed in quotation marks.

What exactly does the browser do with this list of font families? As explained in the section called "The `font-family` Property", it takes the first font family in your list and looks for it on the user's system. If it finds the first font, it uses it to display the text that's associated with the `font-family` property. If it fails to find the first font, it moves to the second, then to the third, and so on.

More specifically, the browser looks through the operating system's collection of fonts in search of the font families you specify. Some applications come with their own fonts and store them in nonstandard places; those fonts will remain invisible to the browser.

This left-to-right, sequential font family searching technique produces two basic guidelines that affect the order in which you list font families in your styles.

First, you want to arrange the fonts in order from the most desirable to the least desirable appearance of the text.

Second, you want the last font on the list to be the generic name for the style of font family you're using (usually serif, sans-serif, or monospace). This ensures that even if none of the fonts you specify is found on the user's system, at least the appearance won't be completely wrong.

As a rule, then, you won't want to mix serif, sans-serif, monospace, cursive, or fantasy fonts in a single CSS style rule. You'll decide which type of font family you want to use, then list one or more font families in order of preference. Always end with the name of the generic font family that describes your choice of generic style.

The following three CSS style rules are typical of the sequencing you'd likely define:

```
p {
  font-family: "Courier New", Courier, monospace;
}
```

```
p {
  font-family: Georgia, "Times New Roman", serif;
}
```

```
p {
  font-family: Helvetica, Arial, sans-serif;
}
```

The specific font families you specify need not be those shown in the examples, and the sequence is not locked in concrete. The point is that, in each case, I've used font family names that specify a common style, then appended the generic family style name to the end of the list of specific fonts.

Using Nonstandard and Downloadable Fonts

As the user's browser will always display the text you present, no matter how you might mangle the `font-family` property's value, it follows that you can supply font family names that are unlikely to be installed on the user's system. The worst-case scenario is that text may display in a way you would not have specified.

For example, if you have an affinity for a particular font that's not normally installed on Windows machines, and for which there isn't really a good Windows equivalent, you can specify it, then design a sort of gradual degradation of the appearance of the content when the font isn't available.

Below, I've specified the Zapfino font that Apple includes on Macintosh; it isn't supplied with Windows, and is almost never installed there.

```
h1 {
    font-family: Zapfino, "Edwardian Script ITC", fantasy;
}
```

Figure 6.9 shows what the display looks like in Firefox on Mac when the Zapfino font is available. On a Windows machine, this would display as Edwardian Script ITC if that font was available, or, if it wasn't, the default `fantasy` font, which might not be quite as aesthetic (or ugly, depending on your opinion of the Zapfino font), will display. This will be as close as you're likely to come to matching the font cross-platform.

Figure 6.9. Displaying the nonstandard, but specified, Zapfino font on Macintosh

Summary

In this chapter we saw how CSS deals with fonts, before diving in to look closely at the workings of the `font-family` and `font-size` properties. Specifically, we investigated the differences between absolute and relative sizing, and considered the impacts these differing techniques could have on a page's usability.

We reviewed a number of other font properties before taking a closer look at the possibilities for specifying standard and nonstandard font families in CSS.

Chapter 7 moves beyond the issue of which fonts are used to display text, and offers some additional CSS styles and other capabilities to make your text more engaging and lively.

7

Text Effects and the Cascade

This chapter builds on the last, in which we looked at the fonts text can be displayed in. Here, we'll explore a range of other text characteristics, including:

- alignment

- first-line indentation

- horizontal and vertical spacing

- text decorations such as overline and strike-out

The browser treats hyperlinks differently from other text, and as such, we can style them using a number of special techniques. Lists also present a particular set of opportunities for text styling and presentation. We'll be looking closely at both hyperlinks and lists here.

The chapter concludes with a discussion of an important CSS concept: cascading. I've largely ignored the "C" in CSS until now, mainly because its primary use is to control the display of textual elements on the page.

We begin by delving into the `span` element, which I've touched on briefly in previous chapters. As you'll see, this element is very useful for dealing with segments of text within larger text blocks.

Using the span Element

Sometimes, you want to treat some text in a paragraph, or even a headline, differently from the text that surrounds it. For example, you might want to change the font, or some font characteristic—such as size or color—of one or two words in the midst of a paragraph. Obviously, you can't create a new paragraph in the existing paragraph without completely messing up the formatting of the page. What's the solution?

Enter: the span element. A span creates an inline collection of text to which styles can be applied. A span is similar to a div, but is treated as an inline element, instead of a block element, by default.

The span element is most useful for assigning special font properties, and some of the more esoteric text decorations and effects we'll discuss later in this chapter. For example, Figure 7.1 shows a case in which the designer wanted to emphasize a sentence by applying a highlighter effect.

Figure 7.1. Using the span element to highlight a sentence

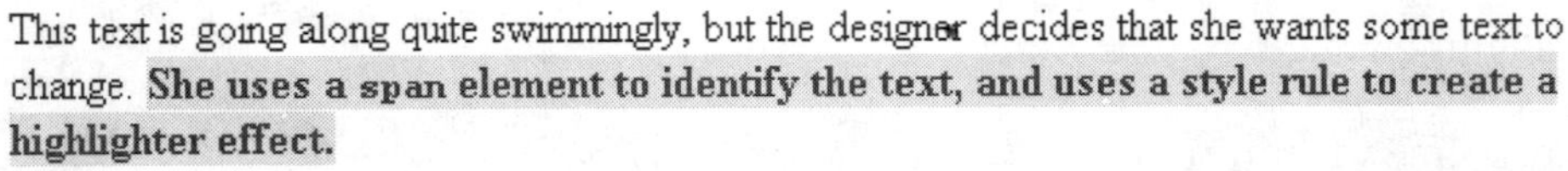

This text is going along quite swimmingly, but the designer decides that she wants some text to change. **She uses a span element to identify the text, and uses a style rule to create a highlighter effect.**

Here's the HTML for the page that produces that result. The style rule and span element are shown in bold, so you can easily spot the important point in this code.

```
<!DOCTYPE html PUBLIC "-//W3C//DTD XHTML 1.0 Strict//EN"
    "http://www.w3.org/TR/xhtml1/DTD/xhtml1-strict.dtd">
<html xmlns="http://www.w3.org/1999/xhtml">
  <head>
    <title>Demonstrating &lt;span&gt; Element Usage</title>
    <meta http-equiv="Content-Type"
        content="text/html; charset=iso-8859-1" />
    <style type="text/css">
      .change {
        background-color: yellow;
        color: maroon;
        font-weight: bold;
      }
```

```
    </style>
  </head>
  <body>
    <p>This text is going along quite swimmingly, but the designer
        decides that she wants some text to change.
        <span class="change">She uses a <code>span</code> element
        to identify the text, and uses a style rule to create a
        highlighter effect.</span></p>
  </body>
</html>
```

As we'll see through this chapter, the span element comes in quite handy when you want to apply any kind of special formatting to fragments within larger bodies of text. However, if you already have in your markup some other tag that you could style to achieve the effect, you should use that existing tag rather than adding spans for this single purpose.

For example, in the markup presented above, we used the code element to mark up the word "span" to indicate that it was computer code. By default, the browser displayed it in a monospace font, but we could use CSS to change the display to just about anything we might want. If we wanted to emphasize some text, we would have used a strong or an em element, and written a CSS rule for that element.

Text Alignment as a Design Technique

Professional artists and designers know that any design—be it a web page, print ad, or painting—comprises negative and positive space. Positive space consists of places in the design that are occupied by an object. On a web page, text, graphics, forms, and other content and user interface elements make up positive space. Negative space, on the other hand, is space that is empty, or not occupied by any object.

Good design dictates that a balance should exist between positive and negative space. We're not about to get into this subject in detail, but suffice it to say that pages that are "designed" as a lot of closely packed text content, with few (if any) "breaks" for negative space, are pretty ugly and hard to use. Even text-only pages can be made more inviting by the application of negative space. And one of the best ways to create negative space on a web page is through the judicious use of text alignment.

Examples of text alignment have appeared in numerous places in this book. Viewed at its most basic level, text alignment is hardly rocket science, so explanations of those examples have not been necessary. However, the time has come for us to understand precisely how text alignment works in CSS.

Text Alignment in CSS vs HTML

In HTML, text alignment was typically handled using the `center` element and the `align` attribute. Both are deprecated in HTML 4.0 as part of the move toward CSS becoming the preferred presentation model.[1]

As we adopt CSS, we use the `text-align` property to describe the alignment of text. The `text-align` property can take any of the following values:

☐ `left`

☐ `center`

☐ `right`

☐ `justify`

The default value is `left`. Support for the `justify` value is not required in the W3C's CSS Recommendations, and support for it is spotty in older browsers. But you can use it with impunity, if not always with the intended effect, because browsers that don't support it generally resort to left alignment.

Moving from Crowded to Airy Design Using Alignment

To see how you can use `text-align` to create more pleasing effects on your pages, let's look at an example. We'll start with the simple page shown in Figure 7.2, in which no alignment styles are included.

---

[1] Actually, the `align` attribute is still permitted in HTML 4.0, but only within the context of table cells.

Figure 7.2. A simple text page layout with no alignment styles

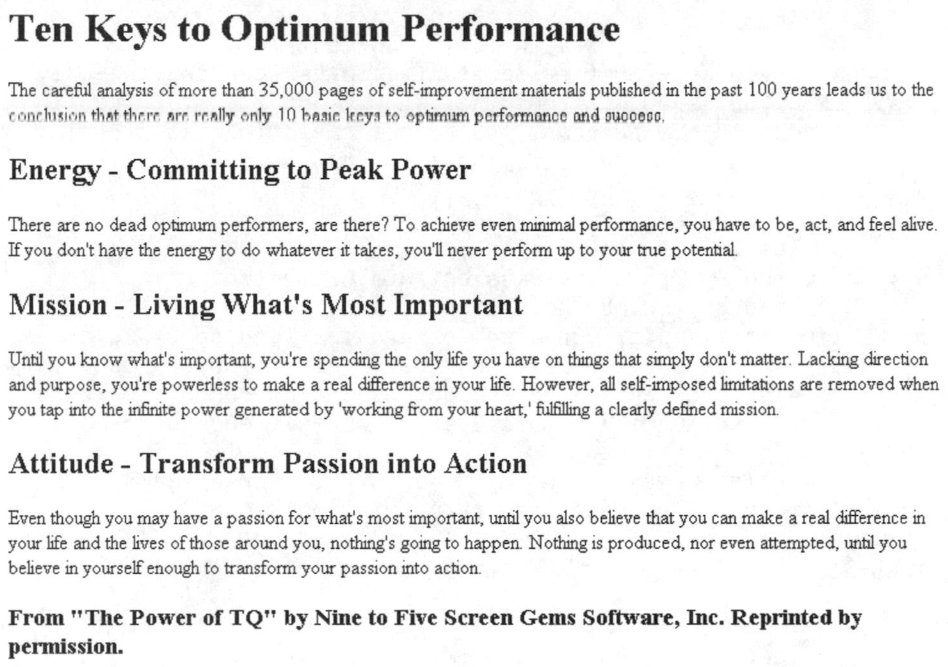

Ten Keys to Optimum Performance

The careful analysis of more than 35,000 pages of self-improvement materials published in the past 100 years leads us to the conclusion that there are really only 10 basic keys to optimum performance and success.

Energy - Committing to Peak Power

There are no dead optimum performers, are there? To achieve even minimal performance, you have to be, act, and feel alive. If you don't have the energy to do whatever it takes, you'll never perform up to your true potential.

Mission - Living What's Most Important

Until you know what's important, you're spending the only life you have on things that simply don't matter. Lacking direction and purpose, you're powerless to make a real difference in your life. However, all self-imposed limitations are removed when you tap into the infinite power generated by 'working from your heart,' fulfilling a clearly defined mission.

Attitude - Transform Passion into Action

Even though you may have a passion for what's most important, until you also believe that you can make a real difference in your life and the lives of those around you, nothing's going to happen. Nothing is produced, nor even attempted, until you believe in yourself enough to transform your passion into action.

From "The Power of TQ" by Nine to Five Screen Gems Software, Inc. Reprinted by permission.

Here's the HTML that produced Figure 7.2:

File: **tenkeys.html (excerpt)**

```
<!DOCTYPE html PUBLIC "-//W3C//DTD XHTML 1.0 Strict//EN"
   "http://www.w3.org/TR/xhtml1/DTD/xhtml1-strict.dtd">
<html xmlns="http://www.w3.org/1999/xhtml">
  <head>
    <title>Text Layout Sample 1</title>
    <meta http-equiv="Content-Type"
        content="text/html; charset=iso-8859-1" />
  </head>
  <body>
    <h1>Ten Keys to Optimum Performance</h1>
    <p>The careful analysis of more than 35,000 pages of
        self-improvement materials published in the past 100 years
        leads us to the conclusion that there are really only 10
        basic keys to optimum performance and success.</p>
    <h2>Energy - Committing to Peak Power</h2>
```

```
    <p>There are no dead optimum performers, are there? To achieve
        even minimal performance, you have to be, act, and feel
        alive. If you don't have the energy to do whatever it
        takes, you'll never perform up to your true potential.</p>
    <h2>Mission - Living What's Most Important</h2>
    <p>Until you know what's important, you're spending the only
        life you have on things that simply don't matter. Lacking
        direction and purpose, you're powerless to make a real
        difference in your life. However, all self-imposed
        limitations are removed when you tap into the infinite
        power generated by 'working from your heart,' fulfilling
        a clearly defined mission.</p>
    <h2>Attitude - Transform Passion into Action</h2>
    <p>Even though you may have a passion for what's most
        important, until you also believe that you can make a real
        difference in your life and the lives of those around you,
        nothing's going to happen. Nothing is produced, nor even
        attempted, until you believe in yourself enough to
        transform your passion into action.</p>
    <h3>From "The Power of TQ" by Nine to Five Screen Gems
        Software, Inc. Reprinted by permission.</h3>
  </body>
</html>
```

There's nothing too complicated here. Nor is there anything very interesting to look at, even though the content itself might interest someone.

Now, let's see what happens when we center the top headline, and move the subheadings so they're aligned to the right side of the page rather than the left. The result is shown in Figure 7.3.

The style sheet rules that produce the effect in Figure 7.3 are pretty simple:

File: **tenkeys.css**

```
h1 {
  text-align: center;
}
h2 {
  text-align: right;
}
```

Figure 7.3. Applying headline alignment to basic text layout

Ten Keys to Optimum Performance

The careful analysis of more than 35,000 pages of self-improvement materials published in the past 100 years leads us to the conclusion that there are really only 10 basic keys to optimum performance and success.

Energy - Committing to Peak Power

There are no dead optimum performers, are there? To achieve even minimal performance, you have to be, act, and feel alive. If you don't have the energy to do whatever it takes, you'll never perform up to your true potential.

Mission - Living What's Most Important

Until you know what's important, you're spending the only life you have on things that simply don't matter. Lacking direction and purpose, you're powerless to make a real difference in your life. However, all self-imposed limitations are removed when you tap into the infinite power generated by 'working from your heart,' fulfilling a clearly defined mission.

Attitude - Transform Passion into Action

Even though you may have a passion for what's most important, until you also believe that you can make a real difference in your life and the lives of those around you, nothing's going to happen. Nothing is produced, nor even attempted, until you believe in yourself enough to transform your passion into action.

From "The Power of TQ" by Nine to Five Screen Gems Software, Inc. Reprinted by permission.

While the layout of the page is admittedly unorthodox, you have to admit that it's more interesting than what we started with. The "air," or negative space, created to the left of the subheadings is attention-getting.

Figure 7.4. Centering text in paragraphs for a different effect

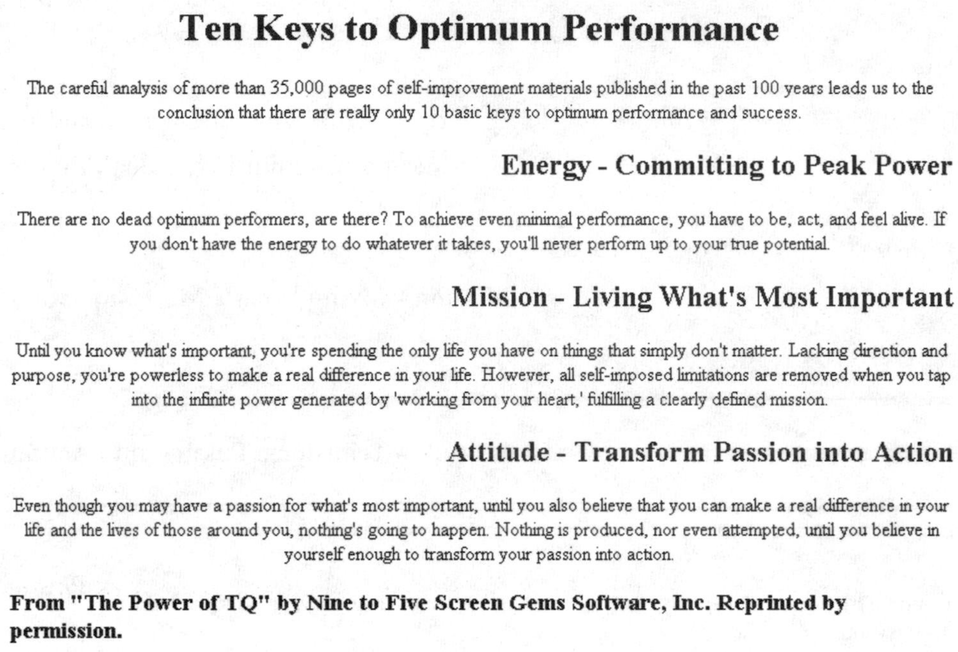

Ten Keys to Optimum Performance

The careful analysis of more than 35,000 pages of self-improvement materials published in the past 100 years leads us to the conclusion that there are really only 10 basic keys to optimum performance and success.

Energy - Committing to Peak Power

There are no dead optimum performers, are there? To achieve even minimal performance, you have to be, act, and feel alive. If you don't have the energy to do whatever it takes, you'll never perform up to your true potential.

Mission - Living What's Most Important

Until you know what's important, you're spending the only life you have on things that simply don't matter. Lacking direction and purpose, you're powerless to make a real difference in your life. However, all self-imposed limitations are removed when you tap into the infinite power generated by 'working from your heart,' fulfilling a clearly defined mission.

Attitude - Transform Passion into Action

Even though you may have a passion for what's most important, until you also believe that you can make a real difference in your life and the lives of those around you, nothing's going to happen. Nothing is produced, nor even attempted, until you believe in yourself enough to transform your passion into action.

From "The Power of TQ" by Nine to Five Screen Gems Software, Inc. Reprinted by permission.

This page consists of headlines that are followed by associated paragraphs of pithy advice. The whole scheme seems to lend itself to something more closely resembling a promotional design. Let's try centering the paragraph text. Now the page looks like Figure 7.4.

The style sheet that generates Figure 7.4 is shown here:

File: **tenkeys.css**

```css
h1 {
  text-align: center;
}
h2 {
  text-align: right;
}
p {
  text-align: center;
}
```

Whether or not you like your paragraphs centered, you can probably see where I'm heading with this concept. By altering the `text-align` property of text elements on the page, we can create more negative space and more pleasing page layouts—even if we don't do anything else.

That said, I couldn't resist making one last change that involves color, not alignment. Figure 7.5 shows you what putting a background color behind the heading text does for the additional negative space. I've used a yellow background—though you can't tell—but the fact that it's a solid color produces the same effect as negative space, while providing yet another way for us to guide readers' eyes to the content we want them to see: the main subheadings.

Figure 7.5. Adding a color background to subheadings to emphasize negative space

Ten Keys to Optimum Performance

The careful analysis of more than 35,000 pages of self-improvement materials published in the past 100 years leads us to the conclusion that there are really only 10 basic keys to optimum performance and success.

Energy - Committing to Peak Power

There are no dead optimum performers, are there? To achieve even minimal performance, you have to be, act, and feel alive. If you don't have the energy to do whatever it takes, you'll never perform up to your true potential.

Mission - Living What's Most Important

Until you know what's important, you're spending the only life you have on things that simply don't matter. Lacking direction and purpose, you're powerless to make a real difference in your life. However, all self-imposed limitations are removed when you tap into the infinite power generated by 'working from your heart,' fulfilling a clearly defined mission.

Attitude - Transform Passion into Action

Even though you may have a passion for what's most important, until you also believe that you can make a real difference in your life and the lives of those around you, nothing's going to happen. Nothing is produced, nor even attempted, until you believe in yourself enough to transform your passion into action.

From "The Power of TQ" by Nine to Five Screen Gems Software, Inc. Reprinted by permission.

Here's the style sheet that creates the effect in Figure 7.5:

File: **tenkeys.css**

```
h1 {
  text-align: center;
}
h2 {
  text-align: right;
  background-color: yellow;
}
p {
  text-align: center;
}
```

First-line Indentation

In the example in the previous section, I centered the text in the explanatory paragraphs under each subheading. As I said at the time, that wasn't necessarily a great design, but it did demonstrate how alignment can produce "air" or negative space. Another, perhaps more conventional, way to accomplish this objective with blocks of text is to *indent* the first line of each paragraph.

The `text-indent` property controls the amount of extra left padding that's applied to the first line of a block of text. The property requires as its value a measurement or percentage of the element width.

Let's put `text-indent` to work. Replace the style rule for paragraphs in the above CSS with a new one, like this:

File: **tenkeys.css** (excerpt)

```
p {
  text-indent: 2em;
}
```

The result will look like Figure 7.6.

Figure 7.6. Indenting the first line of text in each paragraph

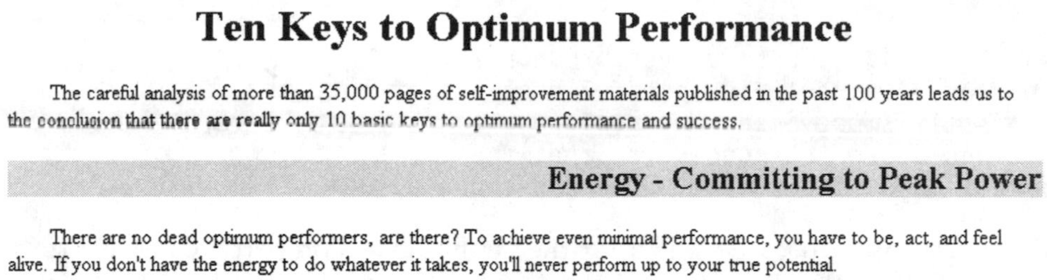

Ten Keys to Optimum Performance

The careful analysis of more than 35,000 pages of self-improvement materials published in the past 100 years leads us to the conclusion that there are really only 10 basic keys to optimum performance and success.

Energy - Committing to Peak Power

There are no dead optimum performers, are there? To achieve even minimal performance, you have to be, act, and feel alive. If you don't have the energy to do whatever it takes, you'll never perform up to your true potential.

Figure 7.7. Outdenting the first line of text in a paragraph

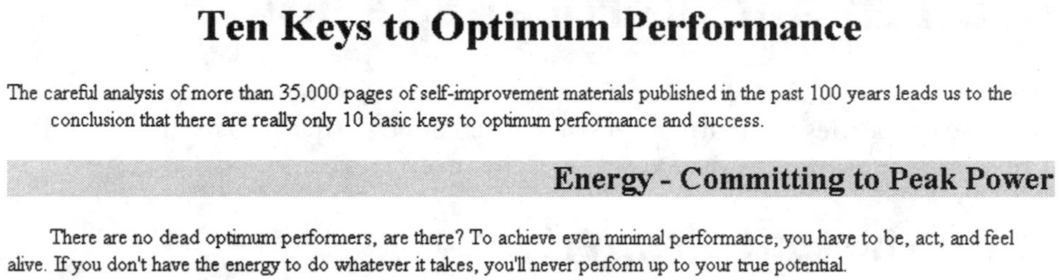

Ten Keys to Optimum Performance

The careful analysis of more than 35,000 pages of self-improvement materials published in the past 100 years leads us to the conclusion that there are really only 10 basic keys to optimum performance and success.

Energy - Committing to Peak Power

There are no dead optimum performers, are there? To achieve even minimal performance, you have to be, act, and feel alive. If you don't have the energy to do whatever it takes, you'll never perform up to your true potential.

A variation on first-line indent is **first-line outdent**, also called a **hanging indent**, where the first line is closer to the left margin than the rest of the paragraph. You can see this effect in the first paragraph of Figure 7.7.

Here are the CSS rules that we add to the style sheet to accomplish the styling shown in Figure 7.7:

File: **tenkeys.css (excerpt)**

```
p.outdent {
  padding-left: 2em;
  text-indent: -2em;
}
```

Here, I've assigned a left padding value of two ems to the entire paragraph, then removed that padding from the first line by setting a negative `text-indent` of the same amount.

In the HTML, I've simply assigned the outdent class to the first paragraph of the document:

File: tenkeys.html (excerpt)

```
<h1>Ten Keys to Optimum Performance</h1>
<p class="outdent">The careful analysis of more than 35,000 pages
  of self-improvement materials published in the past 100 years
  leads us to the conclusion that there are really only 10 basic
  keys to optimum performance and success.</p>
```

When you use a negative value for the text-indent property, you have to be careful that the first line of text doesn't end up falling outside the boundaries of the browser window. In general, this means you need to assign a padding-left of at least the same size as the negative indent you choose.

Horizontal and Vertical Spacing

CSS rules allow you to control spacing between lines, letters, and words. You can use these properties to create interesting visual effects, to improve the readability of text, or sometimes, to fit text into a tight spot.

The line-height Property

All elements in a web page are affected by a line-height property. This property refers to the total distance between the **baselines** of two adjacent lines of text. The baseline of a line of text is the imaginary horizontal line most letters sit on—you can see this line clearly in the word "baseline" itself.

By default, browsers create a line-height that ensures the readability of vertically adjacent lines or elements. For example, if the text in a paragraph is set in a 12-point font, the browser will usually provide one point of spacing above and another point of spacing below the line, creating a total line-height of 14 points.

When you explicitly set the line-height for an element such as a heading or paragraph, you effectively tell the browser to increase or decrease the amount of space between that line and those that are vertically adjacent to it. This space is called **leading** (pronounced like "heading," not like "reading"), a term that's left over from the days when type was set using molten lead formed into bars of type, one for each line. Spacing was created by placing thin, blank slugs between the lines.

Leading can create additional negative space in a web page layout. Figure 7.8 shows how the page we've been working with looks if the following style rule is applied:

File: **tenkeys.css** (excerpt)

```
p {
  text-indent: 2em;
  line-height: 1.5em;
}
```

This effectively creates text that is one and one-half line spaced.

Figure 7.8. Using the `line-height` property to create 1.5-line spaced text

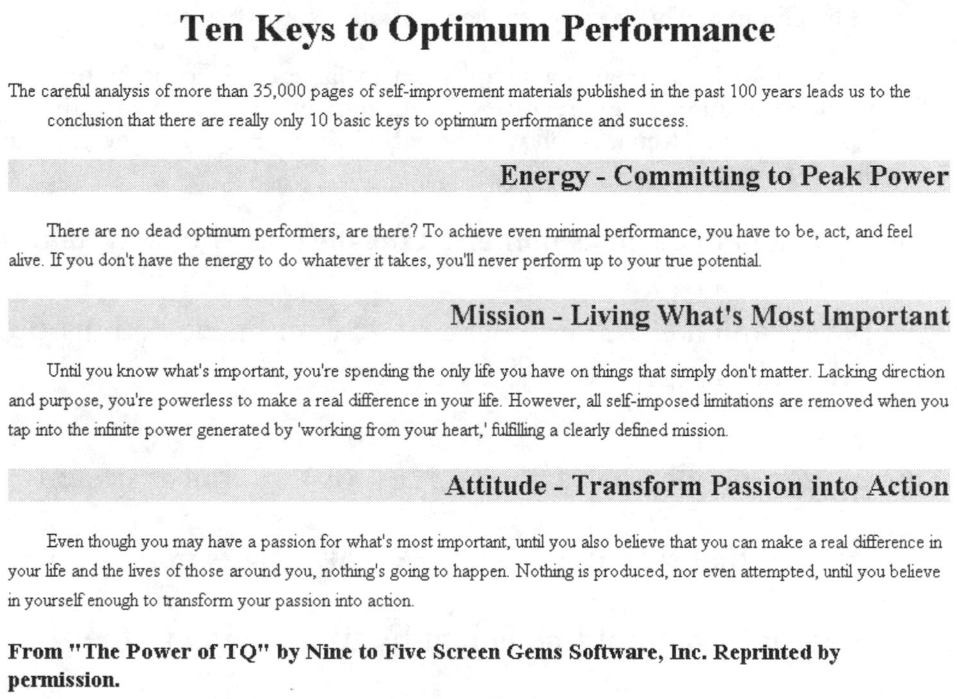

Ten Keys to Optimum Performance

The careful analysis of more than 35,000 pages of self-improvement materials published in the past 100 years leads us to the conclusion that there are really only 10 basic keys to optimum performance and success.

Energy - Committing to Peak Power

There are no dead optimum performers, are there? To achieve even minimal performance, you have to be, act, and feel alive. If you don't have the energy to do whatever it takes, you'll never perform up to your true potential.

Mission - Living What's Most Important

Until you know what's important, you're spending the only life you have on things that simply don't matter. Lacking direction and purpose, you're powerless to make a real difference in your life. However, all self-imposed limitations are removed when you tap into the infinite power generated by 'working from your heart,' fulfilling a clearly defined mission.

Attitude - Transform Passion into Action

Even though you may have a passion for what's most important, until you also believe that you can make a real difference in your life and the lives of those around you, nothing's going to happen. Nothing is produced, nor even attempted, until you believe in yourself enough to transform your passion into action.

From "The Power of TQ" by Nine to Five Screen Gems Software, Inc. Reprinted by permission.

It's important to realize that when you set the `line-height` property using a relative measurement (such as an em value or percentage), that value is applied on the basis of the current element's font settings, not on those of the parent, as is the case with most other font control properties. Thus, if you have a paragraph with a 12-pixel font that's contained in a `div` with an 18-pixel font, for example, a `line-height` value of two ems for the paragraph would produce an actual line height of 24 pixels, not 36.

The `line-height` property is the first CSS property we've encountered that can take a pure numerical argument, as in this example:

```
p {
  line-height: 1.5;
}
```

This has the same visual effect as would supplying a value of 1.5em, or a value of 150%. The difference between a numeric value and a CSS measurement is that a numeric value is inherited directly by child elements, which will apply it to their own font sizes, while relative values cause the actual line height to be inherited by children. This is easier to demonstrate than to explain.

Figure 7.9 shows two different paragraphs, set in large type, to dramatize the different effects of numeric and relative `line-height` properties. The text in the figure explains how each paragraph was formatted relative to the `div` container of which it is part.

Figure 7.9. Relative versus numeric `line-height` property values

This paragraph has a `font-size` of 2em and is nested inside a `div` that has a `line-height` of 2em.

This paragraph also has a `font-size` of 2em, but is nested inside a `div` that sets a `line-height` of 2. This multiplies the paragraph's natural line height by two, giving us the double-spaced effect we probably wanted.

The first paragraph is contained in a `div` with a `line-height` of 2em. The paragraph therefore inherits the line height that results when you double the default line height produced by the div element's font (in this case, the browser's default font size, which is usually 12 points). As the paragraph uses a larger font than the div, the line spacing looks very crowded.

The second paragraph is contained in a div with a line-height of 2. Instead of passing on the exact line height, the inherited value of 2 is used by the paragraph to determine a line-height based on its own, larger font. This produces the double-spaced effect we probably intended.

For this reason, it is generally best to stick to numeric values for the line-height property, unless you know you're striving for a really different vertical spacing effect, and understand the consequences of using CSS measurement values.

The letter-spacing and word-spacing Properties

The letter-spacing property defines the amount of space between the letters in the text element to which it is applied. It can take an absolute or relative value, and its default setting is normal.

Figure 7.10 shows an extreme example of letter-spacing created so you can see the effect.

Figure 7.10. Using letter-spacing to define distance between letters

All paragraphs identified with the class 'spacy' on this page are set to 0.5 ems of letter spacing. You can see here the effect of that setting.

This paragraph is not an instance of the class 'spacy' so it has default letter spacing.

Here's the HTML page that generates Figure 7.10:

File: **spacy.html**

```
<!DOCTYPE html PUBLIC "-//W3C//DTD XHTML 1.0 Strict//EN"
    "http://www.w3.org/TR/xhtml1/DTD/xhtml1-strict.dtd">
<html xmlns="http://www.w3.org/1999/xhtml">
  <head>
    <title>Letter and Word Spacing</title>
    <meta http-equiv="Content-Type"
```

```
         content="text/html; charset=iso-8859-1" />
  <style type="text/css">
    .spacy {
      letter-spacing: 0.5em;
    }
  </style>
</head>
<body>
  <p class="spacy">All paragraphs identified with the class
      'spacy' on this page are set to 0.5 ems of letter spacing.
      You can see here the effect of that setting.</p>
  <p>This paragraph is not an instance of the class 'spacy' so
      it has default letter spacing.</p>
</body>
</html>
```

Notice that the spacing between words is elongated as well, so the words continue to appear as a grouping of letters that are closer together than the words are to one another.

You can also apply negative values to the `letter-spacing` property to cause letters to appear closer to one another.

One situation in which `letter-spacing` comes in particularly handy occurs where a headline appears to have a bit too much inter-letter spacing. This often happens with monospaced fonts, but it can be annoying or distracting with sans-serif fonts as well. In Figure 7.11, this effect is put to good use. The top headline on the page does not use any letter-spacing. Notice how the words containing the letters "i" and "l" and "t," in particular, look a little too "airy." This is a characteristic of monospaced fonts, but with the CSS `letter-spacing` property, you can overcome this problem and continue to use this type of font where it's most appropriate.

Figure 7.11. Using negative `letter-spacing` to tighten up monospace fonts

```
This Is a Little Too Spread Out

This Is a Little Bit Better
```

Here's the HTML that produces the page in Figure 7.11. Notice that I defined a class called "compress," then applied it to one of the h1 heading elements:

File: **compress.html**

```
<!DOCTYPE html PUBLIC "-//W3C//DTD XHTML 1.0 Strict//EN"
    "http://www.w3.org/TR/xhtml1/DTD/xhtml1-strict.dtd">
<html xmlns="http://www.w3.org/1999/xhtml">
  <head>
    <title>Letter Spacing in Headlines</title>
    <meta http-equiv="Content-Type"
        content="text/html; charset=iso-8859-1" />
    <style type="text/css">
      h1 {
        font-family: "Courier New", Courier, monospace;
      }
      .compress {
        letter-spacing: -0.05em;
      }
    </style>
  </head>
  <body>
    <h1>This Is a Little Too Spread Out</h1>
    <h1 class="compress">This Is a Little Bit Better</h1>
  </body>
</html>
```

As you can see, I decreased letter spacing only by a small amount (5% of the width of a character) to achieve the desired result. You'll need to experiment with the effects of the letter-spacing property with various fonts and type sizes to know what will work best in a given situation.

Another case in which letter-spacing is particularly effective is in creating a different visual effect for a page heading. Figure 7.12 shows a heading that makes effective use of letter spacing to create a graphically interesting effect without the use of graphic tools.

Figure 7.12. Using letter-spacing to create an interesting visual effect

j o e   c o o l ' s   w e b   h a n g o u t

The stretched-out headline above almost acts like a logo for Joe Cool's web site, but it is created without a graphics tool.

The HTML that creates the effect shown in Figure 7.12 is simplicity itself:

File: **joecool.html**

```
<!DOCTYPE html PUBLIC "-//W3C//DTD XHTML 1.0 Strict//EN"
    "http://www.w3.org/TR/xhtml1/DTD/xhtml1-strict.dtd">
<html xmlns="http://www.w3.org/1999/xhtml">
  <head>
    <title>Cool Headline With Letter Spacing</title>
    <meta http-equiv="Content-Type"
        content="text/html; charset=iso-8859-1" />
    <style type="text/css">
    h1.pageheading {
      font-family: 'Courier New', Courier, monospace;
      font-size: 18pt;
      letter-spacing: 0.7em;
      text-transform: lowercase;
    }
    </style>
  </head>
  <body>
    <h1 class="pageheading">Joe Cool's Web Hangout</h1>
    <p>The stretched-out headline above almost acts like a logo
        for Joe Cool's web site, but it is created without a graphics
        tool.
    </p>
  </body>
</html>
```

The word-spacing property determines the spacing between words. However, versions of Internet Explorer earlier than 6 don't support this property.[2]

Figure 7.13 depicts the effect a word-spacing setting of 1em has on an oversized sentence.

Figure 7.13. The word-spacing property at work

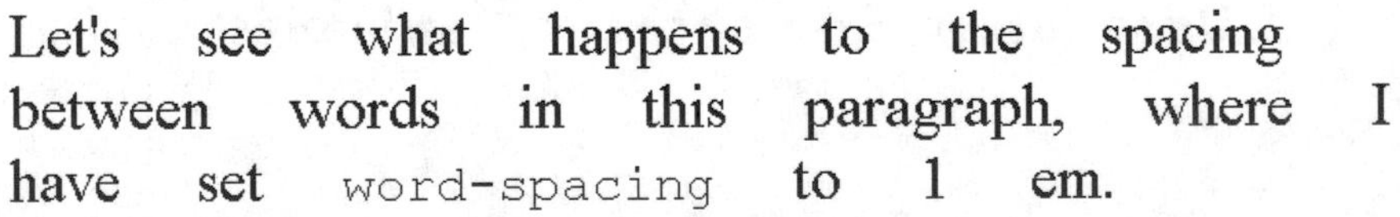

Let's see what happens to the spacing between words in this paragraph, where I have set word-spacing to 1 em.

---

[2]Internet Explorer version 5 for the Macintosh does support this property, but its implementation is buggy and results in word overlap in some circumstances.

Here's the HTML that produces the page shown in Figure 7.13:

File: **wordspacing.html (excerpt)**

```
<!DOCTYPE html PUBLIC "-//W3C//DTD XHTML 1.0 Strict//EN"
    "http://www.w3.org/TR/xhtml1/DTD/xhtml1-strict.dtd">
<html xmlns="http://www.w3.org/1999/xhtml">
  <head>
    <title>Word-Spacing Demonstration</title>
    <meta http-equiv="Content-Type"
        content="text/html; charset=iso-8859-1" />
  </head>
  <body>
    <p style="word-spacing: 1em; font-size: 2em;">Let's see what
        happens to the spacing between words in this paragraph,
        where I have set <code>word-spacing</code> to 1 em.</p>
  </body>
</html>
```

Text Decorations

The text-decoration property allows you to add any of four specific effects to text:

❑ underline

❑ overline

❑ blink

❑ line-through

In addition, the text-decoration property can take a value of none, which can be used in one specific situation I'll discuss in a moment.

I'm going to ignore blinking and underlining as a text decoration. Many mainstream browsers ignore blinking text, because it fell into almost immediate disrepute when Netscape first introduced it as a nonstandard HTML tag. Blinking text is widely considered annoying, amateurish, and the epitome of bad design. Underlining, on the other hand, is still widely supported by browsers, but that doesn't make it a good idea. Users are accustomed to seeing hyperlinks underlined. Underlining text that is not a hyperlink only creates confusion for the user.

Overlining can be used to create an interesting and potentially useful effect in which a line appears above the text, extending to the full width of the text itself. This makes it different from the top border line we learned about in Chapter 3. Figure 7.14 shows the effect; the HTML that produces the effect follows.

Figure 7.14. Using `overline` on a headline

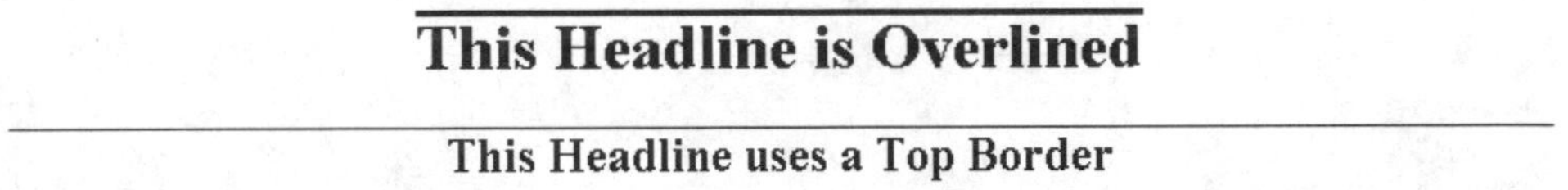

This Headline is Overlined

This Headline uses a Top Border

File: **overline.html**

```
<!DOCTYPE html PUBLIC "-//W3C//DTD XHTML 1.0 Strict//EN"
    "http://www.w3.org/TR/xhtml1/DTD/xhtml1-strict.dtd">
<html xmlns="http://www.w3.org/1999/xhtml">
  <head>
    <title>Showing Off Overlining</title>
    <meta http-equiv="Content-Type"
        content="text/html; charset=iso-8859-1" />
    <style type="text/css">
      h1 {
        text-align: center;
        text-decoration: overline;
      }
      h2 {
        text-align: center;
        border-top: 1px solid black;
      }
    </style>
  </head>
  <body>
    <h1>This Headline is Overlined</h1>
    <h2>This Headline uses a Top Border</h2>
  </body>
</html>
```

The border over the second headline extends the full width of the page because that marks the top of the box containing the headline. The top heading on the page uses a `text-decoration` declaration with a value of `overline` to create a decidedly different result.

Another value the `text-decoration` property can take is `line-through`. An example of this effect is shown in Figure 7.15.

Figure 7.15. Using the `line-through` value of the `text-decoration` property

~~Lorem Ipsum Dolor Sit Amet~~

Tip **The `del` Element**

This strikethrough effect is commonly used to indicate text that has been deleted from a document as part of an edit. HTML includes the `del` element for this purpose, and browsers will generally render it with a strikethrough by default.

If you're using a strikethrough effect to indicate that text has been deleted, you should make use of the `del` element to preserve the semantic meaning of your markup. If you're using the strikethrough effect for some other reason, you should avoid the `del` element and use a `span`, a `div`, or some other semantically correct element.

Also, the `ins` element goes hand in hand with the `del` element, and is used to mark up text that has been inserted into a document.

The last `text-decoration` value I'll describe is `none`. Given that, unless told otherwise, text doesn't display any decoration, you might wonder why you'd ever want to use this value. You can assign the `none` value to the `text-decoration` property to turn off underlining of hyperlinks. This usage can be more or less effective depending on whether the user has already turned off underlining of hyperlinks as a browser preference. Most modern browsers offer this option and many users take advantage of it.

Styling Hyperlinks

Hyperlinks are a special category of text used on a web page. Links are active elements that create navigational points from which users can change their locations to another point on the same page, another page on the same site, or another site entirely. Links can, in fact, be used for many tasks if you call on the capabilities of JavaScript, but those uses are beyond the scope of this book.

There are two ways to control the style of hyperlinks. You can treat links like any other text for the purposes of styling their initial, static appearance. Or you can take advantage of the four widely supported pseudo-classes to style the appearance of links in the four different states in which they can exist. These four states and their corresponding pseudo-classes are shown in Table 7.1.[3]

Table 7.1. The anchor pseudo-classes explained

Anchor Pseudo-class	Corresponding Hyperlink State
`a:link`	not yet visited
`a:visited`	visited
`a:hover`	cursor positioned over link but mouse not being clicked
`a:active`	being clicked on at the moment

Although most links appear inline with text and take on the same basic characteristics (font family and size, for example) as the text in which they're embedded, hyperlinks are blue and underlined by default. Sometimes, you want to have some links appear in a different font or color. In addition, site navigation links can be presented more effectively if you style them differently from normal text on the page. You can use all the normal text identification schemes to alter the appearance of links. For example, you might define a class called, say, `majorlink`, which creates a specialized font and color combination, and then define a link as belonging to that class. Here's how you'd do it:

```
<a class="majorlink" href="http://www.google.com/">Google</a>
```

Figure 7.16 shows two separate hyperlinks. The top one is a normal link, displayed when either the user or the style sheet has turned off underlining; the second is an instance of the class `majorlink`, where I've identified a different font family, size, background color, and text color.

Figure 7.16. Two hyperlinks with different formatting

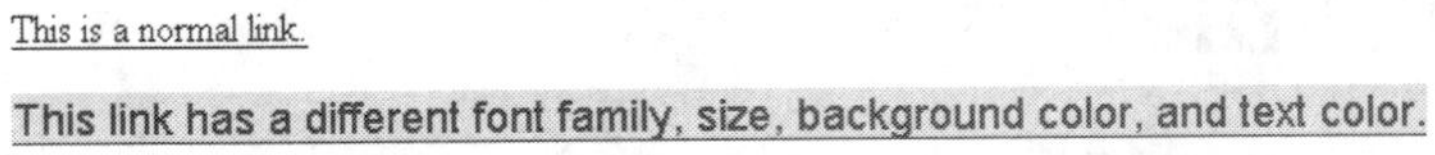

This is a normal link.

This link has a different font family, size, background color, and text color.

---

[3]While I'm discussing these pseudo-classes in conjunction with anchors, the CSS recommendation allows `:hover` and `:active` to be applied to other types of HTML elements, as well. A fifth pseudo-class, `:focus`, also exists. Unfortunately, none of these are supported by Internet Explorer version 6; therefore they're not commonly used.

The anchor pseudo-classes can be used in style sheets to create specific designs that are associated with each condition in which a hyperlink can be found. Here's a typical style sheet that provides for the special treatment of hyperlinks:

```css
a:link {
  color: darkgreen;
  background-color: transparent;
}
a:visited {
  color: lightgreen;
  background-color: transparent;
}
a:hover {
  color: green;
  background-color: black;
}
a:active {
  color: black;
  background-color: green;
}
```

The order in which you declare each of these pseudo-classes is important because, given the rules of cascading (which we'll discuss in the final section of this chapter), each of these sets of rules will be overridden by an earlier rule of the same importance. Thus, if you declare a rule for a :hover pseudo-class before you define a rule for the :link or :visited pseudo-classes, the color you choose for :hover links will never appear, as all links are either visited or unvisited. In the above code fragment, if you relocated the a:hover rule to the first position in the list, it would never be used, because the subsequent :link or :visited rule (whichever applied to the link in question) would override it. Some people find it helpful to use the mnemonic "*love–hate*" to remember that the pseudo-classes should be used in the order :link, :visited, :hover, and :active.

It is possible to specify two pseudo-classes in one rule. For example, you can apply a special "hover" color to visited links with this rule:

```css
a:visited:hover {
  color: blue;
  background-color: transparent;
}
```

You can turn off the underlining of all hyperlinks in a document with a single style rule:

```
a {
  text-decoration: none;
}
```

However, unless your link is otherwise very obviously a link—for example, it appears in a navigation bar styled using CSS instead of images—it is not good practice to remove underlines from links. Without underlines, it's difficult to tell the links from ordinary text.

Styling Lists with CSS

Lists in HTML begin with one of two tags: `<ul>` is used for an unordered or bulleted list; `<ol>` denotes a numbered or ordered list.[4] The items within each of these lists are marked up with `<li>` and `</li>` tags.

Apart from headings and paragraphs, lists are probably the most commonly used of the elements intended to present textual content to the web user. There are three styling properties in CSS that apply only to lists:

❏ `list-style-type`

❏ `list-style-position`

❏ `list-style-image`

There is also a `list-style` shorthand property with which we can set multiple properties for a list.

The `list-style-type` Property

The `list-style-type` property defines the kind of marker that is to be associated with each item in the list. The property takes a constant value that's chosen from the options shown in Table 7.2 and Table 7.3.

---

[4]There are other types of lists for glossary items or definitions, directories, and menus, but they're seldom used, so I've omitted them from this discussion. For the most part, they're styled identically to the two major kinds of lists we'll discuss here.

Table 7.2. Values for the `list-style-type` property and unordered lists

Constant Value	Meaning
circle	open circle
disc	filled circle (bullet)
square	filled square

Table 7.3. Values for the `list-style-type` property and ordered lists

Constant Value	Meaning
decimal	1, 2, 3, 4, 5 ...
decimal-leading-zero	01, 02, 03, 04, 05 ...
lower-alpha	a, b, c, d, e ...
lower-roman	i, ii, iii, iv, v ...
upper-alpha	A, B, C, D, E ...
upper-roman	I, II, III, IV, V ...

There are a number of other possible values for the `list-style-type` property, including those that define item markers in languages such as Hebrew, Armenian, Japanese, and Chinese.

Figure 7.17. Nested lists to which the page author applied no CSS rules

- list item 1
- list item 2
  - sub-list item 1
  - sub-list item 2
    - sub-sub-list item 1
    - sub-sub-list item 2
    - sub-sub-list item 3
  - sub-list item 3
- list item 3

By default, an unordered list displays with an item marker of a filled circle, or bullet. In nested unordered lists, the item marker changes to an open circle for the first level of indentation, and a square for the second level, as shown in Figure 7.17.

What if you prefer to have the item marker be a square for the outermost list, a bullet for the next one, and an open circle for the third? Apply a set of style sheet rules like the ones below, and you can accomplish this objective quite easily:

```
ul {
  list-style-type: square;
}
ul ul {
  list-style-type: disc;
}
ul ul ul {
  list-style-type: circle;
}
```

Notice that I've used contextual selectors to define the three nesting levels of lists and their associated styles. Figure 7.18 shows the result.

Figure 7.18. Applying `list-style-type` property to nested unordered lists

- list item 1
- list item 2
  - sub-list item 1
  - sub-list item 2
    - sub-sub-list item 1
    - sub-sub-list item 2
    - sub-sub-list item 3
  - sub-list item 3
- list item 3

Figure 7.19. Nested ordered lists with a single CSS `list-style-type`

    I. list item 1

   II. list item 2

        I. sub-list item 1

       II. sub-list item 2

           I. sub-sub-list item 1

          II. sub-sub-list item 2

         III. sub-sub-list item 3

      III. sub-list item 3

  III. list item 3

Ordered lists appear more complex because of the wide variety of markers that can be used, but essentially they're the same as unordered lists. If you use CSS to set the types of list item markers for a given kind of list, those same marker types will be used for nested lists. For example, Figure 7.19 shows the effect of assigning uppercase Roman numerals as the `list-style-type` on a set of nested ordered lists.

Not very attractive or helpful, is it? Let's fix it by applying some different `list-style-type` values to nested lists with the CSS rules shown here:

```
ol {
  list-style-type: upper-roman;
}
ol ol {
  list-style-type: upper-alpha;
}
ol ol ol {
  list-style-type: decimal;
}
```

This results in the much-improved output shown in Figure 7.20.

The `list-style-position` Property

Both ordered and unordered lists are displayed so that their item markers align vertically, and the text associated with each item is indented from the marker. This gives a neat, orderly appearance and is almost always the right design choice.

Figure 7.20. Nested ordered lists to which CSS styling has been applied

    I. list item 1
   II. list item 2
        A. sub-list item 1
        B. sub-list item 2
            1. sub-sub-list item 1
            2. sub-sub-list item 2
            3. sub-sub-list item 3
        C. sub-list item 3
  III. list item 3

CSS permits you to define a list in such a way that the item markers line up vertically, but text in the line items wraps under each item marker as it returns to the left margin. To create this effect, use the `list-style-position` property and give it a value of `inside`. Figure 7.21 shows two lists, one of which uses the default `list-style-position` value of `outside`, while the second has a value of `inside`.

Figure 7.21. Two different settings for the `list-style-position` property

- This list uses the default outsidesetting for the list-style-position property. Thus, the item marker is outdented from the text, and appears to be outside the text area.
- This list uses the default outsidesetting for the list-style-position property. Thus, the item marker is outdented from the text, and appears to be outside the text area.

  - This list sets a value of inside for the list-style-position property. As you can see, wrapped list item text appears immediately under the item marker.
  - This list sets a value of inside for the list-style-position property. As you can see, wrapped list item text appears immediately under the item marker.

Here's the HTML that generates the page in Figure 7.21:

```
<ul style="list-style-position: outside;">
  <li>This list uses the default <code>outside</code>setting for
      the <code>list-style-position</code> property. Thus, the
      item marker is outdented from the text, and appears to be
      outside the text area.</li>
  <li>This list uses the default <code>outside</code>setting for
      the <code>list-style-position</code> property. Thus, the
```

```
      item marker is outdented from the text, and appears to be
      outside the text area.</li>
</ul>
<ul style="list-style-position: inside;">
  <li>This list sets a value of <code>inside</code> for the
      <code>list-style-position</code> property. As you can see,
      wrapped list item text appears immediately under the item
      marker.</li>
  <li>This list sets a value of <code>inside</code> for the
      <code>list-style-position</code> property. As you can see,
      wrapped list item text appears immediately under the item
      marker.</li>
</ul>
```

The `list-style-image` Property

You can replace the bullets in front of list items with any graphic image that the browser is capable of rendering. This includes GIF, JPEG, and PNG images, at a minimum.

The `list-style-image` property takes as a value a full or relative URL that points to the image you wish to use. Figure 7.22 shows the use of an image as an item marker in a list.

Figure 7.22. Using an image as an item marker with `list-style-image` property setting

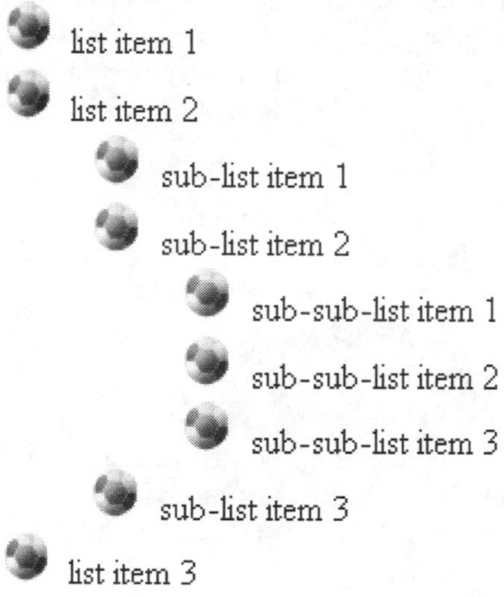

list item 1

list item 2

   sub-list item 1

   sub-list item 2

      sub-sub-list item 1

      sub-sub-list item 2

      sub-sub-list item 3

   sub-list item 3

list item 3

Here's the style sheet that creates the effect:

```
ul {
   list-style-image: url(images/ball.gif);
}
```

Notice that you must supply the image's location as a URL in CSS format, which requires that you use the url operator and provide the location in parentheses, without using quotation marks. This URL can be a relative URL, as shown here, or an absolute URL, which is the image's full address.

Cascading and Inheritance

The "C" in CSS stands for "cascading." Until now, we haven't dealt with any aspect of CSS that required an understanding of that term. However, now that we're dealing with relatively complex display-related issues, the time has come to devote some serious attention to this topic.

Cascading is not confined to text components, objects, and elements. It applies across the board to CSS usage on a web page. The reason why it's often discussed in conjunction with textual elements is because its impact is most apparent and most easily demonstrable in this context.

Inheritance is related to cascading in terms of its impact, but the two terms have quite different meanings.

Cascading addresses the question of how any given element will be displayed if there are multiple style rules that *could* be applied to it. Inheritance addresses the question of how any given element will be displayed if one or more of its properties is defined in a style rule that applies to an ancestor element, but is omitted in the element itself.

This sounds much more complicated than it usually is in practice. I'm going to start by providing a couple of simple examples that will clearly demonstrate the difference. Then, I'll drill down more deeply into both of these subjects.

Basic Principles of Cascading

If you keep your use of CSS simple, you'll rarely have a need to understand cascading on a deep level. For example, if you always use external style sheets, and override the settings in those style sheets with embedded style rules only in specific situations, you probably won't need to spend a great deal of time ferreting out the nuances in the cascading process.

But, when you begin to design pages of any complexity—and to use style sheets across multiple pages and sites in the interests of efficiency and ease of maintenance—you will almost certainly run into situations where what you see isn't what you intended. If you're designing complex pages and sites, you can take advantage of the basic rules of cascading to apply CSS rules logically, consistently, and effectively.

There are four basic factors involved in creating what is called the "cascade" in CSS:

❑ weight

❑ origin

❑ specificity

❑ sort order

These factors are taken into account in the order in which I've listed them.

To sort out possible conflicts in style rules that could be applied to any element in an HTML page, think of the browser as going through a set of decisions about each element. This decision-making process follows this path, in precisely this order:

1. Scan through the declarations that apply to the element and look for declarations that contain the keyword !important. Assign each of those declarations a greater weight than those without the symbol. This is the "weight" factor referred to above.

    !important is simply a keyword that you can add to a CSS declaration, as shown in the example below, to make it override other declarations when usually it wouldn't:

    ```
    div.warning {
      background-color: red !important;
    }
    ```

    We'll see !important in action throughout this section.

2. Within the declarations marked as !important, assign a greater weight to those that come from the user's style sheet (if there is one) than those that come from the author's style sheet. This is the "origin" factor referred to above.

3. Within the declarations that are *not* marked !important, assign a greater weight to those that come from the author's style sheet than to those that have come from the user's style sheet. This is also the "origin" factor at work.

4. To resolve any remaining ties, examine each rule to see how narrowly it applies to the specific element in question. If, for example, you have a paragraph element of class warning, a declaration inside a style rule that applies to paragraphs in general will be given less weight than one that applies to paragraphs of the class warning. Rules declared inline (with the style attribute in your markup) apply only to one element, and therefore always win out at this stage. This is the "specificity" factor at work.

5. Finally, if any ties still remain after all the above steps, sort things out based on the order in which the declarations are defined in the document, with later declarations taking precedence over earlier ones. This is the "sort order" factor referred to above.

At the end of all this processing, all applicable declarations are applied in the order established above, with the property values that are assigned in declarations of greater weight overriding those assigned in declarations of lesser weight.

Generally, you think about this process in the reverse order from that which the browser uses. Most often, you have only to deal with the sort order issue on pages of relatively low complexity. As designs and sites become more complex and your use of style sheets becomes more involved, specificity will become the next major concern for you. You'll typically use !important very rarely, if ever. I'll discuss the cascading rules in the order in which you are most likely to think of them, rather than in the order in which the browser uses them.

Sort Order

As you know, styles can be defined in three different places: an external style sheet, an embedded style sheet, or an inline style attribute as part of a markup tag for a particular HTML element. The sort order factor in the cascade ensures that, regardless of whether a style sheet is embedded in the head of the document or is loaded with a link element, it's the order in which it appears that determines its relative precedence.

For example, let's say that you have an external style sheet called `mylayout.css`. Among other rules, it has this entry:

```
h2 {
  color: green;
}
```

Within a particular document, you decide that you don't want to use the normal site-wide style of green second-level headings. So, you embed a style sheet (using a `style` element in the document header); the following rule appears after the `link` element that loads `mylayout.css`:

```
h2 {
  color: blue;
}
```

In this case, where I've used only one declaration, it's pretty easy to see how cascading works. The external style sheet declaration is overruled by the embedded rule: `h2` elements within the document will appear in blue.

It's important to realize that the second rule doesn't overrule the first because it's declared in an embedded style sheet—it overrules it because the embedded style sheet comes *after* the linked style sheet. Move that `style` element above the `link` element, and `h2` elements will turn green again.

Usually, things are not quite so clean and obvious. Look back to the external (green) style sheet rule above; let's change our rules so we have something like this:

```
h2 {
  color: green;
  background-color: transparent;
  margin-left: 10px;
  font-family: Arial, Helvetica, sans-serif;
  text-decoration: overline;
}
```

In an embedded style sheet in another document, assume we have a rule that looks like this:

```
h2 {
  margin-left: 20px;
  text-decoration: none;
}
```

Once again, let's assume the embedded style sheet is declared *after* the linked style sheet. In this case, any second-level heading in this specific document will be displayed in green on a transparent background, offset from the left margin by 20 pixels, using the font set identified in the external style sheet, with no decoration.

One way of thinking about this process is that a style rule is like a waterfall. It starts out with certain declarations (for `color`, `background-color`, `left-margin`, `font-family`, and `text-decoration`, in the example). Then, that style sheet's rules fall like a waterfall cascading over rocks. When it encounters rocks with declarations that have different values from those in the waterfall, the cascade effect substitutes the new value for the old.

In resolving any conflict between two or more style rules that could apply to a given element, and which are tied on the specificity, origin, and weight factors, the rule declared last will be applied.

Specificity

Specificity refers to the issue of how closely a style rule's selector describes a particular element in your document. On one level, this is pretty easy to understand. As I mentioned earlier, when I listed the factors involved in the cascade decision-making process, a style that applies to paragraph elements is less specific to a paragraph of class `warning` than is a rule that specifically applies to paragraphs of that class. In other words, given the following code fragment, the paragraph will be displayed in red type on a white background rather than white type on a blue background, despite the order of the rules. Remember, specificity has greater impact in the cascade than sort order:

```
<!DOCTYPE html PUBLIC "-//W3C//DTD XHTML 1.0 Strict//EN"
    "http://www.w3.org/TR/xhtml1/DTD/xhtml1-strict.dtd">
<html xmlns="http://www.w3.org/1999/xhtml">
  <head>
    <title>Warning</title>
    <meta http-equiv="Content-Type"
        content="text/html; charset=iso-8859-1" />
    <style type="text/css">
      p.warning {
        color: red;
        background-color: white;
      }
      .warning {
        color: yellow;
```

```
      background-color: red;
    }
    p {
      color: white;
      background-color: blue;
    }
   </style>
  </head>
  <body>
    <p class="warning">This is a warning paragraph.</p>
  </body>
</html>
```

The more closely the rule's selector matches the element, the more specific it is, and the more likely it is to be applied to that element.

But the CSS Recommendation that describes specificity does so in a generic way that you may find useful to understand if you get into something really tricky, with potentially conflicting style rules. Every selector in your style sheet is given a specificity rating that's calculated by the browser using a strict formula. That formula can be expressed as follows:

$(100 \times IDCount) + (10 \times OtherTypeCount) + NamedElements$

In other words, the CSS-compliant browser looks at a rule selector and processes it like this:

1. If it has one or more ID selectors (e.g. `#critical`), count those selectors and multiply the count by 100.

2. If it has any other types of selectors (e.g. class name or pseudo-class), count those selectors and multiply that count by ten. Do not count pseudo-elements.

3. If it has any named elements (e.g. `p` or `div`), count those selectors.

4. Now add all the values together.

Table 7.4 provides examples of different types of selectors, and what their specificity ratings would be.

Table 7.4. Sample specificity ratings for CSS rule selectors

Selector	IDs	Others	Names	Specificity
em	0	0	1	1
p em	0	0	2	2
.critical	0	1	0	10
a:hover	0	1	1	11
div p span.critical	0	1	3	13
#critical	1	0	0	100
p#critical	1	0	1	101

Style properties declared inline (with the `style` HTML attribute) have the highest specificity, since they apply to one element and one element only. No property declared elsewhere can overrule an inline style property based on specificity.

In resolving any conflict between two or more style rules that *could* apply to a given element, and which are tied on the origin and weight factors, the rule with higher specificity will be applied.

Note that the specificity number in the final column is not a definitive value. For example, 11 classes will not outweigh one ID. It might be useful to think of this specificity table as being similar to the Olympic medals table. A country with one gold medal will always come higher up the table than a country with no gold medals, but 11 silver ones.

Origin

The origin factor in the cascade resolves conflicts between rules declared by the page author and rules declared by the user of the browser (e.g. in a user's style sheet). In general, any property setting assigned by the page author takes precedence over a conflicting property setting assigned by the user of the browser.

The exception to this occurs when the two conflicting property settings are assigned greater weight with the `!important` modifier, as described below. In such cases, the origin factor is reversed, and the user's property setting takes precedence over the page author's. In effect, style properties that the user considers important are *more* important than style rules that the page author considers important.

In resolving any conflict between two or more property settings that could apply to a given element, and which are tied on the weight factor (i.e. they're all marked `!important`, or none are), the origin of the property decides which is applied.

Weight

If you give a declaration a weight that's greater than usual by following it with the key word `!important`, it will always override a contradictory setting in the cascade that's not marked `!important`. For example, you might decide that it is really essential for all level-three headings to be blue and indented 20 pixels. If so, you'd code a rule like this:

```
h3 {
  color: blue !important;
  margin-left: 20px !important;
}
```

If, in rendering your page, the browser encounters a situation where a specific level-three heading has a different color setting (for example, because of the way a grouped selector defines the layout), it will ignore that setting and make the heading blue.

Recall that if you increase a declaration's weight with the `!important` symbol, and the user specifies a conflicting style to which he also applies an `!important` symbol, the user's declaration will trump yours, according to the origin factor described above.

However, this doesn't mean that you won't find uses for `!important`. In the vast majority of cases, the user doesn't define or use a style sheet. In such instances, your use of `!important` will ensure that if there are conflicts among the style rules you've declared in various external style sheets, and perhaps also in an embedded style sheet, the one that is most crucial to your design will prevail.

Summary

This chapter demonstrated a number of techniques for using CSS styles to spruce up the otherwise ordinary text on a web page. From the basic use of alignment, indentation, and other techniques, the chapter demonstrated the use of positioning to create shadowed text effects, and described how to manipulate the display of lists as well.

This chapter also provided a detailed description of the role of the cascade in CSS. You now understand how to control the impact of style rules in complex page designs, where display rules may be coming from multiple sources.

In Chapter 8 we'll take a look at how to use CSS in relation to graphics on a web page.

8

Simple CSS Layout

We now have some sound theory under our belts. The rest of this book will concentrate on how you can put CSS into practice when developing your own sites. Along the way, we'll be learning how to lay out pages using CSS—moving from simple layouts to more complex ones—and how you can combine some of the concepts you've already read about to create great-looking sites.

This chapter will start with the creation of a simple two-column layout. Along the way, we'll discover how to use absolute and relative positioning, and see how margins, padding, and borders work together. Then, we'll get an understanding of how all these tools can be used together in practice by creating a two-column layout that uses many of the techniques we have discussed already in this book.

While the layout we'll create in this chapter is a relatively simple one, it's a structure that's used by many web sites; the layout we'll develop here could easily form the basis for a production site.

The Layout

Many web site designs start life as mock-ups in a graphics program. Our first example site is no exception: we have an example layout or "design comp" created in Fireworks as a starting point.

Figure 8.1. Creating the layout as an image file

Starting out with a visual like this enables us to think about the way we're going to build the site *before* we start to write any XHTML or CSS. It gives us the opportunity to decide how best to approach this particular layout before we code a single line.

This layout divides the page into three main sections: a header, which contains the site logo and some main navigation; a main content area comprising a large image above a list of news stories; and a sidebar, which presents some additional items.

Figure 8.2. Marking the main sections on the layout

This layout could be described as a two-column layout with a header area. Being able to visualize a design as being a combination of its main sections eases the process of deciding how to approach the page layout.

Creating the Document

Having decided what the basic components of our page will be, we can start work. The first thing we'll do is create an XHTML document that contains all of the text elements we can see in our layout image, marked up using the correct XHTML elements.

Working this way might seem a little strange at first, particularly if you have been used to working in a visual environment, such as Dreamweaver, and simply concentrating on how the design looks. However, one of the advantages of using CSS for layout is that we're able to separate the structure of the page from its appearance. This allows us to concentrate on building a good solid document as the basis of our site, before adding the design using CSS.

We start out with the basic requirements for an XHTML Strict document. As we're going to use CSS for all of the presentational information on this site, there's no reason not to use a Strict DOCTYPE. The Transitional DOCTYPEs (for both XHTML and HTML 4.01) allow you to use attributes and elements that are now deprecated in the W3C Recommendations. The deprecated elements and attributes are mainly used for presentation, and as we're going to use CSS—not XHTML—for presentation, we won't need to use these anyway.

File: **index.html**

```
<!DOCTYPE html PUBLIC "-//W3C//DTD XHTML 1.0 Strict//EN"
    "http://www.w3.org/TR/xhtml1/DTD/xhtml1-strict.dtd">
<html xmlns="http://www.w3.org/1999/xhtml">
  <head>
    <title>Footbag Freaks</title>
    <meta http-equiv="Content-Type"
        content="text/html; charset=iso-8859-1" />
  </head>
  <body>
  </body>
</html>
```

Declaring the Character Set

In our pages, we've used the `meta` element with the `http-equiv="Content-Type"` attribute to declare our document's character set. This makes it easy for browsers (and the W3C validator) to determine which character set is being used in the document. If this information was missing, a browser could misinterpret the characters in your page, which could see your pages rendered as unintelligible garbage.

All of the examples in this book use ISO-8859-1 encoding, which is the default for most popular text editors and programs such as Dreamweaver. If you're dealing with a different character set, such as Unicode, you'll need to change the `meta` elements accordingly.

The Header

Let's start to add the content of this page to our document. As we do so, we'll split it up into the various sections identified above, containing each page section between `<div>` and `</div>` tags. We'll give each `div` an `id` to identify that section; we'll use these `id`s to address each section and style it using CSS.

After the `<body>` tag, add the following markup:

File: **index.html** (excerpt)

```
<div id="header">
  <p>The Home of the Hack</p>
  <ul>
    <li><a href="">Contact Us</a></li>
    <li><a href="">About Us</a></li>
    <li><a href="">Privacy Policy</a></li>
    <li><a href="">Sitemap</a></li>
  </ul>
</div> <!-- header -->
```

We won't worry about any image elements at this point, because there are numerous ways in which we can add images to the page using CSS; we'll make the decision as to the best way to add each image as we create our CSS. Thus, the header area simply contains the tag line, "The Home of the Hack," and a list that includes the main navigation links.

The Main Content Section

The main content section comes next, contained in a `div` with an `id` of `content`:

File: **index.html** (excerpt)

```
<div id="content">
  <h2>Simon Says</h2>
  <p>Simon Mackie tells us how a change of shoes has given him new
      moves and a new outlook as the new season approaches.</p>
  <p><a href="">Read More</a></p>
  <h2>Recent Features</h2>
  <ul>
    <li>
      <h3>Head for the Hills: Is Altitude Training the
          Answer?</h3>
      <p>Lachlan 'Super Toe' Donald</p>
      <p>Vestibulum ante ipsum primis in faucibus orci luctus et
```

```
          ultrices posuere cubilia Curae; Praesent hendrerit
          iaculis arcu.</p>
      <p><a href="">Full Story</a></p>
    </li>
    <li>
      <h3>Hack up the Place: Freestylin' Super Tips</h3>
      <p>Jules 'Pony King' Szemere</p>
      <p>Vestibulum ante ipsum primis in faucibus orci luctus et
          ultrices posuere cubilia Curae; Praesent hendrerit
          iaculis arcu.</p>
      <p><a href="">Full Story</a></p>
    </li>
    <li>
      <h3>The Complete Black Hat Hacker's Survival Guide</h3>
      <p>Mark 'Steel Tip' Harbottle</p>
      <p>Vestibulum ante ipsum primis in faucibus orci luctus et
          ultrices posuere cubilia Curae; Praesent hendrerit
          iaculis arcu.</p>
      <p><a href="">Full Story</a></p>
    </li>
    <li>
      <h3>Five Tricks You Didn't Even Know You Knew</h3>
      <p>Simon 'Mack Daddy' Mackie</p>
      <p>Vestibulum ante ipsum primis in faucibus orci luctus et
          ultrices posuere cubilia Curae; Praesent hendrerit
          iaculis arcu.</p>
      <p><a href="">Full Story</a></p>
    </li>
  </ul>
</div> <!-- content -->
```

This area will contain the large image with a text overlay that highlights a feature story. Four news items will be listed below this.

The Sidebar

Finally, let's add the sidebar, which contains a search box and some important dates:

File: **index.html (excerpt)**

```
<div id="sidebar">
  <h3>Site Search</h3>
  <form method="post" action="" id="searchform">
    <div>
      <label for="keywords">Keywords</label>:
```

```
      <input type="text" name="keywords" id="keywords" />
    </div>
    <div>
      <input type="submit" name="btnSearch" id="btnSearch" />
    </div>
  </form>
  <h3>Coming Events</h3>
  <ul>
    <li>10 Apr 06 -<br /><a href="">Seattle Zone
        Qualifier</a></li>
    <li>13 Apr 06 -<br /><a href="">World Cup - Round 8</a></li>
    <li>21 Apr 06 -<br /><a href="">FootbagOOM 05 - NY</a></li>
    <li>28 Apr 06 -<br /><a href="">WFPA AGM - Hong Kong</a></li>
    <li>3 May 06 -<br /><a href="">World Cup - Round 9</a></li>
  </ul>
  <h3>Move of the Month</h3>
  <h4>The Outer Stall</h4>
  <p>Eti bibendum mauris nec nulla. Nullam cursus ullamcorper
      quam. Sed cursus vestibulum leo.</p>
  <p><a href="">more</a></p>
</div> <!-- sidebar -->
```

This completes our markup for the homepage of the site. Save your page and view it in your browser. The content of your document will display using the default styles for the elements that we've used, as Figure 8.3 illustrates. It won't be pretty, but it should be easily readable!

Our last job before we start to add the CSS that will create the design we see in the example graphic is to validate our markup. By validating the document at this point, we'll know that we're adding CSS to a valid document: we won't come up against problems caused by existing invalid markup.

Figure 8.3. Displaying the page after the content is added

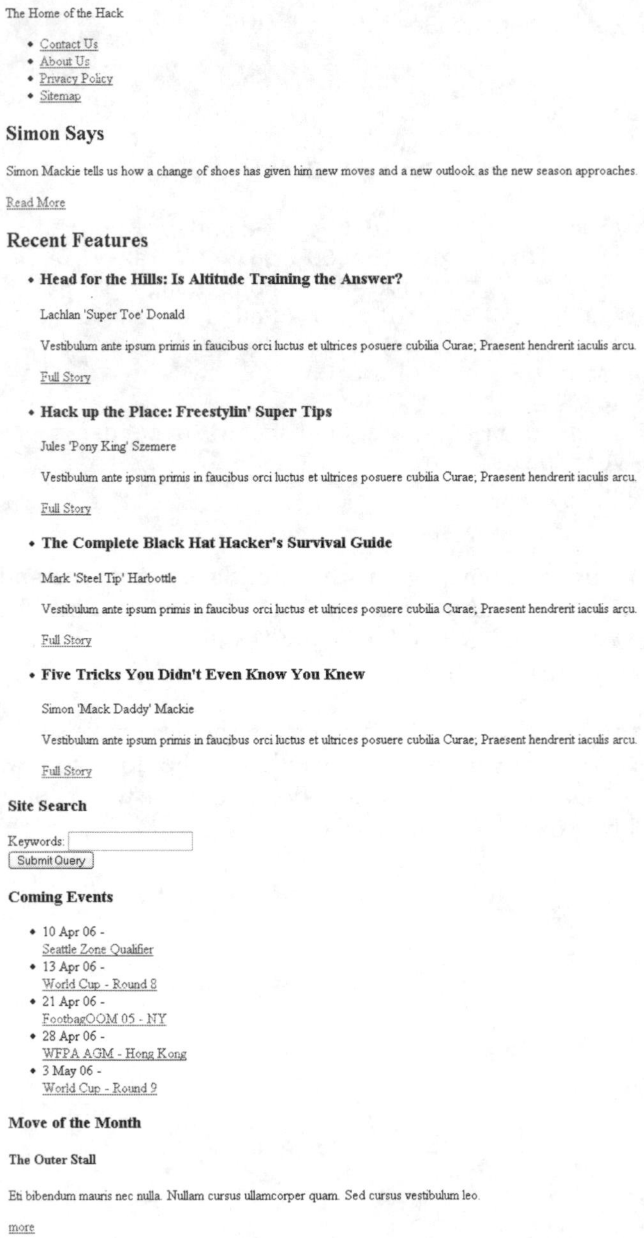

The Home of the Hack

* Contact Us
* About Us
* Privacy Policy
* Sitemap

Simon Says

Simon Mackie tells us how a change of shoes has given him new moves and a new outlook as the new season approaches.

Read More

Recent Features

* **Head for the Hills: Is Altitude Training the Answer?**

  Lachlan 'Super Toe' Donald

  Vestibulum ante ipsum primis in faucibus orci luctus et ultrices posuere cubilia Curae; Praesent hendrerit iaculis arcu.

  Full Story

* **Hack up the Place: Freestylin' Super Tips**

  Jules 'Pony King' Szemere

  Vestibulum ante ipsum primis in faucibus orci luctus et ultrices posuere cubilia Curae; Praesent hendrerit iaculis arcu.

  Full Story

* **The Complete Black Hat Hacker's Survival Guide**

  Mark 'Steel Tip' Harbottle

  Vestibulum ante ipsum primis in faucibus orci luctus et ultrices posuere cubilia Curae; Praesent hendrerit iaculis arcu.

  Full Story

* **Five Tricks You Didn't Even Know You Knew**

  Simon 'Mack Daddy' Mackie

  Vestibulum ante ipsum primis in faucibus orci luctus et ultrices posuere cubilia Curae; Praesent hendrerit iaculis arcu.

  Full Story

Site Search

Keywords:
Submit Query

Coming Events

* 10 Apr 06 -
  Seattle Zone Qualifier
* 13 Apr 06 -
  World Cup - Round 8
* 21 Apr 06 -
  FootbagOOM 05 - NY
* 28 Apr 06 -
  WFPA AGM - Hong Kong
* 3 May 06 -
  World Cup - Round 9

Move of the Month

The Outer Stall

Eti bibendum mauris nec nulla. Nullam cursus ullamcorper quam. Sed cursus vestibulum leo.

more

Positioning the Page Elements

We can now begin to create our style sheet. But, before we do, we need to take a moment to understand some basic concepts that come into play when creating layouts such as this (and many others): the `display` property, the concept of positioning, and the CSS Box Model technique.

The `display` Property

Before we can move on to look at CSS positioning issues, we should take a quick look at the `display` property, as it can have a significant impact on page layout.

The `display` property determines how a browser displays an element—whether it treats it as a block, an inline text fragment, or something else. Although it can be assigned any of 17 legal values, browser support realities confine the list to six, only four of which are really important. For a full reference to `display` see Appendix C.

The six possible values for the `display` property are:

- `block`

- `inline`

- `list-item`

- `none`

- `table-footer-group`

- `table-header-group`

The default value varies from element to element. Block elements such as `p`, `h1`, and `div` default to `block`, while inline elements (those that would normally occur within a section of text), such as `strong`, `code`, and `span`, default to `inline`. List items default to `list-item`. Assigning non-default settings to elements can produce interesting and useful effects. Later in this book, we'll see how we can use `display: inline` to cause a list to display horizontally.

If you supply a value of `none`, the element to which it applies will not display, and the space it would normally occupy will be collapsed. This differentiates the display: none declaration from the visibility: hidden declaration, which is commonly used to hide an element but preserve the space it would occupy if it were visible.

Absolute, Relative, and Positioning Contexts

The CSS position property takes on a single, constant value that determines how the block is positioned on the page. The two most frequently used values are absolute and relative. Another value, static, is the default value for this property; the fourth value, fixed, is not supported by Internet Explorer 6.

Positioning in CSS can be confusing because the points that are referenced to guide a block's placement on the page change in accordance with the **positioning context** of the block. There's no universal set of coordinates to guide placement, even when you're using the absolute positioning value. Each time a block is positioned on the page with a position setting other than static, it creates for its descendants a new positioning context in which the upper left corner of its content area has the coordinates (0,0). So, if you use CSS to position an element within that block, its position will be calculated relative to that new coordinate system—its "positioning context."

The best way to understand this concept is to look at a few simple, interrelated examples. Let's start with a blank page. In this context, the upper left corner of the viewport—the viewable area of the browser window—is where the initial (0,0) coordinates are located. Let's place a simple piece of text in a div, as shown in Figure 8.4.

Figure 8.4. The first line of text

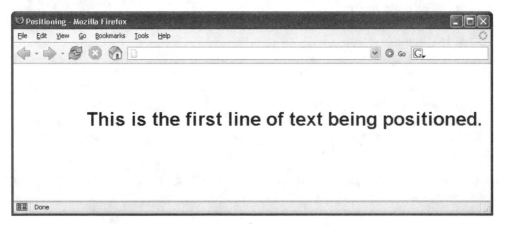

Here's the HTML fragment that produces the result shown above. The CSS properties `top` and `left` are used to position the `div` on the page, locating it 75 pixels from the top of the page, and indenting it from the left of the page by 125 pixels:

File: **positioning.html** (excerpt)

```
<div style="position: absolute; left: 125px; top: 75px;"
    class="big">
  This is the first line of text being positioned.
</div>
```

Now, put a second `div` inside the first one, as shown here:

File: **positioning.html** (excerpt)

```
<div style="position: absolute; left:125px; top: 75px;"
    class="big">
  This is the first line of text being positioned.
  <div style="position: absolute; left: 25px; top: 30px;"
      class="big">
    This is a second line.
  </div>
</div>
```

Figure 8.5. An element positioned inside a positioned block

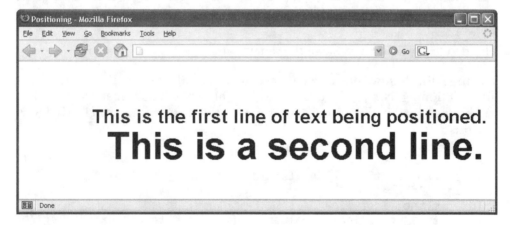

The result is shown in Figure 8.5. Notice that the second line of text is indented 25 pixels from the left of the first line of text, because that first line sets the positioning context for the second: it's the parent element of the second line. Both lines are positioned absolutely; however, the first line is positioned from the top and left of the viewport, and the second line is positioned absolutely from the top and left of the first. Notice, too, that its font size is huge. Why? Take a look at the style rule for the `big` class, and you'll understand:

File: **positioning.html (excerpt)**

```
.big {
  font-family: Helvetica, Arial, sans-serif;
  font-size: 2em;
  font-weight: bold;
}
```

As the second `div` is a child of the first, its font size is calculated relative to that of the first `div`. The style rule defines the font as being of size two ems, which instructs the browser to render the text at twice the size it would otherwise appear. When that two em rule is applied to the first line, its size is doubled. But when it is applied to the second line, the font size of the first line is doubled to calculate that of the second.

We can correct this using an absolute font size constant:

File: **positioning.html (excerpt)**

```
.big {
  font-family: Helvetica, Arial, sans-serif;
  font-size: large;
  font-weight: bold;
}
```

The two `div`s should now share the same font size.

The page now has two `div` elements, one nested inside the other. Both use absolute positioning. Now, let's add a third element—this time, a `span` element that will be contained in the second `div`. Using relative positioning, the HTML looks like this:

File: **positioning.html (excerpt)**

```
<div style="position: absolute; left: 125px; top: 75px;"
    class="big">
  This is the first line of text being positioned.
  <div style="position: absolute; left: 25px; top: 30px;">
    This is <span
        style="position: relative; left: 10px; top: 30px;">an
        example of</span> a second line.
  </div>
</div>
```

The result of this markup can be seen below. Notice that the words "an example of," which are contained in the span, appear below and slightly to the right of their original position. *Relative positioning is always based on the positioned element's original position on the page*. In other words, the positioning context of an element that uses relative positioning is provided by its default position. In this example, the span is positioned as shown in Figure 8.6. It appears below and to the right of where it would normally be if no positioning was applied—a case that's illustrated in Figure 8.7.

Figure 8.6. Example of relative positioning

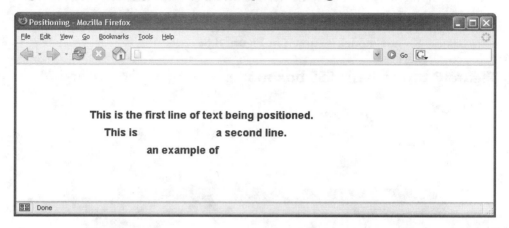

Figure 8.7. The same example with the positioning removed

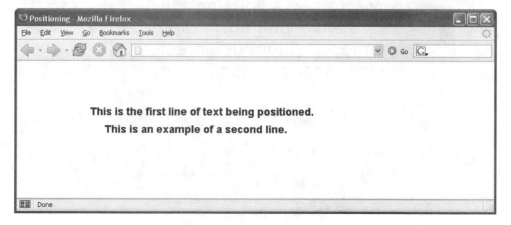

Don't worry if this concept still seems a bit confusing; we'll be looking at how these concepts work in practice as we create our layouts.

The Box Model

From the perspective of a style sheet, every item you deal with in an HTML page can be viewed as existing inside a box. This fact is generally far more obvious when you're formatting large chunks of content, like the three main page areas we've identified in our design. But it's true even when you're dealing with individual components of those elements, like headings, lists, list elements, and even segments of text.

The basic CSS box model is shown in Figure 8.8.

Figure 8.8. The basic CSS box model

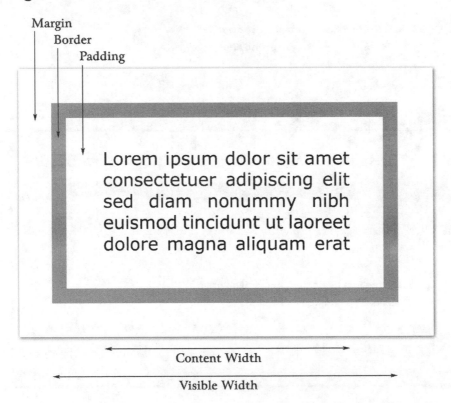

At the center of the CSS box model is the content itself. Don't think of this "content" as being the same as words or images that might comprise the content of a news story or a set of links. "Content" describes any item that's contained within the area of the box.

Notice from the diagram that the visible width of the box is determined by adding together the content width, the padding, and the border. The margin determines the distance between each side of the visible box and adjacent elements. Similarly, the visible height of the box is determined by adding the height of the content to the padding and border settings. Once again, the margin determines how far the box will be separated from adjacent objects vertically.

The width of each of these elements—margin, border, and padding—can be set using four CSS properties (one for each side of the box), or a single shorthand property. Border behavior is slightly more complicated because, in addition to width, a border can have characteristics such as line style and color.

In this discussion, I'll begin by explaining and demonstrating the use of padding in some detail. Then, I'll move on to a discussion of margins, which will be briefer, as it's so similar to padding. Finally, I'll discuss borders.

For the next few sections, I'll use a basic, single-box layout to demonstrate CSS rule techniques. It starts out as the layout shown in Figure 8.9, with no padding, border, or margin: the content is the same size as the box.

Figure 8.9. Starting point for the box model demonstration

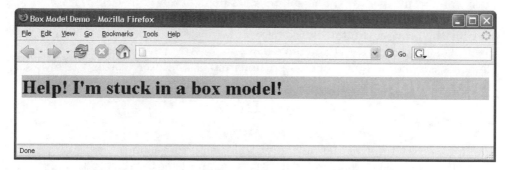

I've given the h1 element a gray background so you can see more easily the impact of the effects I'll be demonstrating. The HTML below produces the page shown in Figure 8.9:

File: **boxmodel.html**

```
<!DOCTYPE html PUBLIC "-//W3C//DTD XHTML 1.0 Strict//EN"
    "http://www.w3.org/TR/xhtml1/DTD/xhtml1-strict.dtd">
<html xmlns="http://www.w3.org/1999/xhtml">
  <head>
    <title>Box Model Demo</title>
    <meta http-equiv="Content-Type"
        content="text/html; charset=iso-8859-1" />
    <style type="text/css">
      h1 {
        background-color: #c0c0c0;
        color: black;
      }
    </style>
  </head>
  <body>
    <h1>Help! I'm stuck in a box model!</h1>
  </body>
</html>
```

Throughout the rest of this discussion, I'll be modifying only the style sheet information, so I'll reproduce only that section of the code, indicating any changes in bold.

Pixels vs Percentages

As the box model deals with the display of content on the screen, the pixel is the most commonly used of the absolute measurement units in CSS. However, if you need to create a layout that takes up all of the available space, regardless of how big the browser window is, it's necessary to use the percentages rather than pixels. Such layouts are characterized by their "stretchy" behavior—the page elements expand and contract proportionately as the user resizes the browser window.

Padding Properties

Four properties together define the padding around an object in a CSS rule: `padding-left`, `padding-right`, `padding-top`, and `padding-bottom`.

Let's change just one of the padding settings to get a feel for how this works. Modify the style sheet in the sample file, so that it replicates the following fragment (remember that the new material is presented in bold text below):

File: **boxmodel.html** (excerpt)

```
h1 {
  background-color: #c0c0c0;
  color: black;
  padding-left: 25px;
}
```

The result of this change is shown in Figure 8.10. Notice that the text now begins 25 pixels from the left side of the box, resulting in 25 pixels of blank, gray space to the left of the text.

Figure 8.10. Demonstrating `padding-left`

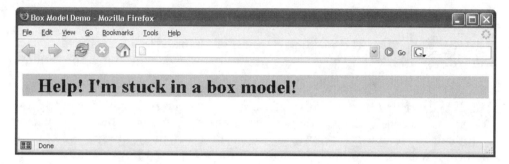

As you'd expect, you can set the other padding sizes the same way, as this code fragment shows:

File: **boxmodel.html** (excerpt)

```
h1 {
  background-color: #c0c0c0;
  color: black;
  padding-left: 25px;
  padding-top: 15px;
  padding-bottom: 30px;
  padding-right: 20px;
}
```

Figure 8.11. Defining all four padding properties

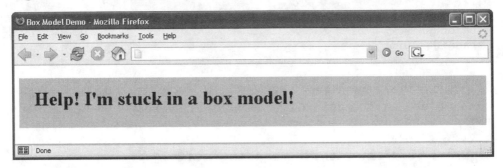

You can see the effects of these changes in Figure 8.11.

You may notice that the padding on the right-hand side appears not to have worked. You asked for 20 pixels, but no matter how wide you stretch the window, the gray area that defines the box containing our h1 element just goes on and on.

This is because padding-right creates a space between the right edge of the text and the right edge of the heading, as represented by the gray box. The spacing is difficult to see in this case, because the heading automatically spans the width of the browser window, leaving plenty of room for the text to breathe on the right-hand side. If you make the browser narrow enough, though, you can see the padding take effect.

Figure 8.12. Demonstrating the effect of padding-right

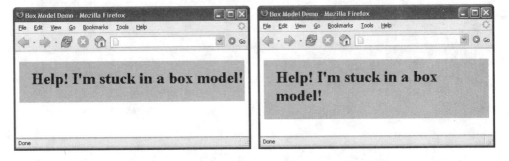

Figure 8.12 demonstrates this principle. The first screenshot shows how the page from Figure 8.11 looks if padding-right is set to 0 and the browser window is resized so there is barely enough room for the text. The second screenshot shows the same page with padding-right set to 20px. Because the box now incorporates 20 pixels of padding on the right-hand side, the text can no longer run all the

way to the right hand border of the gray box, and the end of the sentence is forced onto the next line.

Because it's often necessary to adjust padding around objects in HTML, the CSS standards define a shorthand property that's simply called `padding`. You can give this property up to four values; Table 8.1 identifies how the properties will be assigned in each case.

Table 8.1. Effects of multiple values on `padding` shorthand property

Number of Values	Interpretation
1	Set all four padding values to this value.
2	Set the top and bottom padding to the first value, and left and right padding to the second.
3	Set the top padding to the first value, right and left to the second value, and bottom to the third value.
4	Set the top padding to the first value, right padding to the second, bottom padding to the third, and left padding to the fourth value.

Tip

Remembering the Order

To remember the order in which these values are specified, simply recall that they're identified in clockwise order from the top, or remember the mnemonic *trouble* (top, right, bottom, and left).

For example, the style rule above could be rewritten using the padding shorthand property as follows:

File: **boxmodel.html** (excerpt)

```
h1 {
  background-color: #c0c0c0;
  color: black;
  padding: 15px 20px 30px 25px;
}
```

To create equal top and bottom padding, and equal left and right padding, you could use:

File: **boxmodel.html** (excerpt)

```
h1 {
  background-color: #c0c0c0;
  color: black;
  padding: 15px 25px;
}
```

Finally, to create equal padding on all four sides of the h1 element, you could use this markup:

File: **boxmodel.html** (excerpt)

```
h1 {
  background-color: #c0c0c0;
  color: black;
   padding: 25px;
}
```

What would happen if you used either ems or percentages for the padding values? The two units have slightly different effects: the em unit scales the padding according to the size of the font of the content, while the percentage unit scales the padding according to the width or height of the block that contains the element. To demonstrate these effects, let's work with a new HTML page that displays two headings against colored backgrounds on a page of a contrasting color.

Here's the HTML for that demonstration page:

File: **boxmodel2.html**

```
<!DOCTYPE html PUBLIC "-//W3C//DTD XHTML 1.0 Strict//EN"
    "http://www.w3.org/TR/xhtml1/DTD/xhtml1-strict.dtd">
<html xmlns="http://www.w3.org/1999/xhtml">
  <head>
    <title>Box Model Demo</title>
    <meta http-equiv="Content-Type"
      content="text/html; charset=iso-8859-1" />
    <style type="text/css">
      body {
        background-color: #808080;
        color: black;
      }
      h1, h4 {
        background-color: #c0c0c0;
        color: black;
      }
    </style>
  </head>
```

```
<body>
  <h1>Help! I'm stuck in a box model!</h1>
  <h4>But it's not too crowded if you're just a little old
      heading like me! In fact, it's kind of cozy in here.</h4>
</body>
</html>
```

Notice that I've given the page a dark grey background, and I've added an **h4** element, which I've styled in the same CSS rule as the **h1** element.

This HTML page displays as shown in Figure 8.13.

Figure 8.13. Proportional **padding** page starting point

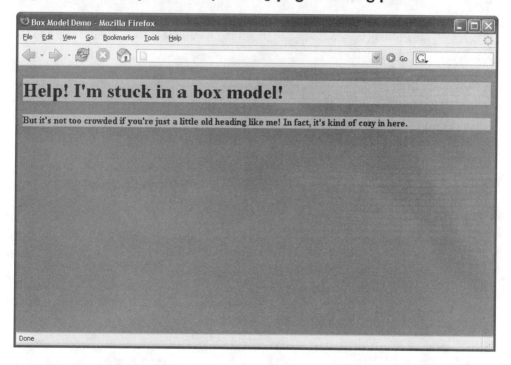

Now, let's change the style sheet for this page so that it uses the **padding** property to create a single-em padding space around the objects. The following code fragment will do the trick:

File: **boxmodel2.html** (excerpt)

```
body {
  background-color: #808080;
```

```
  color: black;
}
h1, h4 {
  background-color: #c0c0c0;
  color: black;
  padding: 1em;
}
```

As you can see in Figure 8.14, the amount of padding that appears around the two heading elements is proportional to the size of the font used in the elements themselves.

em: a Height Measurement

Remember that one em is equal to the height of the font in use. Consequently, much more space is placed around the h1 element than around the h4 element.

Let's see what happens if we use a percentage, rather than an em, for the proportional padding value. Change the HTML so that the style sheet looks like this:

File: **boxmodel2.html (excerpt)**

```
body {
  background-color: #808080;
  color: black;
}
h1, h4 {
  background-color: #c0c0c0;
  color: black;
  padding: 10%;
}
```

The result of this change can be seen in Figure 8.15. Wow! There's a huge amount of space around those elements. The browser has applied 10% of the width of the page as padding on all four sides.

Figure 8.14. Using ems for proportional padding

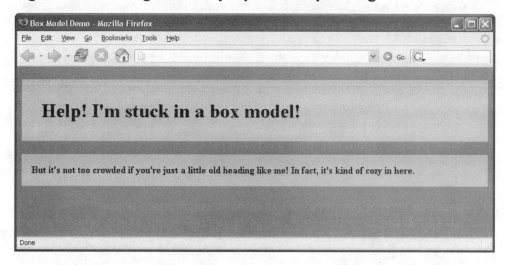

Figure 8.15. Using percentage for proportional spacing

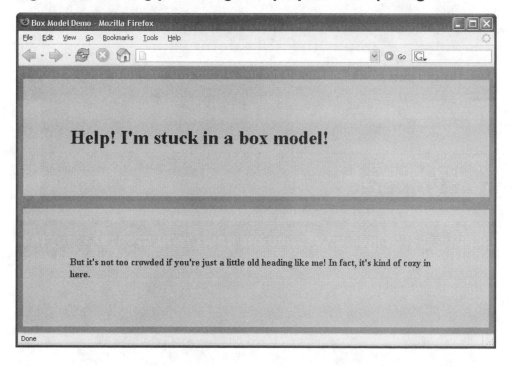

I've been using a background color behind the text of these elements to make it easy to see the effect of the different padding settings, but the background colors aren't required. Figure 8.16 uses the same HTML code as Figure 8.15; the only difference is that I've removed the background colors from the body, h1, and h4 elements. As you can see, these elements maintain their relative spacing.

Figure 8.16. Demonstrating `padding` without colored backgrounds

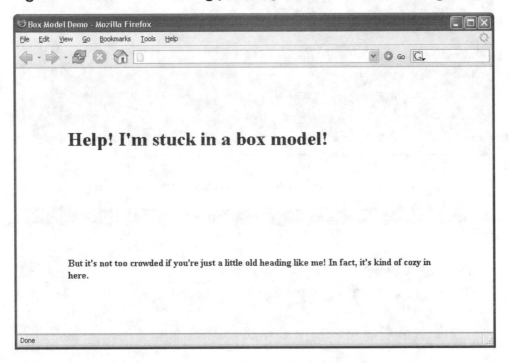

Margin Properties

The difference between margins and padding is that margins exist outside the boundaries of the object, while padding exists inside those boundaries. Figure 8.17 illustrates this difference according to the style sheet rules that are set in the code fragment below. Margins are set in the same way as padding; the only difference is the substitution of the word "margin" for the word "padding."

```
body {
  background-color: #808080;
  color: black;
}
```

```
h1 {
  background-color: #c0c0c0;
  color: black;
}
h2 {
  background-color: #c0c0c0;
  color: black;
  margin-left: 5%;
}
p {
  background-color: #c0c0c0;
  color: black;
  margin-left: 20%;
}
```

Figure 8.17. `margin-left` settings pushing the content and background right

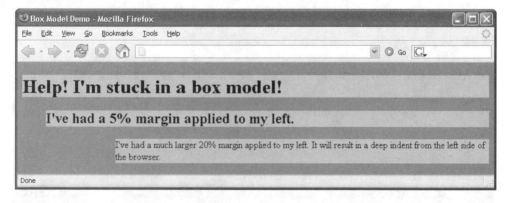

Notice that the second-level heading and the paragraph, both of which have `margin-left` properties, are indented from the left edge of the browser. But, unlike the example in which we set the `padding-left` property, the text and its background color block are indented in this case. This is because the padding, the color block, and the text are inside the content box, while the margin is outside that box.

Next, let's apply `padding-left` and `margin-left` settings to the code fragment:

```
body {
  background-color: #808080;
  color: black;
}
```

```
h1 {
  background-color: #c0c0c0;
  color: black;
}
h2 {
  background-color: #c0c0c0;
  color: black;
  margin-left: 5%;
  padding-left: 1em;
}
p {
  background: #c0c0c0;
  color: black;
  margin-left: 20%;
  padding-left: 10%;
}
```

As you can see in Figure 8.18, the above markup has caused the margin to push the HTML elements and their surrounding background color blocks to the right, while the padding has moved the text to the right within the colored background blocks.

Figure 8.18. Combining `margin-left` with `padding-left`

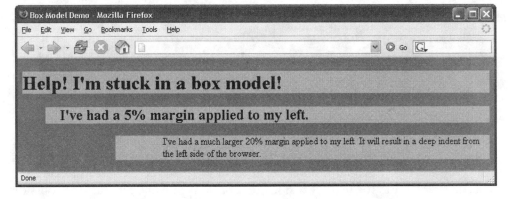

If you load the above HTML (from the file included in the code archive for this book) and resize it, you'll notice that the indentation of the paragraph and the heading changes as the width of the window changes. That's because we used relative values of 20% for the margin and 10% for the padding. Both of these values are calculated relative to the width of the containing block, which in this case is the browser window. The bigger the browser window, the bigger the margin and padding on the paragraph. The padding on the heading doesn't change, as it's specified in ems.

Margins, Padding, and Lists

By default, all visual browsers will apply a 50-pixel margin to the left edge of a list. This allows room for the list item markers (bullets in the case of a bulleted list; numbers in the case of an ordered list). Unfortunately, the CSS Specification doesn't say explicitly whether this space should be implemented as left margin or left padding in the browser's default style rules. However, the description of the `marker-offset` property does imply that margin is the way to go.

Whatever the intent of the specification, Firefox and Safari apply a default padding to the left side of lists, while most other browsers (including Internet Explorer and Opera) use a margin. You can test this easily by applying a `background-color` to an `ol` or `ul` element. On most browsers, the background will not cover the list item markers; on Firefox and Safari, they will.

For this reason, whenever you apply your own left margin or padding value to a list, you must be sure to specify both. If you applied only a margin, for example, the default list indentation would display in Firefox, but be overridden on all other browsers. If you applied a padding value only, the default 50-pixel margin would display on Internet Explorer. Only by specifying both margin and padding (usually by setting `padding: 0` and using `margin` to do the job) can you ensure consistent rendering across current browsers.

You can set vertical margins with the `margin-top` and `margin-bottom` properties. Here's another HTML page that demonstrates vertical margins:

File: **boxmodel3.html**

```
<!DOCTYPE html PUBLIC "-//W3C//DTD XHTML 1.0 Strict//EN"
    "http://www.w3.org/TR/xhtml1/DTD/xhtml1-strict.dtd">
<html xmlns="http://www.w3.org/1999/xhtml">
  <head>
    <title>Box Model Demo</title>
    <meta http-equiv="Content-Type"
        content="text/html; charset=iso-8859-1" />
    <style type="text/css">
      body {
        background-color: #808080;
        color: black;
      }
      h1 {
```

```
      background-color: #c0c0c0;
      color: black;
      margin-bottom: 5cm;
    }
    h2 {
      background-color: #c0c0c0;
      color: black;
      margin-left: 5%;
      margin-top: 5cm;
      margin-bottom: 5cm;
      padding-left: 1em;
    }
    p {
      background: #c0c0c0;
      color: black;
      margin-left: 20%;
      padding-left: 10%;
      margin-top: 5cm;
      margin-bottom: 5cm;
    }
  </style>
</head>
<body>
  <h1>No top margin but a 5cm bottom margin</h1>
  <h2>Top and bottom margins are set to 5cm</h2>
  <p>A paragraph with top and bottom margins set to 5cm</p>
</body>
</html>
```

This page renders as shown in Figure 8.19.

Unlike horizontal margins, vertical margins are not cumulative. If you have two elements stacked one atop the other, like the h1 and h2 elements shown in Figure 8.19, the vertical spacing between them will be the greater of the margin-bottom setting of the top element, and the margin-top setting of the bottom element. In this case, they are both 5cm, so the distance between the two elements is 5cm (not 10cm, as you might have supposed). If I had defined the margin-bottom of the h1 as 10cm, then the vertical distance separating the two elements would have been 10cm. The containing block in this case is the body, which is, for all practical purposes, the same as the browser window's client area.

It is possible to use negative values for margin property settings. This comes in handy when you've set a margin-left property for the body of an HTML page, but you want to move an element closer to the left margin of the page. The following HTML results in the display shown in Figure 8.20:

Figure 8.19. Demonstrating vertical margins

File: **boxmodel4.html**

```
<!DOCTYPE html PUBLIC "-//W3C//DTD XHTML 1.0 Strict//EN"
    "http://www.w3.org/TR/xhtml1/DTD/xhtml1-strict.dtd">
<html xmlns="http://www.w3.org/1999/xhtml">
  <head>
    <title>Box Model Demo</title>
    <meta http-equiv="Content-Type"
      content="text/html; charset=iso-8859-1" />
    <style type="text/css">
      body {
        background-color: #808080;
        color: black;
        margin-left: 5cm;
      }
      h1 {
        background-color: #c0c0c0;
        color: black;
        margin-left: -3cm;
      }
      h2 {
        background-color: #c0c0c0;
        color: black;
      }
```

```
    </style>
  </head>
  <body>
    <h1>The body's margin-left is 5cm, but mine is -3cm. </h1>
    <h2>I have no margin-left setting, so I use the body's 5cm
        setting.</h2>
  </body>
</html>
```

Figure 8.20. Negative margin setting in practice

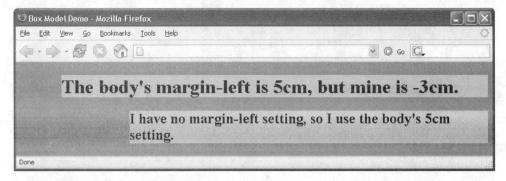

As with the padding property, the margin shorthand property lets you set all four margins with a single declaration, and interprets multiple values using the rules shown in Table 8.1.

Border Properties

Border properties are more complex than padding and margin properties because they affect not only the spacing between objects, but the appearance of that intervening space. A border can be, and usually is, visible. In most ways, managing border properties is similar to the process for managing margins and padding, but there are some key differences.

Borders have three types of properties: style, width, and color. By default, a border's style is set to none, its width to medium,[1] and its color to the text color of the HTML element to which it is applied.

---

[1] Netscape 4 sets a default border width of 0, so you can't rely on the default value if you wish to target that browser.

The border-style property can take any one of a range of constant values. The available values are solid, dashed, dotted, double, groove, ridge, inset, outset, hidden, and none.

The hidden value has the same effect as none, except when applied to table layouts. Refer to the border-style property in Appendix C for further details.

W3C specifications largely leave the issue of the precise appearance of these borders up to the browsers, so don't be surprised if the results of using these characteristics vary a bit from browser to browser, and platform to platform. But, as is the case with default behaviors for other border settings, generally speaking, the browsers treat this issue predictably and satisfactorily within reason.

The width of a border around an object can be set either with four individual declarations, or with the border-width shorthand syntax. The four properties are border-top-width, border-right-width, border-bottom-width, and border-left-width. Each of these properties can be set with an absolute or relative length unit (such as pixels, ems, percentages, or inches), or with one of three descriptive settings: thin, medium, or thick.

If you use the descriptive settings of thin, medium, and thick, the results are browser-dependent. However, they are fairly predictable and consistent across browsers and operating systems, within a pixel or so for each of the three descriptive settings.

Specific Border Measurements

If you wish to use specific measurements for border widths, you should use pixels. This is the most meaningful unit of measurement for screen layouts, which is where border-width is an important property.

You can control the colors associated with all four borders using the border-top-color, border-right-color, border-bottom-color, and border-left-color properties, or you can just use the border-color shorthand property.

As we discovered in Chapter 5, you can supply a color argument in any of the standard ways: using a hexadecimal RGB code (as in #ff9900), using a three-digit hexadecimal RGB shortcut (as in #f90), via the rgb function (as in rgb(102,153,0)), or using a standard color name (as in red).

The shorthand properties border-style, border-width, and border-color all accept multiple values.

There is one additional shorthand property that's probably the most widely used. The `border` property allows you to specify the style, width, and color of all four borders of an object in a compact form. Since a border that's uniform on all sides is most often your desire, this is an efficient way to set border property values.

The following style rule will produce a uniform, three-pixel, solid, red border around any element with a `class="warning"`:

```
.warning {
  border: 3px solid red;
}
```

Constructing the Layout

Now that we have some background knowledge of the ways in which elements behave when they're positioned using CSS, we can put our learning into practice with our first layout.

Create a new style sheet named `styles.css` and link it to the Footbag Freaks document we created earlier by adding the following markup to the `head` of the document:

File: **index.html (excerpt)**

```
<head>
  <title>Footbag Freaks</title>
  <meta http-equiv="Content-Type"
      content="text/html; charset=iso-8859-1" />
  <link rel="stylesheet" type="text/css" href="styles.css" />
</head>
```

The first element to which we'll add CSS is the `body` element. The design has a background image that starts with a pattern but gradually blends into a deep blue. To create this effect on our page, we'll apply the image as a tiled background, and give the page a blue background color. This way, when the background image finishes, it seamlessly merges into the blue page background.

Download Footbag Freaks

The Footbag Freaks web site, including all images, is available for download as part of the code archive for this book.

Let's also set a font family and size, and set the margin and padding for the page (the space between the edge of the viewport and your content) to 0, using the markup below.

File: **styles.css**

```
body {
  margin: 0;
  padding: 0;
  background-color: #050845;
  color: white;
  background-image: url(img/bg.jpg);
  background-repeat: repeat-x;
  font: small Arial, Helvetica, Verdana, sans-serif;
}
```

Setting Freaks `font-size`

I've set the `font-size` on the `body` using the keyword `small`. As we create the rest of the style sheet, I'll use percentage font sizes to make the size of each element a percentage of `small`.

Now, your background image should tile across the width of the page, as shown in Figure 8.21.

Figure 8.21. The background image tiling across the width of the page

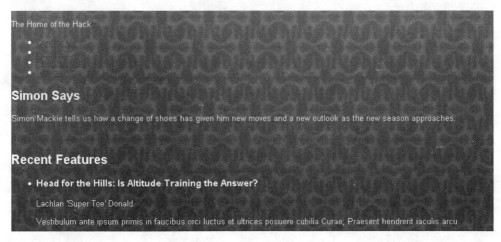

In our layout image, the content of the page is contained in an off-white box. To create this box, we need to add another div in which we can wrap the content. So, immediately after the opening `<body>` tag in your document, add the markup shown in bold below:

File: **index.html** (excerpt)

```
<body>
  <div id="wrapper">
    <div id="header">
      <p>The Home of the Hack</p>
```

Don't forget to close this div immediately before the document's closing `</body>` tag, like so:

File: **index.html** (excerpt)

```
      <p><a href="">more</a></p>
    </div> <!-- main -->
  </div> <!-- wrapper -->
</body>
```

Now, let's add to the style sheet the rules that will give the box an off-white background. We'll also insert rules that add a margin to the wrapper area, creating a space between the wrapper and the body element to let the background image show through:

File: **styles.css** (excerpt)

```
#wrapper {
  background-color: #fdf8f2;
  color: black;
  margin: 30px 40px 30px 40px;
}
```

Figure 8.22 shows the results of our work. The margin has created a space that lets the background show through, but the content inside the wrapper bumps right up against the edge of the off-white area. We can create some extra space here by adding padding to the #wrapper rule, as shown in the markup below. The resulting display is shown in Figure 8.23.

File: **styles.css** (excerpt)

```
#wrapper {
  background-color: #fdf8f2;
  color: black;
  margin: 30px 40px 30px 40px;
```

```
    padding: 10px;
}
```

Figure 8.22. The effect of the styled wrapper `div`

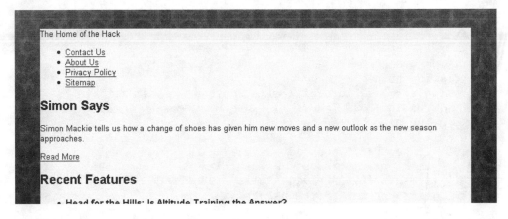

Figure 8.23. Extra padding creating space between the box's edge and its content

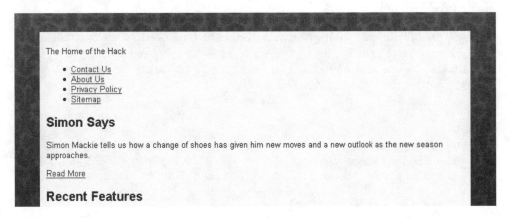

The Header Area

Let's turn our attention to the header area of our layout, which contains the site logo and main navigation. You'll remember that when we created our HTML document, we didn't add any images: we were going to decide how best to include our images as we developed the layout. But now, let's add the logo image using the `img` element. We'll also include the site name as `alt` text for the image, so that users who are browsing the site with images turned off, and those with screen readers, can read the name of the site.

In your document, insert the image directly below the opening `header` div, like this:

File: **index.html** (excerpt)

```
<body>
  <div id="wrapper">
    <div id="header">
      <img src="img/logo.gif" alt="Footbag Freaks" height="77"
          width="203" />
      <p>The home of the hack</p>
      <ul>
        <li><a href="">Contact Us</a></li>
        <li><a href="">About Us</a></li>
        <li><a href="">Privacy Policy</a></li>
        <li><a href="">Sitemap</a></li>
      </ul>
    </div> <!-- header -->
```

If you view the page in a browser, you should see the image in the top, left corner of the off-white box.

The graphic for our page layout shows a thin, light-blue border that appears above and below the site's tagline and navigation. How will we create this effect? Let's contain the tagline and navigation in another `div` to which we can apply a top and bottom border. Add the `div` like so:

File: **index.html** (excerpt)

```
<body>
  <div id="wrapper">
    <div id="header">
      <img src="img/logo.gif" alt="Footbag Freaks" height="77"
          width="203" />
      <div id="header-bottom">
        <p>The home of the hack</p>
        <ul>
          <li><a href="">Contact Us</a></li>
          <li><a href="">About Us</a></li>
          <li><a href="">Privacy Policy</a></li>
          <li><a href="">Sitemap</a></li>
        </ul>
      </div> <!-- header-bottom -->
    </div> <!-- header -->
```

We can now address `#header-bottom` as we add the top and bottom borders:

File: **styles.css** (excerpt)

```css
#header-bottom {
  border-top: 1px solid #b9d2e3;
  border-bottom: 1px solid #b9d2e3;
}
```

To style the navigation list and tagline, we'll use some simple text formatting properties that should now be fairly familiar!

File: **styles.css** (excerpt)

```css
#header-bottom ul {
  margin: 0;
  padding: 0;
}
#header-bottom li {
  display: inline;
}
#header-bottom a:link, #header-bottom a:visited {
  text-decoration: none;
  background-color: #fdf8f2;
  color: #050845;
}
#tagline {
  font-weight: bold;
  background-color: #fdf8f2;
  color: #050845;
  font-style: italic;
}
```

We also need to add an `id` attribute to the paragraph that contains our tagline:

File: **index.html** (excerpt)

```html
<p id="tagline">The home of the hack</p>
```

Figure 8.24. Styling navigation list items with `display: inline`

We set the `margin` and `padding` on the list within this area to 0, then set the `li` element's `display` property to `inline`, which will cause the list items to display on the same line, rather than having each item display on a new line. Figure 8.24 shows this effect in action. We also styled the navigation links—again using the dark blue and removing the underlines from them—and the tagline, which we made bold, italic, and the same blue as our navigation items.

The problem with the display shown in Figure 8.24 is that it's difficult to distinguish the links in the navigation list from one another. The recommended solution[2] to this problem is to add a visible character—such as the pipe character (|)—between each of the links, as I've done in the markup below:

File: **index.html (excerpt)**

```
<ul>
  <li><a href="">Contact Us</a> | </li>
  <li><a href="">About Us</a> | </li>
  <li><a href="">Privacy Policy</a> | </li>
  <li><a href="">Sitemap</a></li>
</ul>
```

We can also set the color of the list items to dark blue (#050845), so that the pipe character that sits outside of the anchor element will be blue, too. Our refined header design is shown in Figure 8.25.

File: **styles.css (excerpt)**

```
#header-bottom li {
  display: inline;
  background-color: #fdf8f2;
```

---

[2]This recommendation was made as part of the Web Content Accessibility Guidelines (WCAG) 1.0. The checkpoint that covers this specific issue can be seen at http://www.w3.org/TR/WCAG10/wai-pageauth.html#tech-divide-links.

```
   color: #050845;
}
```

Figure 8.25. After styling the text elements in the header area

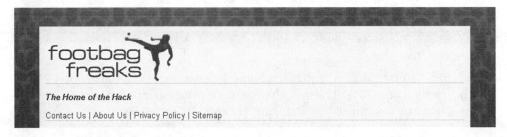

The header is really starting to take shape now! Our next step is to move the tagline and navigation up onto the same line. To do this, we'll have to use a property that, while we haven't discussed it in detail yet, will become more important to us as we progress through these layouts. That property is `float`.

The `float` Property

`float` is one of the most interesting and often-used CSS properties. It takes a value of `left`, `right`, or `none` (though `none`, the default, is rarely used). `float` forces the element to which it's applied to display outside its natural position in the containing box; a `float` value of `left` or `right` pushes the element to the left or the right of its natural position, respectively. This property can be used within any block element.

The `float` property is designed to replace the `align` attribute that's associated with the HTML `img` element, and has, for all practical purposes, precisely the same effect. The `align` attribute is deprecated in favor of the `float` property in recent releases of HTML Recommendations from the W3C. The following HTML fragment uses the `float` property to produce the result shown in Figure 8.26:

```
<p><img src="logo.gif" alt="Footbag Freaks Logo"
    width="203" height="77"
    style="float: left; padding-right: 1em;" />The Footbag Freaks
    logo appears to the left of this paragraph. Depending on
    whether or not I use the CSS <code>float</code> property, I
    may see more than one line of text beside the logo. The CSS
    <code>float</code> property replaces the deprecated
    <code>align</code> attribute of the HTML <code>img</code>
    element and has an identical effect.</p>
```

Figure 8.26. Achieving image-text alignment using the CSS `float` property

 The Footbag Freaks logo appears to the left of this paragraph. Depending on whether or not I use the CSS `float` property, I may see more than one line of text beside the logo. The CSS `float` property replaces the deprecated `align` attribute of the HTML `img` element and has an identical effect.

The `float` property has one major advantage over the `align` attribute: `float` can be applied to elements other than images, whereas application of the old `align` attribute was limited to `img`, `applet`, and `object` elements.

No Dimensions? Declare a `width`

When using the `float` property on elements that don't have well-defined dimensions, you must include a `width` declaration in your CSS. An `img` is an example of an element with well-defined dimensions, whereas a paragraph, a heading, or a `div` doesn't.

Using `float` in our Header

We'll be exploring the `float` property in more detail in the next chapter, when we create a layout that relies on `float` for the positioning of the page's main sections. However, at this point we can use our knowledge of `float` to align the tagline and navigation correctly. The element that we're going to float is the tagline paragraph, so add the rules marked in bold below to your tagline rule:

File: **styles.css** (excerpt)

```
#tagline {
  font-weight: bold;
  background-color: #fdf8f2;
  color: #050845;
  font-style: italic;
  margin: 0;
  padding: 0 0 0 20px;
  width: 300px;
  float: left;
}
```

We set `margin` to `0` so that the paragraph's default margin is removed. We then add 20 pixels of left padding to move the tagline in from the left-hand side, and give it a width of 300 pixels to provide a bit of space to its right, as is indicated in the page's original layout graphic. We then set the value of `float` to `left`, so it sits to the left of the rest of the content, which in this case, is our navigation list.

After making this change to the rules for the tagline paragraph, save your style sheet and view your page in a browser. You should see the navigation display alongside the tagline. These elements behave in exactly the same way as the paragraph that wraps around the image in the example we discussed above. All we need to do now is to align the list of navigation items to the right, and alter the padding on the list to move it in slightly from the right-hand edge. Here's the markup you'll need; the resulting display is depicted in Figure 8.27.

File: **styles.css (excerpt)**

```
#header-bottom ul {
  margin: 0;
  padding: 0 30px 0 0;
  text-align: right;
}
```

Figure 8.27. The display after floating the tagline and aligning the navigation

If you've been working through this example in Internet Explorer 6, you may already have noticed that things aren't going quite to plan. Sometimes, as if by magic, the navigation list that's aligned to the right just seems to disappear, along with part of the light blue borders above and below the list. Then, if you switch to another window, the list magically reappears! Well, sometimes it does; other times, it stays hidden.

If you've experienced this problem, welcome—you've stepped through the looking glass into the wonderful world of Internet Explorer CSS bugs. This one is called the peekaboo bug, as the content disappears and reappears in an almost completely random fashion.

There are quite a few of these Internet Explorer CSS bugs, but the majority seem to revolve around a mysterious, non-standard DOM property called `hasLayout`. The galaxy of `hasLayout` bugs is vast and difficult to understand, but thankfully, these bugs aren't too tricky to squash. Usually, eradicating them is just a matter of adding one of a number of inconsequential declarations to the style rules of the element that's giving you trouble. For example, it can be as simple as adding a `height` declaration to `#header-bottom`, as shown here:

File: **styles.css (excerpt)**

```
#header-bottom {
  border-top: 1px solid #b9d2e3;
  border-bottom: 1px solid #b9d2e3;
  height: 1%;
}
```

This declaration is named the **Holly Hack**, after its inventor, Holly Bergevin.

Add this declaration to your style sheet, and voila! Problem solved. The `height` declaration doesn't really affect the display of the page in any browser, as the content of this `div` "overflows" its height, effectively correcting the height. Don't worry if you don't understand what's going on here. All you need to know is that when you add such declarations either to the element that's giving you trouble, or its parent element, those declarations will often fix bizarre behavior in Internet Explorer 6.

The final task that will complete the heading is to add the little footbag image that displays to the right of the navigation in our layout image. First, add the actual image to your document, beneath the navigation list. In the markup below, I gave this image an empty `alt` attribute, so that nothing about this image would be read out by a screen reader—this image is included for display purposes only. I've also given the image an `id` of `ball`.

File: **index.html (excerpt)**

```
<div id="header">
  <img src="img/logo.gif" alt="Footbag Freaks" height="77"
      width="203" />
  <div id="header-bottom">
    <p id="tagline">The home of the hack</p>
    <ul>
      <li><a href="">Contact Us</a> | </li>
      <li><a href="">About Us</a> | </li>
      <li><a href="">Privacy Policy</a> | </li>
      <li><a href="">Sitemap</a></li>
    </ul>
    <img src="img/header-ball.gif" height="24" width="20" alt=""
        id="ball" />
```

```
  </div> <!-- header-bottom -->
</div> <!-- header -->
```

Now, let's use our first bit of absolute positioning in the CSS to get the image to line up properly. We know the location at which the image should be positioned relative to the top and right-hand sides of the document, as we know the height of the logo and width of the margin on the wrapper div. The following CSS will place the ball in the correct position at the end of the navigation:

```
#ball {
  position: absolute;
  top: 110px;
  right: 55px;
}
```

The header section is now complete! It's displayed in Figure 8.28.

Figure 8.28. The completed header section of the layout

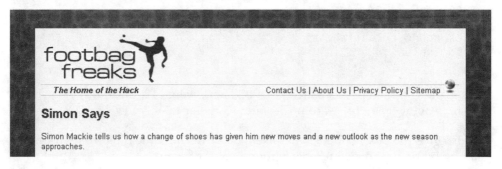

The Content Area

Let's move on to create the look and feel of the main content area of the page. The first thing we'll do is contain the sidebar and content divs within another div that has an id of main. This will help us to line up the sidebar and content divs beneath the header. Add the opening <div id="main"> just after the header's closing </div>:

File: **index.html (excerpt)**

```
    <img src="img/header-ball.gif" height="24" width="20" alt=""
      id="ball" />
  </div> <!-- header-bottom -->
</div> <!-- header -->
<div id="main">
```

```
<div id="content">
  <h2>Simon Says</h2>
```

Close this `div` immediately after the closing `</div>` tag of the `sidebar div`. In the style sheet, give `#main` a `margin-top` of ten pixels to separate the content and header areas, as shown in the snippet below. We'll return to `#main` later, as we create our layout.

File: styles.css (excerpt)

```
#main {
  margin-top: 10px;
}
```

Now, let's create a rule for `#content`. Add the following set of declarations to your style sheet:

File: styles.css (excerpt)

```
#content {
  margin: 0 240px 0 0;
  border: 1px solid #b9d2e3;
  background-color: white;
  color: black;
}
```

We set the top margin of `#content` to 0. Then, we add a 240-pixel right-hand margin, leaving space for us to position our sidebar later.

We also give the box a solid, single-pixel border in the same blue we used for the heading borders, and give it a background color of white.

The Main Feature

At the very top of the page is a "boxout": an area that's visually contained within a box that highlights it. This particular boxout highlights the main feature article. Let's look at that now.

Create a container for the main feature area by adding a `div` with an `id` of `mainfeature`; wrap it around the heading, paragraph, and link of the main feature:

File: index.html (excerpt)

```
<div id="content">
  <div id="mainfeature">
    <h2>Simon Says</h2>
    <p>Simon Mackie tells us how a change of shoes has given him
```

```
         new moves and a new outlook as the new season approaches.
      </p>
   <p><a href="">Read More</a></p>
 </div> <!-- mainfeature -->
 <h2>Recent Features</h2>
```

Now you can style the main feature area in your style sheet:

File: **styles.css** (excerpt)

```
#mainfeature {
  background-image: url(img/mainimg.jpg);
  background-repeat: no-repeat;
  background-color: #112236;
  color: white;
  padding: 2em 2em 1em 200px;
}
```

Here, we add the background image, `maining.jpg`, and set it to `no-repeat`. But if a user has the browser open to dimensions that are wider than the image, we don't want the exposed areas of the page to display white. To prevent this from happening, we add a background color of `#112236`; this is the same color as the far right-hand side of the image, so the image should appear to fade into the background color seamlessly. We then set the text color to `white` and use padding to position the text two ems from the top of the box, two ems from the right, one em from the bottom, and 200 pixels from the left-hand side, so that it's clear of the image of the footbag player.

Next, we style the heading and the paragraphs within the boxout:

File: **styles.css** (excerpt)

```
#mainfeature h2 {
  margin: 0;
  font-weight: normal;
  font-size: 140%;
}
#mainfeature p {
  font-size: 110%;
}
```

Finally, we need to style the "Read More" link that leads readers to the full article. Let's start by adding a `class="more"` attribute to the paragraph element so that we can target it with our style rules:

File: **index.html (excerpt)**

```
<div id="mainfeature">
  <h2>Simon Says</h2>
  <p>Simon Mackie tells us how a change of shoes has given him new
      moves and a new outlook as the new season approaches.</p>
  <p class="more"><a href="">Read More</a></p>
</div>
```

First, we remove the top margin from the paragraph that contains the link, to decrease the space between it and the paragraph. Then, we set text-align to right:

File: **styles.css (excerpt)**

```
#mainfeature p.more {
  margin-top: 0;
  text-align: right;
}
#mainfeature p.more a:link, #mainfeature p.more a:visited {
  color: white;
  background-image: url(img/more-bullet.gif);
  background-repeat: no-repeat;
  background-position: center left;
  padding-left: 14px;
}
```

We then style the link and visited pseudo-classes, changing their color to white and adding the more-bullet.gif background image. We only want to see the bullet once, so we set repeat to no-repeat, then position the background center and left. This positions the image in the center of the link's text. Finally, in order to stop the text from displaying over the top of the background image, we set padding-left to 14 pixels. The impact of these changes is shown in Figure 8.29.

If you load this page in Internet Explorer 6, you'll see that the peekaboo bug that affected our right-aligned navigation bar has reared its ugly head once more, and is randomly causing our feature area to display as a white rectangle. Again, it's simple to fix this issue by adding the declaration height: 1% to our #mainfeature rule.

Figure 8.29. After styling the main feature section

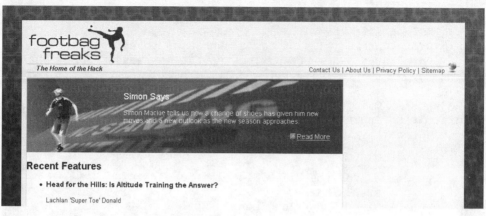

```
#mainfeature {
  background-image: url(img/mainimg.jpg);
  background-repeat: no-repeat;
  background-color: #112236;
  color: white;
  padding: 2em 2em 1em 200px;
  height: 1%;
}
```

Reload the page and the main feature area will display as reliably in Internet Explorer as it does in Firefox, Opera, and Safari.

The Features List

Our layout is really starting to take shape now! Let's spend some time styling the main content on this page: the list of feature articles.

At the moment, the text inside the content area butts up against the border of the box. I want to create some space between that border and the content. The contents of the home page content div are enclosed in an unordered list, so one option we have is to add a margin to that list and to the h2 above it. However, another page might have a different kind of main content, so in order that all of the pages can be dealt with in the same way, let's add another div, which wraps around the heading and features list, and give it a class of inner:

```
<div id="content">
  <div id="mainfeature">
    <h2>Simon Says</h2>
    <p>Simon Mackie tells us how a change of shoes has given him
        new moves and a new outlook as the new season approaches.
        </p>
    <p class="more"><a href="">Read More</a></p>
  </div> <!-- mainfeature -->
  <div class="inner">
    <h2>Recent Features</h2>
    <ul>
      <li>
        <h3>Head for the Hills: Is Altitude Training the
            Answer?</h3>
        <p>Lachlan 'Super Toe' Donald</p>
       <p>Vestibulum ante ipsum primis in faucibus orci luctus et
            ultrices posuere cubilia Curae; Praesent hendrerit
            iaculis arcu.</p>
        <p><a href="">Full Story</a></p>
      </li>
      <li>
        <h3>Hack up the Place: Freestylin' Super Tips</h3>
        <p>Jules 'Pony King' Szemere</p>
       <p>Vestibulum ante ipsum primis in faucibus orci luctus et
            ultrices posuere cubilia Curae; Praesent hendrerit
            iaculis arcu.</p>
        <p><a href="">Full Story</a></p>
      </li>
      <li>
        <h3>The Complete Black Hat Hacker's Survival Guide</h3>
        <p>Mark 'Steel Tip' Harbottle</p>
       <p>Vestibulum ante ipsum primis in faucibus orci luctus et
            ultrices posuere cubilia Curae; Praesent hendrerit
            iaculis arcu.</p>
        <p><a href="">Full Story</a></p>
      </li>
      <li>
        <h3>Five Tricks You Didn't Even Know You Knew</h3>
        <p>Simon 'Mack Daddy' Mackie</p>
       <p>Vestibulum ante ipsum primis in faucibus orci luctus et
            ultrices posuere cubilia Curae; Praesent hendrerit
            iaculis arcu.</p>
        <p><a href="">Full Story</a></p>
      </li>
    </ul>
```

```
    </div>
  </div> <!-- content -->
```

To create some space between the features list and the border of the containing box, let's add a margin to `#content .inner` in the style sheet:

File: **styles.css** (excerpt)

```
#content .inner {
  margin: 10px 20px 10px 40px;
}
```

If you view your layout in the browser, you should see the space that this margin creates. We can now address the content of this section.

First, let's style the heading. In our layout image, the heading has a blue underline that stretches across the entire width of the content—an effect we can create using a bottom border. Let's also add a small amount of padding to the bottom of the h2, to insert some space between the text and this border:

File: **styles.css** (excerpt)

```
#content .inner h2 {
  color: #245185;
  padding-bottom: 0.2em;
  border-bottom: 1px solid #b9d2e3;
  font-size: 110%;
}
```

Next, let's add a rule to remove the margin and list bullets from the list of feature items. While we could simply create this rule for `#content .inner ul`, as there's only one list in this page's layout, that approach might cause problems on other pages whose content includes lists that are not like this special features list. So let's add a `class="features"` attribute to the ul element first, so we can style this particular list—and others like it—without affecting any normal, non-feature lists within page content:

File: **index.html** (excerpt)

```
<div class="inner">
  <h2>Recent Features</h2>
  <ul class="features">
    <li>
```

File: **styles.css** (excerpt)

```
#content .inner ul.features {
  margin: 0;
```

```
    padding: 0;
    list-style: none;
}
```

Each feature has a level three heading; we'll style these by increasing the font size:

File: **styles.css (excerpt)**

```
#content .inner h3 {
    font-size: 130%;
}
```

Let's also make each of these headings act as a link to the appropriate article on the Footbag Freaks site. We can style the link and visited pseudo-classes, as well:

File: **index.html (excerpt)**

```
<li>
  <h3><a href="">Head for the Hills: Is Altitude Training the
      Answer?</a></h3>
  <p>Lachlan 'Super Toe' Donald</p>
  <p>Vestibulum ante ipsum primis in faucibus orci luctus et
      ultrices posuere cubilia Curae; Praesent hendrerit iaculis
      arcu.</p>
  <p><a href="">Full Story</a></p>
</li>
<li>
  <h3><a href="">Hack up the Place: Freestylin' Super
      Tips</a></h3>
  <p>Jules 'Pony King' Szemere</p>
  <p>Vestibulum ante ipsum primis in faucibus orci luctus et
      ultrices posuere cubilia Curae; Praesent hendrerit iaculis
      arcu.</p>
  <p><a href="">Full Story</a></p>
</li>
```

File: **styles.css (excerpt)**

```
#content .inner h3 a:link, #content .inner h3 a:visited {
    color: #245185;
}
```

Finally, let's style the page's paragraph text by making it a dark gray and decreasing the font size to 90%:

File: **styles.css (excerpt)**

```
#content .inner p {
  color: #666666;
  font-size: 90%;
}
```

The Author Images

We want to display an image of the author alongside each feature article listing. Add the image to each feature item, after the heading, like so:

File: **styles.css (excerpt)**

```
<li>
  <h3><a href="">Head for the Hills: Is Altitude Training the
      Answer?</a></h3>
  <img src="img/lachlan.jpg" alt="Lachlan Donald" height="48"
      width="35" />
  <p>Lachlan 'Super Toe' Donald</p>
  <p>Vestibulum ante ipsum primis in faucibus orci luctus et
      ultrices posuere cubilia Curae; Praesent hendrerit iaculis
      arcu.</p>
  <p class="more"><a href="">Full Story</a></p>
</li>
```

Figure 8.30. Displaying author images in the document

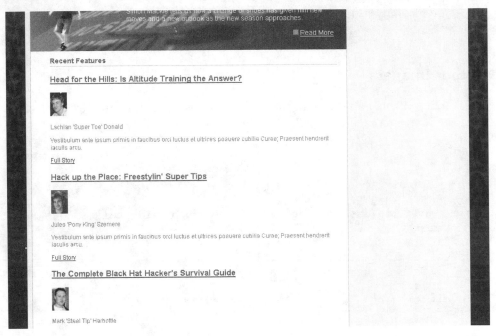

This markup produces the display shown in Figure 8.30.

Let's use the `float: left` declaration to move these author shots to the left of the paragraph text. Note that we don't need to include the image's width here, as each `img` already has a width defined.

File: **styles.css (excerpt)**

```
#content .inner .features li img {
  float: left;
  margin: 0 5px 5px 0;
}
```

Here, we've used a selector that will address only those images that are within an `li` element with the `class="features"` attribute. This way, we avoid affecting any other images that might be added to your content.

We've set the image to float left, and added a margin so that the text doesn't sit right next to the image—it has a little breathing room, as Figure 8.31 shows.

Figure 8.31. Floating the author image

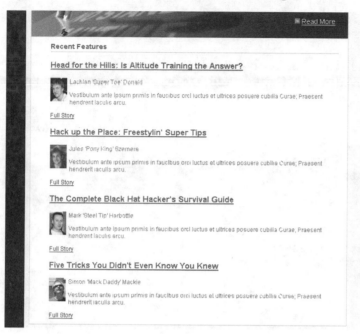

In our layout graphic, author names appear in bold text, so let's give the paragraph surrounding the author name a `class` attribute with the value `author`, and use a CSS rule to style it bold. We're not doing this with any `<strong>` or `<b>` tags because we're styling the author names purely for aesthetic reasons—not for any structural purpose. By keeping the author name styles out of the page markup, we're sticking to our goal of separating content from presentation. And, since we're using CSS, if we want to change the way the author name displays in future, we can simply edit the rules for the appropriate class, instead of finding every page on which an author's name is displayed and changing it there. Here's the change we need to make to the page markup, followed by the CSS rule that will make all suitably marked-up author names bold:

File: **index.html** (excerpt)

```
<img src="img/lachlan.jpg" alt="Lachlan Donald" height="48"
    width="35" />
<p class="author">Lachlan 'Super Toe' Donald</p>
<p>Vestibulum ante ipsum primis in faucibus orci luctus et ultrices
    posuere cubilia Curae; Praesent hendrerit iaculis arcu.</p>
```

File: **styles.css (excerpt)**

```
#content .inner p.author {
  font-weight:  bold;
}
```

The final page element that we need to style for this section is the "Full Story" links that appear beneath each feature. Add a `class` of `more` to each link's opening <p> tag, then add the following rules to your style sheet:

File: **styles.css (excerpt)**

```
#content .inner p.more{
  margin-top: 0;
  text-align: right;
}
#content .inner p.more a:link, #content .inner p.more a:visited {
  color: black;
  background-image: url(img/more-bullet.gif);
  background-repeat: no-repeat;
  background-position: center left;
  padding-left: 14px;
  font-size: 90%;
  color: #1e4c82;
}
```

As I'm sure you've noticed, this styling is very similar to that of the "Read More" link within the feature article section at the top of the page.

Your layout should now look a lot like the original layout graphic. Our progress is shown in Figure 8.32. The page is very close to completion: we have only the sidebar left to style!

Figure 8.32. Displaying the page after styling the main content area

The Sidebar

Figure 8.33. The unstyled sidebar

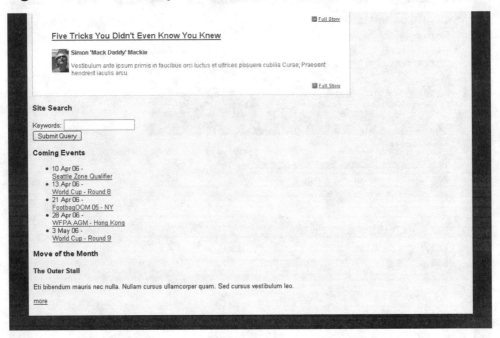

The content of the sidebar is languishing beneath the main content area, as Figure 8.33 illustrates. No rules have been applied to it, so it's just sitting in its natural location in the document.

Our first job is to move the sidebar from this position to the space we've created for it on the right of the content area.

First, let's see what happens if we position the sidebar using absolute positioning from the top and right. Add the following rules to your style sheet:

File: **styles.css** (excerpt)

```
#sidebar {
  position: absolute;
  top: 0;
  right: 0;
  width: 220px;
  background-color: #256290;
```

```
  color: white;
  margin: 0;
  padding: 0;
}
```

View your page in the browser. The sidebar is stuck to the top, right corner of the viewport as in Figure 8.34.

Figure 8.34. Positioning the sidebar top and right

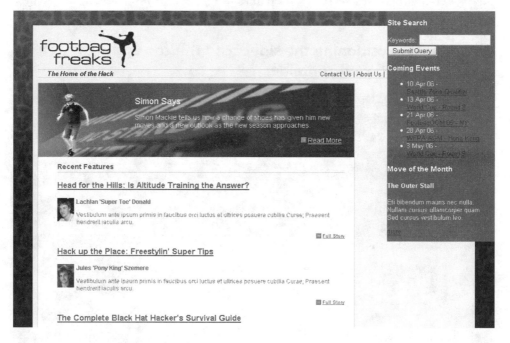

When we discussed absolute and relative positioning earlier, I explained that an element is always positioned relative to its parent element's position, and that this concept was described as an element's positioning context. In this case, #sidebar doesn't have a positioned parent element, so it takes the viewport as its positioning context.

However, we do have an element that can be positioned to provide us with a useful positioning context—the div with id="main".

Find #main in your style sheet and add the following declarations:

File: **styles.css** (excerpt)

```
#main {
  position: relative;
  top:0;
  left:  0;
  width: 100%;
  margin-top: 10px;
}
```

The sidebar now takes #main as its parent, so it falls into place within the area defined by the div with that id, as Figure 8.35 illustrates.

Figure 8.35. Positioning the sidebar to the top and right of a relatively positioned container

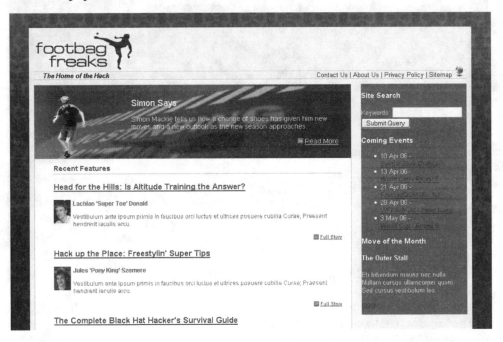

With our sidebar now in position, we can start to style its contents. To start, we'll style the h3 headings that head the different sections of the sidebar:

File: **styles.css** (excerpt)

```
#sidebar h3 {
  font-size: 110%;
  background-image: url(img/sidebar-header-bg.jpg);
```

```
  background-repeat: no-repeat;
  margin: 0;
  padding: 0.2em 0 0.2em 10px;
  font-weight: normal;
}
```

Here, we're displaying a background image behind the heading to create the gradient effect we saw in our design comp.

Good Looks in the Background

Using a background image behind a heading is a great way to make your headings more attractive without resorting to using an image for the actual heading text. Using an image to display headings makes your site more difficult to maintain, as you need to manipulate those images every time you want to make even minor changes.

Let's have a closer look at the sections of content that display below each of the headings in the sidebar. We need to add a div with a class of inner to each of these, in order to create a little space and move the text content away from the border. Add this div to each of the three sections, as shown here:

File: **index.html (excerpt)**

```
<div id="sidebar">
  <div class="inner">
    <h3>Site Search</h3>
    <form method="post" action="" id="searchform">
      <div>
        <label for="keywords">Keywords</label>:
        <input type="text" name="keywords" id="keywords" />
      </div>
      <div>
        <input type="submit" name="btnSearch" id="btnSearch" />
      </div>
    </form>
  </div>
  <div class="inner">
    <h3>Coming Events</h3>
    <ul>
      <li>10 Apr 06 -<br /><a href="">Seattle Zone
          Qualifier</a></li>
      <li>13 Apr 06 -<br /><a href="">World Cup - Round 8</a></li>
      <li>21 Apr 06 -<br /><a href="">FootbagOOM 05 - NY</a></li>
      <li>28 Apr 06 -<br /><a href="">WFPA AGM - Hong
          Kong</a></li>
```

```
      <li>3 May 06 -<br /><a href="">World Cup - Round 9</a></li>
    </ul>
  </div>
  <div class="inner">
    <h3>Move of the Month</h3>
    <h4>The Outer Stall</h4>
    <p>Eti bibendum mauris nec nulla. Nullam cursus ullamcorper
        quam. Sed cursus vestibulum leo.</p>
    <p><a href="">more</a></p>
  </div>
</div> <!-- sidebar -->
```

Now, let's add ten pixels of padding to `inner`:

File: **styles.css** (excerpt)

```
#sidebar .inner {
  padding: 10px;
}
```

As you can see in Figure 8.36, the sidebar is starting to take shape.

Figure 8.36. The display after styling the headings and `inner` class

Now, let's address the list of events.

File: **styles.css (excerpt)**

```
#sidebar ul {
  list-style-image: url(img/more-bullet.gif);
  margin-left: 0;
  padding-left: 20px;
}
```

In the markup above, we use the `more-bullet.gif` image as the list bullet, remove the margin, and add left padding of 20 pixels in order to display the list in line with the headings.

File: **styles.css (excerpt)**

```
#sidebar p, #sidebar li {
  font-size: 90%;
  line-height: 1.4em;
}
```

Next up, we decrease the font size of the paragraph and list item text by reducing it to 90%. We also create a little more spacing between the lines with the help of the `line-height` property.

File: **styles.css (excerpt)**

```
#sidebar ul a:link, #sidebar ul a:visited {
  color:  white;
}
```

The links in the sidebar are white and underlined in the mock-up, so we set them to white with the rule above.

Finally, let's make all the dates in the event list bold. Add a `span` with `class="date"` to each of the dates in the list, then style them using the selector `#sidebar .date`, like this:

File: **index.html (excerpt)**

```
<ul>
  <li><span class="date">10 Apr 06</span> -<br />
      <a href="">Seattle Zone Qualifier</a></li>
  <li><span class="date">13 Apr 06</span> -<br /><a href="">World
      Cup - Round 8</a></li>
  <li><span class="date">21 Apr 06</span> -<br />
      <a href="">FootbagOOM 05 - NY</a></li>
  <li><span class="date">28 Apr 06</span> -<br /><a href="">WFPA
      AGM - Hong Kong</a></li>
  <li><span class="date">3 May 06</span> -<br /><a href="">World
```

```
        Cup - Round 9</a></li>
</ul>
```

File: **styles.css** (excerpt)

```
#sidebar .date {
  font-weight: bold;
}
```

The events in the sidebar now display as shown in Figure 8.37.

Figure 8.37. Displaying the styled events in the sidebar

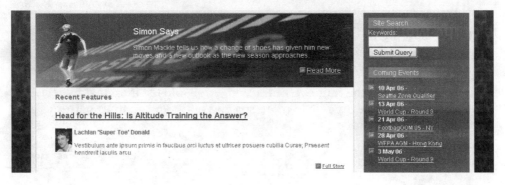

The Form

It's time to create some rules for the search form at the top of the sidebar. Add class="text" to the input type="text" element, then create a rule for #searchform .text that gives the text box a width of 196 pixels and a border. Here's the markup:

File: **styles.css** (excerpt)

```
#searchform .text {
  width: 196px;
  border: 1px solid #45bac0;
}
```

Apply the searchbutton class to the div that surrounds the submit button, and add a rule for it to styles.css, setting text-align to right and adding a top margin so the button doesn't bump right up against the text box.

File: **styles.css** (excerpt)

```
#searchform .searchbutton {
  text-align: right;
```

```
    margin-top: 4px;
}
```

Finally, let's style the button itself, giving it a border the same color as the text field, a background color that matches the blue used for the background of the sidebar, and a text color of white, as defined in the rules below. You'll also need to add a `class` attribute with the value `btn` to the `input` element. The results of your work should look like Figure 8.38.

File: **styles.css (excerpt)**

```
#searchform .btn {
  border: 1px solid #45bac0;
  background-color: #256290;
  color:  white;
}
```

Figure 8.38. Displaying the styled site search

Move of the Month

The final element of the sidebar that we need to consider is the Move of the Month section at its bottom. This section includes an image; we need to add this to the document first. Insert it below the `h4` and give it a `class` of `motm-image`:

File: **index.html (excerpt)**

```
<h3>Move of the Month</h3>
<h4>The Outer Stall</h4>
<img src="img/sidebar-player.gif"
    alt="player demonstrating the outer stall move" height="110"
    width="60" class="motm-image" />
<p>Eti bibendum mauris nec nulla. Nullam cursus ullamcorper quam.
    Sed cursus vestibulum leo.</p>
<p><a href="">more</a></p>
```

Let's float this image to the right so that we can display the text to one side of the image:

File: **styles.css** (excerpt)

```
#sidebar .motm-image {
  float: right;
  margin: 0 30px 0 20px;
}
```

As you can see, we've also added left and right margins to the image. The very last thing we need to do is to format the "more" link, which is very similar to the "Read More" and "Full Story" links in the rest of the layout. However, unlike those links, this link will normally appear next to a floated image. We want to ensure that it doesn't appear alongside the image: we want it always to display below. So, as you can see in the markup below, we use the clear: right declaration to ensure there are no floated elements to the right of the image. We'll also need to add the more class to the paragraph that contains the link:

File: **styles.css** (excerpt)

```
#sidebar p.more {
  clear: right;
  margin: 0 30px 0 0;
  text-align: right;
}
```

We'll be looking at clear in more detail in the next chapter. For now, note that it can take the values of left (clearing a left float), right (clearing a right float), and both (clearing both left and right floats). If you're using floated elements in your layouts, you'll find this a useful property.

The final rules, below, should be familiar to you from the other "Read More" and "Full Story" links:

File: **styles.css** (excerpt)

```
#sidebar p.more a:link, #sidebar p.more a:visited {
  color: white;
  background-image: url(img/more-bullet.gif);
  background-repeat: no-repeat;
  background-position: center left;
  padding-left: 14px;
}
```

This markup completes your two-column layout! The finished page display is shown in Figure 8.39.

Figure 8.39. The completed two-column layout

Repositioning the Sidebar

We can really start to appreciate the flexibility of CSS layouts when we decide to experiment! For instance, imagine that we want to see how this layout would look if we positioned the sidebar on the left, rather than the right. To do this, you'd need to make only two changes in your CSS.

First, locate the #content rule and change the values for margin: give it a 240-pixel *left* margin, rather than a 240-pixel right margin. Then, set the right margin to 0:

```
#content {
  margin: 0 240px 0 0;
  border: 1px solid #b9d2e3;
  background-color: white;
  color: black;
}
```

Now, find the `#sidebar` rule and change the positioning declaration `right: 0` to `left: 0`:

File: **styles.css (excerpt)**

```
#sidebar {
  position: absolute;
  top: 0;
  left: 0;
  width: 220px;
  background-color: #256290;
  color: white;
  margin: 0;
  padding: 0;
}
```

Save your style sheet and refresh the page in your browser. The sidebar will now appear on the left-hand side of the content, as Figure 8.40 shows.

Summary

We've covered a lot in this chapter! We began with an unstyled XHTML document, and after learning a little bit about the theory of using CSS for layout—in particular, absolute and relative positioning, margins, padding, and borders—we began to create a two-column layout using an absolutely positioned sidebar.

You now have a complete page layout that uses CSS positioning; it's the basic layout used by many of the sites we see on the Web every day. This layout method does have its limitations, though—we'll discover those, and discuss some alternative layouts, in the next chapter. However, if you need a two-column layout, this structure is robust and can be used as the basis for countless attractive site designs.

Figure 8.40. Repositioning the sidebar

Three-column Layouts

By the end of the last chapter, we'd developed a two-column layout in which we used absolute positioning to create the sidebar column.

We'll start this chapter by adding a third column to our existing layout. Then, we'll discuss the issues that arise when we want to add a footer that runs along the bottoms of all the columns in a multi-column layout. Along the way, we'll find out how to use the `float` property to build multi-column layouts, and see how to create full-length columns using CSS, again considering some of the issues that can occur when we work with these types of layouts.

Adding a Third Column

The two-column layout we created in the last chapter looks great! However, in the web projects you undertake, you may find that you have additional information that would display well in a third column, as illustrated in Figure 9.1.

Figure 9.1. Mockup of a three-column layout

At the end of the last chapter, I demonstrated how we could move the right column to the left simply by creating a margin that was large enough for it on the left-hand side, and positioning it there instead. We'll be able to use exactly the same technique to drop in our new left-hand column. Let's look at that now.

The Markup

First, add the markup for this column directly below the closing tag of the sidebar `div` and inside the wrapper and main `div`s.

File: **index.html (excerpt)**

```
    <h3>Move of the Month</h3>
    <h4>The Outer Stall</h4>
    <img src="img/sidebar-player.gif"
        alt="player demonstrating the outer stall move"
        height="110" width="60" class="motm-image" />
    <p>Eti bibendum mauris nec nulla. Nullam cursus
        ullamcorper quam. Sed cursus vestibulum leo.</p>
    <p class="more"><a href="">more</a></p>
  </div>
</div> <!-- sidebar -->
<div id="sidebar2">
  <div class="inner">
    <ul id="nav">
      <li><a href="">Freestyle</a></li>
      <li><a href="">Tournaments</a></li>
      <li><a href="">Results</a></li>
      <li><a href="">Rules</a></li>
      <li><a href="">Blog</a></li>
      <li><a href="">FAQ</a></li>
      <li><a href="">Forums</a></li>
      <li><a href="">Organisations</a></li>
    </ul>
    <h3>The BagBlog</h3>
    <div id="bloglatest">
      <h4>10 Apr 06</h4>
      <p><a href="">A New Season: On the Road
        Again</a></p>
      <p>Vestibulum ante ipsum primis in faucibus orci
        luctus et ultrices posuere cubilia Curae;
        Praesent henrerit iaculis arcu.</p>
    </div>
    <ul id="blog">
      <li>5 Apr: <a href="">Ouch... That Really
        Hurt</a></li>
      <li>3 Apr: <a href="">Experimental Moves From
        Spain</a></li>
      <li>29 Mar: <a href="">5 Ways to Lighten Up
        Training</a></li>
    </ul>
    <h3>Newsletter</h3>
    <p>To get all the latest news, tips, results and new
        footbag products sign up to our free
        newsletter.</p>
    <form method="post" action="" id="newsletterform">
      <div>
```

```
            <input type="text" name="email"
                id="newsletter-email" value="email@here"
                class="text" />
        </div>
        <div class="searchbutton">
            <input type="submit" name="btnSubmit"
                id="newsletter-submit" value="SUBSCRIBE"
                class="btn" />
        </div>
      </form>
    </div>
  </div> <!-- sidebar2 -->
  </div> <!-- main -->
  </div> <!-- wrapper -->
 </body>
</html>
```

You can see that I've wrapped this section in a div with the id sidebar2; within that is a div with a class of inner. I've also added some classes to the different elements, so they're ready for us to add the CSS. Once we add this markup, the column will display below the main content area in the browser, as shown in Figure 9.2.

Figure 9.2. Viewing the page in the browser after adding the `sidebar2 div` and contents

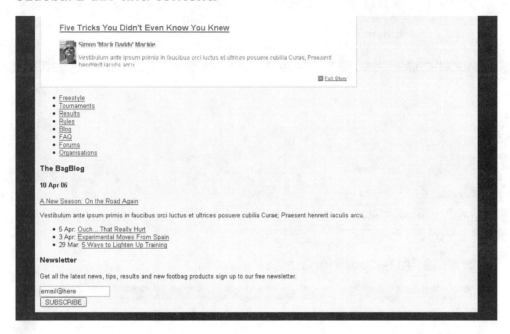

Positioning the Sidebar

We can now use CSS to position this sidebar and style its contents. Using the CSS file for the two-column layout as a starting point, find the rules for #content. Our first task is to create some space into which we can drop the sidebar.

Check your Sidebar's Location

At the end of the last chapter, we showed how easy it was to move a column that was on the right over to the left by changing only two CSS properties. However, the layout we're working toward here assumes that the sidebar sits to the right of the content, so you may need to move it back.

File: **styles.css (excerpt)**

```
#content {
  margin: 0 240px 0 160px;
  border: 1px solid #b9d2e3;
  background-color: white;
```

```
  color: black;
}
```

Change the value for the left margin from 0 to 160px, to create a 160-pixel left margin on the content.

Now, create a rule for #sidebar2 to position it within the 160 pixel margin to the left of the content area:

File: **styles.css (excerpt)**

```
#sidebar2 {
  position: absolute;
  top: 0;
  left: 0;
}
```

This will position the sidebar to the top and left of the relatively positioned div with the id main, as Figure 9.3 illustrates.

Figure 9.3. After positioning the sidebar2

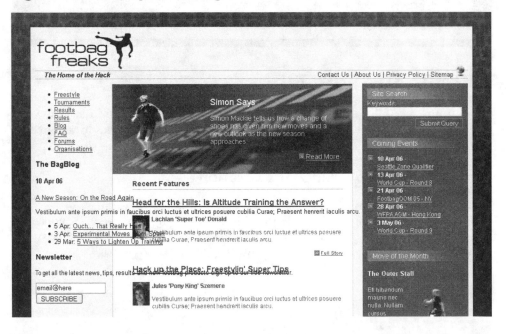

The content of sidebar2 now appears to overlap the content div, as you'd expect. All we're doing is placing the sidebars over a space created by content's margins.

If the sidebar is wider than that margin, it will continue to display over the top of the content div. To prevent this overlap, we give sidebar2 a width value:

File: **styles.css** (excerpt)

```
#sidebar2 {
  position: absolute;
  top: 0;
  left: 0;
  width: 159px;
  border-top: 1px solid #b9d2e3;
  border-left: 1px solid #b9d2e3;
  border-bottom: 1px solid #b9d2e3;
  background-color: white;
  color: black;
  margin: 0;
  padding: 0;
}
```

I have also started to style this sidebar, giving it top, left, and bottom borders, and a background color of white. Figure 9.4 shows our progress so far.

Figure 9.4. Giving `sidebar2` a width so that it doesn't overlap the content

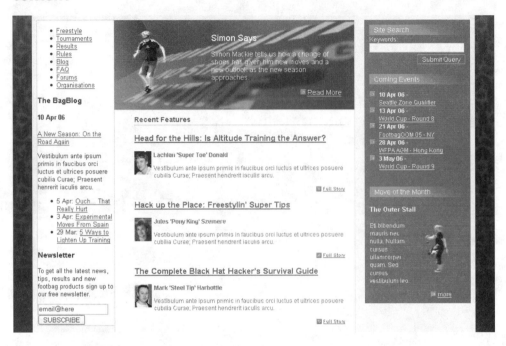

We can now style the individual elements within `sidebar2`.

File: **styles.css (excerpt)**

```
#sidebar2 .inner {
  margin:  10px;
}
```

`#sidebar2 .inner` selects the wrapper around the sidebar contents (those that have a class of `inner`) and applies a ten-pixel margin between the contents of the sidebar and its border.

File: **styles.css (excerpt)**

```
#sidebar2 p {
  font-size: 90%;
  color: #666666;
}
#sidebar2 a:link, #sidebar2 a:visited {
  color: #245185;
```

```
    font-weight: bold;
}
```

Let's also create rules for the paragraphs within `sidebar2`, setting the text to 90% and a dark gray color. We can also set the links within the `sidebar2 div` to be blue and bold.

File: **styles.css (excerpt)**

```
#sidebar2 h3 {
  color: #245185;
  padding-bottom: 0.2em;
  border-bottom: 1px solid #b9d2e3;
  font-size:  110%;
}
```

The headings for the blog and newsletter are marked up as level three headings, so we make these blue and give them a bottom border so that they look similar to the text in these areas of the design. Figure 9.5 shows how these styles display.

Figure 9.5. After the text elements are styled

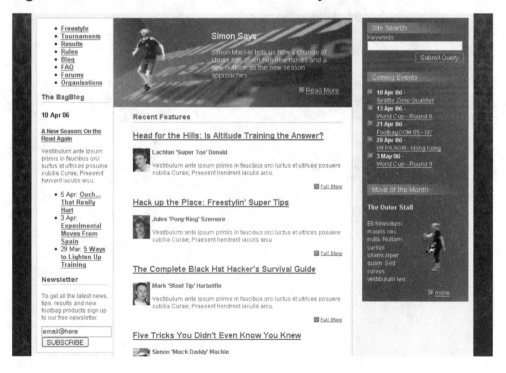

The Navigation

At the top of this sidebar is a list that contains navigation items. Let's add some specific rules to style these list items to fit with our design.

Set the list style to `none` to remove the bullets, then set `margin` and `padding` to 0 to line the list up with the paragraph text:

File: **styles.css (excerpt)**

```
#nav {
  list-style: none;
  margin: 0;
  padding:  0;
}
```

We'll also add a bottom border to each list item, and apply padding to create space between the items (and between each item and its border):

File: **styles.css (excerpt)**

```
#nav li {
  border-bottom: 1px solid #b9d2e3;
  padding: 0.4em 0 0.2em 0;
  font-size:  90%;
}
```

Finally, we can style the links, removing the underline from each, and setting its weight to `normal` (previously, we set all links in `sidebar2` to display in bold). The results of this work are depicted in Figure 9.6.

File: **styles.css (excerpt)**

```
#nav li a:link, #nav li a:visited {
  text-decoration: none;
  color: #245185;
  font-weight: normal;
}
```

Figure 9.6. Styling the navigation

The Blog

Next, we have the blog section of the page. This area contains a featured item, which we've wrapped in a `div` with an `id` of `bloglatest`, and a list of the three most recently posted blog items. These listings would link through to the full blog entries on the completed site.

To style the date on the featured blog entry, we need to style the `h4` within the `div` `bloglatest` to make it orange:

File: **styles.css** (excerpt)

```
#bloglatest h4 {
  color: #ff4e00;
  font-size: 100%;
  font-weight: bold;
}
```

On our list of blog entries, let's set `margin` to `0` and `padding` to 20 pixels. We'll also set the list bullets to use the `more-bullet.gif` image that we used elsewhere in the layout:

```
#blog {
  margin: 0;
  padding: 0 0 0 20px;
  list-style: url(img/more-bullet.gif);
}
```

Finally, we'll style the list items. For each item, the date displays in orange; the link to the article appears in blue next to it. As we've already styled links to display in blue font, we can make the entire list item appear in orange: the links will still be blue. Figure 9.7 shows the finished display.

File: **styles.css** (excerpt)

```
#blog li {
  font-size: 90%;
  padding-bottom: 0.5em;
  color: #ff4e00;
  font-weight: bold;
}
```

Figure 9.7. The blog section of `sidebar2`

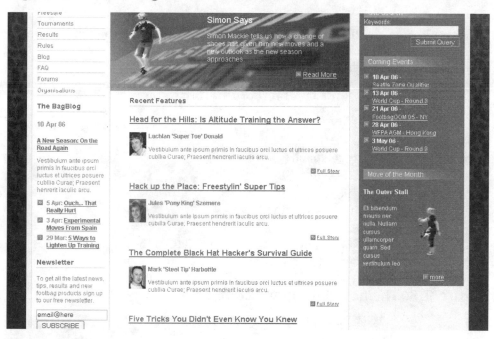

The Newsletter

The newsletter subscription form is the very last thing we need to consider in this layout. First, let's create a rule to address the text field.

Style the text field: create a rule with the selector `#newsletterform .text`, then set the text field's `width` to prevent it from spilling out of the sidebar into the content area:

File: **styles.css (excerpt)**

```
#newsletterform .text {
  width: 135px;
  border: 1px solid #45bac0;
}
```

Next, add a rule for `#newsletterform .searchbutton`:

File: **styles.css (excerpt)**

```
#newsletterform .searchbutton {
  text-align: right;
```

```
    margin-top: 4px;
}
```

Here, we create a rule that will be applied to the `div` that wraps the submit button. This rule aligns the button to the right; we need to align the content of the button's parent to the right to achieve this.

Finally, let's add a rule for `#newsletterform .btn` to the style sheet:

File: **styles.css** (excerpt)

```
#newsletterform .btn {
  border: 1px solid #45bac0;
  background-color: #256290;
  color: white;
  font-size: 80%;
}
```

These rules style the submit button, and are similar to those we created for the search form in the other sidebar. Figure 9.8 shows our progress.

Figure 9.8. The newsletter subscription form

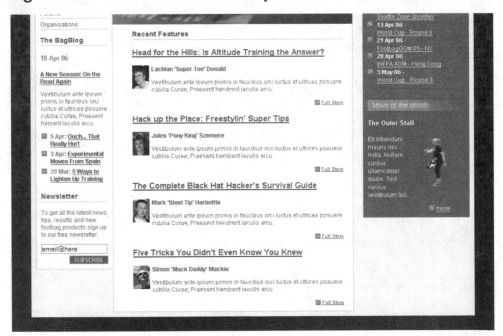

Great work! We've completed a three-column layout that displays in Internet Explorer 6 as illustrated in Figure 9.9. I tend to develop CSS layouts using Firefox—one of the more standards-compliant browsers—then check that my design displays as expected in Internet Explorer. But as you can see, this layout is relatively simple, and holds together well in IE6.

Figure 9.9. The completed three-column layout in IE 6 on Windows

This layout is a great choice for projects for which you need a basic three-column layout with, or without, a header area. Absolute positioning provides good control over the widths of the different columns, and makes it relatively easy to get consistent results across browsers. However, there are times when this layout isn't the best choice. In the next section, we'll take a look at the most common problem designers experience with three-column layouts.

Adding a Footer

The layout we've created works really well … until you want to add a footer that spans all three columns, that is. This variation on our layout is shown in the mock-up in Figure 9.10.

If your center column is the longest of all three, then at first glance, adding the footer seems pretty easy. To demonstrate, let's add the following markup just before the closing `</div>` tag of the wrapper div.

File: **index.html (excerpt)**

```
    </div> <!-- main -->
    <div id="footer">
      <p>Copyright 2006 - All Rights Reserved</p>
    </div> <!-- footer -->
  </div> <!-- wrapper -->
  </body>
</html>
```

Add the following rules to your style sheet, to style the footer to match our design:

File: **styles.css (excerpt)**

```
#footer {
  width: 100%;
  border-top: 1px solid #b9d2e3;
  border-bottom: 1px solid #b9d2e3;
  margin-top: 10px;
}
#footer p {
  font-size: 90%;
  color: #256290;
  margin: 0;
  padding: 0.2em 0 0.2em 0;
}
```

So what's the problem? As Figure 9.11 illustrates, the layout seems to work fine in the browser!

Figure 9.10. The three-column layout with a footer

Figure 9.11. Adding a footer to the layout

Don't be fooled: there *is* a problem here. To see it in action, remove a couple of the articles from the content area so that that part of the page is shorter than the sidebars. Reload the page in the browser, and you'll see that the footer has moved up the page to sit at the bottom of the main content area. But as Figure 9.12 shows, the sidebars now run over the top of our footer. Whoops!

Figure 9.12. The sidebars overlapping the footer

The footer appears beneath the sidebars because the sidebars are absolutely positioned, so they're outside of the **flow** of the document—that is, the sidebars don't appear immediately below the previous element as they would if they weren't positioned. The content is not positioned, so the footer naturally displays underneath the content and the sidebars continue to display where they've been placed, regardless of any other parts of the document. Once you've taken a page element out of the document flow using `position: absolute`, that element will display in complete disregard of other page elements: it will simply overlap them if they're in its way.

When you create a site, you can't be certain that one column will always display longer than another. If you want to use a footer as part of your layout, you'll need to take a different approach. However, before we can look at this new approach, we'll need to know a bit more about the `float` property.

The `float` Property

We discussed `float` briefly in the last chapter, where we used it to position elements in the page header, and float images so that text would wrap around them. In the next example, we'll use `float` to create a multi-column layout. But before we dive into rebuilding our layout using `float`, let's look at a simple example that will give us a more thorough understanding of how this property works.

The document we'll use for this example, replicated below, contains the same areas that we'll include in the project site's layout.

File: **floatexample.html**

```
<!DOCTYPE html PUBLIC "-//W3C//DTD XHTML 1.0 Strict//EN"
    "http://www.w3.org/TR/xhtml1/DTD/xhtml1-strict.dtd">
<html xmlns="http://www.w3.org/1999/xhtml">
  <head>
    <meta http-equiv="Content-Type"
        content="text/html; charset=iso-8859-1" />
    <link rel="stylesheet" type="text/css"
        href="floatexample.css" />
    <title>Floated column example</title>
  </head>
  <body>
    <div id="wrapper">
      <div id="header">
        <p>Header</p>
      </div>
      <div id="main">
        <div id="sidebar">
          <p>First Sidebar</p>
        </div>
        <div id="sidebar2">
          <p>Second Sidebar</p>
        </div>
        <div id="content">
          <p>Content</p>
        </div>
      </div>
      <div id="footer">
        <p>Footer</p>
      </div>
    </div>
  </body>
</html>
```

The first thing you might notice about this document is that the order of the divs differs from the order we used in our positioned layout: here, the two sidebar divs appear before the content div. However, all of the sections of the page are included here. Before we apply any CSS, let's see how this document displays in the browser: Figure 9.13 illustrates.

Figure 9.13. Displaying the example file with no style sheet attached

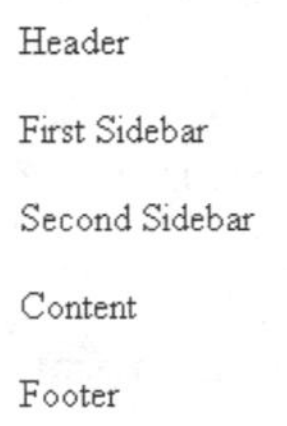

Header

First Sidebar

Second Sidebar

Content

Footer

Now let's create the style sheet `floatexample.css`, and add the following rules to it:

File: **`floatexample.css`**

```
body {
  margin: 0;
  padding: 0;
  font: small Helvetica, Arial, sans-serif;
}
#header {
  margin: 0;
  padding: 0;
}
#main {
  margin-top: 10px;
}
#sidebar {
  float: right;
  width: 220px;
  border: 1px solid black;
  background-color: #dddddd;
}
#sidebar2 {
  float: left;
  width: 159px;
  border: 1px solid green;
```

```
  background-color: #99ff99;
}
#content {
  border: 1px solid blue;
  background-color: #9999ff;
  margin: 0 240px 0 160px;
}
#footer {
  clear: both;
  border: 1px solid red;
  background-color: #ff9999;
}
```

Once you apply this style sheet, the page should display with three bordered columns, a header, and a footer, as shown in Figure 9.14.

Figure 9.14. Displaying the page after the style sheet is added

As you can see, this display reflects the main constituents of our project site's layout: a header, two sidebars, a liquid content area that expands and contracts depending on the width of the browser window, and a footer. Insert additional content into any of these columns, and you'll note that the footer always stays below all three columns, as Figure 9.15 shows. In fact, it's always located at the bottom of the longest column.

Figure 9.15. It doesn't matter how much text is in a column—the footer stays beneath all three

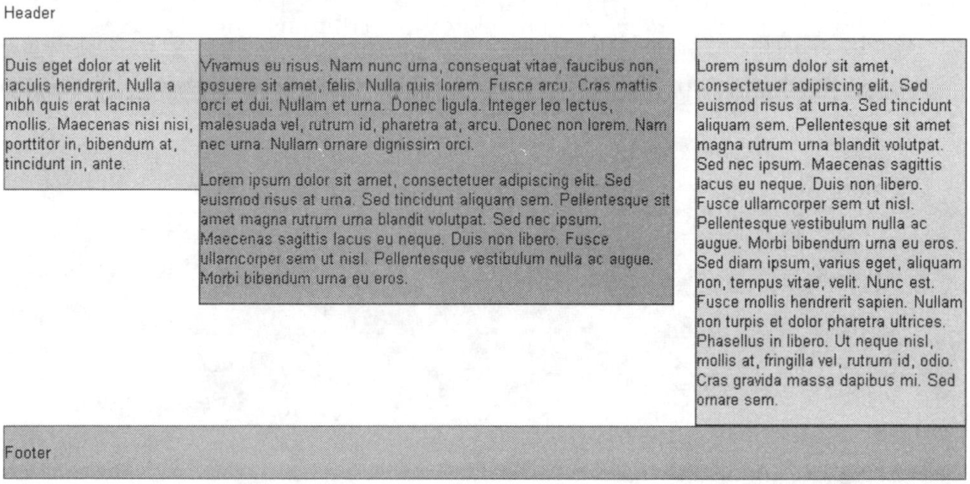

Header

Duis eget dolor at velit iaculis hendrerit. Nulla a nibh quis erat lacinia mollis. Maecenas nisi nisi, porttitor in, bibendum at, tincidunt in, ante.	Vivamus eu risus. Nam nunc urna, consequat vitae, faucibus non, posuere sit amet, felis. Nulla quis lorem. Fusce arcu. Cras mattis orci et dui. Nullam et urna. Donec ligula. Integer leo lectus, malesuada vel, rutrum id, pharetra at, arcu. Donec non lorem. Nam nec urna. Nullam ornare dignissim orci. Lorem ipsum dolor sit amet, consectetuer adipiscing elit. Sed euismod risus at urna. Sed tincidunt aliquam sem. Pellentesque sit amet magna rutrum urna blandit volutpat. Sed nec ipsum. Maecenas sagittis lacus eu neque. Duis non libero. Fusce ullamcorper sem ut nisl. Pellentesque vestibulum nulla ac augue. Morbi bibendum urna eu eros.	Lorem ipsum dolor sit amet, consectetuer adipiscing elit. Sed euismod risus at urna. Sed tincidunt aliquam sem. Pellentesque sit amet magna rutrum urna blandit volutpat. Sed nec ipsum. Maecenas sagittis lacus eu neque. Duis non libero. Fusce ullamcorper sem ut nisl. Pellentesque vestibulum nulla ac augue. Morbi bibendum urna eu eros. Sed diam ipsum, varius eget, aliquam non, tempus vitae, velit. Nunc est. Fusce mollis hendrerit sapien. Nullam non turpis et dolor pharetra ultrices. Phasellus in libero. Ut neque nisl, mollis at, fringilla vel, rutrum id, odio. Cras gravida massa dapibus mi. Sed ornare sem.

Footer

How Does it Work?

When we discussed `float` in the last chapter, I explained that it causes the floated content to move outside of its natural position in the containing box; non-floated content that's also in the box will wrap around the floated content.

In our layout, the two sidebars are floated to the left and right of the content area, which effectively wraps around the two columns. In this instance, we don't want the content to appear to wrap around the sidebars, so we keep wide margins on the content `div`, making it run down the center of the page even if the columns are shorter than the content.

The final piece of the puzzle is the use of the `clear` property on the footer `div`, which causes the footer always to display below the content and sidebars, without overlapping any parts of the layout. As we saw in the last chapter, `clear` can have a value of `left`, `right`, or `both`. Applying the `clear: both` declaration to the footer will clear the left- and right-hand sidebars. The footer will naturally clear the content `div`, as it's still within the flow of the document.

Putting `float` into Practice in our Layout

Having looked at a simple example of how `float` works to create a multi-column layout, we can adapt our layout to display three columns using `float`.

First, we need to adapt the document to place the sidebar sections above the main content section.

File: **`index.html`** (excerpt)

```
<body>
  <div id="wrapper">
    <div id="header">
      ⋮
    </div> <!-- header -->
    <div id="main">
      <div id="sidebar">
        ⋮
      </div> <!-- sidebar -->
      <div id="sidebar2">
        ⋮
      </div> <!-- sidebar2 -->
      <div id="content">
        ⋮
      </div> <!-- content -->
    </div> <!-- main -->
    <div id="footer">
      <p>Copyright 2006 - All Rights Reserved</p>
    </div> <!-- footer -->
  </div> <!-- wrapper -->
</body>
```

Let's take the `floatexample.css` file used in the example above as a starting point, and simply copy and paste the rest of our rules into it. First, we'll identify the declarations that are used to position the parts of the page.

File: **`floatexample.css`** (excerpt)

```
#sidebar {
  float: right;
  width: 220px;
  border: 1px solid black;
  background-color: #dddddd;
}
#sidebar2 {
  float: left;
```

```
  width: 159px;
  border: 1px solid green;
  background-color: #99ff99;
}
    ⋮
#footer {
  clear: both;
  border: 1px solid red;
  background-color: #ff9999;
}
```

Next, we replace the existing positioning declarations in styles.css (the position, top, left, and right properties) with the float and clear declarations.

File: **styles.css (excerpt)**

```
#sidebar {
  float: right;
  width: 220px;
  background-color: #256290;
  margin: 0;
  padding: 0;
  color:  white;
}
```

File: **styles.css (excerpt)**

```
#sidebar2 {
  float: left;
  width: 159px;
  border-top: 1px solid #b9d2e3;
  border-left: 1px solid #b9d2e3;
  border-bottom: 1px solid #b9d2e3;
  background-color: white;
  color: black;
  margin: 0;
  padding: 0;
}
```

File: **styles.css (excerpt)**

```
#footer {
  width: 100%;
  border-top: 1px solid #b9d2e3;
  border-bottom: 1px solid #b9d2e3;
  margin-top: 10px;
```

```
    clear: both;
}
```

Finally, remove the position, top, and left declarations from the #main rule. Remember that the position: relative declaration was used to set the positioning context for the sidebar—we can remove it now that the sidebars aren't making use of it.

File: **styles.css (excerpt)**

```
#main {
  margin-top: 10px;
  width: 100%;
}
```

You'll now be able to see how these adjustments have moved the different portions of our page into the correct locations. Figure 9.16 shows how our page looks now.

Figure 9.16. After using `float` to lay out the columns

You should finish up with a layout that looks the same as our original, absolutely positioned layout. However, whether you increase the amount of content in the sidebars, or decrease the amount of content in the center column, the footer will always display below all three columns. Figure 9.17 shows the page display in IE.

Figure 9.17. The floated layout in Internet Explorer 6

Achieving Full-height Columns

The layout above doesn't quite get us to the point identified by the original page mockup, in which all of the columns were the same length regardless of the amount of content each contained. With some layouts, that won't be a problem, but if full-length columns are your goal, here's a method that will let you achieve it.

To create this effect, we need to "fake" the appearance of full-length columns using background images. The technique, popularized by Dan Cederholm's article "Faux Columns,[1]" basically relies on applying background images to `div`s in your document, to create the appearance of columns. We'll be applying this technique twice: once to the `div` with `id="main"`, to simulate the right column, and once to a new `div` just inside the main `div`, to simulate the left column.

Create a background image that contains the blue of the right-hand sidebar, plus a stripe of the cream background color and the single-pixel light-blue line, as shown in Figure 9.18.

Figure 9.18. The background image containing our faux columns for the layout's right-hand side

In the CSS, find the `#main` selector and add this image to it as a background image. Make sure the image repeats vertically by setting the `background-repeat` property to `repeat-y`. To ensure that it sticks to the right-hand side of the area, add the `background-position: top right` declaration.

```
#main {
  margin-top: 10px;
  width: 100%;
  background-image: url(img/sidebarbg.gif);
  background-position: top right;
  background-repeat: repeat-y;
}
```

Next, we need to ensure that the `div` with `id="main"` is the full height of the tallest of our three columns, as our background is applied to this `div`. Currently, the `div` is only guaranteed to be as tall as our content `div`—the floated sidebars have no bearing on its height, as is illustrated in Figure 9.19.

---

[1] http://www.alistapart.com/articles/fauxcolumns/

Figure 9.19. The floated element has no effect on its parent's height

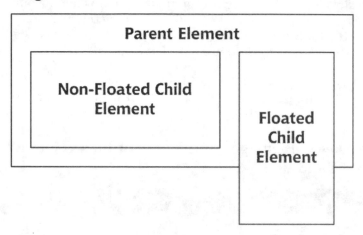

We can get around this issue by adding an empty div, to which clear: both is applied, just before we close our id="main" div. This empty div will appear below all of our columns, just like the footer div. But, as it's inside our id="main" div, it will ensure that this div is as tall as our tallest column, as Figure 9.20 illustrates.

Figure 9.20. Adding a clearing element to extend the parent element's height

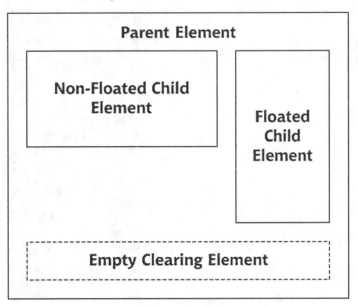

To create this effect, add the following to `index.html`:

File: **index.html (excerpt)**

```
  </div> <!-- content -->
  <div id="clearone"> </div>
</div> <!-- main -->
```

Add the following rule to your style sheet:

File: **styles.css (excerpt)**

```
#clearone {
  clear: both;
  height: 1px;
}
```

If you view the page in your browser now, you'll see that the right-hand column stretches down to the same level as the bottom of the longest column. The effect is depicted in Figure 9.21.

Figure 9.21. After adding the background image to create the right-hand column

For our left column, we'll need to add another `div` to which we can apply our background. Add a `div` with `id="main2"`, as shown below:

File: **index.html** (excerpt)

```
<div id="main">
  <div id="main2">
    <div id="sidebar">
      ⋮
    <div id="clearone"> </div>
  </div> <!-- main2 -->
</div> <!-- main -->
```

Create another image, this time for the left column. It will be 161 pixels wide and four pixels tall, and will have a one-pixel, light-blue line down both its left- and right-hand edges.

Now, create the rule `#main2`, applying our new image as the background image. Position it bottom and left, and make the background color of this area white.

File: **styles.css** (excerpt)

```
#main2 {
  background-image: url(img/leftbg.gif);
  background-position: bottom left;
  background-repeat: repeat-y;
}
```

If you view this page now, you'll see that our full-length faux columns are almost complete, as Figure 9.22 shows. However, the bottom of each of the columns needs a little tidying up.

Figure 9.22. Our faux columns are almost complete

Edit the style sheet to remove the content div's bottom border by replacing the border property with border-top, border-right, and border-left declarations:

File: **styles.css** (excerpt)

```
#content {
  margin: 0 240px 0 160px;
  border-top: 1px solid #b9d2e3;
  border-right: 1px solid #b9d2e3;
```

```
  border-left: 1px solid #b9d2e3;
  background-color: white;
  color: black;
}
```

Also remove the border from the bottom of the left-hand sidebar by removing the `border-bottom` declaration from the `#sidebar2` rule:

File: **styles.css (excerpt)**

```
#sidebar2 {
  float: left;
  width: 159px;
  border-top: 1px solid #b9d2e3;
  border-left: 1px solid #b9d2e3;
  background-color: white;
  color: black;
  margin: 0;
  padding: 0;
}
```

If you view your layout in the browser, you should find that your columns appear to run the full length of the screen, as shown in Figure 9.23.

Figure 9.23. Full-length columns

Admittedly, this effect does require some fiddling around in your graphics program to prepare the background images so that they line up. However, once you've created your images, the effect works very well.

The Content Order Problem

The floated layout we created above looks fantastic. However, the absolutely positioned layout does have one point in its favor: in the markup for the absolutely positioned version of our page, the columns can appear in any order we like. This might not seem important to you, but it's important to those who use browsers that don't support CSS, and users of screen readers. If we use the floated layout, these people will have to wade through all of the content of the sidebars before they get to the page's main content, which sits at the bottom of our markup.

The effect is more marked if you remove the style sheet so that you can see the markup for the content sections in order. Comment out the link to your style sheet and reload the page: you'll be able to see how much "junk" content occurs before the main page content (Figure 9.24 illustrates). Now imagine that your site displayed the same sidebar content on every page—it would be pretty tiresome for site users to have to listen to a screen reader read out that same content for every page of your site they visited!

Figure 9.24. Displaying the page without a style sheet

One solution to this problem is to implement a "skip navigation" link. This link enables the user to skip over repeated or unimportant content in order to get to the real meat of the page. To effect this solution, we simply link to an `id` that's located at the top of the page's important content.

To see this technique in action, add a link to the navigation list in the page's header:

File: **index.html (excerpt)**

```
<ul>
  <li><a href="">Contact Us</a> | </li>
  <li><a href="">About Us</a> | </li>
  <li><a href="">Privacy Policy</a> | </li>
  <li><a href="">Sitemap</a> | </li>
  <li><a href="#content">Jump to content</a></li>
</ul>
```

Load the page in your browser and click the link, as shown in Figure 9.25. The page will jump down a little, so that the top of the content `div` is as close as possible to the top of the viewport.

Anchors Away

You might be used to achieving this effect using an `<a>` tag with a `name` attribute, but modern browsers now support linking directly to an element's `id`, which spares you having to insert additional and otherwise useless anchor elements.

Figure 9.25. Clicking the link enables users to skip easily to the main content

Simon Says

Simon Mackie tells us how a change of shoes has given him new moves and a new outlook as the new season approaches.

Read More

Recent Features

- **Head for the Hills: Is Altitude Training the Answer?**

  Lachlan 'Super Toe' Donald

  Vestibulum ante ipsum primis in faucibus orci luctus et ultrices posuere cubilia Curae; Praesent hendrerit iaculis arcu.

  Full Story

- **Hack up the Place: Freestylin' Super Tips**

  Jules 'Pony King' Szemere

  Vestibulum ante ipsum primis in faucibus orci luctus et ultrices posuere cubilia Curae; Praesent hendrerit iaculis arcu.

  Full Story

- **The Complete Black Hat Hacker's Survival Guide**

These links aren't particularly useful for visitors who don't use screen readers or text-only browsers, though, and various methods have been devised to hide these links so they're available only via screen readers and browsers that don't support CSS. Unfortunately, due to the way that some screen readers interpret CSS and JavaScript, these methods can be problematic. So, for optimum accessibility, it's recommended that you keep the link visible and locate it somewhere near the top of the content. Some site owners, such as Molly Holzschlag,[2] have devised ways of partially hiding the links. On Molly's site, pictured in Figure 9.26, the link doesn't appear until you hover your mouse over the area at the top of the screen.

---

[2] http://www.molly.com/

Figure 9.26. The "skip to content" link on molly.com

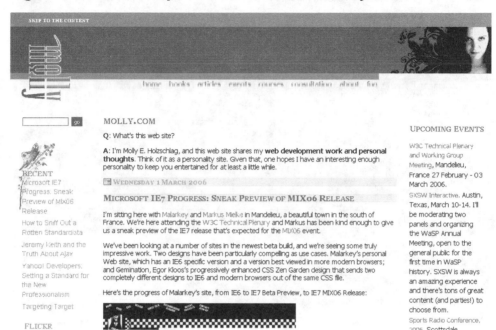

Other Layout Methods

There are other methods of creating multiple-column layouts with a footer that can allow you to order your source code more usefully. However, these techniques tend to entail other compromises. For example, the Source Ordered Columns example on Position is Everything,[3] pictured in Figure 9.27, offers one alternative layout method. The compromise is that all of the columns need to be liquid: they must be set with percentage widths, rather than set with fixed widths that use pixel values.

---

[3] http://positioniseverything.net/ordered-floats.html

Figure 9.27. Source ordered columns on Position is Everything

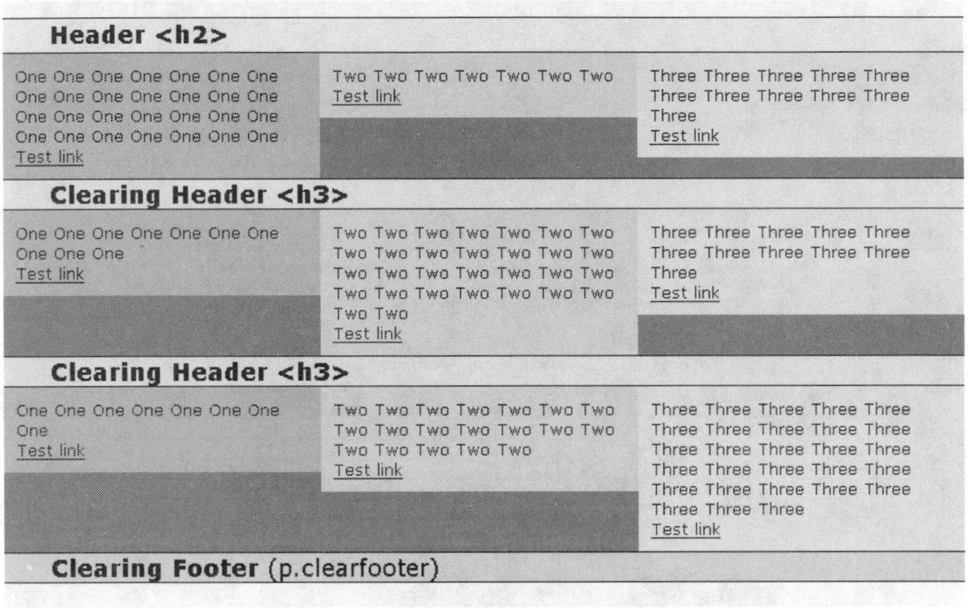

Position is Everything is an excellent source of demos and new ideas for creating CSS layouts. The site also offers an article called "In Search of the One True Layout",[4] which provides an example of a three-column layout with a footer that behaves as required for the example above. However, it uses some complex techniques and many browser hacks. As you continue to work with CSS and develop your confidence with this technology, these examples can be invaluable in helping you to solve problems, but they're also fun to experiment with in your spare time.

Summary

In this chapter, we learned how to change an existing layout by adding another column. Then, we added a footer to our layout and experienced first-hand the problems footers can cause within an absolutely positioned layout. By recreating the same layout from a slightly different starting point, we overcame these problems and produced a layout that positioned elements in a very different way—without needing to redevelop our style sheet from the ground up!

---

[4] http://positioniseverything.net/articles/onetruelayout/

No doubt, you've already realized that there's no single, ideal way to address the problems posed by CSS layouts. Whenever you tackle a new design, you'll need to make a decision as to which type of layout best suits your needs. However, as we saw in this chapter, in most cases it's not too difficult to change your mind later, and switch to a different layout method if you need to.

In the next chapter, we'll look at another type of layout—the fixed-width layout—and consider some of the ways in which we can create these types of layouts. Of course, we'll also address the issues that you're likely to encounter as you do so.

10 Fixed-width Layouts

In the last two chapters, we've been creating layouts that we call **liquid layouts**—those that stretch to fit the size of the user's browser window. This approach gives the user control over the size at which they view the design, as it allows them to resize their window. The other type of layout you may wish to build is a **fixed-width layout**. In this type of layout, we fix the width of the content area to a measurement that will allow the user to avoid scrolling horizontally on most screens.

In this chapter, we'll create a fixed-width layout that's centered in the user's browser window. Along the way, we'll look at a few techniques that we can use to style tables of data effectively, and we'll discuss a method by which you can enable your site visitors to use a different layout if they find your fixed-width layout difficult to read.

The Layout

Figure 10.1. A mockup of the fixed-width layout

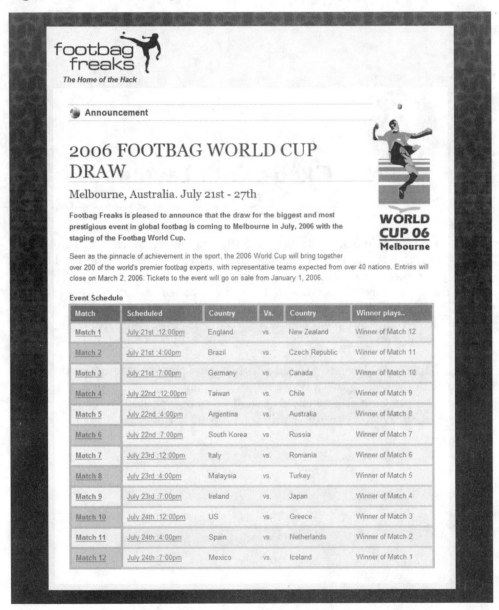

We will start, as in the last chapters, with a mockup that our designer has created in Fireworks; this is presented in Figure 10.1. As you can see, this layout doesn't have a great deal of content. If the table was stretched to the full width of the page, it might look a little sparse and be difficult to read in a wide browser window. This is a situation where we might choose to use a fixed-width layout.

Creating the Document

Once again, create an XHTML or HTML document and save it as `fixed-width.html`. Ensure that all of the content in the document is marked up correctly, then submit it to the W3C validator so you can be certain that the file doesn't contain any markup errors that will create problems when you start to add CSS.

A Tabular Layout

Although we discourage using tables for page layout purposes, remember that using tables is perfectly valid—in fact, it's recommended—for the display of tabular data such as might be stored in a spreadsheet. The match schedule shown in Figure 10.1 is tabular data, so a table is the best way to mark it up.

File: **fixedwidth.html (excerpt)**

```
<!DOCTYPE html PUBLIC "-//W3C//DTD XHTML 1.0 Strict//EN"
    "http://www.w3.org/TR/xhtml1/DTD/xhtml1-strict.dtd">
<html xmlns="http://www.w3.org/1999/xhtml">
  <head>
    <title>Footbag Freaks</title>
    <meta http-equiv="Content-Type"
        content="text/html; charset=iso-8859-1" />
    <link rel="stylesheet" type="text/css"
        href="fixedwidth.css" />
  </head>
  <body>
    <div id="header">
      <img src="img/logo.gif" alt="Footbag Freaks" height="77"
          width="203" />
      <p>The Home of the Hack</p>
    </div> <!-- header -->
    <div id="content">
      <img src="img/player.gif" height="272" width="111"
          alt="World Cup 06 Melbourne" />
      <h1>Announcement</h1>
      <h2>2006 FOOTBAG WORLD CUP DRAW</h2>
      <p>Melbourne, Australia. July 21st - 27th</p>
```

```
      <p>Footbag Freaks is pleased to announce that the draw for
          the biggest and most prestigious event in global footbag
          is coming to Melbourne in July, 2006 with the staging of
          the Footbag World Cup.</p>
      <p>Seen as the pinnacle of achievement in the sport, the
          2006 World Cup will bring together over 200 of the
          world's premier footbag experts, with representative
          teams expected from over 40 nations. Entries will close
          on March 2, 2006. Tickets to the event will go on sale
          from January 1, 2006.</p>
      <table class="schedule" summary="Schedule of matches for the
          Footbag 2006 World Cup">
        <caption>Event Schedule</caption>
        <thead>
          <tr>
            <th scope="col">Match</th>
            <th scope="col">Scheduled</th>
            <th scope="col">Country</th>
            <th scope="col">Vs.</th>
            <th scope="col">Country</th>
            <th scope="col">Winner plays..</th>
          </tr>
        </thead>
        <tbody>
          <tr>
            <th scope="row"><a href="#">Match 1</a></th>
            <td><a href="#">July 21st :12:00pm</a></td>
            <td>England</td>
            <td>vs.</td>
            <td>New Zealand</td>
            <td>Winner of Match 12</td>
          </tr>
          <tr>
            :
            <th scope="row"><a href="#">Match 12</a></th>
            <td><a href="#">July 24th :7:00pm</a></td>
            <td>Mexico</td>
            <td>vs.</td>
            <td>Iceland</td>
            <td>Winner of Match 1</td>
          </tr>
        </tbody>
      </table>
    </div> <!-- content -->
  </body>
</html>
```

Pay special attention to the table's markup. This table has headings along its top and down its left-hand side (the title of each match). These headings are marked up using the th element, while the rest of the cells are marked up using td. We also use the scope attribute on the headings to explain whether the heading describes a column (scope="col") or a row (scope="row"). The heading area of the table is wrapped in a thead element and the body in a tbody element. These attributes are useful for describing the table correctly, but they'll also come in very handy when we come to apply CSS to the page.

I've added two divs to the document: one is wrapped around the header area with the ID header, while the other is wrapped around the content whose ID is content. Figure 10.2 shows how this unstyled layout displays in the browser.

Figure 10.2. The document before any CSS is applied

The Home of the Hack

Announcement

2006 FOOTBAG WORLD CUP DRAW

Melbourne, Australia. July 21st - 27th

Footbag Freaks is pleased to announce that the draw for the biggest and most prestigious event in global footbag is coming to Melbourne in July, 2006 with the staging of the Footbag World Cup.

Seen as the pinnacle of achievement in the sport, the 2006 World Cup will bring together over 200 of the world's premier footbag experts, with representative teams expected from over 40 nations. Entries will close on March 2, 2006. Tickets to the event will go on sale from January 1, 2006.

Event Schedule

Match	Scheduled	Country	Vs.	Country	Winner plays..
Match 1	July 21st :12:00pm	England	vs.	New Zealand	Winner of Match 12
Match 2	July 21st :4:00pm	Brazil	vs.	Czech Republic	Winner of Match 11
Match 3	July 21st :7:00pm	Germany	vs.	Canada	Winner of Match 10
Match 4	July 22nd :12:00pm	Taiwan	vs.	Chile	Winner of Match 9
Match 5	July 22nd :4:00pm	Argentina	vs.	Australia	Winner of Match 8
Match 6	July 22nd :7:00pm	South Korea	vs.	Russia	Winner of Match 7
Match 7	July 23rd :12:00pm	Italy	vs.	Romania	Winner of Match 6
Match 8	July 23rd :4:00pm	Malaysia	vs.	Turkey	Winner of Match 5
Match 9	July 23rd :7:00pm	Ireland	vs.	Japan	Winner of Match 4
Match 10	July 24th :12:00pm	US	vs.	Greece	Winner of Match 3
Match 11	July 24th :4:00pm	Spain	vs.	Netherlands	Winner of Match 2
Match 12	July 24th :7:00pm	Mexico	vs.	Iceland	Winner of Match 1

Centering the Content Area

The first thing we'll do is center the layout and set its width. We need to insert an additional `div` that wraps the entirety of the document's content, so open this new `div` after the opening `<body>` tag and close it before the closing `</body>`. Give this `div` an ID of `wrapper`.

File: **fixedwidth.html** (excerpt)

```
<body>
  <div id="wrapper">
    <div id="header">
    ⋮
    </div> <!-- content -->
  </div> <!-- wrapper -->
</body>
```

Now, create an external style sheet named `fixedwidth.css` and add the following rules to it:

File: **fixedwidth.css** (excerpt)

```
body {
  margin: 0;
  padding: 0;
  text-align: center;
  min-width: 740px;
}
#wrapper {
  text-align: left;
  width: 740px;
  margin-left: auto;
  margin-right: auto;
}
```

This is all that you need to fix the page's width and center its content. Let's step through these rules.

The first rule affects the `body` element. It sets the `margin` and `padding` to `0`, and the `min-width` of the layout to 740 pixels. It also sets the `text-align` property to `center`.

We then add a rule for the new wrapper `div` that we just inserted into our document. Here, we set the right and left margins to `auto` and the width to 740 pixels. The width value in both rules should be changed to reflect the width of your layout. 740 pixels is a good width in that it will allow some of the background to show through even if users' monitors are set to a resolution of 800×600 pixels.

If you view your document in a browser you should see that the content is centered in the browser window, and is 740 pixels wide.

Let's add some more declarations to the `body` rule to insert the background image and color that appears in our design mockup.

File: **fixedwidth.css (excerpt)**

```
body {
  margin: 0;
  padding: 0;
  text-align: center;
  min-width: 740px;
  background-color: #050845;
  color: white;
  background-image: url(img/bg.jpg);
  background-repeat: repeat-x;
  font: small Arial, Helvetica, Verdana, sans-serif;
}
```

With this markup, we add a background color and image, as we did for our liquid layouts. We also set the text to display in a small sans-serif font.

Currently, the background image will display across the whole page. Let's use the wrapper `div` to set the content area to display a lighter, more readable background color, and have the background color display only around the content's edges.

File: **fixedwidth.css (excerpt)**

```
#wrapper {
  text-align: left;
  width: 740px;
  margin-left: auto;
  margin-right: auto;
  background-color: #fdf8f2;
  color: #01407a;
  padding: 10px;
}
```

In the markup above, I've also added ten pixels of padding in order to create some space between the edge of the wrapper `div` and the content. Figure 10.3 shows how the page looks now.

Figure 10.3. The design starting to take shape with the addition of a background image

The Header Area

The header area in this layout is very simple—it contains just the logo and tagline. The logo falls into its correct place by virtue of the natural flow of the document, so let's skip to styling the tagline beneath it using the following rule:

File: **fixedwidth.css** (excerpt)

```
#tagline {
  font-weight: bold;
  color: #050845;
  font-style: italic;
  margin: 0 0 0.5em 0;
  padding: 0 0 0 20px;
}
```

Note that you'll need to add id="tagline" to the tagline's opening <p> tag.

This markup sets the color to a deep blue, the font weight to bold, and its style to italic. We add a bottom margin to provide some space below the tagline and set left-hand padding to position it beneath the logo. Figure 10.4 shows the results of our work on the header.

Figure 10.4. The styled header

The Content

With the header complete, let's move on to style the content area of the page. This area is already wrapped in a `div` with an ID of `content`. If you refer to the design mockup, you'll see that this section has a white background. A darker border sets it out against the off-white background of the wrapper.

Let's begin by creating a CSS rule for `#content` by adding the following to the style sheet:

File: **fixedwidth.css (excerpt)**

```
#content {
  background-color: white;
  border: 1px solid #f0f0f0;
  padding: 0;
}
```

These rules should be fairly self-explanatory by now: we've given the `div` a white background and a border that's slightly darker than the background color of the wrapper. We've also set the padding to zero. Because we added padding of ten pixels to the wrapper, an area that's ten pixels wide shows the darker color around the `div` with `id="content"`—this is the effect that we are trying to reproduce from the design mockup.

Next, let's add some space between the content `div` and the border. We could try to remember to apply a margin to every element within this area, but it's simpler just to add a new `div` within the content `div` and give it a `class="inner"` attribute. We can then give `#content .inner` a 30-pixel margin to create that space.

File: **fixedwidth.css** (excerpt)

```
#content .inner {
  margin: 30px;
}
```

We can now start to look at the contents of the content `div`. The first thing we need to deal with is the World Cup '06 image that sits at the top of the content area. I inserted it there because I want to use `float` to position it to the right of the content.

Add the following rule for `#worldcuplogo`. It sets `float` to `right`, and specifies left and bottom margins for the logo, inserting space between it and the content that will wrap around it:

File: **fixedwidth.css** (excerpt)

```
#worldcuplogo {
  float: right;
  margin: 0 0 20px 40px;
}
```

Once we add `id="worldcuplogo"` to the image in our XHTML, the logo will display to the right of the layout, the content flowing around it as shown in Figure 10.5.

Figure 10.5. Floating the logo image

The layout is really taking shape now. With the addition of some very simple CSS, a few `divs`, and an `id`, we're coming close to replicating the mockup layout we started with. One of the things I enjoy about using CSS for layout is that it gives us the ability to put together simple pages that look attractive very quickly. When the need arises, you can create a news page or simple layout for an announcement like this one in a very short space of time.

The heading "Announcement" is an `h1` element. We can address it using a selector that addresses any `h1` elements that are contained within another element that has the ID `content`.

File: **fixedwidth.css (excerpt)**

```
#content h1 {
  font-size: 120%;
  color: #01407a;
  padding: 0.3em 0 0.3em 30px;
  background-image: url(img/ball.gif);
  background-repeat: no-repeat;
```

```
background-position: left center;
border-top: 1px solid #c5d6e2;
border-bottom: 1px solid #c5d6e2;
}
```

Here, we've added as a background image the ball image that displays to the left of the heading in our mockup. We want to display it just once—by default, it would tile beneath the heading—so we set `background-repeat` to `no-repeat`. We're also using the `background-position` property to push the image to the left and center it vertically.

To stop the heading from appearing on top of the image, we've added padding of 30 pixels to the left of the heading. The top and bottom padding values apply extra space between the heading and the borders. The current page display is shown in Figure 10.6.

Figure 10.6. The heading with the background image

We can now spend some time on the `h2` below the page header. The mockup indicates that this second-level heading should display in a larger font than the h1. The properties that we need to add to the `#content h2` rule in order to achieve this are fairly straightforward.

File: **fixedwidth.css** (excerpt)

```
#content h2 {
  font-size: 260%;
  font-weight: normal;
  font-family: Georgia, Times, "Times New Roman", serif;
  color: #032469;
  border-bottom: 1px solid #c5d6e2;
  margin: 1em 0 0 0;
}
```

We've specified a serif font for the second-level heading in an effort to match the font used in the mockup. The rest of the text content that appears before the Event Schedule table is marked up as paragraphs. The first thing I want to do is to add a bit more space between the lines of text within those paragraphs. We can do so with the help of the `line-height` property.

File: **fixedwidth.css** (excerpt)

```
#content p {
  line-height: 1.6em;
}
```

The text that appears directly below the `h2` identifies the dates to which the article is relevant. Add an `id="dateline"` attribute to this dateline's opening `<p>` tag, and create a CSS rule for it:

File: **fixedwidth.css** (excerpt)

```
#dateline {
  font-size: 160%;
  font-weight: normal;
  font-family: Georgia, Times, "Times New Roman", serif;
  color: #032469;
  margin: 0.3em 0 0 0;
}
```

The next paragraph of text displays in a bold font in the mockup. Let's add `class="intro"` to this text's opening `<p>` tag, then style that class to create the bold look:

File: **fixedwidth.css** (excerpt)

```
.intro {
  font-weight: bold;
}
```

Fantastic! We've styled all of the content on the page, with the exception of the Event Schedule table. We'll address that next, but first, let's take a moment to enjoy the fruits of our labors so far. View your work in a browser; the content area should look a lot like Figure 10.7.

Figure 10.7. The styled content area

The Table

The finalsection of this layout is the Events Schedule table that's used to display the information about the matches that will be played during the tournament. As we've already discussed, though tables should not be used for page design layouts, they are the ideal way to mark up tabular data, like the kind of information you might find displayed in a spreadsheet. We have a nice chunk of tabular data on this page, and we've already marked it up correctly using the various table elements to ensure that the content can be styled easily.

Tip — Looking for Inspiration?

The designer of this layout has taken inspiration from the CSS Table Gallery.[1] This is an excellent reference for those researching the different ways in which tabular data can be presented.

Our unstyled table currently displays in a very usable and accessible manner, as Figure 10.8 shows, but it's not very attractive.

Figure 10.8. The unstyled table

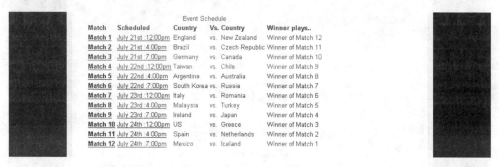

We can start by addressing the table itself. The first thing we should do is ensure that the table cannot move up next to the floated image if the content above it becomes shorter than it is currently. To do so, we use the `clear` property, setting its value to `right`.

File: **fixedwidth.css** (excerpt)

```
table.schedule {
  clear: right;
  width: 100%;
  line-height: 1.4em;
  border-collapse: collapse;
  border: 4px solid #adbbca;
  color: #4f6480;
  background: #f0f0f0;
}
```

---

[1] http://icant.co.uk/csstablegallery/

As Figure 10.9 shows, we've also set the width to 100% and a line height of 1.4em. We've set a chunky border, as well as background and text colors.

Figure 10.9. After styling the `table` element

Event Schedule

Match	Scheduled	Country	Vs.	Country	Winner plays..
Match 1	July 21st :12:00pm	England	vs.	New Zealand	Winner of Match 12
Match 2	July 21st :4:00pm	Brazil	vs.	Czech Republic	Winner of Match 11
Match 3	July 21st :7:00pm	Germany	vs.	Canada	Winner of Match 10
Match 4	July 22nd :12:00pm	Taiwan	vs.	Chile	Winner of Match 9
Match 5	July 22nd :4:00pm	Argentina	vs.	Australia	Winner of Match 8
Match 6	July 22nd :7:00pm	South Korea	vs.	Russia	Winner of Match 7
Match 7	July 23rd :12:00pm	Italy	vs.	Romania	Winner of Match 6
Match 8	July 23rd :4:00pm	Malaysia	vs.	Turkey	Winner of Match 5
Match 9	July 23rd :7:00pm	Ireland	vs.	Japan	Winner of Match 4
Match 10	July 24th :12:00pm	US	vs.	Greece	Winner of Match 3
Match 11	July 24th :4:00pm	Spain	vs.	Netherlands	Winner of Match 2
Match 12	July 24th :7:00pm	Mexico	vs.	Iceland	Winner of Match 1

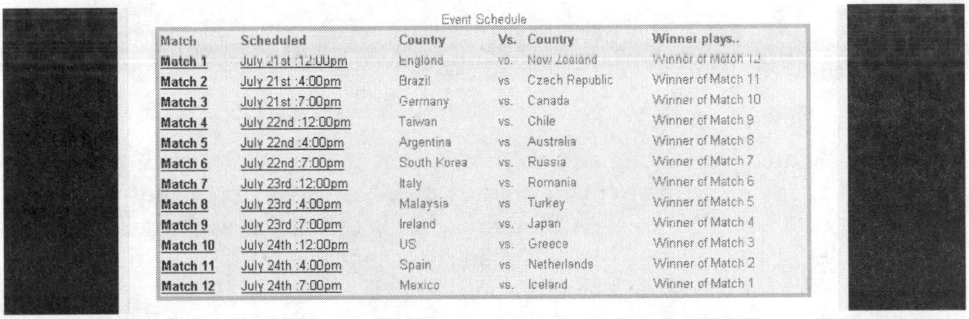

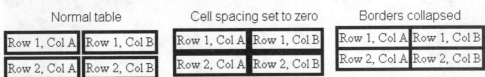

The `border-collapse` property, which is set to `collapse`, ensures that no space appears between the table cells. Normally, some spacing does exist between cells in a table. It's controlled by the `cellspacing` attribute of the `table` element.

Now, you might think that we could set this cell spacing to zero, and solve the problem that way. But even then, if we then set a four-pixel border on each table cell, the borders will combine to produce an eight-pixel border between cells, but a four-pixel border around the outside of the table. By setting `border-collapse: collapse`, we ensure that this cell spacing disappears completely. The borders "collapse" into each other, leaving us with the four-pixel border we intended. This effect is illustrated in Figure 10.10.

Figure 10.10. Demonstration of cell spacing and the `border-collapse` property

Normal table
Row 1, Col A
Row 1, Col B
Row 2, Col A
Row 2, Col B
Cell spacing set to zero
Row 1, Col A
Row 1, Col B
Row 2, Col A
Row 2, Col B
Borders collapsed
Row 1, Col A
Row 1, Col B
Row 2, Col A
Row 2, Col B

When I marked up the Event Schedule table, I used the `caption` element to add the caption that reads "Event Schedule." The `caption` element is the most appropriate element in which to put our table description. Let's now style the `caption` so that it looks like the heading in the mockup.

File: **fixedwidth.css** (excerpt)
```
table.schedule caption {
  margin: 0;
  padding: 0;
  color: #032469;
  line-height: 2em;
  text-align: left;
  font-weight: bold;
}
```

When we created our document, we noted that it was appropriate to use the thead and tbody elements to mark up the table. Now we can use those elements to help us to apply CSS to the different sections of the Events Schedule. If we create a rule for the selector table.schedule thead tr, we can set background and text colors for the table's header row.

File: **fixedwidth.css** (excerpt)
```
table.schedule thead tr {
  color: white;
  background: #5e7796;
}
```

As you can see in Figure 10.11, the table's already starting to look a lot more attractive, but we've got a long way to go before it looks as good as the mockup.

Figure 10.11. Using the thead element to create a blue heading area

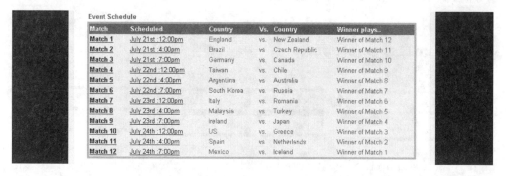

The next rule addresses the th element in thead. We do have other th elements running down the left-hand side of the page. However, they won't be affected by these properties, which apply padding and a four-pixel border to the top, header row of the table.

File: **fixedwidth.css** (excerpt)

```
table.schedule thead tr th {
  padding: 0.4em 0.6em 0.4em 0.6em;
  border: 4px solid #adbbca;
}
```

We now move on to the tbody, which contains the cells that comprise the body of the table. We don't want each individual cell to have borders all the way around it—we just want the table's rows to have top and bottom borders. To achieve this effect, we can add a border to the tr element within tbody:

File: **fixedwidth.css** (excerpt)

```
table.schedule tbody tr {
  border: 4px solid #adbbca;
}
```

Then, we can style the th elements within tbody.

File: **fixedwidth.css** (excerpt)

```
table.schedule tbody th {
  padding: 0.6em;
  border: 4px solid #adbbca;
}
```

This should leave your page looking like the one shown in Figure 10.12.

Figure 10.12. Marking the table rows clearly

In the page mockup, the table looks stripey because of the way coloring is applied to alternate table rows. As well as looking cool, this effect helps make the table more readable. To achieve the striped effect, we'll add a class called odd to alternate rows in our table. We'll then be able to use that class to style those rows differently from their neighbors.

File: **fixedwidth.html** (excerpt)

```
<tr>
  <th scope="row"><a href="#">Match 1</a></th>
  ⋮
  <td>Winner of Match 12</td>
</tr>
<tr class="odd">
  <th scope="row"><a href="#">Match 2</a></th>
  ⋮
  <td>Winner of Match 11</td>
</tr>
<tr>
  <th scope="row"><a href="#">Match 3</a></th>
  ⋮
  <td>Winner of Match 10</td>
</tr>
<tr class="odd">
  <th scope="row"><a href="#">Match 4</a></th>
```

```
    ⋮
  <td>Winner of Match 9</td>
</tr>
```

First, we set a background color on the `td` elements within `tbody`. While working on this element, I added some left padding to move the `td`s away from the border, and line them up with the headings:

File: **fixedwidth.css** (excerpt)

```
table.schedule tbody td {
  background: #e9ecee;
  padding-left:  0.6em;
  border-bottom: 4px solid #ccc;
}
```

Now, let's create a rule for the `tr` elements that have a `class` of `odd`. We can set the background color on these rows:

File: **fixedwidth.css** (excerpt)

```
table.schedule tbody tr.odd {
  background: #c4cfdb;
}
```

Now we can address the `td` elements within the `<tr class="odd">` and `</tr>` tags, giving them a color and background color that match those in our mockup:

File: **fixedwidth.css** (excerpt)

```
table.schedule tbody tr.odd td {
  background: #f0f0f0;
  color: #4f6480;
}
```

If the selectors in these rules are starting to seem a bit confusing, just remember to work from left to right:

1. We have a `table` with a class of `schedule`, which is `table.schedule` in the CSS.

2. We then have the `tbody` element, which sits inside the `table`.

3. Then we have a `tr` element, to which we'll add a class of `odd`.

4. There are `td` elements within those `tr`s.

Figure 10.13 shows the results of our work.

Figure 10.13. After styling the odd rows

Finally, let's style the links that appear in this table. There are two sets of links: those in the row headings down the side of the table, and those associated with the dates in the table cells.

First, we style the links within the th element:

File: **fixedwidth.css** (excerpt)

```
table.schedule tbody tr th a:link {
  font-weight: bold;
  color: #5e7796;
  text-decoration: underline;
}
table.schedule tbody tr th a:visited {
  font-weight: bold;
  color: #5e7796;
}
table.schedule tbody tr th a:hover {
  font-weight: bold;
  color: #5e7796;
  text-decoration: none;
}
```

We then complete our table by styling the links within the td element:

File: **fixedwidth.css (excerpt)**

```
table.schedule tbody td a:link {
  color: #808000;
  text-decoration: underline;
}
table.schedule tbody td a:visited {
  color: #808000;
}
table.schedule tbody td a:hover {
  color: #808000;
  text-decoration: none;
}
```

Your table, and as a result, your layout, is now complete. It should look great—like Figure 10.14.

Figure 10.14. The completed table

Multiple-column Fixed-width Layouts

The layout we've focused on in this chapter really contains just a single column of content. It's possible to create multiple-column fixed-width layouts in much the same way as you created your multiple-column liquid layouts: by either positioning or floating the columns.

Positioned Columns

To use absolute positioning to add a second column to this layout, we need first to add the column—or sidebar—text to the page in its own `div`. Let's add an ID of `extras` just after the closing `</div>` tag of this `div`. On a real site, this sidebar might contain advertising, or additional information about the matches or venue, but for our purposes, dummy text will be fine.

In the natural flow of the document, this text displays below the white box, as Figure 10.15 illustrates.

Figure 10.15. The sidebar `div` before any CSS is added

As with the liquid layouts we created previously, we need to wrap this sidebar content inside two `div`s—one will provide our positioning context, while the other will help us make room for the sidebar. Add the two `div`s as shown in the code excerpt below: the content wrapper `div` wraps the content `div`, while the `div` with the ID `main` wraps the `div`s with IDs `content-wrapper` and `extras`.

File: **fixedwidth.html** (excerpt)

```
</div> <!-- header -->
<div id="main">
  <div id="content-wrapper">
    <div id="content">
      ⋮
    </div> <!-- content -->
  </div> <!-- content-wrapper -->
```

```
  <div id="extras">
   ⋮
  </div> <!-- extras -->
 </div> <!-- main -->
</div> <!-- wrapper -->
```

We can now add style rules for these divs. The content wrapper applies a 200-pixel left margin to the sidebar, while the main div provides its positioning context.

File: **fixedwidth.css (excerpt)**

```
#content-wrapper {
  margin: 0 0 0 200px;
}
#main {
  position: relative;
}
```

Refresh your page in the browser, and you should see that a space has been created for the sidebar. Our next step is to position the column within this space. Simply use the following CSS to position this sidebar from the top and left, or top and right, of the browser's viewport:

File: **fixedwidth.css (excerpt)**

```
#extras {
  position: absolute;
  top: 0;
  left: 0;
  width: 180px;
  background-color: white;
  border: 1px solid #f0f0f0;
}
```

This CSS positions the column and gives it the same white background color and border that the content div displays. Figure 10.16 shows the finished product.

Figure 10.16. The completed layout with a positioned sidebar

Floated Columns

There are a number of reasons why you might want to use floated columns, rather than positioned columns, in this layout. For example, if you want to add a footer that will always remain beneath both the columns, floating the columns will enable you to do that. You might want to wrap your content around the column, rather than have the content take up only the column's width. Again, floating the columns makes this possible.

If you wish to float the sidebar, you'll need to move it to occur just before the `<div id="content-wrapper">` tag.

File: **fixedwidth.html** (excerpt)

```
<div id="main">
  <div id="extras">
  ⋮
  </div> <!-- extras -->
  <div id="content-wrapper">
```

Now, to float this column, all we need to do is replace the positioning declarations in our #extras rule with a float: left declaration. Figure 10.17 shows the impact of this markup.

File: **fixedwidth.css** (excerpt)

```
#extras {
  float: left;
  width: 180px;
  background-color: white;
  border: 1px solid #f0f0f0;
}
```

Figure 10.17. The floated column displaying as expected in Firefox

That's all you need to do to float your sidebar column alongside your main content column in Firefox. However, as Figure 10.18 illustrates, Internet Explorer 6 proves a little more troublesome.

Figure 10.18. Internet Explorer 6 failing to display our world cup image, and pushing the events schedule below the sidebar

As you can see in Figure 10.18, the world cup logo is no longer being displayed, and our events schedule table has been pushed down below the bottom of the sidebar. Occasionally, as you test your pages in Internet Explorer 6, you'll encounter bugs in its application of your CSS rules. Most of these problems have been fixed in IE 7, but unfortunately, it will likely be some time before most users upgrade to IE 7 and IE 6 can be ignored.

One of the most common causes of these bugs has to do with Internet Explorer's concept of "haying layout," which is discussed in the article "On Having Layout".[2] A simple work-around for such bugs is to apply one of a number of declarations

---

[2] http://www.satzansatz.de/cssd/onhavinglayout.html

to one of the problematic element's ancestors. In our case, adding `display: in-line-block`[3] to the `#content` rule fixes our problem, as Figure 10.19 shows.

File: **fixedwidth.css** (excerpt)

```css
#content {
  background-color: white;
  border: 1px solid #f0f0f0;
  padding: 0;
  display: inline-block;
}
```

A list of the properties that can be used, and a discussion of their side-effects, is available in the "On Having Layout" article mentioned above.

Figure 10.19. The floated column displaying as desired in Internet Explorer 6

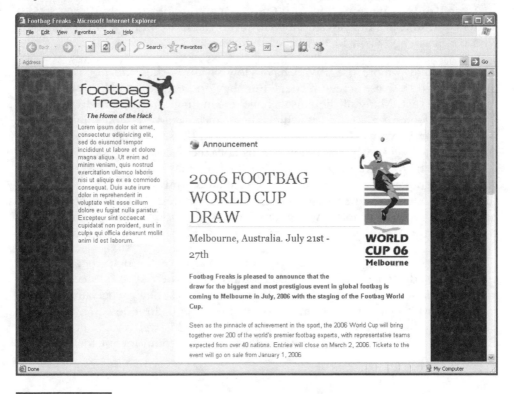

---

[3]Theoretically, this declaration changes the content `div`'s behavior when it's adjacent to other elements, but in this specific case, as it's wrapped in the content wrapper `div`, it has no effect.

These examples have shown just how flexible a CSS layout can be. Instead of needing to rebuild your nested table layout to add new columns, you can make big changes to your layouts with just a few additional CSS properties.

"Zoom" Layouts

Before we wrap up this chapter, let's spend a few moments discussing a technique that can make your site much more usable to users with various accessibility needs. That technique involves the provision of one or more alternate style sheets that give a different look and feel to the site in order to address particular difficulties that some users experience as they work with the Web.

When we discuss accessibility, we often consider users who employ some kind of text-only device—a screen reader that reads the content of the site aloud, perhaps. By using semantic markup, and separating a document's content and structure from its presentation with CSS, we can do a lot to help these users to understand and use our sites easily. However, these are not the only site users who we can help by considering accessibility issues.

There are many more users who have "low vision"—they are not completely blind, nor do they use screen readers, but they do need some help to be able to see web site text. Many of these users have screen magnifiers that help to enlarge on-screen elements to a size at which they can be read. As you might expect, these users have very different requirements than those who use screen readers. For instance, users with low vision can usually see the layout of your site, and with the help of their magnifier, they may find diagrams, images, and other visual elements useful. These users don't want a text-only page—that would deny them visual elements like images, which they can understand once they're magnified. However, the problem with many layouts is that, once they are magnified, columns of text disappear off the edge of users' screens, never to be found again!

Since we know how to build site layouts using CSS, we can help these users by creating an additional style sheet that's tailored to their specific needs. These kinds of style sheets have been called "zoom layouts," as they're specially designed for people who magnify or zoom into web sites. The technique is detailed comprehensively by web accessibility guru Joe Clark on his web site,[4] but let's take a brief look at what we would need to do to create a zoom layout for our fixed-width design.

---

[4] http://www.joeclark.org/access/webaccess/zoom/

Figure 10.20. The layout we're creating

Zoom layouts need to achieve the following:

☐ Switch the text to a large font.

☐ Change the colors used in the design to light text on a dark background, as low-vision users find this easier to read.

❑ Rearrange the content so that it all falls into one column. This way, there's no danger of users missing out on content that has disappeared off the edge of the screen.

Let's take the layout with the floated left-hand column, and create an alternate "zoom layout" style sheet for it. The finished layout will look like Figure 10.20. It's not quite as pretty as our original layout, but it is a lot easier for the target users to read.

Creating the Style Sheet

While you're working on your alternate style sheet, it's not a bad idea to link it as the main style sheet attached to your document, so you can see your changes easily. Take your existing style sheet and save it as `zoom.css`, then attach it to your document. Now, disable your existing style sheet by wrapping it in a comment, as shown below.

File: **fixedwidth.css (excerpt)**

```
<head>
  <title>Footbag Freaks</title>
  <meta http-equiv="Content-Type"
      content="text/html; charset=iso-8859-1" />
  <!--<link rel="stylesheet" type="text/css"
      href="fixedwidth.css" />-->
  <link rel="stylesheet" type="text/css" href="zoom.css" />
</head>
```

We don't want to use fixed widths in our zoom layout. As the text in a fixed-width layout gets larger, one of two things will happen: either the text will become too large for the fixed-width columns (imagine a very long word becoming longer than the fixed-width column), or, if the column grows wider as the text gets larger, the column will become wider than the screen itself, necessitating a horizontal scroll bar.

First, edit the CSS rule for the `body` element to remove the `min-width` declaration as well as the background image and color. In addition, make the base font size `large`:

File: **zoom.css (excerpt)**

```
body {
  margin: 0;
  padding: 0;
  background-color: #333;
```

```
  color: white;
  font: large Arial, Helvetica, Verdana, sans-serif;
}
```

Then, delete everything but the `padding` property from the `#wrapper` rule.

Let's make the header—which contains no text other than the tagline and the image—into a white top banner for the page. To do this, add a CSS rule `#header`:

File: **zoom.css** (excerpt)

```
#header {
  background-color: white;
}
```

To make the content `div` the full width of the page, and to remove the pale background color, delete the `#content` rule. We can also get rid of the `#main` and `#content-wrapper` rules, as we used them only for positioning purposes.

Then, to move the sidebar above the page's main content, remove the existing declarations in the `#extras` rule, and style this `div` so it appears with a white border:

File: **zoom.css** (excerpt)

```
#extras {
  border: 2px solid white;
  padding: 0.2em;
}
```

The rest of the changes that we need to make will affect the colors that are used in the document, and remove some of the background image, margin, and padding settings. My `zoom.css` file now contains the following rules:

File: **zoom.css**

```
body {
  margin: 0;
  padding: 0;
  background-color: #333;
  color: white;
  font:large Arial, Helvetica, Verdana, sans-serif;
}
#wrapper {
  padding: 10px;
}
#header {
  background-color: white;
```

```
}
#tagline {
  font-weight: bold;
  color: #050845;
  font-style: italic;
  margin: 0 0 0.5em 0;
  padding: 0 0 0 20px;
}
#extras {
  border: 2px solid white;
  padding: 0.2em;
}
#content .inner {
  margin: 30px;
}
#worldcuplogo {
  float: right;
  margin: 0 0 20px 40px;
  width: 111px;
}
#content h1 {
  font-size: 120%;
  color: #ccc;
}
#content h2 {
  font-size: 260%;
  font-weight: normal;
}
#content p {
  line-height: 1.6em;
  font-family: Georgia, Times, "Times New Roman", serif;

}
#dateline {
  font-size: 160%;
  font-weight: normal;
  font-family: Georgia, Times, "Times New Roman", serif;
}
.intro {
  font-weight: bold;
}
table.schedule {
  clear: right;
  width: 100%;
  line-height: 1.4em;
  border-collapse: collapse;
```

```
  border: 4px solid #ccc;
  color: white;
  background: #333;
}
table.schedule caption {
  margin: 0;
  padding: 0;
  color: white;
  line-height: 2em;
  text-align: left;
  font-weight: bold;
}
table.schedule thead tr {
  color: white;
  background: #333;
}
table.schedule thead tr th {
  padding: 0.4em 0.6em 0.4em 0.6em;
  border: 4px solid #ccc;
}
table.schedule tbody tr {
  border: 4px solid #ccc;
}
table.schedule tbody th {
  padding: 0.6em;
  border: 4px solid #ccc;
}
table.schedule tbody td {
  background: #333;
  padding-left: 0.6em;
  border-bottom: 4px solid #ccc;
}
table.schedule tbody tr.odd {
  background: #999;
}
table.schedule tbody tr.odd td {
  background: #666666;
  color: white;
}
table.schedule a:link {
  font-weight: bold;
  color: #fc0;
  text-decoration: underline;
}
table.schedule a:visited {
  font-weight: bold;
```

```
  color: #fc0;
}
table.schedule a:hover {
  font-weight: bold;
  color: #fc0;
  text-decoration: none;
}
```

When the layout, styled with zoom.css, is displayed by the browser, it looks like Figure 10.21.

Figure 10.21. The finished "zoom" layout

Attaching Alternate Style Sheets

Many modern browsers, such as Firefox and Opera, already give users the ability to select from multiple style sheets that are attached to a document, provided the style sheets are linked correctly. To offer your users a choice of style sheets, first uncomment your main style sheet to include it in the document once more, and give the `link` element a `title` attribute with a value of `default layout`.

Then, move to the `link` element that refers to `zoom.css`. Change the `rel` attribute to `alternate stylesheet`, and add `zoom layout` as its `title`:

```
<head>
  <title>Footbag Freaks</title>
  <meta http-equiv="Content-Type"
      content="text/html; charset=iso-8859-1" />
  <link rel="stylesheet" type="text/css" href="fixedwidth.css"
      title="default layout" />
  <link rel="alternate stylesheet" type="text/css" href="zoom.css"
      title="zoom layout" />
</head>
```

In Firefox, which supports alternate style sheets, you'll now be able to switch between style sheets: simply select View > Page Style, then choose the style sheet you want. The options you're provided will reflect the names that you entered as the `title` attributes of the linked style sheets, as Figure 10.22 shows.

Figure 10.22. Switching style sheets in Firefox

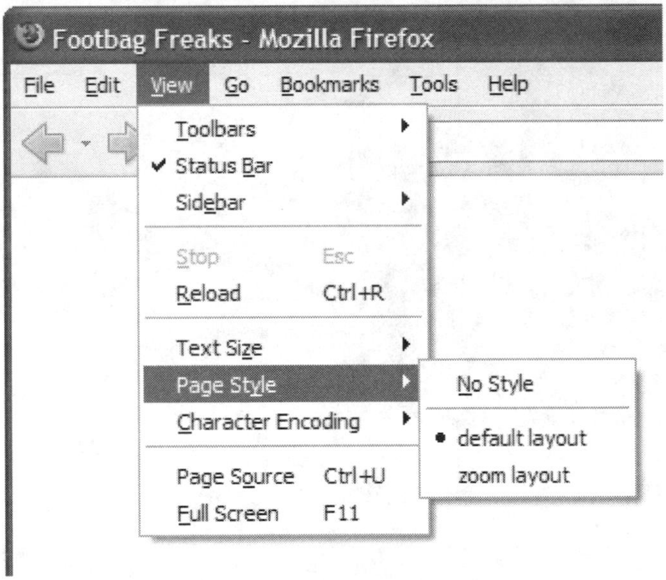

What about people whose browsers don't offer this switching functionality? Well, you can also implement your own "style switcher" to enable those users to switch styles easily. While a discussion of how to build a switcher is beyond the scope of this book, there are a number of ways to create this functionality using

JavaScript or a server-side language such as PHP or ASP. A popular JavaScript method of switching style sheets is explained on A List Apart in the article "Alternative Style: Working With Alternate Style Sheets"[5] by Paul Sowden.

Summary

In this chapter we've learned how to build fixed-width and centered layouts, but I've also shown you how you can start to combine the techniques we've discussed in this book to create many different kinds of layouts. CSS is a powerful tool that can create for designers opportunities that would not have been easy to achieve using a table-based layout. Consider, for example, the ease with which we can create a zoom layout that's tailored for users with low vision capabilities, while still being able to provide a standard layout that meets our branding and visual design aims.

By using the different layout concepts that we've discussed in these last three chapters, along with the many different styling techniques we've explored in this book, you'll find that you can create a variety of layouts on which you might wish to base your site designs. We have discussed here the basic building blocks of CSS layout, and as you explore further and look at some of the examples available on the Web, you'll find that a good understanding of the basics will stand you in good stead as you start to create more complex layouts using CSS.

---

[5] http://www.alistapart.com/articles/alternate/

Appendix A: CSS Miscellany

This appendix pulls together information about CSS that I thought was particularly interesting and potentially useful, but which didn't fit the main flow of the text. The operative word in the title of this appendix is "miscellaneous." There's no particular order to the information here. The following list identifies the topics covered in this appendix, shown in the order in which they're presented:

☐ at-rules

☐ aural style sheets

☐ CSS and JavaScript

At-rules

The CSS 2 recommendation from the W3C defines a new type of CSS rule. It's called an "at-rule" because all the rules of this type start with an "at" symbol (@). This type of rule is meant to be extensible. In other words, future editions of the W3C recommendation, browser developers, and others may define new sets of rules that begin with @.

For now, there are four groups of @ rules:

☐ `@import`

☐ `@media`

☐ `@page`

☐ `@font-face`

The `@media` rule allows you to define different output options for various media in a single style sheet. Browser support is somewhat inconsistent, though it seems to be getting better with each release. Right now, support for this rule is at least usable in most modern browsers (the most notable exception being IE 5.2 on Macintosh).

Initially, W3C defines that the following media types are valid for use with the `@media` rule. However, you should note that the list is not guaranteed to be complete. As new technologies and display platforms emerge, more keywords will undoubtedly be added.

- ❑ `all`

- ❑ `aural` (deprecated in CSS 2.1)

- ❑ `braille`

- ❑ `embossed`

- ❑ `handheld`

- ❑ `print`

- ❑ `projection`

- ❑ `screen`

- ❑ `TTY`

- ❑ `TV`

The purpose of all of these is largely self-explanatory, with the exception of `embossed`, which is intended to define output for a Braille printer. The following HTML produces two decidedly different appearances, depending on whether you're viewing the page on your monitor or printing it out. It demonstrates the syntax and use of the `@media` rule.

```
<!DOCTYPE html PUBLIC "-//W3C//DTD XHTML 1.0 Transitional//EN"
  "http://www.w3.org/TR/xhtml1/DTD/xhtml1-transitional.dtd">
<html xmlns="http://www.w3.org/1999/xhtml">
<head>
  <title>Demonstrating @media Rules</title>
  <style type="text/css">
  <!--
  @media print {
    body {
      font-size: 12pt;
      font-family: courier;
    }
  }

  @media screen {
```

```
    body {
      font-size: 36px;
      font-family: arial;
    }
  }

  @media screen, print {
    body {
      line-height: 1.2;
    }
  }
  -->
  </style>
</head>
<body>
  Let's see if this actually works and, if so, in which browsers.
  I've defined an @media rule for print that makes it print
  12-point Courier, but another @media rule that displays in
  36-pixel Arial on the screen. Both devices produce output with a
  line-height 120% of the default value.
</body>
</html>
```

Notice that it's okay to define a single @media rule for application to multiple media. In that case, the names of the media must be separated by commas. There are two other ways to specify the medium to be used with a given style sheet or rule. You can use the @import rule and supply the media type as a parameter, as in this example:

```
@import url(bossvoice.css) aural;
```

This rule tells the browser to import the CSS style sheet called bossvoice.css, and to apply it to aural output devices.

The second way to define a style's medium is to use the media attribute of the style tag, shown here:

```
<style type="text/css" media="projection">
body {
  color: blue;
  background-color: white;
}
</style>
```

If you define a style sheet for a medium that understands the notion of a "page," you can use the @page at-rule to declare sizes, borders, page breaks, and the presence or absence of crop marks on the output page.[1]

For example, to define an eight and a half-inch by 11-inch page with a half-inch border all the way around, you would write an @page rule like this:

```
@page {
  size: 8.5in 11in;
  margin: 0.5in;
}
```

The size property can be given one of three constant values, in addition to the specific size values shown earlier:

□ auto, which tells the browser to use the default page size for the browser application

□ landscape, where the larger dimension is the width

□ portrait, where the larger dimension is the height

The margin property is a shorthand for the following, more specific properties, which may be specified individually:

□ margin-top

□ margin-right

□ margin-bottom

□ margin-left

You can also define special, overriding dimensions and margins for the first page of a document, as well as separate dimensions for left- and right-hand pages using the :first, :left, and :right pseudo-classes.

Here's a set of @page rules that defines the layout for a document to be printed on both sides, with a special setting for the front page:

---

[1] The @page rule has some complexity associated with it, but I'm not going to attempt to cover that here. If you're curious, I suggest you go to the W3C page where the @page rule is defined. [http://www.w3.org/TR/REC-CSS2/page.html#page-box]

```
@page {
  margin: 2cm; /* All margins set to 2cm */
}
@page:first {
  margin-top: 10cm; /* Top margin on first page 10cm */
}

/* 1cm larger margins near binding */
@page:left {
  margin-left: 3cm;
  margin-right: 4cm;
}
@page:right {
  margin-left: 4cm;
  margin-right: 3cm;
}
```

Under the CSS 2 Recommendation, you can control page breaks in paged output as well. Page control is a very complex topic and one that is probably beyond not only the scope of this discussion, but also the interest level of the vast majority of web designers. So I'm not going to go into it here, except to say that if you ever get into a position where you want or need to prepare a web page for printed (or other paged) output, you can confidently state that you can control the page break. The relevant properties are described in detail in Appendix B.

Aural Style Sheets

Many web designers agree that sound is a vastly under-utilized aspect of communication on the Internet. Flash movies, streamed video, and podcasts are all examples of ways in which sound is becoming a key part of the Web's content. However, opinions differ on how aural cues should be used to improve navigation and user interfaces, particularly with regards to visually impaired users. In the future, I anticipate that we'll see far greater use of spoken language, background music, and mixtures of voice and music to enliven the user experience and improve the accessibility of web content, independent of screenreader software.

The CSS 2 Recommendation from the W3C defines a whole range of sound (aural) presentation qualities that can be defined in CSS. Collectively, these make up the components of an aural style sheet.

Here's a snippet of an aural style sheet, borrowed directly from the W3C's web page on aural style sheets:[2]

```
h1, h2, h3, h4, h5, h6 {
  voice-family: paul;
  stress: 20;
  richness: 90;
  cue-before: url(ping.au);
}
p.heidi {
  azimuth: center-left;
}
p.peter {
  azimuth: right;
}
p.goat {
  volume: x-soft;
}
```

Let's go over this style sheet fragment, line by line.

All headings will be spoken using a voice-family called "paul." A voice family is much like a font family; it contains a collection of minor variations on a voice. The headings will apply a stress value (determining the "contour" of a voice, i.e. the degree of difference in inflection in various parts of the sentences) of 20, which is pretty low.

The code defines a richness of 90, which is very high. Richness determines how far a voice carries, and affects what we might think of as "loudness." Before any heading is pronounced, an "auditory icon" called `ping.au` will be played. You can define cues to be played before and after any sound segment.

Any paragraph marked as an instance of the class "heidi" will appear to originate from the listener's left, in a vertical center of space. Paragraphs that are instances of the class "peter" will come from the listener's right side. All paragraphs spoken by the "goat" voice will be extremely soft.

You get the idea. Again, a full treatment of this topic is beyond the scope of this book, but I wanted you to gain something of an appreciation for the scope of what *can* be done.

---

[2] http://www.w3.org/TR/REC-CSS2/aural.html

With aural style rules, you can control the following characteristics of a voice or the spoken presentation of the information on your web page:

- ❏ volume

- ❏ whether to speak words or spell them out

- ❏ pausing

- ❏ cue sounds before and after

- ❏ mixing (playing two sounds simultaneously)

- ❏ spatial location of the sound in three-dimensional space

- ❏ speech rate

- ❏ pitch and range of pitch

- ❏ stress

- ❏ richness

- ❏ how to speak punctuation (pronounce it or use it as pause cues)

- ❏ how to speak numerals (separate digits or numerical values)

The properties that control all of these factors are listed in Appendix C.

CSS and JavaScript

When you combine XHTML, JavaScript and CSS, you get something called Dynamic HTML, or DHTML. Many people mistakenly believe that DHTML is a technology. It's not. It's a term used to refer to the potential for high levels of interactivity (dynamism) in pages generated using (X)HTML.

Many books have been written about DHTML including *DHTML Utopia: Modern Web Design using JavaScript and DOM*,[3] which was written by Stuart Langridge and published by SitePoint.

---

[3] http://www.sitepoint.com/books/dhtml1/

I've omitted teaching you JavaScript or DHTML here because the subject is so vast. This book is intended principally for beginning-to-intermediate web designers, not advanced folks using scripting and programming techniques.

Still, it's important, as you begin to move beyond what's in this book and develop your skills as a web designer, that you have a basic appreciation of the potential for DHTML. So let me provide a brief overview of the topic, just to whet your appetite and perhaps forestall some of your budding questions about what is possible.

At the core of DHTML is something called the Document Object Model, or DOM. While the comparison is a bit simplistic, you can think of the DOM as a specification or definition of the way you can refer to individual pieces of your web pages. This, in turn, enables you to tell them to change something about their display or behavior. JavaScript is the language that's most often used to write these instructions.

Essentially, each CSS property can be accessed and modified from a JavaScript. Within the JavaScript code, you simply refer to the object by its ID or name, identify the property whose value you wish to retrieve or change, and, if appropriate, supply a new value. When the script is executed, the CSS modification occurs.

For example, you could create a button on a web page that would hide some particular piece of content (whose ID we'll assume to be `hereandgone`). You would define a JavaScript function called, for example, `hideshow`. It would look something like this:

```
function hideShow() {
  document.getElementById("hereandgone").style.visibility="hidden";
}
```

Where you define the script, when and how it gets executed, and other similar details are beyond the scope of our discussion here. The point is simply that you can access and modify element styles in an HTML page, even after the page has been rendered in the user's browser using JavaScript. The syntax varies very little from the example above, which is one of the reasons why the DOM has been defined as it has. It seems cumbersome to have to type `getelementById` every time you want to get an element's style or other property, but the fact is that since this operator is the same in every instance, you can quickly learn to handle lots of different scripting situations with very little additional knowledge.

Appendix B: CSS Color Reference

As we discussed in detail in Chapter 7, there are five methods that specify color values in CSS:

❏ descriptive color names

```
color: red;
```

❏ RGB hexadecimal values (including a three-character shorthand)

```
color: #ff0000;
color: #f00;
```

❏ RGB decimal values

```
color: rgb(255, 0, 0);
```

❏ RGB percentage values

```
color: rgb(100%, 0%, 0%);
```

❏ system color names

```
color: AppWorkspace;
```

This appendix provides a complete reference to the first three methods. The CSS 2 Recommendation[1] prescribes a set of 17 descriptive color names, which are presented in Table B.1. Netscape proposed an additional 124 color names, which are supported by practically every graphical browser available today, and are presented in Table B.2. Finally, CSS 2 also provides a set of 28 system color names, which correspond to the colors used for different parts of the GUI presented by the user's operating system, and are presented in Table B.3. System color names are supported in most current browsers, but older browsers typically do not support them.

---

[1] http://www.w3.org/TR/REC-CSS2/syndata.html#color-units

Table B.1. Standard CSS color names

Color Name	Hex Equivalent	Red	Green	Blue
aqua	#00FFFF	0	255	255
black	#000000	0	0	0
blue	#0000FF	0	0	255
fuchsia	#FF00FF	255	0	255
gray	#808080	128	128	128
green	#008000	0	128	0
lime	#00FF00	0	255	0
maroon	#800000	128	0	0
navy	#000080	0	0	128
olive	#808000	128	128	0
purple	#800080	128	0	128
red	#FF0000	255	0	0
silver	#C0C0C0	192	192	192
teal	#008080	0	128	128
white	#FFFFFF	255	255	255
yellow	#FFFF00	255	255	0
orange	#FFA500	255	156	0

Table B.2. Netscape extended color names

Color Name	Hex Equivalent	Red	Green	Blue
aliceblue	#F0F8FF	240	248	255
antiquewhite	#FAEBD7	250	235	215
aquamarine	#7FFFD4	127	255	212
azure	#F0FFFF	240	255	255
beige	#F5F5DC	245	245	220
bisque	#FFE4C4	255	228	196
blanchedalmond	#FFEBCD	255	235	205
blueviolet	#8A2BE2	138	43	226
brown	#A52A2A	165	42	42
burlywood	#DEB887	222	184	135
cadetblue	#5F9EA0	95	158	160
chartreuse	#7FFF00	127	255	0
chocolate	#D2691E	210	105	30
coral	#FF7F50	255	127	80
cornflowerblue	#6495ED	100	149	237
cornsilk	#FFF8DC	255	248	220
crimson	#DC143D	220	20	61
cyan	#00FFFF	0	255	255
darkblue	#00008B	0	0	139
darkcyan	#008B8B	0	139	139
darkgoldenrod	#B8860B	139	134	11
darkgray	#A9A9A9	169	169	169
darkgreen	#006400	0	100	0
darkkhaki	#BDB76B	189	183	107
darkmagenta	#8B008B	139	0	139
darkolivegreen	#556B2F	85	107	47
darkorange	#FF8C00	255	140	0
darkorchid	#9932CC	153	50	204

Color Name	Hex Equivalent	Red	Green	Blue
darkred	#8B0000	139	0	0
darksalmon	#E9967A	233	150	122
darkseagreen	#8FBC8F	143	188	143
darkslateblue	#483D8B	72	61	139
darkslategray	#2F4F4F	47	79	79
darkturquoise	#00CED1	0	206	209
darkviolet	#9400D3	148	0	211
deeppink	#FF1493	255	20	147
deepskyblue	#00BFFF	0	191	255
dimgray	#696969	105	105	105
dodgerblue	#1E90FF	30	144	255
firebrick	#B22222	178	34	34
floralwhite	#FFFAF0	255	250	240
forestgreen	#228B22	34	139	34
gainsboro	#DCDCDC	220	220	220
ghostwhite	#F8F8FF	248	248	255
gold	#FFD700	255	215	0
goldenrod	#DAA520	218	165	32
greenyellow	#ADFF2F	173	255	47
honeydew	#F0FFF0	240	255	240
hotpink	#FF69B4	255	105	180
indianred	#CD5C5C	205	92	92
indigo	#4B0082	75	0	130
ivory	#FFFFF0	255	255	240
khaki	#F0E68C	240	230	140
lavender	#E6E6FA	230	230	250
lavenderblush	#FFF0F5	255	240	245
lawngreen	#7CFC00	124	252	0
lemonchiffon	#FFFACD	255	250	205

Color Name	Hex Equivalent	Red	Green	Blue
lightblue	#ADD8E6	173	216	230
lightcoral	#F08080	240	128	128
lightcyan	#E0FFFF	224	255	255
lightgoldenrodyellow	#FAFAD2	250	250	210
lightgreen	#90EE90	144	238	144
lightgrey	#D3D3D3	211	211	211
lightpink	#FFB6C1	255	182	193
lightsalmon	#FFA07A	255	160	122
lightseagreen	#20B2AA	32	178	170
lightskyblue	#87CEFA	135	206	250
lightslategray	#778899	119	136	153
lightsteelblue	#B0C4DE	176	196	222
lightyellow	#FFFFE0	255	255	224
limegreen	#32CD32	50	205	50
linen	#FAF0E6	250	240	230
magenta	#FF00FF	255	0	255
mediumaquamarine	#66CDAA	102	205	170
mediumblue	#0000CD	0	0	205
mediumorchid	#BA55D3	186	85	211
mediumpurple	#9370DB	147	112	219
mediumseagreen	#3CB371	60	179	113
mediumslateblue	#7B68EE	123	104	238
mediumspringgreen	#00FA9A	0	250	154
mediumturquoise	#48D1CC	72	209	204
mediumvioletred	#C71585	199	21	133
midnightblue	#191970	25	25	112
mintcream	#F5FFFA	245	255	250
mistyrose	#FFE4E1	255	228	225
moccasin	#FFE4B5	255	228	181

Color Name	Hex Equivalent	Red	Green	Blue
navajowhite	#FFDEAD	255	222	173
oldlace	#FDF5E6	253	245	230
olivedrab	#6B8E23	107	142	35
orange	#FFA500	255	165	0
orangered	#FF4500	255	69	0
orchid	#DA70D6	218	112	214
palegoldenrod	#EEE8AA	238	232	170
palegreen	#98FB98	152	251	152
paleturquoise	#AFEEEE	175	238	238
palevioletred	#DB7093	219	112	147
papayawhip	#FFEFD5	255	239	213
peachpuff	#FFDAB9	255	218	185
peru	#CD853F	205	133	63
pink	#FFC0CB	255	192	203
plum	#DDA0DD	221	160	221
powderblue	#B0E0E6	176	224	230
rosybrown	#BC8F8F	188	143	143
royalblue	#4169E1	65	105	225
saddlebrown	#8B4513	139	69	19
salmon	#FA8072	250	128	114
sandybrown	#F4A460	244	164	96
seagreen	#2E8B57	46	139	87
seashell	#FFF5EE	255	245	238
sienna	#A0522D	160	82	45
skyblue	#87CEEB	135	206	235
slateblue	#6A5ACD	106	90	205
slategray	#708090	112	128	144
snow	#FFFAFA	255	250	250
springgreen	#00FF7F	0	255	127

Color Name	Hex Equivalent	Red	Green	Blue
steelblue	#4682B4	70	130	180
tan	#D2B48C	210	180	140
thistle	#D8BFD8	216	191	216
tomato	#FF6347	255	99	71
turquoise	#40E0D0	64	224	208
violet	#EE82EE	238	130	238
wheat	#F5DEB3	245	222	179
whitesmoke	#F5F5F5	245	245	245
yellowgreen	#9ACD32	154	205	50

Table B.3. Standard CSS system color names

Color Name	Description
ActiveBorder	active window border color
ActiveCaption	active window caption color
AppWorkspace	background color of a multiple document interface
Background	desktop background color
ButtonFace	face color for three-dimensional display elements
ButtonHighlight	highlight color for three-dimensional display elements (edges facing light source)
ButtonShadow	shadow color for three-dimensional display elements (edges opposite light source)
ButtonText	text color on push buttons
CaptionText	text color in caption, size box, and scroll bar arrow box
GrayText	grayed-out (disabled) text color
Highlight	background color for selected items in a control
HighlightText	text color for selected items in a control
InactiveBorder	inactive window border color
InactiveCaption	inactive window caption color
InactiveCaptionText	inactive caption text color
InfoBackground	tooltip background color
InfoText	tooltip text color
Menu	menu background color
MenuText	menu text color
Scrollbar	scroll bar background color
ThreeDDarkShadow	dark shadow color for three-dimensional display elements
ThreeDFace	face color for three-dimensional display elements
ThreeDHighlight	highlight color for three-dimensional display elements
ThreeDLightShadow	light color for three-dimensional display elements

Color Name	Description
ThreeDShadow	shadow color for three-dimensional display elements
Window	window background color
WindowFrame	window frame color
WindowText	text color in windows

Appendix C: CSS Property Reference

This appendix contains a complete reference to all CSS properties at the time of this writing. This includes properties defined in the CSS1[1] and CSS 2.1[2] specifications, as well as browser-specific extensions to the CSS recommendations.

Where a browser-specific extension exposes the same functionality as a planned feature in CSS3, which is currently a working draft, this is indicated with a reference to the relevant draft.

A note on browser versions: compiling an exhaustive list of browser compatibility in a field that is constantly changing would result in a printed resource that is out-of-date immediately after going to print. The notes here on compatibility should therefore be used as a guide, based on browser versions that were available when going to print. Versions for Internet Explorer (Windows) are listed due to the percentage of the population still persisting with older versions of IE. Version 7 was not available for download at the time this book went to print, so mentions of that browser are based on tests using the Beta 2 release. Internet Explorer on the Macintosh platform has been officially retired by Microsoft, and was not included in these tests.

For Mozilla browsers, testing was performed using the latest version of the two primary browsers that share the Gecko rendering engine, namely Firefox 1.5.0.1 and Seamonkey 1.0 (formerly the Mozilla Application Suite). Other browsers that use the Gecko engine (e.g. Netscape, Flock, Camino) can generally be relied upon to support the same subset of CSS properties as those supported by Firefox and Seamonkey.

Opera and Safari users also tend to update regularly, and the versions used for testing this appendix were Opera 8.52 and Safari 2.0. The popular Konqueror browser for Linux supports a similar subset of CSS properties as Safari. For a continually updated and comprehensive list of CSS browser support, visit http://en.wikipedia.org/wiki/Comparison_of_layout_engines_(CSS).

---

[1] http://www.w3.org/TR/REC-CSS1
[2] http://www.w3.org/TR/CSS21/

azimuth

`azimuth` sets the direction in horizontal space from which sound originates when the content is presented aurally (e.g. in a speaking browser for the blind).

For full details on this property, see the CSS 2.1 specification.[3]

Inherited: Yes

See also: `elevation`

Value

This property takes as its value an angle (`-360deg` to `360deg`, where `0deg` is in front of the listener), or a descriptive constant (e.g. `far-right behind`).

Initial value: `center`

Compatibility

CSS Version: 2.1

The property is not yet supported by any browser.

Examples

The following style rule will cause all headings to be heard from the front-left of the sound field:

```
h1, h2, h3, h4, h5, h6 {
  azimuth: -45deg;
}
```

background

This shorthand property allows you to set all the background properties of an element with a single property declaration.

Inherited: No

---

[3] http://www.w3.org/TR/REC-CSS2/aural.html#spatial-props

See also: `background-attachment`, `background-color`, `background-image`, `background-position`, and `background-repeat`

Value

You can specify any of the values permitted by the five `background-` properties, in any order, separated by spaces. If a property is not specified, its default is used.

Initial value: none

Compatibility

CSS Version: 1

The property is supported by Internet Explorer 4 or later, Opera, Safari, and all Mozilla browsers.

Examples

This rule gives the page a fixed (non-scrolling) background image, which will display over a solid white background:

```
body {
  background: #fff url(/images/texture.gif) fixed;
}
```

background-attachment

This property determines whether the background image assigned to an element scrolls in synchronization with the element's content, or remains fixed in relation to the browser window. For example, if you wanted the top-left corner of your page background image to remain in the top-left corner of the browser window, even as the page was scrolled, you would set `background-attachment` to `fixed`.

Inherited: No

See also: `background-image`

Value

`fixed` or `scroll`

Initial value: `scroll`

Compatibility

CSS Version: 1

The property is supported by Internet Explorer 4 or later, Opera, Safari and all Mozilla browsers.

Internet Explorer for Windows, prior to version 7, and Opera browsers (up to version 6), do not correctly support `background-attachment: fixed` on elements other than `body`. Internet Explorer 7, Opera, Safari, and Mozilla browsers all get this right.

Examples

This style rule applies a background image to the page, and specifies that the image should not scroll with the page content:

```
body {
  background-image: url(/images/texture.gif);
  background-attachment: fixed;
}
```

background-color

This property sets the background color for an element.

Note that the default background color is `transparent`, so even though this property is not inherited, nested elements will allow the background to show through by default. The reason for this arrangement is to allow background images to be displayed behind nested elements.

It is considered good practice always to specify a foreground color (with the `color` property) whenever you specify a background color, and vice versa.

Inherited: No

See also: `color`

Value

The property takes any CSS color value (see Appendix B) or `transparent`.

Initial value: `transparent`

Compatibility

CSS Version: 1

This property works in all CSS-compatible browsers.

Example

This style rule fills `blockquote` tags of class `warning` with a tomato-red background color:

```
blockquote.warning {
  background-color: #ff6347;
  border: 0 solid #ff6347;
}
```

background-image

This property sets the background image for an element. By default, element backgrounds are transparent, so the background image will show through nested elements, unless they have been assigned background colors or images of their own.

The positioning and tiling of a background image may be customized with the `background-position` and `background-repeat` properties, respectively.

Inherited: No

See also: `background-attachment`, `background-color`, `background-position`, `background-repeat`

Value

The property takes as its value a URL or `none`. In CSS, URLs must be surrounded by the `url()` wrapper, not quotes. See the examples below.

Initial value: none

Compatibility

CSS Version: 1

Works in all CSS-compatible browsers.

Example

These style rules demonstrate the assigning of background images with relative, absolute, and fully qualified URLs, respectively:

```
body {
  background-image: url(../images/texture.gif);
}

body {
  background-image: url(/images/texture.gif);
}

body {
  background-image: url(http://www.mysite.com/images/texture.gif);
}
```

background-position

By default, an element's background image (assigned with the background-image property) is aligned so that its top and left edges are flush with the top and left edges of the element (including any padding), respectively. With the background-position property, you can assign a different position for the image.

Inherited: No

See also: background-image

Value

The property takes one position specifier, or two position specifiers separated by a space.

Each of the position specifiers may be a CSS length measurement (pixels, points, ems, etc.), a percentage, or one of the constants from Table C.1.

Table C.1. `background-position` constants

Vertical	Horizontal
top, center, bottom	left, center, right

If you specify only one measurement or percentage, it applies to the horizontal position; the vertical position of the image will default to 50%. If you specify two measurements or percentages, the first specifies the horizontal position, while the second specifies the vertical. Negative measurements/percentages are allowed, but are rarely useful.

If you specify only one constant, the other dimension defaults to center. The order of constants is not significant.

You can mix length measurement types and percentages (i.e. specify vertical position in one format, horizontal in another). However, you cannot mix lengths/percentages with constants.

Percentages and constants differ from length measurements in the way they position the image. In an element that's 500 pixels wide, a horizontal position of center or 50% will center the image within the horizontal area of the element. However, a horizontal position of 250px (or any equivalent length measurement) positions the *left edge* of the image exactly 250 pixels from the left edge of the element.

Initial value: 0 0

Compatibility

CSS Version: 2.1

The property works in Internet Explorer 4 or later, Opera, Safari, and Mozilla browsers.

Examples

In this style rule, the background image is centered in the element area:

```
body {
  background-position: center;
}
```

In both of these style rules, the background image is placed flush against the bottom-right corner of the element:

```
body {
  background-position: 100% 100%;
}

body {
   background-position: bottom right;
}
```

In this style rule, the background image's left edge will be positioned 20 pixels from the left of the element, and the image will be centered vertically:

```
body {
  background-position: 20px;
}
```

In this style rule, the background image's top edge is 20 pixels from the top of the element, and the image will be centered horizontally across the element's width:

```
body {
  background-position: 50% 20px;
}
```

The following style rule is illegal, as it mixes a length measurement with a constant:

```
body {
  background-position: 20px center; /* This is illegal! */
}
```

background-position-x, background-position-y

These nonstandard properties are supported only by Internet Explorer browsers, and let you individually specify the two components of the `background-position` property. These properties are most useful in Dynamic HTML scripting in an Internet Explorer-only environment.

Inherited: No

See also: `background-position`

Value

Both of these properties support values specified in CSS lengths and percentages. Additionally, `background-position-x` and `background-position-y` support the horizontal and vertical position constants listed in Table C.1. Important differences between positions specified with CSS length measurements and positions specified with percentages or constants are described under `background-position`.

Initial value: 0

Compatibility

CSS Version: n/a

The properties are supported by Internet Explorer 4 or later only.

Example

This style rule places the background image 20 pixels from the top, and centers it horizontally on the page:

```
body {
  background-position-x: center;
  background-position-y: 20px;
}
```

background-repeat

By default, a background image, specified with the `background-image` property, will repeat horizontally and vertically to fill the element (this is often referred to as *tiling*). The `background-repeat` property lets you override that behavior with your own preferences.

Inherited: No

See also: `background-image`, `background-position`

Value

The property takes as a value `repeat`, `no-repeat`, `repeat-x`, or `repeat-y`.

The first two options are self-explanatory. `repeat-x` causes the image to repeat only horizontally, effectively forming a horizontal band with the background image. `repeat-y` causes the image to repeat only vertically, forming a vertical band.

Initial value: `repeat`

Compatibility

CSS Version: 1

The property works in all CSS-compatible browsers.

Example

This style rule uses `background-repeat` and `background-position` to create a horizontal band 50 pixels below the top of the page:

```
body {
  background-repeat: repeat-x;
  background-position: 0 50px;
}
```

behavior

An Internet Explorer-only property, `behavior` lets you assign packaged Dynamic HTML code to HTML elements in bulk. For a full description of the behaviors feature in Internet Explorer, refer to the MSDN web site.[4]

Inherited: No

Value

The property takes a URL (specified with the CSS `url()` wrapper) or an object ID.

---

[4] http://msdn.microsoft.com/workshop/author/behaviors/overview.asp

Initial value: none

Compatibility

CSS Version: n/a

Attached behaviors are supported by Internet Explorer 5 for Windows or later. Other behavior types are supported by Internet Explorer 5.5 for Windows or later.

Example

The following style rule applies the behavior defined in the `draganddrop.htc` file to any element of class `draganddrop`:

```
.draganddrop {
  behavior: url(draganddrop.htc);
}
```

border

This is a shorthand property that lets you set the same width, color, and style for all four borders of an element with a single property declaration. This property sets up identical borders on all four sides, but can be followed by side-specific border properties that modify them.

Inherited: No

See also: `border-width`, `border-style`, and `border-color`

Value

You can specify a `border-width` value, a `border-style` value, and a `border-color` value, or any combination of the three, in any order, separated by spaces.

Initial value: none

Compatibility

CSS Version: 1

The property works on all CSS-compatible browsers, with the same browser-specific limitations as the individual `border-` properties.

Example

This style rule puts a dashed, yellow, single-pixel border around `div` tags of class `advertisement`:

```
div.advertisement {
  border: dashed yellow 1px;
}
```

border-bottom, border-left, border-right, border-top

These are shorthand properties that let you set the style, width, and color of the border on a particular side of an element with single property declaration.

Inherited: No

See also: `border-width`, `border-style`, and `border-color`

Value

You can specify a `border-width` value, a `border-style` value, and a `border-color` value, or any combination of the three, in any order, separated by spaces.

Initial value: none

Compatibility

CSS Version: 1

The properties work in all CSS-compatible browsers.

Example

Applies a single-pixel, dashed, blue border to the bottom of elements with a `title` attribute:

```
[title] {
  border-bottom: dashed blue 1px;
}
```

Note that attribute selectors are not yet supported by many browsers.

border-bottom-color, border-left-color, border-right-color, border-top-color

Each of these properties sets the color of the border along one side of an element.

Inherited: No

See also: `border-color`

Value

The properties take any CSS color value (see Appendix B).

Initial value: none

Compatibility

CSS Version: 2.1

The properties work in all CSS-compatible browsers.

Example

```
p.funky {
  border-style: solid;
  border-top-color: blue;
  border-right-color: yellow;
  border-bottom-color: #ff0000;
  border-left-color: #0f0;
}
```

border-bottom-style, border-left-style, border-right-style, border-top-style

Each of these properties sets the style of the border along one side of an element.

Inherited: No

See also: `border-style`

Value

Any of the constants allowed for `border-style`.

Initial value: `none`

Compatibility

CSS Version: 2.1

The properties work in all CSS-compatible browsers.

Example

This style rule puts double lines along the left and right, and single lines along the top and bottom, of `blockquote` elements:

```
blockquote {
  border-top-style: solid;
  border-bottom-style: solid;
  border-left-style: double;
  border-right-style: double;
}
```

border-bottom-width, border-left-width, border-right-width, border-top-width

Each of these properties sets the width of the border along one side of an element.

Inherited: No

See also: `border-width`

Value

The value of these properties can be `thin`, `medium`, `thick`, or any CSS length measurement.

Initial value: `medium`

Compatibility

CSS Version: 1

The properties work in all CSS-compatible browsers.

Example

This style rule puts two-pixel borders along the left and right, and one-pixel borders along the top and bottom, of `blockquote` elements:

```
blockquote {
  border-style: solid;
  border-top-width: 1px;
  border-bottom-width: 1px;
  border-left-width: 2px;
  border-right-width: 2px;
}
```

border-collapse

This property lets you choose between two systems that the browser can use to define table borders.

The default system, which you can select with the value `separate`, is the familiar "separate borders" system. Here, each table cell has its own borders, which are separated from those of neighboring cells by the table's cell spacing. The new system, which you can select with the `collapse` value, gets rid of any cell spacing, combines the borders of adjacent cells, and lets you assign borders to row and column groups. For full details, refer to the CSS 2.1 specification.[5]

---

[5] http://www.w3.org/TR/CSS21/tables.html#collapsing-borders

Inherited: Yes

See also: `empty-cells`

Value

`collapse` or `separate`

Initial value: `separate`[6]

Compatibility

CSS Version: 2.1

This property works in Internet Explorer 5 or later for Windows, Opera, Safari, and Mozilla browsers.

Example

This style rule sets tables of class `data` to use the collapsed border model:

```
table.data {
  border-collapse: collapse;
}
```

border-color

The `border-color` property sets the color of the border surrounding the selected element(s).

The colors may be set individually for each side using the `border-bottom-color`, `border-left-color`, `border-right-color`, and `border-top-color` properties.

Inherited: No

---

[6]The initial value prescribed by the CSS 2 specification is actually **collapse**; however, all current browsers' default table rendering systems correspond to **separate**. Therefore, the CSS Working Group has proposed changing the default value of this property to **separate** in a future version of the CSS specification. This proposal may be found in the Errata for the CSS 2 specification.

Value

You can specify from one to four different color values (see Appendix B) to color different sides of the element, as shown in Table C.2.

Table C.2. Effects of multiple values on border properties

Number of Values	Effect on Borders
1	All four borders receive the value specified.
2	The top and bottom (horizontal) borders receive the first value; left and right (vertical) borders receive the second.
3	The top border receives the first value, vertical borders receive the second, and the bottom border receives the third.
4	The values are applied to top, right, bottom, and left borders, respectively.

Initial value: The `color` property of the element, which may be inherited if it's not explicitly specified.

Compatibility

CSS Version: 1

The property works in all CSS-compatible browsers.

Example

This style rule puts blue borders on the top and bottom, and red borders on the left and right sides, of `blockquote` elements:

```
blockquote {
  border-style: solid;
  border-color: blue red;
}
```

border-spacing

This property is the CSS equivalent to the `cellspacing` attribute of the HTML `<table>` tag. It lets you specify the spacing that will appear between cells in a table. This property is ignored if `border-collapse` is set to `collapse` for the table.

Inherited: Yes

See also: `border-collapse`

Value

The property takes a single CSS length measurement, or two lengths separated by a space. A single value will be applied as both the horizontal and vertical spacing between cells. Two values will be applied as horizontal and vertical spacing, respectively.

Initial value: 0

Compatibility

CSS Version: 2.1

The property is supported by Safari, Opera, and Mozilla browsers.

Example

This style rule sets spacing of five pixels between all table cells in tables of class `spacious`:

```
table.spacious {
  border-spacing: 5px;
}
```

border-style

The `border-style` property sets the style of the border surrounding the selected element(s).

The style may be set for each side individually, using the `border-bottom-style`, `border-left-style`, `border-right-style`, and `border-top-style` properties.

Inherited: No

Value

The CSS specifications provide a set of constants for a range of border styles. Table C.3 shows the available constants and the browsers that support them.

You can specify from one to four different style values to style each side of the element differently, as shown in Table C.2.

The difference between none and hidden, though not visible in Table C.3, arises in HTML tables where the border-collapse property is set to collapse. When two cells share a border and one of them specifies a style of none for that border, the other cell's border style takes precedence and the border is drawn.

However, the hidden border style takes precedence over all other border styles; therefore, if the first cell in the previous example specified a style of hidden, the other cell's border style would be ignored and no border would be drawn. See the CSS 2 Specification[7] for a full discussion of table border conflict resolution.

Initial value: none

---

[7] http://www.w3.org/TR/REC-CSS2/tables.html#border-conflict-resolution

Table C.3. CSS border style constants

Constant	CSS Spec	Supporting Browsers	Sample
double	CSS1	All CSS browsers	double
groove	CSS1	All CSS browsers	groove
inset	CSS1	All CSS browsers	inset
none	CSS1	All CSS browsers	none
outset	CSS1	All CSS browsers	outset
ridge	CSS1	All CSS browsers	ridge
solid	CSS1	All CSS browsers	solid
dashed	CSS1	Mozilla, IE 5.5/Win+, Opera, Safari	dashed
dotted	CSS1	Mozilla, IE 5.5/Win+, Opera, Safari	dotted
hidden	CSS 2	Mozilla, IE 5.5/Win+, Opera, Safari	hidden

Compatibility

CSS Version: 1

The property works in all CSS-compatible browsers. For specific compatibility information, see above.

Note that in versions up to and including 6, Internet Explorer rendered a dotted border identically to a dashed one. Internet Explorer 7 corrects this.

Example

This style rule makes any element of class fauxbutton look like a button by giving it an outset border style, a light grey background, and black text:

```
.fauxbutton {
  border-style: outset;
  border-color: grey;
  border-width: medium;
  background: lightgrey;
  color: black;
}
```

border-width

The border-width property sets the width of the border surrounding the selected element(s).

The widths for each side may be set individually using the border-bottom-width, border-left-width, border-right-width, and border-top-width properties.

Inherited: No

Value

The property takes as a value thin, medium, thick, or any CSS length measurement.

You can specify from one to four different values to set different border widths for each side of the element, as shown in Table C.2.

Initial value: medium

Compatibility

CSS Version: 1

The property works in all CSS-compatible browsers.

Example

This style rule puts thick borders on the top and bottom, and thin borders on the left and right sides of blockquote elements:

```
blockquote {
  border-style: solid;
  border-width: thick thin;
}
```

bottom

This property lets you set the distance between the bottom edge of an `absolute` positioned element (including its padding, border, and margin) and the bottom edge of the positioning context in which it resides. The positioning context is the padding area of the element's nearest ancestor that has a `position` property value other than `static`, or the `body` element.

For `relative` positioned elements, this property sets a relative offset from the normal position of its bottom edge. So, a setting of `10px` will shift the bottom edge of the box up by ten pixels, and a setting of `-10px` will shift it down by the same amount.

Inherited: No

See also: `position`, `left`, `top`, and `right`

Value

The property takes a CSS length measurement, a percentage value, or the `auto` constant. Percentages are based on the height of the parent element. The `auto` constant tells the browser to determine the position of the bottom edge itself, based on whatever other constraints may exist on the size/position of the element.

Initial value: `auto`

Compatibility

CSS Version: 2.1

The property works in Internet Explorer 5 or later, Opera, Safari, and Mozilla browsers.

Example

This style rule positions the element with ID `menu` at the bottom of the document:

```
#menu {
  position: absolute;
  bottom: 0;
  width: 100px;
```

```
    height: 200px;
}
```

caption-side

This property lets you specify the side of a table on which that table's caption (specified with the `<caption>` tag) should appear.

Inherited: Yes

Value

The property takes as a value either of the following constants: `top`, `bottom`.

Initial value: `top`

Compatibility

CSS Version: 2.1

The property works in Internet Explorer 5 for Macintosh, Opera, and Mozilla browsers. Mozilla browsers also implement the unofficial values of `left` and `right`.

Example

This style rule places captions at the bottom of all tables that occur within other tables:

```
table table {
  caption-side: bottom;
}
```

clear

Setting a `clear` property on an element lets you specify that it should appear below any floating elements that would normally cut into it. You can specify that the element should be clear of left-floated elements, right-floated elements, or both.

Inherited: No

See also: `float`

Value

The property can take as its value `left`, `right`, `none`, or `both`.

Initial value: `none`

Compatibility

CSS Version: 1

The property works in all CSS-compatible browsers.

Example

This style rule ensures that the element with ID `footer` will be clear of any floating elements that appear above it in the page:

```
#footer {
  clear: both;
}
```

clip

This property clips (or crops) the visible region of the absolute- or fixed-positioned element(s) to which it is applied. The element occupies the same amount of space on the page as usual, but only the area specified by this property is displayed.

In contrast to the `overflow` property, this property affects only the *visible* area of an element (including its padding, borders, etc.). The size and position of the element are not affected by this property.

Inherited: No

See also: `overflow`

Value

The current CSS specification allows only for rectangular clipping regions. You can specify such a region by wrapping four measurement values in the CSS `rect()` wrapper, as follows:

```
clip: rect(top right bottom left);
```

For an element that's *x* pixels wide and *y* pixels high, the default clipping region (assuming it has no borders or padding to increase its rendered area) would be `rect(0px xpx ypx 0)`. To trim ten pixels from each side of the image, you'd change this to `rect(10px x-10px y-10px 10px)`, where you would calculate and substitute the actual values of *x-10* and *y-10*.

The default value, `auto`, lets the browser determine the area of the element to draw, as usual.

Initial value: `auto`

Compatibility

CSS Version: 2.1

The property works in all CSS-compatible browsers.

Note that Opera browsers will clip only the rendered content of the element—not its background. This is actually correct according to the CSS 2.1 specification, although it does not match the established behavior of other browsers.

Example

This style rule will clip ten pixels from the left and right sides of the element with ID `logo`, which is a 100 x 100-pixel image:

```
#logo {
  position: absolute;
  clip: rect(0px 90px 100px 10px);
}
```

color

This property sets the foreground (text) color of the element. It also defines the default border color of the element.

In general, you should always specify a background color when you specify a foreground color, and vice versa.

Inherited: Yes

See also: `background-color`

Value

The property takes as its value any CSS color value (see Appendix B).

Initial value: `black`

Compatibility

CSS Version: 1

The property works in all CSS-compatible browsers.

Example

This style rule sets paragraphs of class `warning` to have white text on a tomato-red background:

```
p.warning {
  color: white;
  background-color: #ff6347;
}
```

content

Sometimes it makes sense to generate some text at the beginning or end of an element as part of that element's style. Termed **generated content**, this text is not part of the HTML document, but is generated purely by the style sheet. The CSS `content` property is intended for this purpose. You must apply it to the `:before` or `:after` pseudo-elements, as shown in the examples below.

Inherited: No

See also: `counter-increment`, `counter-reset`, `quotes`

Value

The CSS 2.1 specification mandates a number of different generated content formats, but not all of them are supported by current browsers. You can use any combination of the following content formats by listing them one after the other, separated by spaces.

`"arbitrary string"`

This format lets you place a string of text before or after the actual content of the element. You cannot format this text by placing HTML code in the string—the browser will display the tags as text. Instead, use CSS to style the string, as in the examples below. The special code `\A` in the string produces a line break (same effect as an HTML `<br>` tag).

Browser support:

Partially supported by: Mozilla browsers (text is displayed but the `\A` code is ignored)

Fully supported by: Opera

`url(http://url.goes.here)`

This format lets you place some external resource before or after the actual content of the element. For example, if you supply a URL to an image, the browser should place that image before/after the content of the element. If you supply a URL to an HTML document, the browser should display the contents of the document before/after the content of the element.

There are obvious complexities that come into play here, but since no browsers support this format yet, any further discussion would be purely academic.

`counter(name)`
`counter(name, style)`
`counters(name, string)`
`counters(name, string, style)`

These formats let you generate numbered elements (for example, numbered section headings) without having to resort to an ordered list (`<ol>`) in the HTML document. You must define, increment, and reset your counters when appropriate using the `counter-increment` and `counter-reset` CSS properties, then use one of the above formats to display the value of a counter where desired.

`counter(name)` will display the value of the named counter in decimal format, while `counter(name, style)` lets you specify the style in which to display the counter value (you can use any style allowed by the `list-style-type` CSS property). You can also define hierarchical counters to produce multiple-level numbering (e.g. "Section 5.2.3"), the values of which you can output with `counters(name, string)` or `counters(name, string, style)`. The `string` argument specifies the string that is used to separate the numbers, and is typically a period (`"."`).

Browser support: Mozilla browsers, Opera

attr(*attribute*)

This format lets you output the value of an attribute of the element (e.g. the title attribute of an <a> tag) before or after the actual content of the element.

Browser support: Mozilla browsers, Opera

open-quote
close-quote

These formats let you display opening or closing quotation marks, the exact appearance of which is dictated by the CSS quotes property.

Browser support: Mozilla browsers, Opera

no-open-quote
no-close-quote

These formats let you put "fake" opening or closing quotes that don't actually display anything, but which still jump in and out of nesting levels defined in the quotes property.

Browser support: Mozilla browsers

normal

This is the default setting of "no generated content."

Initial value: " " (the empty string)

Compatibility

CSS Version: 2.1

Safari and Internet Explorer do not support the content property; refer to each property above for other browser support.

Examples

This style rule puts the text "Note: " in bold at the start of a paragraph of class note:

```
p.note:before {
  content: "Note: ";
```

```
  font-weight: bold;
}
```

These style rules put angle brackets (< >) around span elements of class tagname using generated content and the quotes property:

```
span.tagname {
  quotes: "<" ">";
}
span.tagname:before {
  content: open-quote;
}
span.tagname:after {
  content: close-quote;
}
```

These style rules put quotation marks around <blockquote> elements. The third style rule applies to blockquote elements that have a cite attribute, and modifies the content property to close the quotation marks and display the source of the citation on a new line:

```
blockquote:before {
  content: open-quote;
}
blockquote:after {
  content: close-quote;
}
blockquote[cite]:after {
  content: close-quote "\A from " attr(cite);
}
```

Unsupported by current browsers, these style rules should place a standard HTML header and footer on the current page:

```
body:before {
  content: url(standardheader.html);
}
body:after {
  content: url(standardfooter.html);
}
```

counter-increment

This property increments or decrements a named counter (for display with the content property) for each occurrence of the selected element(s).

On nested elements, a hierarchical counter is automatically created, so that you effectively have a separate counter at each level of the structure.

Inherited: No

See also: `content`, `counter-reset`

Value

The property takes as its value a counter name, optionally followed by a positive or negative integer to indicate how much to increment (positive) or decrement (negative) the counter. If you want to increment/decrement multiple counters for a single element, you can separate their names (and optional integers) by spaces.

The default value, `none`, is also supported, but is of little practical use.

Initial value: `none`

Compatibility

CSS Version: 2.1

The property is supported by Mozilla browsers and Opera.

Examples

This simple example will keep track of the number of `h1` tags in the document, and will output a chapter number at the start of each:

```
h1 {
  counter-increment: chapter;
}
h1:before {
  content: "Chapter " counter(chapter) " - ";
}
```

This example uses a counter to number `div` elements in the document, then displays the counter value in the `h1` tags appearing within them. Because the `counters()` format is used to output the counter value, nested `div` elements will be numbered hierarchically (e.g. "Division 2.1.3"):

```
div {
  counter-increment: division;
}
div > h1:before {
  content: "Division " counters(division,".") ": ";
}
```

counter-reset

This property sets a named counter (for display with the `content` property) to a particular value each time the enclosing style rule is matched.

By default, the counter is reset to zero, but you can specify any value you like.

Inherited: No

See also: `counter-increment`

Value

The property takes a counter name, optionally followed by a positive or negative integer that specifies the new value for the counter (the default is 0). If you want to set multiple counters for a single element, you can separate their names (and optional integers) by spaces.

The default value, `none`, is also supported, but is of little practical use.

Initial value: `none`

Compatibility

CSS Version: 2.1

The property is supported by Mozilla browsers and Opera.

Example

This example lets you use `h1` elements to mark chapters, and `h2` elements to mark subsections and display hierarchical numbering on section headings:

```
h1 {
  counter-increment: chapter;
  counter-reset: section;
```

```
}
h1:before {
  content: "Chapter " counter(chapter) " - ";
}
h2 {
  counter-increment: section;
}
h2:before {
  content: "Section " counter(chapter) "." counter(section) " - ";
}
```

cue

Sound cues are used by aural (speaking) browsers for the visually impaired as "audio icons." This is a shorthand property that lets you specify the `cue-before` and `cue-after` properties with a single property declaration.

Inherited: No

See also: `cue-before`, `cue-after`

Value

The property takes one or two URLs (specified with CSS `url()` syntax) that point to sound files. If one URL is provided, it is assigned to `cue-before` and `cue-after`—the sound is played before and after the element. If two URLs are provided, the first is assigned to `cue-before` and the second to `cue-after`.

Initial value: none

Compatibility

CSS Version: 2.1

The property is not supported by any currently available browser.

Example

This example plays `ding.wav` before and after each `div` element:

```
div {
  cue: url(/sounds/ding.wav);
}
```

cue-after, cue-before

Sound cues are used by aural (speaking) browsers for the visually impaired as "audio icons." `cue-before` and `cue-after` let you set cues to be played before and after an element, respectively.

Inherited: No

See also: cue

Value

These properties take a URL, specified with CSS `url()` syntax, that points to a sound file.

The default value, `none`, is also supported, but is of little practical use.

Initial value: none

Compatibility

CSS Version: 2.1

The properties are not supported by any currently available browser.

Example

This example plays `ding.wav` before each `h1` element, with the exception of `h1` elements of class `silent`:

```
h1 {
  cue-before: url(/sounds/ding.wav);
}
h1.silent {
  cue-before: none;
}
```

cursor

This property lets you modify the appearance of the mouse cursor when the mouse hovers over a selected element.

Inherited: Yes

Value

Table C.4 lists the different cursor values supported by the CSS 2.1 standard, and the major browsers that support them. The special value `auto` is the default, and lets the browser determine automatically what the cursor should look like. The value `default` sets the cursor to its default appearance, as dictated by the operating system.

The value `url(url)`, which is currently supported only in Internet Explorer 6 for Windows, lets you define your own cursor by pointing to a `.cur` (Windows static cursor) or `.ani` (Windows animated cursor) file on your site. Presumably, this property will support more standard image formats when it is implemented in other browsers.

Table C.5 lists the additional, nonstandard cursors supported by various versions of Internet Explorer. These cursors' exact appearances may vary between browsers and operating systems.

Table C.4. CSS 2.1 standard cursors

cursor Value	Appearance (in IE6)
auto	n/a
crosshair	+
default	▷
e-resize	↔
help	▷?
move	✛
n-resize	↕
ne-resize	↗
nw-resize	↖
pointer	☝
s-resize	↕
se-resize	↘
sw-resize	↙
text	I
url(url)	n/a
w-resize	↔
wait	⧖
progress	▷⧖

Table C.5. Internet Explorer-only cursors

cursor Value	Appearance (in IE6)
all-scroll	
col-resize	
hand	
no-drop	
not-allowed	
row-resize	
vertical-text	

Initial value: auto

Compatibility

CSS Version: 1

The property is supported by all CSS-compatible browsers.

Example

The following style rule (which doesn't work in browsers that don't support attribute selectors) displays the `pointer` cursor when the mouse hovers over any element with an `onclick` attribute.

```
[onclick] {
  cursor: pointer;
}
```

direction

Most western languages are written left-to-right (LTR). As you probably know, many other languages (e.g. Hebrew) are written right-to-left (RTL). Documents written with the Unicode character set[8] can contain text from both LTR and RTL languages. The Unicode standard includes a complicated algorithm that should be used for displaying such mixed text. It also defines special characters that let you "group" text.

For example, consider the following imaginary string of text, where the lowercase text represents LTR characters and the uppercase text represents RTL:

```
english1 HEBREW1 english2 HEBREW2 english3
```

Now, the obvious way to render this would be "english1 1WERBEH english2 2WERBEH english3," but what happens if we add some HTML tags to the mix?

```
<p>english1 <q lang="he">HEBREW1 english2 HEBREW2</q> english3</p>
```

As you can see, the text beginning with HEBREW1 and ending with HEBREW2 is intended as an inline quotation in Hebrew, which just happens to contain an English word. Since HEBREW1 and HEBREW2 belong to the same block of Hebrew text, "HEBREW1" should be rendered from right to left, i.e. "1WERBEH." Also, as the quotation is in Hebrew, the sentence should be read from right-to-left, but the English word must remain LTR. With this in mind, the complete paragraph should be rendered as "english1 2WERBEH english2 1WERBEH english3."

The HTML 4.0 standard (which forms the basis of XHTML 1.0) defines the dir attribute and the bdo element to handle these complexities. To obtain the desired rendering in an HTML4-compatible browser, the code should be:

```
<p>english1 <q lang="he" dir="rtl">HEBREW1 english2 HEBREW2</q>
  english3</p>
```

The dir attribute of the q element specifies the rendering order; the lang attribute won't have any actual visible effect. For full details on language and bidirectional text rendering in HTML, refer to Section 8 of the HTML 4.0 standard.[9]

So, where does CSS come into play, you ask? Well, the direction property, in combination with a unicode-bidi property setting of embed, performs the same role as the HTML dir attribute. In combination with a unicode-bidi property setting of bidi-override, direction has the same effect as the HTML bdo tag. However, it is still considered best practice to include bidirectional text attributes as part of the HTML code. The direction and unicode-bidi properties are intended for use in styling XML documents that do not have the benefit of HTML

---

[8] http://www.unicode.org/
[9] http://www.w3.org/TR/REC-html40/struct/dirlang.html

4's bidirectional text features. Since the focus of this book is on web development, I'll therefore refer you to the CSS 2.1 standard[10] for full details on these properties.

Inherited: Yes

See also: `unicode-bidi`

Value

The property takes either of `ltr` or `rtl`.

Initial value: `ltr`

Compatibility

CSS Version: 2

This property is not supported by any currently available browser.

Example

This style rule sets the text direction of an imaginary XML element named `hebrew` to `rtl`. The `unicode-bidi` property is there to ensure that this setting will "group" any elements within it according to this direction, even if `hebrew` is rendered as an inline element:

```
hebrew {
  direction: rtl;
  unicode-bidi: embed;
}
```

display

In HTML, there are different *types* of elements. `div` and `blockquote`, for example, are both block elements, while `strong` and `em` are both inline elements. For each type of element, a browser supports a "display mode." Essentially, all block elements are displayed the same way, but with varying margins, padding, borders, etc. as the default.

---

[10] http://www.w3.org/TR/CSS21/visuren.html#direction

The `display` property lets you set the "display mode" for an element. For example, you can set a hyperlink (`a`) to be displayed as a block instead of inline text.

The most common use for the display property is to show and hide portions of an HTML document. Setting `display` to `none` causes the element not just to be hidden (as with the `visibility` property), but not to occupy any space on the page, either. Using Dynamic HTML to set this property in JavaScript event handlers lets you create, for example, hierarchical menus that expand and collapse to display submenus on the fly.

Inherited: No

See also: `visibility`

Value

block
CSS version: 1

Browser support: The value is supported by all CSS-compatible browsers.

The default display mode for `p`, `div`, `ul`, `blockquote`, and many others, `block` causes the element to occupy a rectangular area of the page, stacked vertically with its sibling elements, so that previous siblings are above it, and subsequent siblings are below it.

inline
CSS version: 1

Browser support: The value is supported by all CSS-compatible browsers.

The default display mode for `strong`, `u`, `a`, `code`, and many others, this value causes the element to flow "inline" as a string of text within the parent block, possibly broken by word wrapping.

list-item
CSS version: 1

Browser support: This value is supported by all CSS-compatible browsers.

The default display mode for `li` elements, `list-item` causes the element to be rendered as a list item. The `list-style` family of properties controls the position and appearance of the list item marker (i.e. the bullet or number).

none
CSS version: 1

Browser support: none is supported by all CSS-compatible browsers.

This display mode causes the element not to be rendered at all. The element will not occupy any space on the page (unlike elements to which visibility: hidden applies: this hides the element but reserves space for it on the page).

run-in
CSS version: 2

Browser support: This value is not supported by any currently available browsers.

This display mode causes the element to appear as an inline element at the start of the block immediately following it. If there is no block following a run-in element, it is displayed as a normal block instead. The effect is illustrated in Figure C.1.

Figure C.1. Effect of run-in display mode

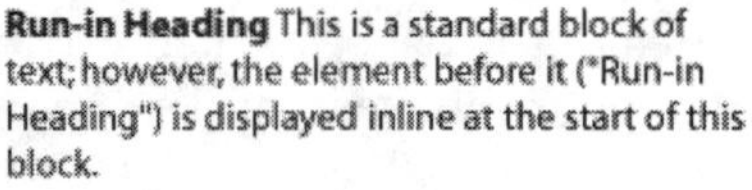

Run-in Heading This is a standard block of text; however, the element before it ("Run-in Heading") is displayed inline at the start of this block.

table
inline-table
table-row
table-column
table-row-group
table-column-group
table-header-group
table-footer-group
table-cell
table-caption
CSS version: 2

Browser support: IE5 for Windows supports only table-header-group, while IE5.5 for Windows adds support for table-footer-group. There is no additional support in Internet Explorer versions 6 or 7.

Mozilla browsers support all of these except `inline-table`, `table-caption`, `table-column`, and `table-column-group`.

These display modes let you display various elements as tables (or parts thereof). The practical utility of these display modes is questionable, which is why most browsers have yet to fully implement them. For full details, refer to the CSS 2.1 Specification.[11]

`inline-block`
  CSS version: 2.1

  Browser support: Support exists in Internet Explorer 5.5 or later for Windows only.

  This display lets you place a block inline with the content of its parent element.

Initial value: `inline`[12]

Compatibility

CSS Version: The property is supported in version 1 (many display modes were added in CSS 2, with more coming in CSS3).

All CSS-compatible browsers support this property, but none yet supports the full range of CSS 2 display modes. See above for full compatibility information.

Example

This style rule hides unordered list (`ul`) elements nested within an unordered list of class `menu`. In a practical application, JavaScript code could be used to display these submenus, by changing the `display` property to `block`, when the user clicks one of the main menu items:

```
ul.menu ul {
  display: none;
}
```

---

[11] http://www.w3.org/TR/CSS21/tables.html

[12] Elements like `p`, `div`, `blockquote`, etc. have a default `display` value of `block`, and other elements have their own default `display` values. These defaults come from the browser's built-in default style sheet, rather than from the CSS specification. If you were to create your own tag (which you can do with XHTML), its `display` property would be `inline` by default.

elevation

elevation is used by aural browsers (e.g. a speaking browser for the blind) to set a position at an angle from a horizontal plane. It's from this position that the sound emanates when the content is presented aurally.

Inherited: Yes

See also: azimuth

Value

The property takes an angle (from -90deg to 90deg, where 90deg is directly above the listener, -90deg is directly below, and 0deg is at the listener's ear level), or a descriptive constant (e.g. above) as its value.

Initial value: level

Compatibility

CSS Version: 2

The property is not yet supported by any browser.

Example

This style rule will cause all elements of class commandment to be heard from 80 degrees above the horizontal:

```
.commandment {
  elevation: 80deg;
}
```

empty-cells

This property lets you set whether or not empty table cells are displayed in a table operating in "separate borders" mode (see border-collapse).

Inherited: Yes

See also: border-collapse

Value

The value of this property can be show or hide. When it's set to hide, empty table cells, their borders, and their backgrounds are not drawn—the table background is visible in their place.

Initial value: show[13]

Compatibility

CSS Version: 2

The property is supported by all CSS-compatible browsers.

Example

This style rule sets tables of class seethru to hide empty table cells:

```
table.seethru {
  border-collapse: separate;
  empty-cells: hide;
}
```

filter

Internet Explorer for Windows offers this property, which lets you apply static special effects, and animated transitions, to any HTML element.

Inherited: No

Value

Internet Explorer 4 or later for Windows supports a set of 14 static filters and two animated transition filters. Internet Explorer 5.5 or later supports a new filter technology that offers all the filters supported by IE4 and a bunch more besides, with a total of two procedural surface filters, 16 static effect filters, and 17 animated transition filters.

Static filters offer effects such as translucent elements, drop shadows, glows, blurs, flips, rotations, lighting, and distortions. Animated transition filters let you wrap

---

[13]Mozilla browsers default to hide when running in "Quirks mode."

an element's change from one appearance to another in an animated effect. Available transitions include simple PowerPoint™-style wipes and slides, smooth fades and gradient wipes, and a fanciful pixelation effect.

You need to apply animated transition filters with CSS, then trigger them with JavaScript code, to see the animated effect.

Internet Explorer 4 filters have the following syntax:

```
filter: filter(param=value, ...)
```

Internet Explorer 5.5 filters look like this:

```
filter: progid:DXImageTransform.Microsoft.filter(param=value, ...)
```

You can apply filters in any sensible combination by specifying them one at a time, separated by spaces, in the value of the `filter` property.

For complete documentation that covers all the available filters, and explains how to use them in various ways, see Microsoft's Introduction to Filters and Transitions[14] and its Visual Filters and Transitions Reference.[15]

Initial value: none

Compatibility

CSS Version: n/a

Internet Explorer 4 or later supports a basic set of filters and transitions. These basic filters are superseded in Internet Explorer 5.5 by an entirely new set of filters, but support for the original set is maintained for backwards compatibility.

Examples

This style rule uses the IE4 static filter `dropShadow` to show a shadow beneath any element of class `floating`:

```
.floating {
  filter: dropShadow(color=#000000, offx=5, offy=5);
}
```

---

[14] http://msdn.microsoft.com/workshop/author/filter/filters.asp
[15] http://msdn.microsoft.com/workshop/author/filter/reference/reference.asp

In the following example, the style rule assigns the IE5.5 animated transition filter **Pixelate** to the element with the ID **toolbar**. The JavaScript code then assigns an event handler that is triggered when the page finishes loading. The event handler enables the filter (it's disabled in the CSS code), sets the starting state for the transition with **Apply()**, makes the element visible (it's hidden in the CSS code), then plays the transition with **Play()**.

```
<style type="text/css">
#toolbar {
  visibility: hidden;
  filter: progid:DXImageTransform.Microsoft.Pixelate(MaxSquare=50,
Duration=1, Enabled=false);
}
</style>
<script type="text/javascript" language="JavaScript">
window.onload = function() {
  var toolbar = document.getElementById('toolbar');
  toolbar.filters[0].enabled = true;
  toolbar.filters[0].Apply();
  toolbar.style.visibility='visible';
  toolbar.filters[0].Play();
}
</script>
```

float

When set to a value besides the default (none), this property causes the element to float against the left or right margin of its parent element. A floated element will not affect the placement of any of the blocks on the page, but the content within those blocks (including other floated elements) will flow around it. The clear property lets you create elements that will be displaced downwards to prevent their content from flowing around floated elements.

Inherited: No

See also: clear

Value

The property can take values of left, right, or none.

Initial value: none

Compatibility

CSS Version: 1

The property is supported by all CSS-compatible browsers.

Example

This style rule sets images of class `headshot` to float against the left side of their parent elements:

```
img.headshot {
  float: left;
}
```

font

This is a shorthand property that allows you to set many font properties of an element with a single property declaration. With this one property, you can set the values of `font-style`, `font-variant`, `font-weight`, `font-size`, `line-height`, and `font-family`.

Unless you use one of the CSS 2 constants (described below), you must specify a `font-size` and `font-family`. All the other properties are optional, and will be reset to their initial values if they are not specified (overriding any previous declarations of equal or lesser precedence for their values). The properties `font-stretch` and `font-size-adjust` are also reset to their default values by this property, even though you don't have the option of specifying your own values.

Inherited: Yes

See also: The individual font properties, listed above.

Value

The syntax of this property is as follows:

```
font: [style] [variant] [weight] size [/ line-height] family
```

The values in square brackets are optional. The first three values—*style*, *variant*, and *weight*—may be specified in any order, and can take values allowed for font-style, font-variant, and font-weight, respectively. *size* is required, and can take any font-size value. *line-height* must come right after *size* if it is specified, can take any line-height value, and must be preceded by a slash (/). Finally, the *family* value can take any font-family value.

As of CSS 2, an alternative syntax is available for this property:

```
font: constant
```

constant is one of the following constants, each of which corresponds to a full font specification (family, size, weight, etc.):

☐ caption

☐ icon

☐ menu

☐ message-box

☐ small-caption

☐ status-bar

The fonts associated with these constants vary between browsers, operating systems, and individual system configurations. The idea is that they should match the fonts in use elsewhere on the system so that user interface elements of the web page can be made to match up with equivalent elements in local applications.

Initial value: none

Compatibility

CSS Version: 1 (constants added in CSS 2)

All CSS-compatible browsers support this property to some extent—generally, one that's compatible with the limits of each browser's support for individual font properties.

Examples

This style rule uses all possible values to define a font for paragraph elements:

```
p {
  normal normal normal 11pt/12pt Myriad, Helvetica, sans-serif;
}
```

This style rule applies the system caption font to caption elements:

```
caption {
  font: caption;
}
```

font-family

This property lets you set the typeface used to display text in an element. Like the HTML `font` tag, this property lets you specify a list of fonts, each of which will be tried in order.

If the first font is not available on the user's system, or if a particular character is not present in the font, the browser will check the second font in the list, and so on. This per-character fallback method (which is specified only as of CSS 2 and, therefore, is not yet supported in all browsers) lets you create multilingual content, then list a font for each language; the browser should pick and choose characters from the fonts in the list, always giving preference to those listed first.

Any time you set this property, the font list should end with a **generic font name** (see below), so that the browser will always have some idea of the type of font you're after.

Be aware that browsers will not fall back on fonts specified in lower-priority style rules. For example, if you set paragraph elements to `Verdana, sans-serif` and paragraphs of class `note` to `Myriad`, a user that does not have Myriad installed will see paragraphs of class `note` displayed in the browser's default font, not Verdana. In this example, you should set paragraphs of class `note` to `Myriad, Verdana, sans-serif` to achieve the desired effect.

Inherited: Yes

See also: `font`

Value

The property takes as its value a comma-separated list of font names. Font names that contain spaces should be quoted (e.g. `"Times New Roman"`).

In addition to actual font names, the list can contain any of the following generic font names:

☐ `serif`

The browser selects a font with serifs.[16]

☐ `sans-serif`

The browser selects a font without serifs.

☐ `cursive`

The browser selects a handwritten font.

☐ `fantasy`

The browser selects an elaborate, stylized font.

☐ `monospace`

The browser selects a font in which all characters have the same dimensions (suitable for showing code).

Since browsers always will be able to find a font for each of these generic font names, it only makes sense for the last font in the `font-family` list to be one of these.

Initial value: browser specific

Compatibility

CSS Version: 1

The property is supported by all CSS-compatible browsers.

Example

This style rule assigns a very common set of fonts to the body of the document:

---

[16]Serifs are those little horizontal flares that you see at the tops and bottoms of vertical lines in fonts like Times New Roman.

```
body {
  font-family: Verdana, Arial, Helvetica, sans-serif;
}
```

font-size

This property lets you set the size of the font displayed in an element.

You can choose from several different methods. You can select an absolute font size, or specify the size relative to the font size of the parent element. If you choose an absolute size, you can specify an exact CSS length (e.g. in pixels or points), or a font size constant (e.g. small), which yields a fixed, browser-specific size. If you choose a relative size, again you have the choice between a relative length in units (e.g. in ems or a percentage), or a relative size constant (larger or smaller).

Inherited: Yes, but in the case of relative measurements, the *computed* value is inherited.

See also: font

Value

As outlined above, this property supports a range of different value formats:

absolute CSS measurements
    a CSS length measurement in pixels (px), points (pt), picas (pi), centimeters (cm), millimeters (mm), or inches (in)

absolute size constants
    any of the following absolute size constants:

    ❑ xx-small

    ❑ x-small

    ❑ small

    ❑ medium

    ❑ large

❑ x-large

❑ xx-large

It's up to the browser to determine the actual sizes of these constants; generally, they're smaller in Mac OS than in Windows browsers. The differences between font sizes are also browser-specific, but the standard suggests a factor of 20% between adjacent values (i.e. large is 20% bigger than medium).

relative CSS measurements
a relative CSS measurement, in ems (em), exes (ex), or percentages (%)

This will set the font size of an element relative to that of its parent element.

relative size constants
either of the following size constants:

❑ smaller

❑ larger

The amount by which to adjust the parent's font size for the element is left up to the browser, but the specification suggests a factor of 20%. According to this suggestion, smaller is roughly equivalent to 80% or 0.8em, and larger is roughly equivalent to 120% or 1.2em.

Initial value: medium (see compatibility note for Internet Explorer for Windows)

Compatibility

CSS Version: 1

All CSS-compatible browsers support this property.

In Internet Explorer for Windows (up to and including version 7), the initial (default) font size is small instead of medium. In other words, Internet Explorer takes a font-size setting of small to mean the user's selected default font size. Therefore, medium becomes one step larger than the default font size. IE corrects this in standards-compliant mode,[17] but if you intend to design for any previous version with absolute font size constants, you'll need to use a separate, browser-specific style sheet.

---

[17] http://msdn.microsoft.com/library/en-us/dnie60/html/cssenhancements.asp

Examples

This style rule sets the default font size for all elements in the document to 11 points. Because `font-size` is inherited, all elements that don't define their own `font-size` should inherit this value:

```css
body {
  font-size: 11pt;
}
```

However, in practice, many older browsers do not allow font properties to be inherited by certain elements (tables, for example), so a more aggressive rule is needed:

```css
body, p, blockquote, li, td, th, pre {
  font-size: 11pt;
}
```

This style rule illustrates a common *faux pas* among inexperienced developers:

```css
ul, ol {
  font-size: 80%;
}
```

Because the *computed* value of the `font-size` property is inherited, not only will lists have a font 20% smaller than the body text, but lists nested within other lists will have a font size 20% smaller than *that*! Similarly, the fonts in lists nested two levels deep will be 20% smaller again (just over half the size of the body text). To avoid this unwanted domino effect, you must add a second style rule so that the lists inherit their parent's font-size:

```css
ul ul, ul ol, ol ul, ol ol {
  font-size: inherit;
}
```

font-size-adjust

If you've ever compared two different fonts at the same point size and thought that one looked considerably smaller than the other, you've encountered the reason for this property. Correctly setting this property lets the browser adjust for font differences to preserve the *apparent* size if it needs to use a different font than the one you specified (e.g. if the font you specified was not available on the user's system).

The apparent size of a font has more to do with the height of lowercase letters (the **x-height**) than with the actual font size. At 100 points, Myriad Web has an x-height of 48 points—lowercase letters are 48% as tall as the font size. This ratio is called the **aspect value** of the font. So in other words, Myriad Web has an aspect value of 0.48. However, Verdana has an aspect value of 0.58. If you specified Myriad Web as your desired font, but the user's browser substitutes Verdana for it because Myriad Web is not available, the text will look larger because of the substitute font's higher aspect value.

If you set the `font-size-adjust` property to the aspect value of your preferred font, the browser should be able to adjust the sizes of substitute fonts to give them the x-height you want. This assumes the browser knows (or can detect) the aspect value of the substitute font.

Inherited: Yes

See also: `font`

Value

The property takes as its value the aspect value of your preferred font. This is used in combination with the `font-size` property to adjust the size of a substitute font so that it's displayed with the desired x-height. The special value `none` disables font size adjustment for the element.

Initial value: `none`

Compatibility

CSS Version: 2

The property is not supported in any currently available browser.

Example

This style rule assigns a set of fonts to the body element and uses `font-size-adjust` to ensure that whatever font is used, it will have the same x-height as Myriad Web (the preferred font) at 11 points:

```
body {
   font-family: "Myriad Web", Verdana, Helvetica, sans-serif;
   font-size-adjust: 0.48; /* The aspect value of Myriad Web */
}
```

font-stretch

Many font families (Futura comes to mind) not only have different weights (e.g. normal, light, bold) and styles (e.g. normal, italic, oblique), but also different densities (e.g. normal, condensed, extended). This property lets you select the density of the font to be displayed in an element.

The CSS 2 specification makes no mention of whether a browser should artificially condense or expand a font for which different density versions are not available; however, since most browsers do this for other font properties (e.g. `font-style`, `font-weight`, `font-variant`), this would not be an unreasonable expectation. The property name certainly suggests that function.

Inherited: Yes

See also: `font`

Value

The property takes as its value one of 11 constants: nine are absolute, while two are relative.

The absolute constants are:

- [ ] `ultra-condensed`

- [ ] `extra-condensed`

- [ ] `condensed`

- [ ] `semi-condensed`

- [ ] `normal`

- [ ] `semi-expanded`

- [ ] `expanded`

- [ ] `extra-expanded`

- [ ] `ultra-expanded`

The relative constants are:

- ❏ `narrower`

- ❏ `wider`

A relative constant takes the `font-stretch` value of the parent element and sets the current element's value to the next narrower or wider value, respectively.

Initial value: `normal`

Compatibility

CSS Version: 2

This property is not supported by any currently available browsers.

Example

This style rule sets any element of class `languid` to be displayed in an extra-expanded font:

```
.languid {
  font-stretch: extra-expanded;
}
```

font-style

This property lets you choose between the normal, italic, and oblique styles of a font.

Inherited: Yes

See also: `font`

Value

`normal`, `oblique`, or `italic`.

Initial value: `normal`

Compatibility

CSS Version: 1

The property is supported by all CSS-compatible browsers.

Most browsers will artificially skew a normal font to create an italic style if none is available. Additionally, most browsers will treat the `oblique` setting as a synonym for `italic`, rather than select or generate an actual oblique font style.

Example

The default style sheets employed by most browsers specify that emphasis (`em`) elements should be displayed in an italic font. If you wanted to display emphasis with an underline instead, you would have to make a point of setting the `font-style` to `normal`:

```
em {
  font-style: normal;
  text-decoration: underline;
}
```

font-variant

This property lets you specify that the current element be rendered with a small-caps version of the font assigned to it. In a small-caps font, the lowercase letters look just like uppercase letters, but smaller.

The Latin alphabet (used by most Western languages) is actually the exception in that it has uppercase and lowercase versions of each letter. Most other writing systems in the world have a single case, and therefore are unaffected by this property.

Inherited: Yes

See also: `font`

Value

The property takes a value of `normal` or `small-caps`.

Initial value: `normal`

Compatibility

CSS Version: 1

This property is supported by most CSS-compatible browsers.

Internet Explorer for Windows (when not running in standards-compliant mode[18]) displays the `small-caps` value as all-caps (i.e. all characters in the element are capitalized). Internet Explorer 6 and later (in standards-compliant mode) artificially shrinks the capitals corresponding to lowercase characters in the text to simulate a `small-caps` font.

No currently available browsers actually will use the small-caps variant of a font if one is available.

Example

This style rule displays all headings on the page in small-caps:

```
h1, h2, h3, h4, h5, h6 {
  font-variant: small-caps;
}
```

font-weight

This property sets the boldness of the font to be displayed in the element.

Inherited: Yes, but in the case of relative settings, the *computed* value is inherited.

See also: `font`

Value

The CSS specification defines the following absolute values:

- ❑ `normal` (equivalent to **400**)

- ❑ `bold` (equivalent to **700**)

- ❑ `100`

---

[18] http://msdn.microsoft.com/library/en-us/dnie60/html/cssenhancements.asp

- ❑ 200

- ❑ 300

- ❑ 400

- ❑ 500

- ❑ 600

- ❑ 700

- ❑ 800

- ❑ 900

Also available are the following relative values:

- ❑ bolder

- ❑ lighter

According to the CSS 2 specification, bolder and lighter should select the version of the font that is a degree bolder or lighter, respectively, than the font inherited from the parent element.

Initial value: normal

Compatibility

CSS Version: 1

This property is supported by all CSS-compatible browsers.

In practice, most browsers only support normal and bold, mapping the numerical and relative values to those two absolute settings.

Example

This style rule overrides the default style sheets of most browsers that specify that strong elements should be rendered bold. On browsers that support more than one level of boldness, such elements will be displayed bolder than the text in the parent element. Thus, a `strong` element inside a heading that is rendered bold will be rendered with even greater boldness:

```
strong {
  font-weight: bolder;
}
```

height

This property sets the height of the contents of a block or replaced element.[19] This height does not include padding, borders, or margins.

If the contents of a block require more vertical space than the height you assign, the behavior is defined by the `overflow` property.

Inherited: No

See also: `max-height`, `min-height`, `overflow`, `width`

Value

The property takes any CSS length value, a percentage of the parent element's height, or `auto` as its value.

Initial value: `auto`

Compatibility

CSS Version: 1

This property is supported in some form by all CSS-compatible browsers. Current, standards-compliant browsers (Opera, Safari, and Mozilla browsers) support it fully.

Internet Explorer for Windows (up to and including version 7) incorrectly includes padding, borders, and margins in the height value. This is known as the **box model bug**. IE corrects this in version 6 and later, when rendering in standards-

---

[19]A replaced element is any element whose appearance and dimensions are defined by an external resource. Examples include images (`img` tags), plug-ins (`object` tags), and form fields (`input` and `select` tags). You can also think of replaced elements as being any element that can be displayed inline with text, and that acts as a single, big character for the purposes of wrapping and layout.

compliant mode,[20] but for all previous versions you'll need to use a separate, browser-specific style sheet or live with smaller boxes whenever borders, margins, or padding come into play (which is almost always). A third alternative is commonly known as the **box model hack**,[21] and exploits a more obscure bug in IE6's CSS support to work around the box model bug.

In Internet Explorer 4, this property is supported for a limited subset of block elements (`div` is a safe bet).

Example

This style rule assigns a fixed height of 100 pixels to paragraphs within the element with ID `blurbs`:

```
#blurbs p {
  height: 100px;
}
```

ime-mode

Chinese, Japanese, and Korean writing systems have more characters than can fit on a typical keyboard. Windows deals with this with an Input Method Editor (IME). When the IME is active, the user can type a few keyboard characters to describe the actual character he or she wishes to insert, then choose it from a popup list. When the IME is inactive, the actual keyboard characters are inserted as typed.

This nonstandard property lets you set the default IME mode for a form field (`input` or `textarea`)—active or inactive—or even disable the IME entirely for that field.

Inherited: No

Value

Values for this property include `active`, `auto`, `disabled`, and `inactive`.

Initial value: auto

---

[20] http://msdn.microsoft.com/library/en-us/dnie60/html/cssenhancements.asp
[21] http://css-discuss.incutio.com/?page=BoxModelHack

Compatibility

CSS Version: n/a

The property is supported in Internet Explorer 5 for Windows or later only.

Example

This style rule sets the IME to inactive by default in `input` and `textarea` elements of class `latin`:

```
input.latin, textarea.latin {
  ime-mode: inactive;
}
```

layout-flow

This nonstandard property lets you choose between two common layout methods for text: left-to-right horizontal lines stacked top to bottom on the page (the usual layout for western languages like English), and top-to-bottom vertical lines stacked right to left on the page (the usual layout for East Asian languages like Chinese).

This property has been deprecated in favour of the more flexible `writing-mode` property.

Inherited: Yes

See also: `writing-mode`

Value

The property can take values of `horizontal` or `vertical-ideographic`.

Initial value: `horizontal`

Compatibility

CSS Version: n/a

The property is compatible with Internet Explorer for Windows version 5 or later only.

Example

This style rule sets the `layout-flow` of the `body` and all its children (unless otherwise specified) to the East Asian style:

```
body {
  layout-flow: vertical-ideographic;
}
```

layout-grid

East Asian writing systems generally call for character layout to be performed in a grid. This nonstandard shorthand property lets you set all the properties associated with that grid in a single property declaration.

Inherited: Yes

See also: `layout-grid-char`, `layout-grid-line`, `layout-grid-mode`, and `layout-grid-type`

Value

The format of this property is as follows:

```
layout-grid: [mode] [type] [line [char]]
```

The values in square brackets are optional, and have the following meanings:

❑ *mode* is a valid value for `layout-grid-mode`

❑ *type* is a valid value for `layout-grid-type`

❑ *line* is a valid value for `layout-grid-line`

❑ *char* is a valid value for `layout-grid-char`

Initial value: `both loose none none`

Compatibility

CSS Version: n/a

The property is compatible with Internet Explorer 5 or later for Windows only.

Equivalent functionality is planned for inclusion in CSS3, but final property names and values are likely to differ. To follow the work on this front, see the CSS Working Group web site.[22]

Example

This is a basic example of the `layout-grid` property in use:

```
div.fullgrid {
  layout-grid: both fixed 12px 12px;
}
```

layout-grid-char

East Asian writing systems generally call for character layout to be performed in a grid. This property sets the character size enforced by that grid.

`layout-grid-mode` must be set to `char` or `both` for this property to have any effect.

Inherited: Yes

See also: `layout-grid`

Value

This property can take a CSS length value, a percentage of the parent element's width, `auto` (use the largest character in the font as the grid size), or `none` (character grid disabled).

Initial value: none

Compatibility

CSS Version: n/a

The property is compatible with Internet Explorer 5 or later for Windows only.

---

[22] http://www.w3.org/TR/2003/WD-css3-text-20030226/#document-grid

Equivalent functionality is planned for inclusion in CSS3, but final property names and values are likely to differ. To follow the work on this front, see the CSS Working Group web site.[23]

Example

This style rule specifies that characters should be positioned according to a 12-point grid:

```
div.monospaced {
  layout-grid-char: 12pt;
}
```

layout-grid-line

East Asian writing systems generally call for character layout to be performed in a grid. This property sets the line size enforced by that grid.

layout-grid-mode must be set to line or both for this property to have any effect.

Inherited: Yes

See also: layout-grid and layout-grid-mode

Value

This property can take a CSS length value, a percentage of the parent element's height, auto (use the largest character in the font as the grid size), or none (line grid disabled).

Initial value: none

Compatibility

CSS Version: n/a

The property is compatible with Internet Explorer 5 or later for Windows only.

---

[23] http://www.w3.org/TR/2003/WD-css3-text-20030226/#document-grid

Equivalent functionality is planned for inclusion in CSS3, but the final property names and values are likely to differ. To follow the work on this front, see the CSS Working Group web site.[24]

Example

This style rule specifies that lines should be positioned according to a 12-point grid:

```
div.monospaced {
  layout-grid-line: 12pt;
}
```

layout-grid-mode

East Asian writing systems generally call for character layout to be performed in a grid. This property lets you set which character dimensions (character width or line height) are regulated by the grid.

Inherited: Yes

See also: `layout-grid`, `layout-grid-char`, and `layout-grid-line`

Value

The property takes any one of the following constants:

❑ `both`

❑ `char`

❑ `line`

❑ `none`

Initial value: `both`

Compatibility

CSS Version: n/a

---

[24] http://www.w3.org/TR/2003/WD-css3-text-20030226/#document-grid

The property is compatible with Internet Explorer 5 or later for Windows only.

Equivalent functionality is planned for inclusion in CSS3, but final property names and values are likely to differ. To follow the work on this front, see the CSS Working Group web site.[25]

Example

This style rule sets `span` elements with the attribute `lang="jp"` to display characters according to a 12-point grid, but leaves the line height alone:

```
span[lang=jp] {
  layout-grid-mode: char;
  layout-grid-char: 12pt;
}
```

Note that since Internet Explorer for Windows doesn't currently support attribute selectors, this style rule has no practical use.

layout-grid-type

East Asian writing systems generally call for character layout to be performed in a grid. Different East Asian languages have different conventions as to which characters should be aligned to the grid. This property lets you set the convention to use.

For full details on this property, see the reference page at MSDN.[26]

Inherited: Yes

See also: `layout-grid` and `layout-grid-mode`

Value

The property takes any one of the following constants:

❑ `fixed`

❑ `loose`

---

[25] http://www.w3.org/TR/2003/WD-css3-text-20030226/#document-grid
[26] http://msdn.microsoft.com/workshop/author/dhtml/reference/properties/layoutgridtype.asp

❑ strict

Initial value: loose

Compatibility

CSS Version: n/a

The property is compatible with Internet Explorer 5 or later for Windows only.

Equivalent functionality is planned for inclusion in CSS3, but final property names and values are likely to differ. To follow the work on this front, see the CSS Working Group web site.[27]

Example

This style rule sets span elements with the attribute lang="jp" to use a strict layout grid:

```
span[lang=jp] {
  layout-grid-type: strict;
}
```

Note that since Internet Explorer for Windows doesn't currently support attribute selectors, this style rule has no practical use.

left

This property lets you set the distance between the left edge of an absolute positioned element (including its padding, border, and margin) and the left edge of the positioning context in which it resides. The positioning context is the padding area of the element's nearest ancestor that has a position property value other than static, or the body element.

For relative positioned elements, this property sets a relative offset from the normal position of its left edge. So, a setting of 10px will shift the left edge of the box ten pixels to the right, and a setting of -10px will shift it ten pixels to the left.

Inherited: No

---

[27] http://www.w3.org/TR/2003/WD-css3-text-20030226/#document-grid

See also: `position`, `bottom`, `top`, and `right`

Value

This property takes a CSS length measurement, a percentage value, or the `auto` constant. Percentages are based on the width of the parent element. The `auto` constant tells the browser to determine the position of the left edge itself, based on whatever other constraints may exist on the size/position of the element.

Initial value: `auto`

Compatibility

CSS Version: 2

The property works in all CSS-compatible browsers.

Example

This style rule positions the element with ID menu 80% of the way from the left edge of the window and gives it a width of 19.9%. We don't use a full 20% for the width to prevent some browsers from generating a horizontal scroll bar, due to rounding errors:

```
#menu {
  position: absolute;
  left: 80%;
  width: 19.9%;
  height: 200px;
}
```

letter-spacing

This property lets you increase or decrease the amount of spacing between characters in an element.

Inherited: Yes

See also: `word-spacing`

Value

The property takes any CSS length, or `normal`, as its value. Percentages are *not* allowed.

Positive lengths increase letter spacing by the specified amount, while negative lengths decrease it. In most cases, it is preferable to specify the spacing in ems (e.g. `0.5em`), as this will preserve the relative spacing of letters, even if you change the font size (one em is equal to the height of the current font).

Initial value: `normal`

Compatibility

CSS Version: 1

The property is supported by all CSS-compatible browsers.

Examples

This style rule sets all elements of class **spacy** to display extra spacing one-half the height of the font between each character:

```
.spacy {
  letter-spacing: 0.5em;
}
```

This style rule sets all elements of class **crowded** to display characters one-half the font size closer together than usual:

```
.crowded {
  letter-spacing: -0.5em;
}
```

line-break

This nonstandard property controls line-breaking policy (*Kinsoku*) for Japanese text.

By default, a relaxed line-breaking routine is used. This is the preferred method for modern typography, especially where narrow columns may exist. With this property, you can specify that a stricter, more traditional method is applied.

Inherited: Yes

Value

The property takes a value of `normal` or `strict`.

Initial value: `normal`

Compatibility

CSS Version: n/a

The property is supported by Internet Explorer 5 or later for Windows only.

Equivalent functionality is planned for inclusion in CSS3, and early drafts indicate that the property name and values will be the same as shown here. To follow the work on this front, see the CSS Working Group web site.[28]

Example

This style rule will instruct the browser to use strict (traditional) line-breaking rules for any element of class `tradbreak`:

```
.tradbreak {
  line-break: strict;
}
```

line-height

By default, the browser will determine the amount of vertical space allocated to a line by simply taking the tallest element (or font). The `line-height` property is used in this process; setting it lets you artificially increase, decrease, or arbitrarily set the line height for an element. If more than one element appears on a line, the one with the highest `line-height` property determines the rendered height of the line.

Inherited: Yes, but see below for differences in inheritance rules based on the value format.

See also: `font` and `font-size`

---

[28] http://www.w3.org/TR/2003/WD-css3-text-20030226/#line-breaking

Value

This property supports any of the following formats for its value:

normal
> This constant is the initial value of this property, and is equivalent to a number setting somewhere between 1.0 and 1.2, according to the CSS 2.1 specification.

number
> This is a number (e.g. 1.5), which is multiplied by the font size to get the rendered height of the line. A setting of 1.0 will crowd the lines together as closely as possible without overlapping characters, while a setting of 1.2 will leave a more natural amount of space between the lines. The value inherited by child elements will be this number, not the resultant line height, so a child element with a larger font will leave a proportionally larger space between lines.

length
> This is a CSS absolute length (e.g. 50px). A setting in ems will look the same as a number setting with the same face value, but child elements will inherit the actual line height, rather than the proportion of the font size.

percentage
> This constant is a percentage, which is multiplied by the font size to obtain the displayed line height. As with a setting in ems, the rendered line height may be proportional to the font size, but child elements inherit the absolute height, rather than the relative percentage.

Initial value: normal

Compatibility

CSS Version: 1

The property is supported by all CSS-compatible browsers.

Example

This style rule sets all elements of class spacy to have line height that's one and a half times the font size:

```
.spacy {
  line-height: 1.5;
}
```

Because a number value is used, child elements will also have line heights that are one and a half times *their* font sizes. If a value of 150% or 1.5em was used here, child elements would instead have the same line height as this element.

list-style

This shorthand property lets you set the three list-style properties with a single property declaration.

All three elements are optional, but any property you do not specify will implicitly be set to its initial value (overriding any value specified in a rule of lesser or equal priority).

For this property to have any effect, the target element (or one of its descendants, which will inherit this property) must have its display property set to list-item. The recommended method for setting the list-style properties of a list is to apply the properties to the list element so that the individual list items inherit them.

Inherited: Yes

See also: list-style-image, list-style-position, and list-style-type.

Value

The syntax for this property is as follows:

```
list-style: [type] [position] [image]
```

Each of the three values is optional (as indicated by the square brackets); however, at least one must appear. *type* is any valid value for list-style-type, *position* is any valid value for list-style-position, and *image* is any valid value for list-style-image. These three values may appear in any order.

If you specify both *type* and *image*, the type will be used when the image fails to load.

Setting this property to none will set both list-style-image and list-style-type to none.

Initial value: none

Compatibility

CSS Version: 1

This property is supported by all CSS-compatible browsers.

Examples

These style rules set an image for unordered lists and a Roman numeral format for ordered lists:

```
ul {
  list-style: url(/images/bullet.gif);
}
ol {
  list-style: upper-roman;
}
```

Compare the rules above to the following:

```
ul {
  list-style-image: url(/images/bullet.gif);
}
ol {
  list-style-type: upper-roman;
}
```

If we had an ordered list (`ol`) nested inside an unordered list (`ul`), the first set of rules above would have the intended effect of displaying Roman numerals for the ordered list. However, the second set of rules would display images for *all* the list elements—in both the ordered and unordered lists—because the nested, ordered list would inherit the `list-style-image` property from the unordered list. This doesn't happen with the first set of style rules because `list-style: upper-roman` implicitly sets the `list-style-image` property to `none`.

list-style-image

This property lets you assign an image to be displayed, instead of a standard marker for list items. You can set this property for individual list items (`li`) if needed; however, the recommended method for specifying an image for all elements in a list is to apply the property to the list element (ol, ul, etc.) and let the list items inherit it.

You should usually specify a list-style-type value with your list-style-image; the browser will use the list-style-type as a fallback if the image fails to load.

Be aware of the fact that this property is inherited by descendant elements, including nested lists. See the discussion in the example for the list-style property to learn how to avoid this pitfall.

Inherited: Yes

See also: list-style, list-style-type

Value

The property takes a CSS URL (using the url() wrapper), or none.

Initial value: none

Compatibility

CSS Version: 1

This property works in all CSS-compatible browsers.

Example

These style rules will set all unordered list (ul) elements to display an image as a marker (with square as the fallback list-style-type). The second rule specifically sets the list-style-image and list-style-type of ordered list elements (ol) to prevent them from inheriting the properties of an unordered list in which they may be nested:

```
ul {
  list-style-image: url(/images/bullet.gif);
  list-style-type: square;
}
ol {
  list-style-image: none;
  list-style-type: decimal;
}
```

list-style-position

As shown in Figure C.2, `list-style-position` controls whether or not the markers for list elements hang in the margin of list items or appear within the block.

Figure C.2. Effects of `list-style-position`

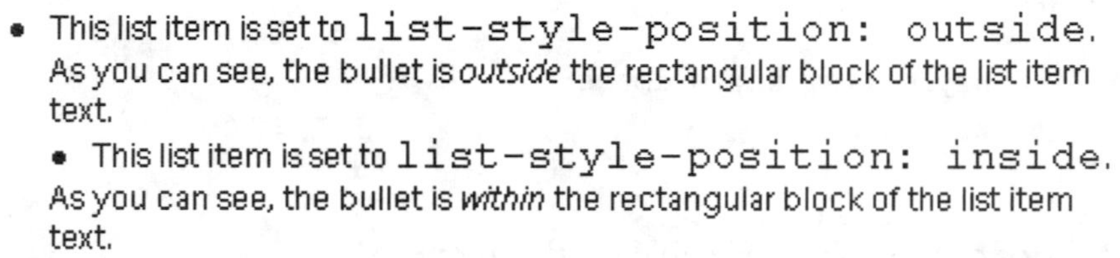

- This list item is set to `list-style-position: outside`. As you can see, the bullet is *outside* the rectangular block of the list item text.
  - This list item is set to `list-style-position: inside`. As you can see, the bullet is *within* the rectangular block of the list item text.

Inherited: Yes

See also: `list-style`

Value

The property takes a value of `inside` or `outside`.

Initial value: `outside`

Compatibility

CSS Version: 1

This property works in all CSS-compatible browsers.

Example

This style rule sets lists of class `compact` to display markers within the rectangular block of the list item text and removes the associated left margin:

```
ul.compact, ol.compact {
  list-style-position: inside;
  margin-left: 0;
}
```

list-style-type

This property lets you set the type of marker displayed alongside list items. This may include actual list item (li) elements, or other elements whose display properties are set to list-item. If an affected element also has a list-style-image value other than none, this property defines the fallback marker to display if the image cannot be loaded.

Inherited: Yes

See also: list-style, list-style-image

Value

A wide range of constants are available for this property.

The following "glyph" markers display a single symbol for all list items, and are commonly used for unordered lists:

❑ circle

❑ disc

❑ square

The following "numbering" markers display a number in the chosen format for each list item:

❑ decimal

❑ decimal-leading-zero

❑ lower-roman

❑ upper-roman

❑ hebrew

❑ georgian

❑ armenian

- ☐ cjk-ideographic

- ☐ hiragana

- ☐ katakana

- ☐ hiragana-iroha

- ☐ katakana-iroha

The following "alphabetic" markers display a letter in the chosen format for each list item:

- ☐ lower-alpha or lower-latin

- ☐ upper-alpha or upper-latin

- ☐ lower-greek

The special constant none displays no marker at all.

Initial value: none[29]

Compatibility

CSS Version: 1 (with multilingual constants added in CSS 2)

This property is supported by all CSS-compatible browsers; however, most support only the CSS1 constants: circle, disc, square, lower-alpha, upper-alpha, lower-roman, upper-roman, and none.

Example

This set of style rules sets top-level unordered lists to use square bullets, nested unordered lists to use circle bullets, and doubly-nested unordered lists to use disc bullets:

```
ul {
  list-style-type: square;
```

---

[29]This initial value applies to generic elements. Web browsers generally use a default internal style sheet that specifies a list-style-type of disc for unordered lists and decimal for ordered lists. Most browsers also assign unique default types to nested lists.

```
    list-style-image: none;
}
ul ul {
  list-style-type: circle;
}
ul ul ul {
  list-style-type: disc;
}
```

margin

This property sets the size of the margins surrounding the selected element(s).

The size for each side may be set individually using the `margin-bottom`, `margin-left`, `margin-right`, and `margin-top` properties.

Inherited: No

See also: `margin-bottom`, `margin-left`, `margin-right`, `margin-top`

Value

You can specify from one to four different values to set different margin sizes for each side of the element, as shown in Table C.6.

Each value can be a CSS length (`px`, `pt`, `em`, etc.), a percentage of the parent element's *width* (even for the top and bottom margins[30]), or the `auto` constant, which tells the browser automatically to calculate and use a margin that will allow the element to assume its default (or assigned) width.

---

[30]This is true with one exception. When the parent element is the **body**, percentage values for top and bottom margins are based on the document's *height* instead. This exception does *not* apply to borders or padding.

Table C.6. Effects of multiple values on `margin` property

Number of values	Effect on margins
1	All four margins receive the value specified.
2	Top and bottom (horizontal) margins receive the first value; left and right (vertical) margins receive the second.
3	Top margin receives the first value, vertical margins receive the second, and bottom margin receives the third.
4	Values are applied to top, right, bottom, and left margins, respectively.

Initial value: 0

Compatibility

CSS Version: 1

The property works in all CSS-compatible browsers.

Example

This style rule sets `blockquote` elements to be 80% of the width of their parent block. The margin property leaves a ten-pixel margin above and below these elements, and sets the left and right margins to `auto` so that the block will be centered horizontally.

```
blockquote {
  width: 80%;
  margin: 10px auto;
}
```

margin-bottom, margin-left, margin-right, margin-top

These properties let you set sizes of the individual margins around an element.

Inherited: No

See also: `margin`

Value

Each value can be a CSS length (px, pt, em, etc.), a percentage of the parent element's *width* (even for the top and bottom margins[30]), or the auto constant, which tells the browser automatically to calculate and use a margin that will allow the element to assume its default (or assigned) width.

Initial value: 0[31]

Compatibility

CSS Version: 1

The property works in all CSS-compatible browsers.

Example

These style rules modify the default margins, assigned by the browser to headings and paragraphs, to make headings "stick to" the first paragraph that follows:

```
h1, h2, h3, h4, h5, h6 {
  margin-bottom: 0;
  margin-top: 12pt;
}
p {
  margin-top: 0;
  margin-bottom: 6px;
}
```

marker-offset

When a :before or :after pseudo-element has its display property set to marker, it is rendered outside the main content box of the element, to the left of the first line (:before), or to the right of the last line (:after) in left-to-right writing systems. This property sets the distance between the two closest border edges of the main content and the marker, as shown in Figure C.3.

---

[31]This initial value is for generic elements. Browsers use an internal style sheet that defines default margins for elements such as headings, paragraphs, block quotes, and list items.

Figure C.3. The effect of `marker-offset`

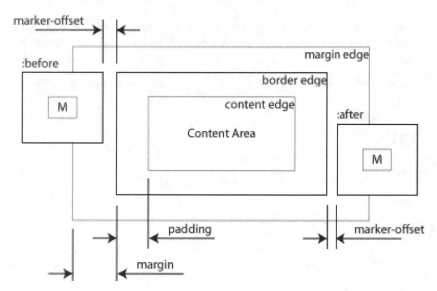

Note that the marker box has padding and borders, but no margins.

Inherited: No

See also: `display`

Value

The property takes any CSS length value (`px`, `pt`, `em`, etc.), or the `auto` constant, which lets the browser choose the distance.

Initial value: `auto`

Compatibility

CSS Version: 2

The property is not supported by any currently available browser.

Example

This style rules place stylistic quotation marks around `blockquote` elements. The `marker-offset` property ensures that there will be five pixels of space between the quotation marks and the content of the element (plus any padding that may be added to the `blockquote`):

```
blockquote:before, blockquote:after {
  display: marker;
  marker-offset: 5px;
  content: '"';
  font-size: 150%;
  color: blue;
}
```

marks

This property, which can appear only within an `@page` at-rule (see the section called "At-rules" in Appendix A) specifies whether crop marks, page alignment crosses, or both should appear on the printed page.

Value

The property takes either the `none` constant, or `crop`, `cross`, or both (separated by a space).

Initial value: none

Compatibility

CSS Version: 2

This property is not supported by any currently available browser.

Example

This at-rule specifies that pages should be printed with crop marks (to indicate where the page should be cut) and crosses (to help in the alignment of pages):

```
@page {
  marks: crop cross;
}
```

max-height, min-height

Instead of setting a fixed height, it is sometimes useful to set *limits* on the height of an element. These two properties let you set a maximum and/or minimum height. The height of the element is calculated normally, and then these limits are applied.

Remember to set the `overflow` property to `hidden` (or another appropriate value) if you set a `max-height`; otherwise, the content will overflow the specified height, even if the element does not.

Inherited: No

See also: `height`, `max-width`, `min-width`

Value

The property takes a CSS length (`px`, `pt`, `em`, etc.), a percentage of the parent element's content area height, or (in the case of `max-height` only) `none`.

Initial value:

☐ `max-height: none`

☐ `min-height: 0`

Compatibility

CSS Version: 2

This property is fully supported on Safari, Opera, and Mozilla browsers only.

Internet Explorer 6 and later supports `min-height` only, and then only on `td`, `th`, and `tr` elements in fixed-layout tables (see `table-layout`). The CSS 2 specification states that this property should *not* apply to table elements (this is corrected when IE renders in standards-compliant mode[32]).

---

[32] http://msdn.microsoft.com/library/en-us/dnie60/html/cssenhancements.asp

Example

This style rule specifies that the element with ID `sidemenu` should have a height between 200 and 1000 pixels, and should display a scroll bar if the content's height is greater than the maximum:

```
#sidemenu {
  min-height: 200px;
  max-height: 1000px;
  overflow: auto;
}
```

max-width, min-width

Instead of setting a fixed width, it is sometimes useful to set *limits* on the width of an element. These two properties let you set a maximum and/or minimum width. The width of the element is calculated normally, and then these limits are applied.

Remember to set the `overflow` property to `hidden` (or another appropriate value) if you set a `max-width`; otherwise, the content will overflow the specified width, even if the element does not.

Inherited: No

See also: `width`, `max-height`, `min-height`

Value

The property takes a CSS length (`px`, `pt`, `em`, etc.), a percentage of the parent element's content area height, or (in the case of `max-height` only) `none`.

Initial value:

❑ `max-height: none`

❑ `min-height: 0`

Compatibility

CSS Version: 2

This property is fully supported on Safari, Opera, and Mozilla browsers only.

Example

This style rule specifies that the element with ID `topmenu` should have a width between 200 and 1000 pixels, and should display a scroll bar if the content's width is greater than the maximum:

```
#topmenu {
  min-width: 200px;
  max-width: 1000px;
  overflow: auto;
}
```

-moz-border-radius

Mozilla-based browsers support a number of nonstandard CSS properties that were implemented for the skinning engines of those browsers. These properties all begin with the prefix `-moz-` to indicate their nonstandard nature. Several of these properties also are useful for general web site design, and have equivalents in current drafts of future CSS standards.

`-moz-border-radius` is a shorthand property that lets you add rounded corners to the border of an element by setting the radius to use for each of the corners of the box. The content of the box is not clipped by these rounded corners, so you'll usually want to define an appropriate amount of padding to prevent overlaps. However, the background *is* clipped.

Inherited: No

See also: `-moz-border-radius-bottomleft`, `-moz-border-radius-bottomright`, `-moz-border-radius-topleft`, `-moz-border-radius-topright`

Value

You can specify from one to four values, separated by spaces, for this property. Each value can be a CSS length value or a percentage of the width of the element from 0% to 50%. The maximum corner radius will always be 50% of the maximum dimension (width or height) of the element. The effects of specifying multiple values are shown in Table C.7.

Table C.7. Effects of multiple values on the `margin` property

Number of values	Effect on margins
1	All four corners receive the value specified.
2	Top-left and bottom-right corners receive the first value; top-right and bottom-left corners receive the second.
3	The top-left corner receives the first value, top-right and bottom-left corners receive the second, and the bottom-right corner receives the third.
4	Values are applied to top-left, top-right, bottom-right, and bottom-left corners, respectively.

Initial value: 0

Compatibility

CSS Version: n/a

This property works in Mozilla-based browsers only.

Equivalent functionality is planned for inclusion in CSS3, but final property names and values are likely to differ. To follow the work on this front, see the CSS Working Group web site.[33]

Example

This style rule creates a circular element that's 100 pixels in diameter:

```
.circle {
  border: 1px solid red;
  width: 100px;
  height: 100px;
  -moz-border-radius: 50%;
}
```

---

[33] http://www.w3.org/TR/2002/WD-css3-border-20021107/#the-border-radius

-moz-border-radius-bottomleft, -moz-border-radius-bottomright, -moz-border-radius-topleft, -moz-border-radius-topright

Mozilla-based browsers support a number of nonstandard CSS properties that were implemented for the skinning engines of those browsers. These properties all begin with the prefix `-moz-` to indicate their nonstandard nature. Several of these properties also are useful for general web site design, and have equivalents in current drafts of future CSS standards.

The `-moz-border-radius-corner` properties let you add rounded corners to the border of an element by setting a radius for each of the corners of the box. The content of the box is not clipped by these rounded corners, so you'll usually want to define an appropriate amount of padding to prevent overlaps. The background *is* clipped, though.

Inherited: No

See also: `-moz-border-radius`

Value

The value can be a CSS length value, or a percentage of the width of the element from **0%** to **50%**. The maximum corner radius will always be 50% of the maximum dimension (width or height) of the element.

Initial value: 0

Compatibility

CSS Version: n/a

This property works in Mozilla-based browsers only.

Equivalent functionality is planned for inclusion in CSS3, but final property names and values are likely to differ. To follow the work on this front, see the CSS Working Group web site.[34]

Example

This style rule creates an interesting rounded shape:

```
.roundthing {
  border: 1px solid red;
  width: 100px;
  height: 100px;
  -moz-border-radius-bottomleft: 25%;
  -moz-border-radius-bottomright: 50%;
  -moz-border-radius-topleft: 50%;
  -moz-border-radius-topright: 25%;
}
```

-moz-opacity

Mozilla-based browsers support a number of nonstandard CSS properties that were implemented for the skinning engines of those browsers. These properties all begin with the prefix -moz- to indicate their nonstandard nature. Several of these properties also are useful for general web site design, and have equivalents in current drafts of future CSS standards.

The -moz-opacity property lets you create translucent elements that allow elements behind them partially to show through.

Inherited: No

See also: filter

Value

You can set the opacity as a decimal number between 0.0 (totally transparent) and 1.0 (totally opaque), or as a percentage between 0% (transparent) and 100% (opaque). You should generally use decimal numbers, as the draft CSS3 standard does not currently allow for percentages.

Initial value: 1.0

---

[34] http://www.w3.org/TR/2002/WD-css3-border-20021107/#the-border-radius

Compatibility

CSS Version: n/a

This property works in Mozilla-based browsers only.

Equivalent functionality is planned for inclusion in CSS3, but final property names and values are likely to differ. To follow the work on this front, see the CSS Working Group web site.[35]

Example

This style rule makes the element with ID `sidebar` 50% transparent:

```
#sidebar {
  -moz-opacity: 0.5;
}
```

orphans

This property affects the position of page breaks, when the user prints the page from his or her browser. With this property, you can specify the minimum number of lines in a block before a page break can occur.

For example, if a paragraph element had six lines and the page size called for a page break to occur after the second line, an `orphans` setting of three would force the page break to occur *before* the paragraph, so that the first three lines could appear on the same page.

Inherited: Yes

See also: `windows`

Value

The property takes as its value a positive integer.

Initial value: 2

---

[35] http://www.w3.org/TR/2003/WD-css3-color-20030214/#transparency

Compatibility

CSS Version: 2

This property is currently supported only by Opera.

Example

This style rule indicates that at least four lines of a broken paragraph must appear at the bottom of the page before a page break occurs:

```
p {
  orphans: 4;
}
```

outline

Outlines are very similar to borders; however, they do not occupy any space in the CSS box model (i.e. turning off and on an element's outline or changing its outline width should not affect the position of that element, or any other elements on the page). Additionally, an outline should follow the actual shape of the element's content (e.g. hugging the jagged right edge of a left-aligned paragraph) rather than forming a rectangular box around it. The outline of an inline element that flows over several lines is closed at the starts and ends of lines, whereas the border is not.

`outline` is a shorthand property that lets you set all three of the outline-related properties for an element with a single property declaration.

Inherited: No

See also: `border`, `outline-color`, `outline-style`, `outline-width`

Value

The syntax for this property is as follows:

```
outline: [color] [style] [width]
```

`color` is any valid value for `outline-color`. `style` is any valid value for `outline-style`. `width` is any valid value for `outline-width`.

All three of the values are optional (as indicated by the square brackets), but you must specify at least one. They can be specified in any order. Any unspecified value causes the corresponding property to be set to its initial value.

Initial value: none

Compatibility

CSS Version: 2

Opera and Mozilla browsers support this property, and they render rectangular outlines only, as opposed to the content-hugging style prescribed by the CSS 2 specification.

Example

This style rule makes use of the `:focus` pseudo-class to draw a medium, dashed, red outline around any form element that has focus:

```
input:focus, select:focus, textarea:focus {
  outline: medium dashed red;
}
```

outline-color

Outlines are very similar to borders; however, they do not occupy any space in the CSS box model (i.e. turning off and on an element's outline or changing its outline width should not affect the position of that element, or any other elements on the page). Additionally, an outline should follow the actual shape of the element's content (e.g. hugging the jagged right edge of a left-aligned paragraph) rather than forming a rectangular box around it. The outline of an inline element that flows over several lines is closed at the starts and ends of lines, whereas the border is not.

The `outline-color` property sets the color of the outline drawn around the selected element(s).

Inherited: No

See also: `border-color`

Value

The property takes any CSS color value, or `invert`, which will reverse the color(s) of the background over which it is drawn.

Initial value: `invert` (`black` in current browsers)

Compatibility

CSS Version: 2

Opera and Mozilla browsers support this property, and they render only rectangular outlines, as opposed to the content-hugging style prescribed by the CSS 2 specification. Both of these browsers use an initial value of `black`, as they do not support `invert`.

Example

This style rule puts red outlines around hyperlinks when the user hovers the mouse over them:

```
a:hover {
  outline-style: solid;
  outline-color: red;
}
```

outline-style

Outlines are very similar to borders; however, they do not occupy any space in the CSS box model (i.e. turning off and on an element's outline or changing its outline width should not affect the position of that element, or any other elements on the page). Additionally, an outline should follow the actual shape of the element's content (e.g. hugging the jagged right edge of a left-aligned paragraph) rather than forming a rectangular box around it. The outline of an inline element that flows over several lines is closed at the starts and ends of lines, whereas the border is not.

The `outline-style` property sets the style of the outline drawn around the selected element(s).

Inherited: No

See also: `border-style`

Value

This property accepts the same set of constants as `border-style` (see Table C.3), with the exception of `hidden`.

Initial value: `none`

Compatibility

CSS Version: 2

Opera and Mozilla browsers support this property, and they render rectangular outlines only, as opposed to the content-hugging style prescribed by the CSS 2 specification.

Example

This style rule adds an outline of style `inset` around active hyperlinks:

```
a:active {
  outline-style: inset;
  outline-color: grey;
  outline-width: medium;
}
```

outline-width

Outlines are very similar to borders; however, they do not occupy any space in the CSS box model (i.e. turning off and on an element's outline or changing its outline width should not affect the position of that element, or any other elements on the page). Additionally, an outline should follow the actual shape of the element's content (e.g. hugging the jagged right edge of a left-aligned paragraph) rather than forming a rectangular box around it. The outline of an inline element that flows over several lines is closed at the starts and ends of lines, whereas the border is not.

The `outline-width` property sets the width of the outline drawn around the selected element(s).

Inherited: No

See also: `border-width`

Value

The property takes `thin`, `medium`, `thick`, or any CSS length measurement as its value.

Initial value: `medium`

Compatibility

CSS Version: 2

Opera and Mozilla browsers support this property, and they render rectangular outlines only, as opposed to the content-hugging style prescribed by the CSS 2 specification.

Example

This style rule adds a three-pixel outline of style `outset` around hyperlinks when the user hovers the mouse over them:

```
a:hover {
  outline-style: outset;
  outline-color: grey;
  outline-width: 3px;
}
```

overflow

This property lets you control how the browser treats an element when it is not big enough to hold all of its content. In practice, this situation occurs only when you have assigned a fixed or maximum width and/or height for the element. Most often, content will overflow the height of the element, because inline content will reflow to accommodate limited width; however, if an element contains children with their own fixed widths, they can overflow the width as well.

When you apply the `overflow` property to an element whose dimensions cause part of its contents to be cropped, the size of the element is cropped for layout purposes, too. Decorations such as borders are applied to the element after cropping has taken place. This is quite different from the `clip` property, which affects only the *visible* area of the element, and which crops borders and other decorations along with the element content.

Inherited: No

See also: `clip`, `height`, `text-overflow`, `max-width`, `max-height`, `width`

Value

This property can be set to any of these four constant values:

auto
> This setting causes scroll bars to appear when needed, to allow the content of the element to be scrolled within the defined width/height limits. Be aware that the scroll bars themselves will occupy a browser-specific amount of space within the element area.

hidden
> This setting hides any overflowing content. Affected content will be invisible and inaccessible to the user.

scroll
> This setting behaves just like `auto`, except that horizontal and vertical scroll bars are displayed, whether they are needed or not. This lends predictability to the appearance of the block, when you're not sure whether the scroll bars will be needed or not.

visible
> This setting specifies that content that overflows the assigned boundaries of the element should be rendered anyway. The overflowing content should be drawn outside the visible box (its background and borders).

Initial value: `visible`

Compatibility

CSS Version: 2

This property works on all CSS-compatible browsers.

Internet Explorer for Windows (up to and including version 6 in standards-compliant mode) incorrectly expands the size of the box to accommodate overflowing content when this property is set to `visible`, rather than drawing the content outside the bounds of the box. This has been corrected in Internet Explorer 7.

Example

This style rule assigns a width and height to the element with ID `mainmenu`, but allows scroll bars to be added, if necessary, to make overflowing content accessible:

```
#mainmenu {
  width: 150px;
  height: 400px;
  overflow: auto;
}
```

overflow-x, overflow-y

These nonstandard properties work the same as the `overflow` property, except that they apply to one dimension only. `overflow-x` controls how/if content that overflows the horizontal limits of the element is rendered; `overflow-y` controls the content protruding from the vertical limits.

Inherited: No

See also: `overflow`

Value

Each of these properties can take any one of the constant values supported by the `overflow` property.

Initial value: `visible`

Compatibility

CSS Version: n/a

These properties work with Mozilla browsers and Internet Explorer for Windows version 5 or later.

Equivalent functionality is planned for inclusion in CSS3, but final property values may differ. To follow the work on this front, see the CSS Working Group web site.[36]

Example

This style rule assigns a width and height to the element with ID mainmenu, and allows a vertical scroll bar to be added if the content is too high to fit within the allocated 400 pixels. Content that does not fit horizontally will be visibly clipped:

```
#mainmenu {
  width: 150px;
  height: 400px;
  overflow-x: hidden;
  overflow-y: auto;
}
```

padding

This shorthand property sets the size of the padding on all four sides of the selected element(s) with a single property declaration. Padding is extra space added around the content—but within the borders—of an element. Any background color or image assigned to an element will also fill the padding area of that element.

Padding may be set individually for each side of an element using padding-bottom, padding-left, padding-right, and padding-top properties.

Inherited: No

See also: padding-bottom, padding-left, padding-right, padding-top

Value

You can specify from one to four different values to set different padding sizes for each side of the element, as Table C.8 indicates.

Each value can be a CSS length (px, pt, em, etc.), or a percentage of the parent element's *width*—even for the top and bottom padding settings.

---

[36] http://www.w3.org/TR/2002/WD-css3-box-20021024/#the-overflow-x

Table C.8. Effects of multiple values on `padding` property

Number of values	Effect on padding
1	All four sides receive the value specified.
2	Top and bottom (horizontal) padding settings receive the first value; left and right (vertical) padding settings receive the second.
3	Top padding receives the first value, vertical padding settings receive the second, and bottom padding receives the third.
4	Values are applied to top, right, bottom, and left padding settings, respectively.

Initial value: 0

Compatibility

CSS Version: 1

The property works in all CSS-compatible browsers.

Examples

This style rule adds a thin border and red background around elements of class `warning`. It also adds five pixels of padding on the top and bottom, and ten pixels of padding on the left and right, between the content and the borders, allowing the content to breathe a little:

```
.warning {
  border: 1px solid;
  background-color: red;
  padding: 5px 10px;
}
```

This style rule sets a padding of three pixels around all cells in tables of class `spacy`. This is the CSS equivalent of `cellpadding="3"` in the `<table>` tag:

```
table.spacy td, table.spacy th {
  padding: 3px;
}
```

padding-bottom, padding-left, padding-right, padding-top

These properties let you set the individual padding sizes around an element. Padding is extra space added around the content—but within the borders—of an element. Any background color or image assigned to an element will also fill the padding area of the element.

Inherited: No

See also: `padding`

Value

Each value can be a CSS length (`px`, `pt`, `em`, etc.), or a percentage of the parent element's *width* (even for the top and bottom padding settings).

Initial value: 0

Compatibility

CSS Version: 1

The property works in all CSS-compatible browsers.

Example

This style rule adds a thin border and red background around elements of class `warning`. It also adds five pixels of padding on the top and bottom and ten pixels of padding on the left and right, between the content and the borders, allowing the content to breathe a little:

```
.warning {
  border: 1px solid;
  background-color: red;
  padding-top: 5px;
  padding-bottom: 5px;
  padding-left: 10px;
  padding-right: 10px;
}
```

See the example for the `padding` property to see how this same effect can be achieved with less typing.

page

The `@page` at-rule can be given an identifier so that you can declare different page types for use by a site when printing. For example, this style rule sets up a page type named `mylandscape`:

```
@page mylandscape {
  size: 11in 8.5in;
  margin: 1in;
  marks: crop;
}
```

The `page` property lets you assign a named page type to selected elements. Those elements will then be printed on the specified page type.

Inherited: Yes

Value

`page` takes as its value an identifier assigned to an `@page` rule declared elsewhere, or `auto`.

Initial value: `auto`

Compatibility

CSS Version: 2

The property is not supported by any currently available browser.

Example

This style rule ensures that all `div` elements of class `overhead` are rendered on a page of type `mylandscape` (as declared above), and are followed by a page break:

```
div.overhead {
  page: mylandscape;
  page-break-after: always;
}
```

page-break-after

When printing a web page, the browser simply places page breaks wherever they need to occur to ensure that all printed pages are as full as possible, by default. This property affords you greater control over the placement of page breaks during printing by letting you manually add or suppress a page break after a given element.

Inherited: No

See also: orphans, page-break-before, page-break-inside, widows

Value

This property can take any of the following values:

always
> The browser will always put a page break after the selected element(s).

avoid
> The browser will try to avoid placing a page break after the selected element(s).
>
> The practical effect of this setting is to keep an element on the same page as the next sibling element.

auto
> The browser will put a page break after the selected element(s) if it ended at the bottom of a page.

left
> The browser will always put one or two page breaks after the selected element(s) so that the next element begins at the top of a left-hand (i.e. even-numbered) page in double-sided printing.

right
> The browser will always put one or two page breaks after the selected element(s) so that the next element begins at the top of a right-hand (i.e. odd-numbered) page in double-sided printing.

Initial value: auto

Compatibility

CSS Version: 2

This property works in Internet Explorer 4 or later, Opera, and Mozilla browsers. All of these browsers treat `left` and `right` the same as `always`.

The `avoid` value is not directly supported by Internet Explorer for Windows; however, if you use JavaScript to set the property to an empty string (`""`), it will have the same effect.

Example

This style rule keeps every heading on the same page as the first element that follows it, whenever possible:

```
h1, h2, h3, h4, h5, h6 {
  page-break-after: avoid;
}
```

page-break-before

When printing a web page, the browser simply places page breaks wherever they need to occur to ensure that all printed pages are as full as possible, by default. This property affords you greater control over the placement of page breaks during printing by letting you manually add or suppress a page break before a given element.

Inherited: No

See also: `orphans`, `page-break-after`, `page-break-inside`, `widows`

Value

This property can take any of the following values:

always
The browser will always put a page break before the selected element(s).

avoid
The browser will try to avoid placing a page break before the selected element(s).

The practical effect of this setting is to keep an element on the same page as the previous sibling element.

auto

The browser will put a page break before the selected element(s) if the previous element ended at the bottom of a page.

left

The browser will always put one or two page breaks before the selected element(s) so that they begin at the top of a left-hand (i.e. even-numbered) page in double-sided printing.

right

The browser will always put one or two page breaks before the selected element(s) so that they begin at the top of a right-hand (i.e. odd-numbered) page in double-sided printing.

Initial value: auto

Compatibility

CSS Version: 2

This property works in Internet Explorer 4 or later, Opera, and Mozilla browsers. All of these browsers treat `left` and `right` the same as `always`.

The `avoid` value is not directly supported by Internet Explorer for Windows; however, if you use JavaScript to set the property to an empty string (`""`), it will have the same effect.

Example

This style rule adds the necessary page breaks to place all `div` elements of class `section` at the top of a right-hand page:

```
div.section {
  page-break-before: right;
}
```

page-break-inside

When printing a web page, the browser simply places page breaks where they need to occur to ensure that all printed pages are as full as possible, by default. This property affords you greater control over the placement of page breaks during printing by letting you manually prevent page breaks from occurring in the middle of selected elements.

Inherited: Yes

See also: orphans, page-break-after, page-break-before, widows

Value

This property can take any of the following values:

avoid
>   The browser will try to avoid placing a page break within the selected element(s).
>
>   The practical effect of this setting is to keep all of an element on one page.

auto
>   The browser will put a page break within the selected element(s) if the bottom of a page is reached while rendering it.

Initial value: auto

Compatibility

CSS Version: 2

Currently Opera is the only browser to implement this.

Example

This style rule keeps pre elements of class programlisting on one page whenever possible:

```
pre.programlisting {
  page-break-inside: avoid;
}
```

pause

Pauses are used by aural (speaking) browsers for the visually impaired to provide clues to document structure. This is a shorthand property that lets you specify the pause-before and pause-after properties with a single property declaration.

Inherited: No

See also: pause-before, pause-after, speech-rate

Value

This property takes one or two time values, each of which is a floating-point number followed by either **s** (seconds) or **ms** (milliseconds), or a percentage of the average word time (which is 1/*rate*, where *rate* is the value of the element's speech-rate property).

If one value is specified, it is applied to both the pause-before and pause-after properties. If two values are specified, the first is applied to pause-before, the second to pause-after.

Initial value: Browser-specific

Compatibility

CSS Version: 2

The property is not supported by any currently available browser.

Example

This example pauses for half the length of the average word before and after each div element:

```
div {
  pause: 50%;
}
```

pause-after, pause-before

Pauses are used by aural (speaking) browsers for the visually impaired to provide clues to document structure. `pause-before` and `pause-after` let you set the amount of time to pause before and after an element, respectively.

Inherited: No

See also: `pause, speech-rate`

Value

Each of these properties takes a time value, which is a floating-point number followed by either **s** (seconds) or **ms** (milliseconds), or a percentage of the average word time (which is 1/*rate*, where *rate* is the value of the element's `speech-rate` property).

Initial value: Browser-specific

Compatibility

CSS Version: 2

The property is not supported by any currently available browser.

Example

This example pauses for half the length of the average word before each h1 element, with the exception of h1 elements of class `minor`:

```
h1 {
  pause-before: 50%;
}
h1.minor {
  pause-before: none;
}
```

pitch

For use by aural (speaking) browsers for the visually impaired, this property sets the average pitch (frequency) of the voice that reads a selected element's content aloud. Typical male voices are around 120 Hz, while female voices average about 210 Hz.

Inherited: Yes

See also: `pitch-range`, `richness`, `stress`, `voice-family`, `volume`

Value

The property takes a frequency in Hertz (`Hz`) or kiloHertz (`kHz`), or any of the following constants, as its value:

- `x-low`

- `low`

- `medium`

- `high`

- `x-high`

The actual frequencies that correspond to these constants depend on the `voice-family` property in use.

Initial value: `medium`

Compatibility

CSS Version: 2

The property is not supported by any currently available browser.

Example

This example causes aural browsers to speak elements of class `ominous` in a low pitch:

```
.ominous {
  pitch: low;
}
```

pitch-range

For use by aural (speaking) browsers for the visually impaired, this property controls the amount of pitch variation (which affects the perceived level of animation and excitement) in the voice that reads a selected element's content aloud.

Inherited: Yes

See also: `pitch`, `richness`, `stress`, `voice-family`, `volume`

Value

The property takes any integer between 0 and 100, where 0 is a complete monotone, 50 is an average speaking voice, and 100 is extremely animated.

Initial value: 50

Compatibility

CSS Version: 2

The property is not supported by any currently available browser.

Example

This example causes aural browsers to speak elements of class `ominous` with an added level of animation:

```
.ominous {
  pitch-range: 75;
}
```

play-during

Intended for use by aural browsers for the visually impaired, this property could have at least one practical use in mainstream browsers: providing a standard way to add background sounds to a page. In aural browsers, this property sets the sound played in the background while the contents of a selected element are read aloud.

Inherited: No

See also: cue

Value

Values for this property can take the following format:

```
play-during: url(uri) [mix] [repeat]
```

uri is the relative or absolute URL of the sound file you wish to have played during the reading of this element. The optional keyword mix, when present, causes the element's background sound to be mixed with the background sound of its parent element, instead of replacing it. The optional keyword repeat, when present, causes the sound to be played repeatedly, if its duration is less than the reading of the element content.

Alternatively, this property may be set to either of the following constants:

❑ auto

❑ none

auto allows the parent element's play-during sound to continue playing while the element is read (as opposed to setting this value to inherit, which would cause it to start again from the beginning). none suppresses the parent element's play-during sound during the reading of the element, allowing it to resume afterward.

Initial value: auto

Compatibility

CSS Version: 2

The property is not supported by any currently available browser.

Example

This example plays dirge.wav in the background of a div element of class epitaph:

```
div.epitaph {
  play-during: url(/sounds/dirge.wav) repeat;
}
```

position

This property sets the method used to position an element on the page.

Inherited: No

See also: `bottom`, `left`, `right`, `top`, `z-index`

Value

This property may be set to any of the following constant values:

`static`

The element is laid out according to normal document flow. The `bottom`, `left`, `right`, and `top` properties have no effect. This is the default.

`absolute`

The element can be precisely positioned within the **positioning context** in which it resides. In other words, a (`top`,`left`) position of (0,0) will place the element against the top-left corner of the nearest ancestor that has a `position` setting other than `static`, or against the top-left corner of the `body` element if there is no such ancestor.

Absolute positioned elements do not occupy any space in the normal document flow.

`fixed`

This setting lets you position the element as with `absolute`, but when the page is scrolled, the element maintains its position in the window instead of scrolling with the rest of the page.

`relative`

The element can be positioned relative to where it would appear if it were positioned normally, with `static`. In other words, a (`top`,`left`) position of (50,-30) will place the element 50 pixels below and 30 pixels to the left of where it would appear if its position were left up to the browser.

Relative positioned elements still occupy the space they would be assigned if they were not positioned to begin with. This may sound like a pain, but it comes in handy in some common page layout situations.

One use of `relative` is to let an element act as a positioning context for one or more `absolute` positioned child elements, without moving it from its normal place in the document flow.

Initial value: `static`

Compatibility

CSS Version: 2

This property works in all CSS-compatible browsers; however, the `fixed` property is supported correctly only by Mozilla, Opera, Safari, and Internet Explorer 7. Internet Explorer 6 (in quirks and standards-compliant mode) treats `fixed` exactly like `absolute`.

Example

This style rule places the element with ID `logo` 30 pixels from the top and right edges of the browser window (assuming the element is in the body's positioning context), and keeps it there even when the user scrolls the document:

```
#logo {
  position: fixed;
  top: 30px;
  right: 30px;
}
```

The chapters of this book that deal with page layout also contain plenty of examples with which you may experiment.

quotes

The `content` property of `:before` and `:after` pseudo-elements lets you specify **generated content** that should appear before and/or after any element. Generated content is presentational text that is rendered on the page but does not form part of the HTML document. Among the types of content that can be generated are quotation marks. The `quotes` property lets you define the format of those quotes.

Since you can have quotes within quotes, this property lets you set the quotes' appearance at each nesting level.

Inherited: Yes

See also: `content`

Value

The property takes as a value a space-separated list of pairs of quote strings (see example below), or `none`. If pairs of strings are provided, the first pair will be used for the first (outermost) level of quotes, the second pair will be used for the first level of nested quotes, and so on. If the `none` constant is specified, the `open-quote` and `close-quote` elements of the `content` property will not generate any content.

The CSS 2 specification does not cover how quotes should be rendered when they appear at a nesting level for which quote strings are not provided; presumably, the final pair of quote strings would be used for all deeper nesting levels as well.

Initial value: A browser-specific series of quote strings.

Compatibility

CSS Version: 2

The best support for this property is provided by recent Mozilla browsers; however, older browsers (including Netscape 6 and Firefox 1.0.7) support this property, though the first pair of quote strings you specify are applied to all nesting levels. This is rectified in Firefox 1.5 and Seamonkey 1.0.

Opera also supports this property reasonably well; however, a bug in version 7 of that browser does affect this feature. If you specify quote strings for n nesting levels, then any quoted elements at nesting level $n+1$ or deeper will have the `close-quote` string of the deepest specified nesting level as its `open-quote` string, and double quotes (") for its `close-quote` string.

Internet Explorer 5 for Macintosh supports the `open-quote` and `close-quote` elements of the `content` property, but it chooses the quote strings itself, ignoring this property.

Internet Explorer for Windows (up to and including version 7 in standards-compliant mode) does not support generated quotes.

Example

This example uses double quotes for the first (outermost) level of quotes, then single quotes for the second level (and presumably for all deeper levels). This setting is applied to the body element (it is inherited by all nested elements), then quotes are added to blockquote and q (inline quote) elements:

```
body {
   quotes: '"' '"' "'" "'";
}
blockquote:before, q:before {
   content: open-quote;
}
blockquote:after, q:after {
   content:close-quote;
}
```

richness

For use by aural (speaking) browsers for the visually impaired, this property controls richness/smoothness in the voice that reads a selected element's content aloud (which affects the degree to which the sound "carries").

Inherited: Yes

See also: pitch, pitch-range, stress, voice-family, volume

Value

The property takes any integer between 0 and 100, where 0 is a soft, mellifluous voice, 50 is an average speaking voice, and 100 is a strident voice.

Initial value: 50

Compatibility

CSS Version: 2

The property is not supported by any currently available browser.

Example

This example causes aural browsers to speak elements of class `ominous` more softly than usual:

```
.ominous {
  richness: 30;
}
```

right

This property lets you set the distance between the right edge of an `absolute` positioned element (including its padding, border, and margin) and the right edge of the positioning context in which it resides. The positioning context is the padding area of the element's nearest ancestor that has a `position` property value other than `static`, or the `body` element.

For `relative` positioned elements, this property sets a relative offset from the normal position of its bottom edge. So a setting of `10px` will shift the right edge of the box ten pixels to the left, and a setting of `-10px` will shift it right by the same amount.

Inherited: No

See also: `position`, `bottom`, `left`, and `top`

Value

This property takes a CSS length measurement, a percentage value, or the `auto` constant. Percentages are based on the width of the parent element. The `auto` constant tells the browser to determine the position of the right edge itself, based on whatever other constraints may exist on the size/position of the element.

Initial value: `auto`

Compatibility

CSS Version: 2

The property works in all CSS-compatible browsers.

Often, the same effect can be achieved by setting the `left` property of a box. Since `left` is supported by more browsers than `right`, this should be done whenever possible.

Example

This style rule positions the element with ID `menu` against the right edge of the document (assuming it is in the body's positioning context):

```
#menu {
  position: absolute;
  right: 0;
  width: 100px;
  height: 200px;
}
```

ruby-align

Ruby text is a new addition in the XHTML 1.1 recommendation and is described by the Ruby Annotation Recommendation[37] of the W3C. Commonly used in Japan and China, ruby text generally appears in a smaller font that overlays the main text as a pronunciation guide, or to provide some other explanatory annotation. It has no relation to the Ruby programming language, other than the fact that they both originated in Japan.

This property sets how the ruby text is aligned with the base text.

Inherited: No

See also: `ruby-overhang`, `ruby-position`

Value

This property accepts any of the following constants:

❏ `auto`

❏ `center`

❏ `distribute-letter`

---

[37] http://www.w3.org/TR/2001/REC-ruby-20010531/

❑ distribute-space

❑ left

❑ line-edge

❑ right

For the meanings of each of these constants, see the CSS3 Ruby module working draft[38] and the Microsoft Internet Explorer documentation for this property.[39]

Initial value: auto

Compatibility

CSS Version: n/a

This property is supported only in Internet Explorer for Windows version 5 or later. In that browser, this property must be applied to the ruby element that contains the ruby text (rt) element for which you wish to set the alignment.

Equivalent functionality is planned for inclusion in CSS3, and the current working draft suggests that this property will be as documented here. To follow the work on this front, see the CSS Working Group web site.[40]

Example

This style rule centers ruby text over the base text:

```
ruby {
  ruby-align: center;
}
```

ruby-overhang

Ruby text is a new addition in the XHTML 1.1 recommendation and is described by the Ruby Annotation Recommendation[41] of the W3C. Commonly used in Japan and China, ruby text generally appears in a smaller font that overlays the

---

[38] http://www.w3.org/TR/css3-ruby/
[39] http://msdn.microsoft.com/workshop/author/dhtml/reference/properties/rubyalign.asp
[40] http://www.w3.org/TR/css3-ruby/
[41] http://www.w3.org/TR/2001/REC-ruby-20010531/

main text as a pronunciation guide, or to provide some other explanatory annotation.

This property controls whether ruby text is allowed to extend over adjacent text or whitespace, if it is longer than the base text it annotates.

Inherited: No

See also: `ruby-align`, `ruby-position`

Value

This property accepts any of the following constants:

❑ `auto`

❑ `none`

❑ `whitespace`

For the meanings of each of these constants, see the CSS3 Ruby module working draft[42] and the Microsoft Internet Explorer documentation for this property.[43]

Initial value: `auto`

Compatibility

CSS Version: n/a

This property is supported only in Internet Explorer for Windows version 5 or later. In that browser, this property must be applied to the `ruby` element that contains the ruby text (`rt`) element for which you wish to set the alignment.

Equivalent functionality is planned for inclusion in CSS3, and the current working draft suggests that this property will be as documented here. To follow the work on this front, see the CSS Working Group web site.[44]

---

[42] http://www.w3.org/TR/css3-ruby/
[43] http://msdn.microsoft.com/workshop/author/dhtml/reference/properties/rubyalign.asp
[44] http://www.w3.org/TR/css3-ruby/

Example

This style rule allows ruby text to overhang whitespace adjacent to the base text only:

```
ruby {
  ruby-overhang: whitespace;
}
```

ruby-position

Ruby text is a new addition in the XHTML 1.1 recommendation and is described by the Ruby Annotation Recommendation[45] of the W3C. Commonly used in Japan and China, ruby text generally appears in a smaller font that overlays the main text as a pronunciation guide, or to provide some other explanatory annotation.

This property controls where the ruby text is positioned in relation to its base text.

Inherited: No

See also: ruby-align, ruby-overhang

Value

In Internet Explorer for Windows version 5 or later, this property accepts the following constants:

❑ above

❑ inline

However, the current working draft of CSS3 proposes the following values:

❑ after

❑ before

❑ right

---

[45] http://www.w3.org/TR/2001/REC-ruby-20010531/

For the meanings of each of these sets of constants, see the Microsoft Internet Explorer documentation for this property[46] and the CSS3 Ruby module working draft,[47] respectively.

Initial value:

❑ Internet Explorer: above

❑ CSS3 draft: before

Compatibility

CSS Version: n/a

This property is supported only in Internet Explorer for Windows version 5 or later. In that browser, this property must be applied to the ruby element that contains the ruby text (rt) element for which you wish to set the alignment.

Equivalent functionality is planned for inclusion in CSS3, but the proposed property values differ from those supported by Internet Explorer for Windows. To follow the work on this front, see the CSS Working Group web site.[48]

Example

This style rule places ruby text inline with, instead of above, the base text in Internet Explorer for Windows:

```
ruby {
   ruby-position: inline;
}
```

scrollbar-base-color

This nonstandard property is provided by Internet Explorer for Windows version 5.5 or later to let the page designer control the overall color of the scroll bar(s) associated with an element. The browser will use the specified color as a basis for choosing the actual colors of all the parts of the scroll bars.

---

[46] http://msdn.microsoft.com/workshop/author/dhtml/reference/properties/rubyalign.asp
[47] http://www.w3.org/TR/css3-ruby/
[48] http://www.w3.org/TR/css3-ruby/

The colors of individual parts of the scroll bars can be controlled precisely with the `scrollbar-`*`element`*`-color` properties.

Inherited: Yes

See also: `scrollbar-`*`element`*`-color`

Value

The property takes any CSS color value. See Appendix B.

Initial value: depends on user configuration

Compatibility

CSS Version: n/a

This nonstandard property works only in Internet Explorer for Windows version 5.5 or later.

Example

This style rule sets the overall scroll bar color to blue on `textarea` elements:

```
textarea {
  scrollbar-base-color: blue;
}
```

scrollbar-element-color

This collection of nonstandard properties is provided by Internet Explorer for Windows version 5.5 or later to let the page designer control the colors of various parts of the scroll bar(s) associated with an element. The actual property names, along with their meanings, are listed in Table C.9.

Table C.9. Internet Explorer `scrollbar` properties

Property	Affected area(s)
scrollbar-3dLight-color	outer top and left edges of the scroll bar buttons and thumb
scrollbar-arrow-color	up and down arrows in the scroll bar buttons
scrollbar-darkShadow-color	outer right and bottom edges of the scroll bar buttons and thumb
scrollbar-face-color	interior areas of the scroll bar buttons and thumb
scrollbar-highlight-color	inner top and left edges of the scroll bar buttons and thumb
scrollbar-shadow-color	inner right and bottom edges of the scroll bar buttons and thumb
scrollbar-track-color	background of the scroll bar, outside the scroll bar buttons and thumb

Inherited: Yes

See also: `scrollbar-base-color`

Value

The property takes any CSS color value. See Appendix B.

Initial values: depend on user configuration

Compatibility

CSS Version: n/a

These nonstandard properties work only in Internet Explorer for Windows version 5.5 or later.

Example

This style rule removes the three-dimensional appearance of the scroll bars around `textarea` elements, displaying them in flat black and white instead:

```
textarea {
  scrollbar-3dLight-color: black;
```

```
    scrollbar-arrow-color: black;
    scrollbar-darkShadow-color: black;
    scrollbar-face-color: white;
    scrollbar-highlight-color: white;
    scrollbar-shadow-color: white;
    scrollbar-track-color: black;
}
```

size

This property, which can appear only within an @page at-rule (see the section called "At-rules" in Appendix A), lets you control the page size and/or orientation as needed.

Value

This property can take a number of constants, or specific page measurements.

Supported constants are:

❑ auto

❑ landscape

❑ portrait

auto tells the browser to use a page size/orientation equal to the printer settings, while landscape and portrait force the browser to rotate the page as necessary to print in the specified orientation on the printer's paper size.

Alternatively, you can specify an exact page size with either one or two CSS length values (separated by spaces). If only one value is specified, it is used as both the width and height; otherwise, the first value is the page width and the second is the page height.

Initial value: auto

Compatibility

CSS Version: 2

The property is not supported by any currently available browser.

Example

This style rule specifies that the page should be printed in landscape orientation on a Letter-sized (8.5-inch by 11-inch) page:

```
@page {
  size: 11in 8.5in;
}
```

speak

For use by aural (speaking) browsers for the visually impaired, this property controls if and how an element's content should be read aloud.

Inherited: Yes

See also: `speak-header`, `speak-numeral`, `speak-punctuation`

Value

This property accepts any of the following constants:

☐ none: The element's content is not read.

☐ normal: The element's content is read normally.

☐ spell-out: The element's content is spelled out one character at a time.

Initial value: `normal`

Compatibility

CSS Version: 2

This property is not supported by any currently available browser.

Example

This example causes aural browsers to spell out `abbr` and `acronym` elements:

```
abbr, acronym {
  speak: spell-out;
}
```

speak-header

For use by aural (speaking) browsers for the visually impaired, this property controls how table headers are read. As the browser reads out the contents of each cell in the table, it can either read all the headers for a cell before that cell's contents, or it may read only those headers that are different from the headers of the previously-read cell.

Inherited: Yes

See also: speak, speak-numeral, speak-punctuation

Value

This property accepts any of the following constants:

❏ always: For each cell, all the headers that apply to it are read first.

❏ once: For each cell, only headers that are different from the previously-read cell are read.

Initial value: once

Compatibility

CSS Version: 2

This property is not supported by any currently available browser.

Example

This example causes aural browsers to read all the headers that apply to each cell in a table of class matrix:

```
table.matrix {
  speak-header: always;
}
```

speak-numeral

For use by aural (speaking) browsers for the visually impaired, this property controls how numbers are read. A number may be read either as a series of digits (e.g. "one, two, three") or as a whole number (e.g. "one hundred twenty-three").

Inherited: Yes

See also: `speak`, `speak-header`, `speak-punctuation`

Value

This property accepts any of the following constants:

❑   `digits`: The number is read as a series of digits.

❑   `continuous`: The number is read as a whole number.

Initial value: `continuous`

Compatibility

CSS Version: 2

The property is not supported by any currently available browser.

Example

This example causes aural browsers to read numbers occurring in any element of class `binary` as a series of digits:

```
.binary {
  speak-numeral: digits;
}
```

speak-punctuation

For use by aural (speaking) browsers for the visually impaired, this property controls how punctuation is read. Punctuation may either be read aloud (e.g. "period"), or represented by pauses in the reading of surrounding text.

Inherited: Yes

See also: `speak`, `speak-header`, `speak-numeral`

Value

This property accepts any of the following constants:

❑ `code`: Punctuation is read aloud.

❑ `none`: Punctuation is implied by natural pauses.

Initial value: `none`

Compatibility

CSS Version: 2

This property is not supported by any currently available browser.

Example

This example causes aural browsers to read aloud punctuation occurring in any element of class `spokenpunct`:

```
.spokenpunct {
  speak-punctuation: code;
}
```

speech-rate

For use by aural (speaking) browsers for the visually impaired, this property controls how quickly (or slowly) the content of an element is read.

Inherited: Yes

See also: `pause`

Value

You can specify the exact speech rate in words per minute as a positive, floating-point number.

This property also accepts any of the constants in Table C.10.

Table C.10. `speech-rate` constants

Constant	Effect
x-slow	80 words per minute
slow	120 words per minute
medium	180 to 120 words per minute
fast	300 words per minute
x-fast	500 words per minute
slower	the inherited rate minus 40 words per minute
faster	the inherited rate plus 40 words per minute

Initial value: medium

Compatibility

CSS Version: 2

This property is not supported by any currently available browser.

Example

This example causes aural browsers to read elements of class ominous more slowly than usual:

```
.ominous {
  speech-rate: slower;
}
```

stress

For use by aural (speaking) browsers for the visually impaired, this property controls stress in the voice that reads a selected element's content aloud. In English, for example, every sentence usually contains particular words that are emphasized more heavily than others. This property controls how great the difference is between emphasized and non-emphasized passages.

Inherited: Yes

See also: `pitch`, `pitch-range`, `richness`, `voice-family`, `volume`

Value

The property takes any integer between 0 and 100; 50 is an average level of stress.

Initial value: 50

Compatibility

CSS Version: 2

The property is not supported by any currently available browser.

Example

This example causes aural browsers to speak elements of class `ominous` with greater stress than usual:

```
.ominous {
  stress: 75;
}
```

table-layout

This property lets you accelerate table rendering by allowing it to take a shortcut in calculating the column sizes. When `table-layout` is set to `fixed`, the browser considers only the cells in the first row when determining the table's cell widths (and the table's overall width). This allows the browser to render the table one row at a time, instead of having to wait for the full table to load before being able to display any of it.

Be aware that wider content in subsequent table rows will be wrapped to the column widths set by the first row when the fixed table layout mode is used: the cell size will not increase to accommodate the data.

Inherited: No

See also: `max-height`, `min-height`

Value

auto or fixed

Initial value: auto

Compatibility

CSS Version: 2

This property is supported by all CSS-compatible browsers.

Example

This style rule sets tables of class thumbnails to the quicker, fixed layout mode:

```
table.thumbnails {
  table-layout: fixed;
}
```

text-align

This property sets the horizontal alignment of text and other inline content within a block element.

If you're looking for a way to set the horizontal alignment of a block (e.g. to center it on the page), you should instead use the margin-left, margin-right, left, and right properties to achieve the desired effect (e.g. you can center a block horizontally by setting its left and right margins to auto).

Inherited: Yes

See also: text-align-last, vertical-align

Value

This property supports the following constant values:

❑ center

❑ justify

- ☐ left

- ☐ right

center, left, and right are self-explanatory. justify should be familiar to users of word processors; it causes the words on each line to be spaced so that each line starts and ends against the edge of the content box, with the exception of the last line.

Initial value: Depends on the language of the browser and/or the element

Compatibility

CSS Version: 1

This property is supported by all CSS-compatible browsers.

In older browsers (most version 4 browsers), justify behaves the same as left; however, this is allowable under the CSS 2.1 standard.

Example

This style rule will justify text within the body and all child elements, unless otherwise specified (thanks to inheritance):

```
body {
  text-align: justify;
}
```

text-align-last

This nonstandard property, supported by Internet Explorer for Windows version 5.5 or later, lets you specifically set the alignment of the last line of text within a block element whose text-align property is set to justify.

This property is ignored when the text-align property is not set to justify.

Inherited: Yes

See also: text-align

Value

This property supports the following constant values:

- ❏ auto
- ❏ center
- ❏ justify
- ❏ left
- ❏ right

auto allows the last line to reflect the alignment set by the `text-align` property.

Initial value: auto

Compatibility

CSS Version: n/a

The property is supported only by Internet Explorer for Windows version 5.5 or later.

Example

This style rule causes the last line of a `blockquote` element to be right-aligned:

```
blockquote {
  text-align: justify;
  text-align-last: right;
}
```

text-autospace

This property lets you choose between a number of methods for increasing the space between ideographic characters (in Asian languages) and non-ideographic characters (non-Asian languages).

Inherited: No

Value

This property accepts any of the following constant values:

- `ideograph-alpha`: extra space between ideographic and non-ideographic characters

- `ideograph-numeric`: extra space between ideographic and numeric characters

- `ideograph-parenthesis`: extra space between ideographic characters and parentheses

- `ideograph-space`: extra space between ideographic characters and whitespace

- `none`: no extra space

Initial value: none

Compatibility

CSS Version: n/a

The property is compatible with Internet Explorer 5 or later for Windows only.

Equivalent functionality is planned for inclusion in CSS3, but combinations of the above values will likely be allowed. To follow the work on this front, see the CSS Working Group web site.[49]

Example

This style rule adds extra spacing between ideographic and non-ideographic characters in paragraphs of class `mixed`:

```
p.mixed {
  text-autospace: ideograph-alpha;
}
```

---

[49] http://www.w3.org/TR/2003/WD-css3-text-20030226/#text-autospace-prop

text-decoration

This property lets you add one or more "decorations" to the text within an element. Decorations include overlining, underlining, striking through, and blinking.

Although this property is not inherited, specifying it on an element will apply the decoration through the whole element, including any child elements.

Inherited: No

Value

This property can be set to none to remove any decoration specified in a lower-priority rule (e.g. to remove the underline applied to hyperlinks in the default style sheets of visual browsers).

Otherwise, it can take any space-delimited combination of the following constants:

☐ blink[50]

☐ line-through

☐ overline

☐ underline

Initial value: none

Compatibility

CSS Version: 1

This property works in all CSS-compatible browsers; however, the blink decoration type is (mercifully) not supported in Internet Explorer browsers.

Example

This style rule removes the underline from hyperlinks in the document and replaces it with a dashed bottom border:

---

[50]The author begs you not to use this.

```
a:link, a:visited {
  text-decoration: none;
  border-bottom: 1px solid dashed;
}
```

text-indent

This property sets the indent applied to the first line of a block element (and its children, thanks to inheritance).

A negative value will result in a hanging indent, with the text of the first line protruding from the content area of the block. You will usually want to balance a negative text-indent with a positive padding-left value of the same or greater size to keep all the text within the border of the block.

Inherited: Yes

See also: padding

Value

The property takes any CSS length value (px, pt, em, etc.), or a percentage of the parent element's width.

Initial value: 0

Compatibility

CSS Version: 1

This property is supported by all CSS-compatible browsers.

Example

This style rule creates a one-centimeter hanging indent on all paragraphs by using a negative text-indent in combination with a padding-left value of the same size:

```
p {
  text-indent: -1cm;
  padding-left: 1cm;
}
```

text-justify

This nonstandard property, supported by Internet Explorer for Windows version 5 or later, controls the algorithm used to calculate spacing in blocks with `text-align` set to `justify`. This property is designed for use with Asian languages where "words" do not necessarily occur, and therefore the adaptive word spacing usually associated with justified text does not have a clear meaning.

Inherited: Yes

See also: `text-align`, `text-kashida-space`

Value

This property will accept any one of the following constant values:

- `auto`: allows the browser to choose which algorithm to use

- `distribute`: increases letter spacing and word spacing by the same amount

- `distribute-all-lines`: same as `distribute`, but also applies to the last line

- `inter-cluster`: same as `distribute`, but does not add space between characters of Southeast Asian grapheme clusters

- `inter-ideograph`: same as `distribute`, but does not add space between non-Chinese/Japanese/Korean characters

- `inter-word`: the familiar method for Latin languages like English; adds only space between words

- `kashida`: uses elongated strokes in Arabic characters to justify text

- `newspaper`: same as `distribute`, but preference is given to inter-word spacing over inter-character spacing

Initial value: `auto`

Compatibility

CSS Version: n/a

The property is available in Internet Explorer 5 or later for Windows only. The `kashida` mode is supported only by version 5.5 or later.

Equivalent functionality is planned for inclusion in CSS3, but final property names and values are likely to differ. To follow the work on this front, see the CSS Working Group web site.[51]

Example

This style rule specifies the `newspaper` justification mode for `div` elements of class `column`:

```
div.column {
  text-align: justify;
  text-justify: newspaper;
}
```

text-kashida-space

This nonstandard property, supported by Internet Explorer for Windows version 5.5 or later, controls the degree to which the browser relies on kashida expansion to achieve justified alignment. This property is designed for use with Arabic languages, where certain horizontal lines in the script can be extended to lengthen words.

For this property to have a useful effect, affected elements must have their `text-align` property set to `justify`, and their `text-justify` property set to a mode that allows kashida expansion (`auto`, `distribute`, `kashida`, or `newspaper`).

Inherited: Yes

See also: `text-align`, `text-justify`

Value

The property takes as its value a percentage ratio between kashida expansion and whitespace expansion, where `100%` will result in only kashida expansion and `0%` will result in only whitespace expansion.

Initial value: `0%`

---

[51] http://www.w3.org/TR/2003/WD-css3-text-20030226/#justification-prop

Compatibility

CSS Version: n/a

This property is supported by Internet Explorer 5.5 or later for Windows only.

Equivalent functionality is planned for inclusion in CSS3, but final property names and values are likely to differ. To follow the work on this front, see the CSS Working Group web site.[52]

Example

This style rule specifies that for every two units of whitespace that are added, one unit of kashida expansion is added:

```
div.column {
    text-align: justify;
    text-kashida-space: 33%;
}
```

text-overflow

This nonstandard property, supported by Internet Explorer 6 or later, lets you handle text that is clipped by the width of an element more elegantly. The portion of the string that would normally overflow the edge of the box is replaced with an ellipsis (...).

The element must have its `overflow` property set to something other than `visible` (although `hidden` is the only value that really makes sense) for this property to have any effect.

Note that this property affects only text that is clipped by the *width* of the element (or the height in vertical writing systems), either because word-wrapping is disabled with the `white-space` property, or because a long word or other non-wrappable text segment is too long to fit in the box.

Inherited: No

See also: `overflow`, `white-space`, `width`

---

[52] http://www.w3.org/TR/2003/WD-css3-text-20030226/#kashida-prop

Value

This property can be set to either of these two constants:

☐ `clip`

☐ `ellipsis`

Initial value: `clip`

Compatibility

CSS Version: n/a

The property is supported in Internet Explorer for Windows version 6 or later only.

Example

This style rule specifies that text within `div`s of class `summary` should not be wrapped, and that text that does not fit within the `div` should be shown with an ellipsis:

```
.summary {
  width: 500px;
  white-space: nowrap;
  overflow: hidden;
  text-overflow: ellipsis;
}
```

text-transform

This property causes the text of selected element(s) to be case-modified for display. Text can be displayed capitalized, uppercase, or lowercase.

Inherited: Yes

Value

This property may be assigned any one of the following constant values:

☐ `capitalize`: The first letter of each word is displayed in uppercase.

□ `lowercase`: All characters in the text are displayed in lowercase.

□ `uppercase`: All characters in the text are displayed in uppercase.

□ `none`: The text is displayed unmodified.

Initial value: `none`

Compatibility

CSS Version: 1

This property is supported by all CSS-compatible browsers.

Example

This style rule displays all headings in capitalized text (the first letter of each word is capitalized):

```
h1, h2, h3, h4, h5, h6 {
  text-transform: capitalize;
}
```

text-underline-position

This nonstandard property, supported by Internet Explorer for Windows version 5.5 or later, controls whether underlines are drawn above or below text inside the selected element(s). This property is designed for use with Asian languages and other vertical writing systems.

For this property to have a visible effect, an affected element (or one of its children) must have its `text-decoration` property set to `underline`.

Inherited: Yes

See also: `text-decoration`

Value

This property will accept either of these three constant values:

- ❑ `auto` or `auto-pos`: The underline is drawn above the text if the language is set to `ja` (Japanese) and `writing-mode` is set to `tb-rl`.

- ❑ `above`: The underline is drawn above the text.

- ❑ `below`: The underline is drawn below the text.

Initial value:

- ❑ Internet Explorer 6 or later: `auto`

- ❑ Internet Explorer 5.5: `below`

Compatibility

CSS Version: n/a

The property is compatible with Internet Explorer for Windows version 5.5 or later only. The `auto` and `auto-pos` values are supported only in version 6 or later.

Equivalent functionality is planned for inclusion in CSS3, but final property names and values are likely to differ. To follow the work on this front, see the CSS Working Group web site.[53]

Example

This style rule specifies that underlines should always be drawn below the text, even in vertical, Japanese text:

```
body {
  text-underline-position: below;
}
```

top

This property lets you set the distance between the top edge of an `absolute` positioned element (including its padding, border, and margin)[54] and the top edge of the positioning context in which it resides. The positioning context is the

---

[53] http://www.w3.org/TR/2003/WD-css3-text-20030226/#text-decoration-other
[54] The CSS 2 specification contains an error that suggests that the padding, border, and margin of the positioned element should not be considered. This has been acknowledged as a mistake by the CSS Working Group in the Errata document for CSS 2.

padding area of the element's nearest ancestor that has a `position` property value other than `static`, or the `body` element.

For `relative` positioned elements, this property sets a relative offset from the normal position of its top edge. So, a setting of `10px` will shift the top edge of the box ten pixels downward, and a setting of `-10px` will shift it ten pixels upward.

Inherited: No

See also: `position`, `bottom`, `left`, and `right`

Value

The property takes a CSS length measurement, a percentage value, or the `auto` constant. Percentages are based on the height of the parent element. The `auto` constant tells the browser to determine the position of the top edge itself, based on whatever other constraints may exist on the size/position of the element.

Initial value: `auto`

Compatibility

CSS Version: 2

The property is supported by all CSS-compatible browsers.

Example

This style rule positions the element with ID `menu` ten pixels from the top edge of the window:

```
#menu {
  position: absolute;
  top: 10px;
}
```

unicode-bidi

Most western languages are written left-to-right (LTR). As you probably know, many other languages (e.g. Hebrew) are written right-to-left (RTL). Documents written with the Unicode character set[55] can contain text from both LTR and RTL languages. The Unicode standard includes a complicated algorithm that should be used for displaying such mixed text. It also defines special characters that let you "group" text.

For example, consider the following imaginary string of text, where the lowercase text represents LTR characters and the uppercase text represents RTL:

```
english1 HEBREW1 english2 HEBREW2 english3
```

Now, the obvious way to render this would be "english1 1WERBEH english2 2WERBEH english3," but what if we add some HTML tags to the mix?

```
<p>english1 <q>HEBREW1 english2 HEBREW2</q> english3</p>
```

As you can see, the text beginning with HEBREW1 and ending with HEBREW2 is intended as an inline quotation in Hebrew, which just happens to contain an English word. Since HEBREW1 and HEBREW2 belong to the same block of Hebrew text, "2WERBEH" should be rendered to the left of "1WERBEH". With this in mind, the complete paragraph should be rendered as "english1 2WERBEH english2 1WERBEH english3."

The HTML 4.0 standard (along with XHTML 1.0) defines the dir attribute and the bdo element to handle these complexities. To obtain the desired rendering in an HTML4-compatible browser, the code should be:

```
<p>english1 <q lang="he" dir="rtl">HEBREW1 english2 HEBREW2</q>
  english3</p>
```

The dir attribute of the q tag is what specifies the rendering order; the lang attribute won't have any actual visible effect. For full details on language and bidirectional text rendering in HTML, refer to Section 8 of the HTML 4.0 standard.[56]

So, where does CSS come into play, you ask? Well, the direction property, in combination with a unicode-bidi property setting of embed, performs the same role as the HTML dir attribute. In combination with a unicode-bidi property setting of bidi-override, direction has the same effect as the HTML bdo tag. However, it's still considered best practice to include bidirectional text attributes as part of the HTML code. The direction and unicode-bidi properties are intended for use in styling XML documents that do not have the benefit of HTML 4's bidirectional text features. Since the focus of this book is on web development,

---

[55] http://www.unicode.org/
[56] http://www.w3.org/TR/REC-html40/struct/dirlang.html

I'll therefore refer you to the CSS 2.1 standard[57] for full details on these properties.

Inherited: No

See also: `direction`

Value

This property will accept any one of these three constant values:

❑ `normal`: The element is treated normally for purposes of bidirectional text rendering; LTR text is rendered LTR and RTL text is rendered RTL. The `direction` property has no effect on the element.

❑ `embed`: The element behaves as an embedded sequence of LTR or RTL text, as set by the `direction` property. This is equivalent to setting the HTML `dir` property on the element.

❑ `bidi-override`: All text inside the element, whether LTR or RTL, is rendered in the direction set by the `direction` property. This is equivalent to using an HTML `bdo` tag with the equivalent `dir` attribute value.

Initial value: `normal`

Compatibility

CSS Version: 2

The property is not supported by any currently available browser.

Example

This style rule sets the text direction of an imaginary XML element named `hebrew` to `rtl`. The `unicode-bidi` property setting in this case ensures that all text within the `hebrew` element (even text that would normally be displayed LTR according to the Unicode standard) will be displayed RTL.

```
hebrew {
  direction: rtl;
```

---

[57] http://www.w3.org/TR/CSS21/visuren.html#direction

```
    unicode-bidi: bidi-override;
}
```

vertical-align

This property sets the vertical alignment of text and other inline content with respect to either its parent element's font, or the line in which it appears.

This value also lets you set the vertical alignment of content within table cells.

Inherited: No

See also: `text-align`

Value

This property supports a range of constant values as well as CSS measurements and percentages.

The majority of the supported constants for this property align text and other inline content with respect to the parent element's font:

baseline
> The baseline[58] of the content will line up with the baseline of the parent element's font. If the content has no baseline (e.g. an image), then the bottom of the content is lined up with the baseline of the parent element's font.

middle
> The content is aligned so that its vertical midpoint lines up with a point that is half the parent element font's x-height[59] above the parent element's baseline.

sub
> The content is aligned so that its baseline is positioned some distance below the parent element's baseline; this is suitable for subscript text. Usually, you'll want to set a smaller `font-size` property for the content as well.

---

[58]The baseline is the imaginary line on which text is written. The bottoms of letters rest on the baseline, with descenders extending below it.
[59]The x-height is the height of lowercase letters in a font.

super

> The content is aligned so that its baseline is positioned some distance above the parent element's baseline, which is suitable for superscript text. You will usually want to set a smaller `font-size` property for the content as well.

text-bottom

> The content is aligned so that its bottom lines up with the bottom of the parent element's font. This position is independent of the actual line height.

text-top

> The content is aligned so that its top lines up with the top of the parent element's font. This position is independent of the actual line height.

As with the above constants, setting the vertical position with a numerical value gives a position relative to the parent element's font:

length

> A CSS length (`px`, `pt`, `em`, etc.) shifts the content's baseline—or bottom, if no baseline exists—up or down from the parent element's baseline for positive or negative values, respectively.

percentage

> A percentage (e.g. `50%`) shifts the content's baseline—or bottom, if no baseline exists—up or down from the parent element's baseline by a percentage of the element's `line-height` property for positive or negative values, respectively.

Finally, two additional constants let you set the content's vertical position with respect to the line in which the content appears. This may be considerably different from the parent element's font (e.g. if the line contains a tall image that increases the overall line height).

bottom

> The content is aligned so that its bottom (not its baseline) rests against the bottom of the line area.

top

> The content is aligned so that its top rests against the top of the line area.

When applied to table cells, this property does not support `sub`, `super`, `text-bottom`, or `text-top`—all of these behave like `baseline`. The constants `bottom`, `middle`, and `top` refer to the cell box, while `baseline` ensures that the first line of each cell shares the same baseline as the other cells in the same row.

Initial value: `baseline`

Compatibility

CSS Version: 1 (the *length* value format was added in CSS 2)

This property is supported by all CSS-compatible browsers.

Internet Explorer for Windows supports only `baseline`, `sub`, and `super` in version 5 or earlier. Version 5.5 or later supports the other constants, but only on HTML elements that support the `valign` attribute (i.e. table cells). Internet Explorer for Windows does not support setting length or percentage values for this property.

Example

This style rule will align content within table header cells (`th`) to the vertical middle of the cell:

```
th {
  vertical-align: middle;
}
```

visibility

This property lets you set whether an element is visible or not. When an element is invisible, it is not displayed at all; however, it still occupies the same space on the page that it would occupy if it were visible. To hide an element so that it does not occupy any space on the page, set the `display` property to `none` instead.

Inherited: Yes

See also: `display`

Value

This property will accept any one of the following constant values:

❑ `collapse`: When applied to a row (`tr`), row group (`thead`, `tbody`, `tfoot`), column (`col`), or column group (`colgroup`) element, this setting causes the row(s) or column(s) to be visibly removed from the table, allowing the table to shrink accordingly. For other elements, this setting has the same effect as `hidden`.

❏ `hidden`: The element is not visible, but still occupies space in the document.

❏ `visible`: The element is displayed as normal.

Initial value: `visible`

Compatibility

CSS Version: 2

All CSS-compatible browsers support this property, but none yet support the `collapse` value.

Example

This style rule hides elements with class `active`. Using dynamic HTML, these elements could be shown in response to some user event:

```
.active {
  visibility: hidden;
}
```

voice-family

For use by aural (speaking) browsers for the visually impaired, this property controls the **voice family** used to read the content of the element. A voice family embodies the vocal attributes of a particular character, and is the aural analogue to the `font-family` property.

Inherited: Yes

See also: `pitch`, `pitch-range`, `richness`, `stress`, `volume`

Value

A comma-separated list of voice names. Voice names that contain spaces should be quoted (e.g. `"Albert Einstein"`).

In addition to actual voice names, the list can contain any of the following generic voice names:

❏ `male`

❏ female

❏ child

Since browsers will always be able to find a voice for each of these generic voice names, it only makes sense for the last name in the `voice-family` list to be one of these.

Initial value: browser specific

Compatibility

CSS Version: 2

The property is not supported by any currently available browser.

Example

This example causes aural browsers to speak elements of class `ominous` in the voice of Igor, or in any male voice if the Igor voice family is not supported:

```
.ominous {
  voice-family: igor, male;
}
```

volume

For use by aural (speaking) browsers for the visually impaired, this property sets the median volume (loudness) of the voice that reads a selected element's content aloud.

Inherited: Yes

See also: `pitch, pitch-range, richness, stress, voice-family`

Value

An absolute volume between 0 and 100 (inclusive), a percentage of the inherited volume, or one of the following constants:

❏ `silent`: no sound at all

- ❏ x-soft: the lowest perceptible volume, the same as 0

- ❏ soft: equivalent to 25

- ❏ medium: equivalent to 50

- ❏ loud: equivalent to 75

- ❏ x-loud: the maximum comfortable volume, the same as 100

Initial value: medium

Compatibility

CSS Version: 2

The property is not supported by any currently available browser.

Example

This example causes aural browsers to speak elements of class ominous in a soft voice:

```
.ominous {
  volume: soft;
}
```

white-space

Experienced HTML designers will be accustomed to the fact that whitespace in HTML source code (sequences spaces, tabs, and line breaks) is collapsed to a single space character in the rendered output, and that line breaks occur only due to normal word wrapping performed by the browser or due to a hard break (<br/>) tag. Non-breaking space characters ( ), the nowrap attribute in table tags, and the HTML <pre> tag can be used to work around this behavior, when necessary.

The white-space property lets you assign the special properties of these work-arounds to other document elements so that the document code need not reflect the intended formatting.

Inherited: Yes

Value

This property will accept any one of the following constant values:

- `normal`: Content is rendered with the default HTML behavior. Whitespace is collapsed and word wrapping is performed.

- `nowrap`: Whitespace is collapsed as with `normal`, but word wrapping does not occur. Line breaks will occur only when specified with `<br/>` tags or when present in generated content (see `content`).

- `pre`: Whitespace is not collapsed and word wrapping does not occur. This type of rendering is the default for `<pre>` tags, except the `font-family` of the element is not set to `monospace`.

- `pre-wrap`: This value prevents user agents from collapsing sequences of whitespace.

- `pre-line`: This value directs user agents to collapse sequences of whitespace.

Initial value: `normal`

Compatibility

CSS Version: 1

CSS Version: 2.1 (pre-wrap and pre-line values)

This property is supported in Opera, Safari, and Mozilla browsers.

Internet Explorer for Windows supports this property as of version 5.5; however, the `pre` value is supported only in version 6 and later, and then only when running in standards-compliant mode.[60]

None of these browsers support the `pre-line` and `pre-wrap` values introduced in CSS 2.1.

Example

This style rule will preserve whitespace and suppress word wrapping on `div` elements of class `screen`:

---

[60] http://msdn.microsoft.com/library/en-us/dnie60/html/cssenhancements.asp

```
div.screen {
  white-space: pre;
}
```

widows

This property affects the position of page breaks when the user prints the page from his or her browser. With this property, you can specify the minimum number of lines that must remain in a block following a page break.

For example, if a paragraph element had six lines and the page size called for a page break to occur after the fourth line, then an `widows` setting of 3 would force the page break to occur *before* the paragraph so that the last three lines could appear on the same page.

Inherited: Yes

See also: `orphans`

Value

A positive integer.

Initial value: 2

Compatibility

CSS Version: 2

This property is currently only supported by Opera.

Example

This style rule indicates that page breaks must allow at least four lines of a broken paragraph to appear at the top of the next page after the break occurs:

```
p {
  widows: 4;
}
```

width

This property sets the width of the contents of a block or replaced element.[61] This width does not include padding, borders, or margins.

If the contents of a block require more horizontal space than the width you assign, the behavior is defined by the overflow property.

Inherited: No

See also: height, max-width, min-width, overflow, text-overflow

Value

The property takes any CSS length value, a percentage of the parent element's width, or auto.

Initial value: auto

Compatibility

CSS Version: 1

This property is supported in some form by all CSS-compatible browsers. Current, standards-compliant browsers (Opera, Safari, Mozilla) support it fully.

Internet Explorer for Windows (up to and including version 7) incorrectly includes padding, borders, and margins in the width value. This is known as the **box model bug**. IE corrects this in version 6 and later when in standards-compliant mode,[62] but for all previous versions you'll need to use a separate, browser-specific style sheet or live with smaller boxes whenever borders, margins, or padding come into play (which is almost always). A third alternative is commonly known as the **box model hack**,[63] which exploits a more obscure bug in IE6's CSS support to work around the box model bug.

---

[61]A replaced element is any element whose appearance and dimensions are defined by an external resource. Examples include images (img tags), plug-ins (object tags), and form fields (input and select tags). Another way to think of replaced elements is as any element that can be displayed inline with text and that acts as a single, big character for the purposes of wrapping and layout.

[62] http://msdn.microsoft.com/library/en-us/dnie60/html/cssenhancements.asp

[63] http://css-discuss.incutio.com/?page=BoxModelHack

In Internet Explorer 4, this property is supported only for a limited subset of block elements (`div` is a safe bet).

Example

This style rule assigns a fixed width of 100 pixels to paragraphs within the element with ID `blurbs`:

```
#blurbs p {
  width: 100px;
}
```

word-break

This nonstandard property, supported by Internet Explorer for Windows version 5 or later, lets you specify different word wrapping behavior for Chinese/Japanese/Korean (CJK) scripts than for other writing systems.

Inherited: Yes

Value

This property will accept any one of the following constant values:

- `break-all`: allows both CJK and non-CJK words to be broken by word wrapping at any point; ideal for CJK text containing non-CJK fragments

- `keep-all`: prevents both CJK and non-CJK words from being broken by word wrapping; ideal for non-CJK text containing CJK fragments

- `normal`: allows CJK words to be broken by word wrapping at any point, but prevents non-CJK words from being broken in the same way

Initial value: `normal`

Compatibility

CSS Version: n/a

The property is supported by Internet Explorer 5 or later for Windows only.

^aEquivalent functionality is planned for inclusion in CSS3, but final property names and values are likely to differ. To follow the work on this front, see the CSS Working Group web site.[64]

Example

This style rule sets the entire document to prevent arbitrary breaking of words in CJK and non-CJK text, in anticipation of the document being primarily non-CJK:

```
body {
  word-break: keep-all;
}
```

word-spacing

This property lets you increase or decrease the amount of spacing between words in an element.

Inherited: Yes

See also: letter-spacing

Value

The property takes any CSS length, or normal. Percentages are *not* allowed.

Positive lengths increase word spacing by the specified amount, while negative lengths decrease it. In most cases, it is preferable to specify the spacing in ems (e.g. 0.5em), as this will preserve the relative spacing of words even if you change the font size (one em is equal to the height of the current font).

Initial value: normal

Compatibility

CSS Version: 1

This property is supported by Internet Explorer for Windows version 6 or later, Safari, Opera, and Mozilla browsers.

---

[64] http://www.w3.org/TR/2003/WD-css3-text-20030226/#wordbreak-props

Examples

This style rule sets all elements of class **spacy** to have extra spacing to half of the font's height between each word:

```
.spacy {
  word-spacing: 0.5em;
}
```

This style rule sets all elements of class **crowded** to display words to half the font size closer together than usual:

```
.crowded {
  word-spacing: -0.5em;
}
```

word-wrap

This nonstandard property, supported by Internet Explorer for Windows version 5.5 or later, lets you specify whether words that are too long to fit within the assigned width of an element should overflow that width (the default behavior), or be wrapped to the next line at the edge of the box.

Inherited: Yes

See also: width, text-overflow

Value

break-word or normal

Initial value: normal

Compatibility

CSS Version: n/a

The property is supported by Internet Explorer 5.5 for Windows or later only.

Example

This style rule allows long words throughout the document to be wrapped forcibly if they overflow the assigned width of their containers:

```
body {
  word-wrap: break-word;
}
```

writing-mode

This nonstandard property lets you choose between two common layout methods for text: left-to-right horizontal lines stacked from top to bottom on the page (the usual layout for western languages like English), and top-to-bottom vertical lines stacked from right to left on the page (the usual layout for East Asian languages like Chinese).

For scripts not designed to be displayed this way (e.g. Latin script as used in English text), the tb-rl setting rotates the text 90 degrees clockwise so that it can be read vertically.

Inherited: Yes

See also: layout-flow

Value

lr-tb or tb-rl

Initial value: lr-tb

Compatibility

CSS Version: n/a

The property is supported by Internet Explorer 5.5 for Windows or later only.

Equivalent functionality is planned for inclusion in CSS3, but final property names and values are likely to differ. To follow the work on this front, see the CSS Working Group web site.[65]

---

[65] http://www.w3.org/TR/2003/WD-css3-text-20030226/#Progression

Example

This style rule sets the `writing-mode` of the `body` and all its children (unless otherwise specified) to the East Asian style:

```
body {
  writing-mode: tb-rl;
}
```

z-index

For any element for which the `position` property is other than `static`, this property sets the stacking order relative to other positioned elements within the same **stacking context**.[66]

Non-positioned elements are always beneath all positioned elements in the same stacking context; they effectively have a `z-index` of 0. Elements in the same stacking context with the same `z-index` are stacked in the order they appear in the document, with later elements overlaying earlier ones.

Inherited: No

See also: `position`

Value

A positive integer, or the `auto` constant. The higher the integer, the higher the element's position in the stacking order.

The `auto` constant causes the element to behave as if it had a `z-index` of 0, except that it does not create a new stacking context.

Initial value: `auto`

Compatibility

CSS Version: 2

This property works in all CSS-compatible browsers.

---

[66]The stacking context of any element is the closest positioned ancestor whose `z-index` property is set.

Example

This style rule positions the element with ID `mainmenu` near the top-left of the browser window and with a `z-index` value that causes it to hover over other elements of lower `z-index` values:

```
#mainmenu {
  position: absolute;
  top: 10px;
  left: 10px;
  width: 100px;
  height: 300px;
  z-index: 10;
}
```

zoom

This nonstandard property, supported by Internet Explorer for Windows version 5.5 or later, lets you magnify or reduce the size of an element and all its contents.

Inherited: No

Value

The property takes as its value the magnification factor, either as a floating point number (`1.0` is the normal size) or as a percentage (`100%` is the normal size), or the constant value `normal`.

Initial value: `normal`

Compatibility

CSS Version: n/a

This property is supported by Internet Explorer for Windows version 5.5 or later only.

Example

This style rule sets all images in the document to appear at half their normal size:

```
img {
  zoom: 50%;
}
```

Recommended Resources

This bibliography provides you with links to, and comments on, some of the better reference sources—online and off—that I've encountered in my adventures with CSS.

I'm absolutely certain that I've left out a lot of great stuff here. The universe of CSS information is too large for one person to know about, and certainly too vast for a single appendix in a book. What I've provided here is a list of the best books and web sites I've personally encountered and used. Each is accompanied by a brief commentary to help you decide which resources will best suit your needs in a given design situation.

The resources appear in no particular order.

Books

DHTML Utopia: Modern Web Design Using JavaScript & DOM[1], 1st Edition
By Stuart Langridge. Published by SitePoint. ISBN: 0-9579218–9–6.

> Stuart started out as a SitePoint blogger, and how he managed to fit the writing of this—which is arguably among the most entertaining and educational books on DHTML—around blogging *and* his day job is anyone's guess. As the publishers comment, the book, "doesn't cover old-style, browser-specific DHTML. Modern DHTML, as presented in this book, utilizes web standards, separates the code from the markup, and degrades gracefully." This is a practical, hands-on, tutorial-style title that shows you how to implement slick DHTML functionality for browsers that can handle it, without causing problems in browsers that can't. It's essential reading for those who want to use DHTML creatively and effectively.

Eric Meyer on CSS: Mastering the Language of Web Design
By Eric N. Meyer. Published by New Riders. ISBN: 0-7357-1245-X.

> Meyer is among the best-known CSS authorities on the planet. This slick, oversized, highly illustrated book is an absolute treasure-trove of teachings about CSS beyond the basics. The text consists of 13 separate projects through which Meyer walks the reader step by step. Meyer leads readers

---

[1] http://www.sitepoint.com/books/dhtml1/

carefully and precisely from converting an existing page to CSS, through styling for print, and applying CSS to HTML forms. Learn to create an online greeting card, a multi-column layout, unusually shaped designs, and translucent-looking scrolling areas atop fixed backgrounds.

Each chapter concludes with several challenges that stretch your skills as you attempt to build on what Meyer has taught in the chapter.

The only criticism I have of this book is its rather weak index, which reduces its value as a reference. But read through any of the projects and work them out on the screen, and I guarantee you'll learn something—no matter how sophisticated a CSS designer you might be!

By the way, if you buy this book, be sure to check out the companion web site[2] (mentioned later in this appendix). There are errors in the first printed edition that you'll need to be aware of if you're to avoid total confusion at some points.

The CSS Anthology: 101 Essential Tips, Tricks & Hacks
By Rachel Andrew. Published by SitePoint. ISBN: 0-9579218–8–8.

Rachel's first book for SitePoint, The CSS Anthology[3] was designed to provide a natural progression for readers of HTML Utopia. It provides solutions to common (and some not-so-common!) CSS problems in an easy-to-use question-and-answer format that has made it a favorite of web designers and interface developers around the world. More than 100 tutorials are provided for experienced CSS developers who want to hone their skills and take their CSS capabilities to the next level. But it's just as well-suited to relative newcomers to CSS who want to ensure they have all the answers—and the right ones at that!

Useful Web Sites and Pages

The usual caveats about things moving around on the Web apply here. I've provided the URL for each site or page that was accurate and current as this book went into production. But there can be no guarantees as to their accuracy beyond that point.

Unfortunately, much of the CSS-related content you'll find by searching the Web is likely out of date before you see it. There was a flurry of articles in

---

[2] http://www.ericmeyeroncss.com/
[3] http://www.sitepoint.com/books/cssant1/

1998–1999 when CSS was new, but very few sites (our own http://www.sitepoint.com/ is one exception) have continued their CSS coverage, or ever extended beyond basics.

A List Apart

> http://www.alistapart.org/
>
> A List Apart has been a cornerstone of the web design community's online world since its inception. The brainchild of Jeffrey Zeldman, this site is chock-full of intriguing information. Zeldman shows exactly how to do things, often by redesigning parts of his own site.
>
> A really awesome repository of articles by many of the best designers and thinkers, this really is a list apart.

HTML Utopia! Design Web Sites Without Tables Parts 1 and 2

> http://www.sitepoint.com/article.php/379
>
> This inspirational two-parter was largely responsible for the decision to write this book, and to treat the topic of CSS the way I have. It's a nice, condensed introduction to the issues in this book, and can serve as a decent refresher when you just want to remind yourself why you're going through all this!

Style Sheet Reference Guide

> http://www.webreview.com/style/
>
> This is the most comprehensive table of CSS compatibility analysis that I know of. It lists virtually every property and feature of CSS 1 and CSS 2, and indicates whether or not the feature is supported. The front page (which appears at the URL above) lets you select which chart you want to look at and work with.
>
> I use this site extensively, because it's so accurate and complete that if I have any question at all about whether a particular CSS trick I'm about to try will work in most browsers, the answer is literally two or three clicks away.

The AnyBrowser Campaign Site Design Guide

> http://www.anybrowser.org/campaign/abdesign3.html

This is one of the sites I love to support and visit. It's part of the "Viewable With Any Browser" Campaign that was launched to encourage web designers and developers to be sure that their sites actually work in all the major browsers. It encourages the use of standards, and discourages relying on browser-specific tricks and techniques.

The page has a ton of links to places where you can validate, check, and get advice about conformance with standards and specifications. It's a good place to remind yourself how best to design web pages using CSS to ensure maximum accessibility.

glish.com: CSS Layout Techniques

http://glish.com/css/

This site provides a brisk, chatty overview of CSS. The best feature is the list of resources included here. Although maintenance of the site has long since stopped, it nonetheless offers a wealth of information that you'll find useful.

The Layout Reservoir at BlueRobot

http://bluerobot.com/web/layouts/default.asp

This site is primarily a code repository for two- and three-column layouts, and provides some helpful information about centering elements in CSS.

Little Boxes at the Noodle Incident

http://www.thenoodleincident.com/tutorials/box_lesson/boxes.html

I find it helpful sometimes to sort of stumble through a series of design mishaps and blind alleys with someone who's already been there and done that. This site is a bit like that. The UI is clean and well planned, and each page gives you useful information about a specific approach to a box layout design problem, how the author approached it, what worked, what didn't, and how he ultimately solved it.

CSS, Cascading Style Sheets, HTML, Web Site Tips at Websitetips.com

http://www.websitetips.com/css/index.shtml

This is a fine repository of links with some commentary. This resource lists lots of sites and other references that I haven't included in this appendix. It may be a good idea to pop over to this site if you need some information about CSS that you don't find in this book, or you want more examples to clarify your understanding.

Complexspiral Demo

http://www.meyerweb.com/eric/css/edge/complexspiral/demo.html

This is a sub-site of Eric Meyer's, but it deserves its own entry because it was, as far as I can tell, the first place on the Web to teach the fixed-background trick that has become de rigeur on many modern sites. It's also an attractive design, and Eric gives you all the information and code you need to adapt the technique to your own use.

Accessibility Features of CSS

http://www.w3.org/TR/CSS-access

Even though the entire W3C set of CSS sites is useful (and cited later), this page is particularly helpful when you're dealing with an accessibility issue and want to know what, if anything, CSS can do to help you make your site more accessible. Contrasted with most W3C recommendations (which are dry, hard to read, and terse to a fault), this discussion is readable and helpful.

Eric Meyer on CSS

http://www.ericmeyeroncss.com/

This site is the supplemental/support site for Eric's book of the same title. It offers errata (very helpful; some of the stuff that slipped through the cracks of the editing and production process are embarrassingly wrong), as well as some information that didn't fit into the book.

Real World Style

http://realworldstyle.com/

A very nice, cleanly designed, and helpful site by Mark Newhouse that's full of tips, insights, opinions, and other goodies. Be sure also to follow the links to his blog, where he holds forth regularly on CSS-related topics.

This is one of my favorites. I visit it often.

NYPL: Style Guide

http://www.nypl.org/styleguide/

The esteemed New York Public Library's site, where styles and rules about the use of XHTML and CSS are linked. Every once in a while, I'll wonder about the proper way to do something (as opposed to the technically correct way) and when I do, this site has been quite useful.

W3C Recommendation for Cascading Style Sheets, level 1
W3C Recommendation for Cascading Style Sheets, level 2

http://www.w3.org/TR/REC-CSS1

http://www.w3.org/TR/REC-CSS2

These are the definitive sites that explain exactly how CSS is supposed to work. The W3C's recommendations appear here in their entirety, are searchable, and are well-organized, too. The main idea is that browser manufacturers understand and consider these recommendations, then make their browsers behave correctly. But, as a friend of mine likes to say: "In theory, there's no difference between theory and practice, but in practice, there is."

Still, it's a good idea to be familiar with the contents of these pages and at least to know your way around them.

W3C CSS Validation Service

http://jigsaw.w3.org/css-validator/

This is the site for the validation service I talk about in Chapter 4.

A CSS-based "Frames" Simulation

http://css.nu/exp/nf-illustration.html

The site is slightly mislabeled. It actually explains how to use CSS to avoid the frames/tables that would otherwise be necessary to create modern layouts. It offers some suggestions and tidbits I didn't find easily elsewhere, and it's quite entertaining.

Fancy Paragraphs with CSS

http://www.sitepoint.com/article.php/942

This article on SitePoint offers good explanations and insights into some of the topics I cover in Chapter 7. Examples are clear, large, bold, and presented in color, so there's value in reading them even if you feel you understand the topic well.

CSS is Easy!

http://www.sitepoint.com/article.php/309

A SitePoint article that offers a quasi-interactive tutorial in CSS. You might find this useful primarily because the author explains things in very small steps, doling out the information carefully.

What is Liquid Design?

http://www.sitepoint.com/article.php/951

A well-organized SitePoint article that teaches the basics of using CSS and tables for liquid (aka "stretchy") design. I found its primary value to be in the clarity with which you could see the distinction between using tables and CSS for this kind of project.

Introduction to CSS Shorthand

http://www.sitepoint.com/article.php/966

As you've learned in the course of this book, many groups of related CSS styles have a shorthand identifier that collects all the individual properties into a single one. For example, `font` is shorthand for `font-family`, `font-size`, `font-weight`, and other related properties.

This brief article discusses shorthand in CSS, and how to use it properly.

Index

Symbols

\#
   hexadecimal string prefix, 80
   ID selector symbol, 46
\+ adjacent selector connector, 52
/* */ comment delimiters, 60
\> parent-child selector, 51

A

\<a\> elements and skip navigation, 253
abbreviated size units, 56
abbreviations, absolute sizing, 56
absolute measurements, 54, 56
   font sizes, 99, 160, 366
absolute positioning
   document flow and, 235
   Footbag Freaks homepage, 191, 204
   multi-column, fixed-width layouts, 282
   text, 158
   three-column layout example, 231
accessibility
   alternate style sheets, 30, 288
   Braille printers, 300
   pixel sizing and, 57, 101
   relative sizing and, 55
   semantic markup and, 34, 288
   tabular layouts and, 6
   transparent gifs and, 5
   "zoom" layouts, 288
adjacent selectors, 52
Adobe Acrobat, 100
Adobe GoLive, 5
Adobe OpenType standard, 104
align attribute, 114, 187
alignment
   of headings, 117
   of list items, 197, 209, 226
   of text, 113–120, 187
alphabets, non-Roman
   Arabic, 452
   Asian languages, 447, 451, 455
   East Asian, 377, 382, 472
   Hebrew, 352, 457
alternate style sheets, 30
   attaching, 295
   semantic markup and, 34
   "zoom" layouts, 288
alternating table rows, coloring, 88, 90, 279
anchors (*see* links)
animation
   pseudo-class simulation of, 28
   transitions filters, 359
asterisk, universal selector, 44
at-rules, 67–68, 299–303
attention-getting color, 85
attribute selectors, 52
attributes, terminology and, 9
aural style sheets, 303–305
   (*see also* screen readers)
author images, Footbag Freaks, 199

B

background colors, 23
   background images with, 91
   fixed-width layouts, 266
   Footbag Freaks web site, 182
   headings, 119
   highlighting alternate table rows, 88, 279
   revealing box model effects, 163, 173, 175
   setting \<body\> color and, 82
   text readability and, 81

O

oblique font styles, 103

<ol> elements, 134

opacity, 404

OpenType font standard, 104

Opera browser
  CSS property support, 317
  CSS support history, 66
  font sizing, 57

operating system-specific colors, 79, 315

origin factor, cascading, 146

outdents, 121, 450

outline property, CSS, 78, 406

overlining, 130

P

padding
  margins, borders and, 163, 172
  padding properties, 164

padding property, CSS, 41, 413
  Footbag Freaks styling, 182
  multiple values and, 167

padding-left property, CSS, 122, 415

@page rule, 302, 398, 416, 438

page styling, 302, 405, 467

paragraphs
  centering, 118
  highlighting text within, 112
  indenting first lines, 120
  initial drop-caps, 48
  removing default margins, 188

parent elements, 43

parent-child selectors, 51

PDF files, 100

percentage sizing
  padding property values, 168
  pixel sizing compared to, 164
  text sizes, 57, 100, 123

period class name prefix, 45

pipe character, 186

pixel sizing, 56, 101
  border widths, 179
  percentages compared to, 164
  point sizes and, 58

Pixy's Color Scheme Generator, 82

placeholder graphics, 4, 53

plus sign, 52

position property, CSS, 158, 426

positioning context, CSS, 158
  absolute positioning, 205, 282
  relative positioning, 160

positioning in CSS, 157–180
  (see also absolute positioning)
  background images, 93
  relative positioning, 161
  repositioning sidebars, 213–214

positioning properties, replacing, 241–242

printed output, 302, 417–418, 420
  @media rule, 300

Profile menu, W3C validator, 64

properties, CSS
  (see also shorthand properties)
  browser compatibility charts, 68
  complete listing, 317–475
  as declaration components, 9
  inclusion in rules, 11
  inherited properties, 43
  JavaScript manipulation, 306
  with multiple values, 10, 41
  uniform application, 31
  working with fonts, 96

proportional spacing
  (see also em measurements; percentage sizing)
  padding property values, 168

prototyping, 12

pseudo-class selectors, 48, 145

pseudo-classes, CSS, 132
  dynamic effects with, 28
  Footbag Freaks link styling, 194, 198

Books for Web Developers from SitePoint

Visit http://www.sitepoint.com/books/
for sample chapters or to order!

3rd Edition
Covers PHP5, MySQL4
and Mac OS X

Build Your Own

Database Driven Website

Using PHP & MySQL

By Kevin Yank

A Practical Step-by-Step Guide

RUN YOUR OWN
WEB SERVER
USING
LINUX & APACHE

BY **STUART LANGRIDGE**
& **TONY STEIDLER-DENNISON**

GET STARTED WITH LINUX AND APACHE — THE EASY WAY!

THE CSS ANTHOLOGY

101 ESSENTIAL TIPS, TRICKS & HACKS

BY RACHEL ANDREW

THE MOST COMPLETE QUESTION AND ANSWER BOOK ON CSS

DHTML UTOPIA: MODERN WEB DESIGN USING JAVASCRIPT & DOM

BY **STUART LANGRIDGE**

PRACTICAL UNOBTRUSIVE JAVASCRIPT TECHNIQUES

THE JAVASCRIPT ANTHOLOGY

101 ESSENTIAL TIPS, TRICKS & HACKS

BY **JAMES EDWARDS**
& CAMERON ADAMS

THE MOST COMPLETE QUESTION AND ANSWER BOOK ON JAVASCRIPT

BUILD YOUR OWN

STANDARDS
COMPLIANT
WEBSITE
USING
DREAMWEAVER 8

BY RACHEL ANDREW

A PRACTICAL STEP-BY-STEP GUIDE TO MASTERING DREAMWEAVER 8

Dreaming of running your own successful Web Design or Development business?

This kit contains everything you need to know!

The Web Design Business Kit

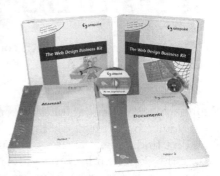

Whether you are thinking of establishing your own Web Design or Development business or are already running one, this kit will teach you everything you need to know to be successful...

Two ring-bound folders and a CD-ROM jam packed with expert advice and proven ready-to-use business documents that will help you establish yourself, gain clients, and grow a profitable freelance business!

Folder 1:
Covers advice on every aspect of running your business:

- *How to sell yourself*
- *How to land bigger jobs*
- *What to charge*
- *How to keep clients for life*
- *How to manage budgets*
- *How to hire & fire employees*
- *And much more*

Folder 2:
Contains 64 essential, ready-to-use business documents:

- *Business Plan*
- *Sample Proposal & Contract*
- *Client Needs Analysis Form*
- *Marketing Surveys*
- *Employment Documents*
- *Financial Documents*
- *And much more*

CD-ROM:
Contains electronic copies of all the business documents in Folder 2, so you can apply them instantly to your business!

- *Ready to apply*
- *Easily customizable*
- *MS Word & Excel format*

The Web Design Business Kit is available exclusively through sitepoint.com. To order, get more information, or to download the free sample chapters, visit:

www.sitepoint.com/books/freelance1/

What our customers have to say about the Web Design Business Kit:

"The Web Design Business Kit (Documents & Manual) is the best marketing tool that I have found! It has changed my business strategies, and my income."

Barb Brown
www.barbbrown.com

"We've already closed 2 deals by following the suggested steps in the kit! I feel like I shouldn't pass the word about this kit to others or risk a lot of good competition!"

Jeneen McDonald
www.artpoststudios.com

"Of everything I have purchased on the Internet, related to business and not, this is (without question) the most value for the money spent. Thank you."

Thom Parkin
www.twice21.com